Making Headlines

Making Headlines

The American
Revolution as
Seen through the
British Press

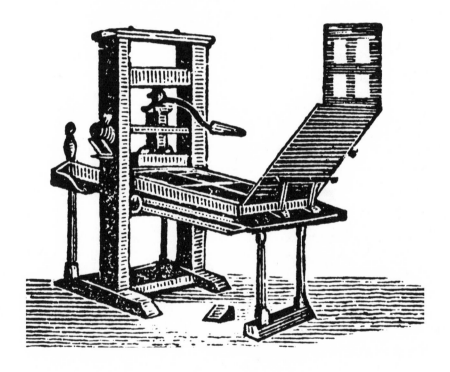

Troy Bickham

NORTHERN
ILLINOIS
UNIVERSITY
PRESS

DeKalb

© 2009 by Northern Illinois University Press

Published by the Northern Illinois University Press, DeKalb, Illinois 60115

Manufactured in the United States using postconsumer-recycled, acid-free paper.

All Rights Reserved

Design by Julia Fauci

Library of Congress Cataloging-in-Publication Data

Bickham, Troy O.

Making headlines : the American Revolution as seen through the British press /
Troy Bickham.

p.   cm.

Includes bibliographical references and index.

ISBN 978-0-87580-393-7 (clothbound : alk. paper)

1. United States—History—Revolution, 1775–1783—Foreign public opinion, British.
2. United States—History—Revolution, 1775–1783—Press coverage. 3. Public opinion—
Great Britain—History—18th century. 4. War—Press coverage—Great Britain—History—18th
century. 5. Press and politics—Great Britain—History—18th century. 6. British newspapers—History—18th century. 7. Journalism—Great Britain—History—
18th century. I. Title.

E249.3.B53 2009

973.3—dc22

2008026483

For Rhobert and Irene

CONTENTS

LIST OF ILLUSTRATIONS

PREFACE

✳ This book concludes a project that began in the first week of my graduate studies during a reception lunch for new graduate students at Lincoln College, Oxford. I had the good fortune to be seated next to Paul Langford (at that time, the tutor for graduates), who mentioned during lunch that in his past research into Britain and the American Revolution he had been surprised at how well the British had thought of George Washington. Whether or not this was simply an observation or a subtle hint for a fruitful research project is unclear, but I certainly took it as the latter and made it the subject of my master's thesis. It has been with me in various forms ever since, even as I pursued a different topic for my doctoral dissertation, wrote my first book, and began still other projects. The subject of the British press and the American Revolution maintained my interest—most intensively over the past three years—and it has constantly informed my teaching and research as a whole.

A few comments should be made about style. The American Revolution was both a transatlantic civil war and a civil war within the colonies. Most groups adhered to a broadly defined, but shared, English political tradition. All of this has served to make nomenclature for various groups and perspectives somewhat difficult—a 'patriot' in America was not the same as a 'patriot' in Britain, and definitions of both were contested at the time. Not all 'Americans' sided with Congress, and not all colonists saw themselves as 'Americans.' Because the book takes the British perspective as its focus, it has largely employed contemporary British terminology for the sake of clarity. In the time period covered, the various British groups selected competing terms. 'Whigs,' 'tories,' and 'patriots' refer to groups in Britain, except otherwise noted. 'Loyalists' are those colonists who generally supported the continuation of British rule. Those colonists who openly supported the cause of independence from Britain are referred to as 'rebels,' supporters of Congress, and sometimes simply as 'Americans.' Spellings within quoted material have not been changed. Newspaper issue dates in the notes are given in the standard European day-month-year format for smoother reading and to reduce punctuation. Newspaper names have been shortened to reflect contemporary usage. For example, *Felix Farley's Bristol Journal* is cited as the *Bristol Journal,* which is how other newspapers and diarists typically referred to it. This is for the sake of simplicity and emphasis on the place of publication rather than the name of the printer associated with it. More often than not, the name was more a tool for brand continuity than a reflection of who owned or ran the paper. For example, by the outbreak of the American Revolution, the original Felix Farley had long been dead and the *Bristol Journal* was owned and produced by a consortium rather than a single man. The exception is the Edinburgh *Ruddiman's Weekly Mercury*, which, in contrast to other newspapers outside of London, did not include its production home within the title.

During the long journey of this project, I have accrued a number of debts. During its earliest days as a master's thesis on representations of George Washington and Congress in the London press, I especially benefited from the direction and advice of Paul Langford, John Stevenson, Joanna Innes, Daniel Walker Howe, Peter Thompson, Dror Wahrman, Sarah Knott, and Jeremy Osborn. An earlier version of Chapter 7 first appeared as "Sympathizing with Sedition? George Washington, the British Press, and British Attitudes during the American War of Independence" in 2002 in the *William and Mary Quarterly*, which granted permission to reproduce it here. Through this experience my broader understanding of the press, public opinion, and the transatlantic nature of the American Revolution benefited from the generous comments of its editors, Philip Morgan and Christopher Grasso, and the anonymous readers. Since expanding the project into a book-length examination of the British press coverage of the American Revolution, I (and the project) have benefited from the advice, conversations, and criticisms of especially Eliga Gould, Stephen Conway, Joanna Innes, Roger Knight, Kathleen Wilson, April Hatfield, James Rosenheim, and the anonymous readers at Northern Illinois University Press. James Bradford generously read the entire manuscript at a late stage and saved me from a number of mistakes. Any errors, either of fact or interpretation, are, of course, my own and more likely than not the consequence of unheeded advice.

The project benefited from the financial support of a number of institutions, including the University of Oxford, Lincoln College, Somerville College, Oxford's Beit Fund for Imperial History, Southeast Missouri State University, and Texas A&M University and its Melbern G. Glasscock Center for Humanities Research. The librarians and archivists at the Bodleian Library and the British Library's Newspaper Reading Room were particularly kind in assisting me with identifying and using the tens of thousands of newspapers and magazines I consulted. No one even once complained about the sometimes weighty bound volumes of newspapers. The project has found a fortunate home with Northern Illinois University Press. Kevin Butterfield, who initially contacted me about pursuing the book and ultimately commissioned it, was helpful in conceptualizing the book. Melody Herr was an ideal editor—simultaneously encouraging, challenging, and patient. Alex Schwartz, Susan Bean, Julia Fauci, and Tracy Schoenle deftly transformed the plain manuscript into a beautiful book.

Throughout the entire process I benefited from the wise and loving counsel of my wife and, more recently, the happy distractions of our two children. My sister, Laura, has made my many research trips to Britain far less lonely and tedious than they otherwise would have been. Rhobert and Irene Hickman have been better grandparents than I could have possibly wished for, making their home my home away from home, and it is to them that I dedicate this book.

Making Headlines

INTRODUCTION

To you all readers turn, and they look
Pleas'd on a paper, who abhor a book;
Those who ne'er design'd their Bible to peruse,
Would think it hard to be deny'd their News;
Sinners and Saints, the wisest with the weak,
Here mingles tastes, and one amusement seek:
This, like the public inn, provides a treat,
Where each promiscuous guest sits down to eat;
And such this mental food, as we may call,
Something to all men, and to some men all.[1]
—*The News-Paper: A Poem* (1785)

There is nothing so easy, or at least nothing that people are so free of, as giving advice to the nation. We have it both from those who have no knowledge of our affairs, and those who have no concern in them. We have it from Foreigners as well as Englishmen, Gentlemen and Tradesmen, and from every corner of England. Now I own I live in this country, and therefore think I have a right to give my opinion in any thing that concerns the Public.
—"Letter to the Printer," *London Chronicle*, December 24, 1774

＊ By the mid-eighteenth century a British newspaper was the world in digest. As the extract from George Crabbe's poem explains, newspapers enabled readers to traverse continents to visit foreign peoples, slip into the sometimes equally alien worlds of royal courts, and sail with armadas across the vast oceans. Throughout the conflict that began in Massachusetts in April 1775, the press kept the British public informed of all angles of the war as it spread across the globe. Speeches from American Indians, letters from soldiers in India, and extracts from West Indian newspapers reached British artisans and aristocrats without discrimination. Yet as the quote above from a reader's letter reveals, opening such worlds to ordinary Britons had consequences—"benefits" in the eyes of some and "prices" in those of others. The British were not passive readers: they digested the information the press provided and then discussed it at home, at the local coffeehouse, or in the press itself. In essence, reading newspapers turned commoners into critics. The editor of the *Edinburgh Magazine* remarked as early as 1756, "There is not perhaps a nation in the world where the people so eagerly calculate events before hand, or so vehemently debate the issue of public operations, as we do on this island." "One would think that there was something in the air of this island, which has the property of infusing political presumption," the editor continued, noting that, "It possesses men of all ranks, professions and degrees."[2]

The British reading public was well-versed in American news even before word of fighting between British troops and colonial militia at Lexington and Concord reached Britain in late May 1775. Heavy press reporting of the Seven Years War and the subsequent growing pains of an empire that stretched from the Mississippi River to Madras had created a lasting, widespread interest in overseas matters among the wider public.[3] Although only a corner of the empire and neither the most populous nor the wealthiest segment of it, the thirteen mainland North American colonies that declared their independence in July 1776 had captured a disproportionate amount of the British public's attention. The American colonists' strategy of answering undesirable imperial taxes with economic boycotts and barrages of pamphlets entrenched in the language of ancient English liberties touched the hearts and pocketbooks of Britons like no other imperial squabble before or since. But it was not just the immediate turmoil that defined British perceptions of North America and its inhabitants. During the Seven Years War and its aftermath, Britons had been persuaded to perceive European-descended Americans as countrymen and the nation as extending beyond the British Isles and into North America.[4] As a future Lord Mayor of London declared in 1771, "As to the Americans, I declare I know no difference between an inhabitant of Boston in Lincolnshire, and Boston in New England."[5] By the eve of the American Revolution, Britons toured museum exhibitions on American Indians, bought tomahawks at auctions, and listened to American Indian converts preach in their churches. Britons knew colonists as family members, friends, customers, business partners, tenants, comrades in the military, and, in some instances, as their elected representatives in local political posts and even in the British Parliament.[6]

In consequence, opinion of American affairs was never in short supply. Some railed against the colonists as ingrates, such as a reader of the *Morning Post* who complained that, "Every child knows that the last war, which cost Great Britain so many millions, and the lives of so many thousands of her people, was undertaken solely for the defence of America."[7] Others lamented the actions of "tyrannical ministers" bent on destroying colonial goodwill. British newspapers and magazines served as national and local forums for discussions and debates throughout the war, disseminating information and chronicling readers' responses. Such an analysis of the press would hardly have been revealing to contemporaries, who recognized the importance of the press to current and future generations alike. As the *General Evening Post* remarked in an announcement printed throughout its January 1778 issues, advertisements might need to be postponed in order to free up space "to enable us to lay before our readers the best and fullest information . . . at a crisis teeming with events of the utmost consequences to every subject of this realm." Such measures were necessary, the paper explained, because, "In times like the present, the Intelligence and Debates are very copious and claim our first attention, as they may probably hereafter contribute to furnish materials for the history of the most interesting disputes ever recorded in the annals of our country."[8]

An examination of Britain in the American Revolution is hardly new. Even before the cannons were silenced, American and British writers had begun publishing histories of the conflict. From the start, however, the thirteen colonies that rebelled were central to any account and have overshadowed the rest of the conflict to the point that even the British made but mere cameo appearances in what had become almost entirely an American drama. Europe, India, and the Caribbean virtually disappeared from the historical accounts along with African slaves and American Indians.

The process of recovering the diversity of experiences has been a slow but important one. Although still America-centered, historians of the second half of the twentieth century have increasingly recognized the heterogeneity of North American societies. As a result, the experiences of America's peoples beyond the white adult males who advocated the cause of independence by taking up arms or joining the rebel government have received greater scrutiny. The diverse experiences of American Indians, Africans, colonial women, and loyalists have all received individual attention and are increasingly part of larger narratives of the American Revolutionary experience. At the beginning of the last century, the British government also re-emerged at the center of the historical stage, playing the key role of the protagonist whose bumbling policies and struggle to take hold of their rapidly expanding and far-flung empire drove the timing and type of colonial resistance.[9] Yet because the global war that began with the American Revolution has still been largely left to scholars of American history, the recognized dynamism of the colonial society has not been extended to its British counterpart. Whereas competing ideologies, gender, race, religion, material interests, and local issues have all been accepted as factors in the American experience of the conflict, consideration for contemporary Britons has generally been reduced to the immediate circumstances and ideological currents that surrounded a handful of the British political and mercantile elite. Thus the ramblings of a few members of Parliament or pamphlet authors have too often been presented as the voice of a nation.

Over the past century, some scholars of British history have sought to redress this gap, beginning with Dora Mae Clark's groundbreaking *British Opinion and the American Revolution* (1930), which attempted to provide an account of British viewpoints from a socially and politically broad perspective. Since then scholars have benefited from the outpouring of scholarship on eighteenth-century British society, culture, and the empire. The outcome has been studies of British roles in the conflict ranging from examinations of London radical politicians to provincial coffeehouse culture. Such studies have rightly rehabilitated the significance of the American Revolution and the wider world war it sparked in British history, and now almost any comprehensive look at the period seems incomplete without the requisite, albeit often too brief, consideration of the conflict from a British perspective.[10] In fact, the American Revolutionary era has most recently served as a springboard for investigations into such broadly diverse topics as the emergence of the "modern self," the functioning of the fiscal-military state, and national identity.[11]

Unfortunately, the vast majority of attention has gone to those Britons who openly sympathized with the American patriot cause. Although individually meritorious, the corpus of scholarship, when taken as a whole, distorts wider British opinion as overly sympathetic and predominately focused on events in North America rather than on the empire as a whole.[12] In consequence, the exceptional positions of men and women such as Josiah Tucker, William Shipley, John Cartwright, John Wilkes, Joseph Priestly, Richard Price, and Catharine Macaulay appear almost mainstream in the array of works that collectively, though unintentionally, misrepresent the broader understanding of British responses to the American Revolution.

The large majorities in Parliament commanded by Lord North as Prime Minister and the marginalization of Edmund Burke, Charles James Fox, and the rest of the fragmented opposition for most of the war seems secondary to these sidelined Britons' public dissatisfaction with the war effort and moderate sympathy for the American colonists.

A study of the discussions and depictions of the war in the British press is important, not only because it assists our understanding of the founding of the United States, but also because it enables a deeper understanding of British history, particularly Britain's development as a modern society and global imperial power. The American Revolution mattered to the vast majority Britons who were not directly involved in the conflict, and the British press, which fueled and satisfied their interest, vividly demonstrates this. For contemporaries, the conflict was as much about Britain losing its colonies as it was about the colonies winning independence, and just as America's revolution was about more than simply evicting its imperial masters, Britain's experience had a deeper significance beyond shedding a few pesky colonies on the way to nineteenth-century imperial greatness. As noted above, American colonists were fellow nationals in the eyes of many Britons, and for those Britons the conflict was nothing short of a tragic civil war. Moreover, rising nationalism in Britain during the second half of the century meant that overseas victories and defeats had an impact on individuals' sense of self-worth at home.[13] As one contemporary French visitor remarked in 1772: "Each citizen identifying himself with the government, must of necessity extend to himself the high idea of which he has of the nation; he triumphs in its victories; he exhausts himself in projects to promote its successes, to second its advantages, and to repair its losses."[14] Essential to remember is that Britons who supported the prosecution of the war, like the Americans who opposed them, fought for a cause. The romanticized "Spirits of 1776" and the enshrined words of the Declaration of Independence have proven to be more historically lasting, but, had the British succeeded in crushing the rebellion, George III's appeal to divine blessings, the rule of law, and the need to protect the weak (i.e. the loyalists) in his speech before Parliament in 1775 came close to being a cornerstone of our collective memory of the conflict.

The American Revolution was perhaps the most nationally divisive event in Britain during the eighteenth century. After all, it marks the first time in modern history that a literate public sustained a major, widespread critique of their government's use of military force as a tool of public policy.[15] Such an unprecedented response did not sit well with many Britons, who interpreted such behavior as disloyal, if not treasonous, and thus the war sometimes split communities and households and provoked civilians to violence. When the news of the British victory at Long Island reached Bristol via the press in October 1776, the port city that had elected conciliationists to Parliament two years earlier, including New Yorker Henry Cruger, erupted into violence as an exuberant mob from across the social ranks took to the streets, attacking the persons, homes, and businesses of both known American sympathizers and anyone who failed to show sufficient visible pleasure at the Americans' defeat. Fearing further violence against his supporters two months later, Edmund Burke, Bristol's other member of Parliament, hesitated to push his conciliation stance too publicly, and so he insisted that the protest to the national fast day for "the success His Majesty's arms in America" on December 13 be subdued and consist of a simple dinner that finished before nightfall.[16] Similar instances of attacks and reprisals spread throughout the country during the war. Sometimes they were collective, as described above, but at other times they were more personal, such as the following year when young Abigail Frost witnessed her father, a successful Nottingham grocer, respond with rage when Robert Denison, an associate, raised a toast to George Washington: "my father got upon the table, crossed it, and leaned on Mr R. Denison's shoulder and crushed him down on the floor."[17]

The British newspaper and periodical press offers a unique opportunity to explore British attitudes toward the American Revolution and the global war it provoked. The press was sufficiently cheap and abundant to touch the lives of most Britons, regardless of rank, gender, or geography. The large numbers of newspapers and magazines made for a great diversity of editorial stances, and the openness and unparalleled freedom of the press meant that it served as the public forum in which these views clashed. Perhaps most importantly, most Britons experienced much of the conflict through the press. Apart from some minor exceptions, the military action transpired on distant lands and oceans that few Britons would ever visit except through their imaginations. The press's vivid accounts made the forests of North America and the coasts of India real and relevant to ordinary Britons. Thus in this instance a tight focus on one type of source material is justifiable, because through the press we can recapture the depth and diversity of British attitudes toward the conflict, America, and the wider empire, as well as show how these issues mingled with domestic concerns.

For the purposes of this study the "press" refers only to newspapers, magazines, and periodicals. Other printed mediums, particularly pamphlets, enabled lengthy commentaries, but they functioned differently. Typically selling for one shilling, a pamphlet cost two-thirds of a day's wages of one of the most skilled and best paid craftsmen at Josiah Wedgwood's factory or as much as a month's subscription to a leading provincial paper.[18] In consequence, pamphlets' circulation was severely limited, and even best-selling ones almost never outsold a single daily issue of a major London newspaper.[19] Moreover, pamphlets were one-time publications focusing on single issues. This eliminated the possibility of the sort of established subscription network that newspapers and magazines enjoyed and, along with it, the sort of casual readers who might acquire a newspaper to follow one story but then stumble onto something else of interest. Besides, unlike the newspaper and periodical press, pamphlets were rarely predominately economic enterprises subject to market demand. More often they existed as the fiercely partisan products of patrons and hired penmen.[20] Nevertheless, pamphlets are undeniably important in that they offer uniquely detailed insights into the arguments for or against a particular issue, and the Anglo-American crisis generated hundreds of them. Some of them appeared in extracted form in newspapers, and in such cases they have been given equal consideration in this study to that of other opinion pieces; however, in terms of assessing broadly held views and experiences, pamphlets on their own fall short of the value of the newspaper and periodical press.

Using the newspaper and periodical press as a tool for investigating British opinion is well established. Studies of Britain and the American Revolution often cite a handful of newspapers and magazines, and Solomon Lutnick's impressive and often-cited *The American Revolution and the British Press* has focused exclusively on the press.[21] However, our understanding of the press and reading practices has improved significantly in the four decades since the publication of Lutnick's study, justifying a fresh, comprehensive consideration. Whereas the London newspapers were once accepted as party bugles operated by corrupt editors in search of bribes or satisfying personal vendettas, scholars have increasingly recognized the British newspapers as profitable businesses run by savvy men and women and backed by advertising revenues, not party funds.[22] Scholars have also widely acknowledged the cultural importance and independence of English and Scottish provincial centers, whose local presses are ignored or summarily dismissed in earlier studies of the press and the American Revolution. Yet provincial cultures were sufficiently dynamic during the second half of the century to engage national and imperial issues in significant and substantive ways.[23] The era of the American Revolution was certainly no exception. Recent studies of eighteenth-century reading practices have also shown how newspaper and magazine readership transcended barriers of social class, geography, and gender.[24] British newspapers found their way into artisans' breakfast-table banter, the hands of shopkeepers' wives, and middling families' evening fireside conversations. With at least one-third of the population having regular access to printed news, the press's viability for recapturing and assessing British public responses and perceptions was unmatched.

The newspaper and periodical press is not, of course, perfect source material, but it remains the best available and is a useful tool for accessing public opinion. The press has never been an exact mirror of public opinion; it leads as well as follows popular discourses, and this era was no exception. I began this study as an examination of state propaganda in the eighteenth century, but what I found was a relatively free press being driven by market forces. Eighteenth-century Britons—including those in power, those printing the news, and those reading it—certainly considered the press as a general reflection, although not a precise mirror, of public opinion. Assessing the precise extent to which the press affected policy is impossible to determine and beyond the scope of this study, but those in power respected, if not feared, the power of the press. Public opinion as reflected in the press certainly mattered both to those who constituted it and to those who were judged by it during the era of the American Revolution. Governing factions and special interest groups on both sides of the Atlantic during the eighteenth century worked hard to sway public opinion via the press. Among the age's fastest recorded crossing of the Atlantic was the ship that Sam Adams arranged to transport copies of Salem's *Essex Gazette* of April 25, 1775, which gave grossly biased American patriot accounts of the battles at Lexington and Concord, to waiting London newspaper editors.[25] Lord North, who, as a leader of George III's government for most of the war, endured more public scrutiny than perhaps any other figure, knew and lamented the power of the press to smear the characters of powerful men. At one point in a House of Commons debate, he rose and declared in frustration: "The first thing we lay our hands on in the morning is a libel; the last thing we lay our hands on the evening is a libel. Our eyes open upon libels; our eyes close upon libels. In short, libels, lampoons and satires, constitute all the writing, printing, and reading, of our time."[26] Upon returning to Britain, unsuccessful generals, such as John Burgoyne and William Howe, mounted extensive printed publicity campaigns to defend their actions and characters, personally writing letters for newspapers and pamphlets.[27]

Yet despite its importance, or perhaps because of it, the press in Britain did not succumb during the war to factional interests to the extent that its credibility as a reasonable barometer of literate public opinion can be impugned. Unlike many of their American counterparts, British printers did not suffer imprisonment, physical violence, or damage to their property by angry mobs in retaliation for their coverage of the American conflict.[28] This is not to suggest that the British press was immune to external influence. Government supporters, the West Indian lobby, and American loyalists, to name but a few, all used the press to convey their messages to a broad British audience in hopes of garnering support. But while bribes, sympathetic editors, and personal connections might have given these groups disproportionate access to the printed discussion, exclusivity was never a possibility. Many of these groups' biggest asset was access to new information that news-hungry readers wanted, such as the American rebels' cartel-like hold on information coming out of the mainland colonies during the 1775–1776 period, but this was a long war, and military battles ensured that such monopolies did not last. Even the most biased of the metropolitan newspapers, which operated in a market large enough to enable niches, carried a diversity of content, and, because readers often perused more than one newspaper particularly in urban markets, such papers did not have the exclusive attentions of their readers. In short, the British press was too large, too profitable, and too diffuse for any single group to control or even manipulate it on a sustained, wide scale. The news output was enormous during this period, with roughly two hundred distinct newspaper and magazine issues being produced per week. This was the beginning of hyper-coverage unlike anything before it, as editors raced and scrounged to fill their pages with the latest and most in-depth coverage of the top story: the American Revolution and everything connected to it and precipitated by it. And it lasted for nine years.

Unfortunately this means that neglect or diligence allows anyone to find quotable material to support virtually any interpretation of the conflict; therefore, for each of my examples and arguments there are often—somewhere in the literally hundreds of thousands of pages of text—counter-examples that might support counterarguments. But the approach here has been to focus on consensus, describing and analyzing the major shifts and clashes in opinion and themes in the press's coverage of the war in order to better understand how British readers generally experienced and engaged with the conflict.

The examination of the press in this study is not exhaustive, but it is comprehensive. With well over one hundred British newspapers and magazines in circulation during the American Revolution, a complete reading of every issue would be too arduous a task, not to mention impossible because so many issues have been lost. Nevertheless, a sufficient sample size has been considered to make the conclusions drawn viable—at least from the standpoint of adequate sources. A total of forty-one British newspapers and magazines have been consulted. This is roughly one-third of the total in operation at the time and an easy majority of those that have survived. The fourteen London newspapers included in the study represent a diversity of political leanings and are a mix of daily, tri-weekly, and weekly papers. Some, such as the government-supporting *Morning Post,* which was notorious at the time for its support of the North ministry, or the *Gazetteer,* which rarely had a kind word for the North government, obviously merit inclusion. Those that enjoyed a wide, almost national circulation, such as the *General Evening Post, Saint James's Chronicle, London Chronicle,* and *Morning Chronicle,* also naturally deserve consideration. The government's official newspaper, the *London Gazette,* was another obvious choice. Complementing the London newspapers are ten metropolitan magazines. Many of these magazines, such as the *Gentleman's Magazine* and the *London Magazine,* enjoyed truly national distributions, but they retained a distinctly metropolitan flavor in both the subjects they covered and their reporting of them.

Of the forty-one newspapers and magazines considered, eighteen were printed outside of London. Considering that about one-third of the total numbers of copies of newspapers and magazines in circulation in Britain were produced outside of London, including a substantial portion in this study seemed appropriate. Half of those considered were printed in Scotland, although many enjoyed readers who were English. Edinburgh printers produced most of the Scottish media, but newspapers and magazines from Glasgow and Dundee are considered, too. The other half of the provincial newspapers and magazines are from England. These were selected on the basis of regional diversity and availability, as the survival rate of the provincial press both in Scotland and England has been significantly lower than their metropolitan counterparts.

This book is divided into three parts: the workings of the press in the era of the American Revolution, an exploration of the press coverage and discussion of the war from a British chronological perspective, and an examination of some of the major themes of the American war. In Part 1, the focus of the first chapter is primarily on the issues of distribution, organization, and readership, while the relationships between the press and politics are investigated in the second chapter. Drawing on business records along with contemporary public and private comment, revealed in these chapters is the notion that the press was a widely available medium that operated predominately outside of the party political system to present socially and geographically diverse British audiences with forums for local and national discussions. Profit from sales and advertising, not politics, drove the men and women who ran the nation's press, which gave the press greater legitimacy in the eyes of its readers and simultaneously made it an arena and a resource for public and private discussions. Also emphasized in these chapters is the importance of the press outside of London, both in terms of readership and news production. Ultimately, the case is made in these chapters that the press's broad readership, independence, and sheer abundance make it not only a legitimate source for recapturing national and local public discourses surrounding the conflict but the best available.

The American Revolution and the global conflict it precipitated are examined within a chronological framework in the next four chapters. Provided in these chapters is an account of how the British press covered and the reading public responded to the American Revolution and the global war into which it grew. Also within these chapters is an attempt to explain the shape and tenor of that coverage and commentary by considering such factors as the availability and manipulation of information. The starting date of the American Revolution was a matter of contention even among those who lived through it: the Seven Years War, the Stamp Act of 1765, the Boston Massacre, the Boston Tea Party, the meeting of the first Continental Congress, the battle of Lexington and Concord, and the Declaration of Independence are all legitimate starting points. Historians have also argued from ideological, political, and social perspectives that the origins of the American Revolution stretched much further back into the seventeenth and eighteenth centuries.[29] In consequence, any starting date is somewhat arbitrary. Mine is the spring of 1774, when in the wake of the escalating measures taken on both sides of the Atlantic, the British press coverage and comment shifted noticeably toward an expectation of armed conflict, and the nation braced itself for war. Chapter 3 thus begins with this starting point and covers the conflict until two and a half years later, when the Declaration of Independence reached Britain, clarifying the aims of the American colonists in arms and confirming once and for all the conflict's stakes. The conclusion of the purely American war, which ended with the surrender of the British army at Saratoga in the autumn of 1777 and the eruption of war with France the following spring, is covered in Chapter 4. For the British, the American Revolution was in many ways two wars: the first being the attempted suppression of rebellion in North America and the second a global war primarily against France and Spain in which the American colonies were but a small part. In the first, which chapters 3 and 4 cover, there was little immediate threat to Britons at home, and the government conducted it so as to have as little impact on Britons as possible—limited tax increases, augmenting rather than raising new regiments and relying heavily on foreign auxiliaries rather than domestic recruiting drives. The second saw mobilization of the economy and populace on a par with the Seven Years War and the later wars against revolutionary France.[30] This global war is explored in chapters 5 and 6. The British press's coverage of this phase of the conflict was akin to that of other wars against the Bourbon monarchs during the eighteenth century. The rhetoric emphasized the war as a necessary and righteous crusade against a foreign culture, and, unlike the war in America, hardly anyone publicly opposed it on moral grounds. Britain suffered enormously in the first round of the global war, but the historically neglected second stage, which effectively began when the American war was recognized throughout Britain as lost in the winter of 1781/2, saw a series of major victories that rehabilitated the nation's confidence in the empire and the armed forces' ability to protect it. This newfound public confidence, explored in Chapter 6, at least partly explains the lack of national mourning and defeatism when Britain formally recognized American independence and agreed to the terms of peace in 1783.

Part 3 consists of chapters that examine the peculiarity of the American conflict in the British imagination. For most Britons the conflict with the colonies was a civil war, and with that outlook came a host of quandaries about how the war should be conducted and how the rebelling colonists, who regularly evinced qualities and goals that appealed to traditional British notions of liberty, patriotism, and good leadership, should be perceived. Considering the size of the British press, the length of the war, and editors' and readers' acute interest in it, there is no shortage of topics that lend themselves to exploring this subject. Those I have chosen are intended therefore to be representative rather than a final word on the subject. Chapter 7 reveals and explains the overwhelming admiration in the British press of George Washington, who, in sharp contrast to his British military counterparts, Parliament, the king, and Congress, enjoyed virtually universal praise in the press from start to finish. Transatlantically shared notions of good leadership, gentlemanliness, public expectations for British military success, disdain for politicians, and access to information from America all worked in the American commander in chief's favor in the British press, making him virtually the only figure on either side to maintain a positive public image throughout the entire conflict. One of the most controversial aspects of the British government's prosecution of the war in America—the inclusion of peoples from outside of the Anglo-American family—is the focus of Chapter 8. The Declaration of Independence listed the enlistment of foreign troops, American Indians, and black slaves as atrocities of the king and justifications for rebellion, but the British response in the press to these measures was mixed. Ultimately the discussion in the press sheds further light on British attitudes toward these outsiders while also revealing the complicated—

and sometimes flexible—view of the legitimate tools of war as well as a genuine reluctance to deploy some of them against the Americans in the same way that the British had done when facing foreign enemies. The discussion in the British press about the future of the Anglo-American relationship and the American republic is the subject of the last chapter. The discussion highlights the prevailing uncertainty surrounding the new United States, the continued sense of a cultural closeness between Britain and America, and a deep suspicion of republicanism and democracy.

Besides providing an improved understanding of the British experience at home and public responses to the conflict, a study of the British press during this period ultimately highlights two key points about wider British attitudes toward America and the empire. First, the British public discourse was far more independent and complicated than historians have hitherto depicted it. Dividing newspapers and magazines definitely according to pro- or anti-American and pro- or anti-ministry, as historians have too often been quick to do, is potentially misleading for all but a handful of publications. Although bias and political leanings were prevalent, virtually every publication carried a mixture of comment on each issue. Besides, the war that began at Lexington lasted more than nine turbulent years for the British and outlasted three ministries, which meant that hardly any newspapers or magazines had the same stance on either the Americans or the British government for the duration of the fighting.

The conflict was divisive, but to depict it as "polarizing" portrays the era as much neater than it truly was. As revealed in the following chapters, one did not have to be an American sympathizer to admire the virtues of George Washington or to loathe Britain's alliances with American Indians. Nor were opinions always predictable. Samuel Curwen, a Massachusetts loyalist refugee living in Britain who had suffered horribly at the hands of the American patriots, remarked in his diary after learning of possible British-allied American Indian raids on New York's frontier, "may it please God to preserve my poor Country from the desolating judgments of a merciless savage Indian war."[31] Charles Goore, a Liverpool merchant, like many British traders in early 1775, waited anxiously in crowded coffeehouses for news of American affairs and "the resolves of Parliament." Despite the economic hardship a war would cause him, he vigorously supported the armed subordination of the colonies in a letter to a friend: "I have upwards of £5000 amongst the Virginians, yet I hope the British Government will not submit to their arbitrary demands. Submit now and always submit for it is evident they are resolved to be independent."[32] Yet throughout the entire crisis he held Parliament's mismanagement responsible for allowing the war and was a harsh critic of the North ministry. The press ultimately offers a more organic view of British attitudes, highlighting the ambiguity in public opinion caused by the fortunes of the military and the heroism and villainy of the major actors.

The second key point is that the empire mattered to the ordinary middling and artisan Britons who constituted the bulk of the press's readership.[33] As one reader remarked in London's *Gazetteer* as early as the summer of 1775, the "affairs of America engross so much of the attention of the public, that every other consideration seems to be laid aside."[34] Religion, commerce, national identity, and rivalry with European powers are but a few of the extremely diverse reasons for popular interest in the empire that historians have identified. The press coverage of the American Revolution and the global war it sparked is a testament to this. Its millions of pages chronicle grassroots petitions to the king protesting and supporting government actions, nationwide laments and celebrations in response to battles, individual readers' opinions, and national debates. Although enormously diverse in sentiment and coverage, the underlying assumption of all of it was that overseas affairs mattered to British readers. The production of newspapers and magazines was, after all, ultimately a massive business run by savvy men and women who knew the profitability of catering to readers' tastes.

Whether or not Britain in the 1770s was a nation of imperialists is up for debate, and it is a subject in need of more attention than can be offered here. Nevertheless, even during their least successful imperial war, the British widely endorsed the material and security benefits of the empire, and throughout the war they associated the nation's health and future with its ability to retain its overseas territorial possessions. This was not a mere exercise in rhetoric. The tens of thousands of newspapers that British presses churned out daily covered these places so acutely that they would have seemed as if they were next-door. To be certain, numerous detractors complained about the costs of the empire—in terms of both its immediate drain on government funds and its long-term negative impact on the morality of the nation. Few Britons openly gloried in turning Britain into another Imperial Rome during this period, but most professed that without an empire the nation would be relegated to second-rate status in Europe. Despite the increasing importance of Asia, Africa, and the West Indies, the mainland North American colonies remained the empire's lynchpin in the minds of many Britons during the 1770s. This changed as Britain regained its footing and successfully stood toe-to-toe with its old enemies without the aid of either America or any major European allies. In consequence, the press reveals how British society at the end of the war was much more imperially minded and in many ways more confident in its position as an imperial power than when the war started.

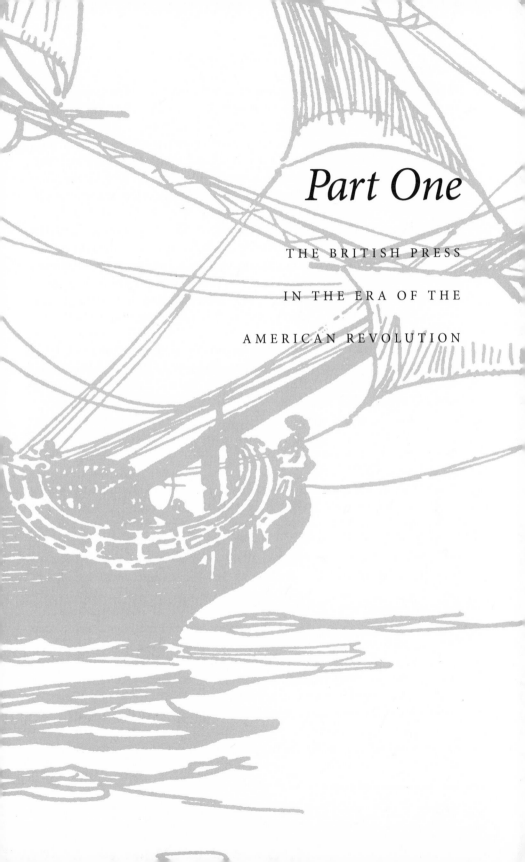

Part One

THE BRITISH PRESS

IN THE ERA OF THE

AMERICAN REVOLUTION

Distribution, Organization, and Readership

✳︎   The newspaper and periodical press was central to Britons' experience of the American Revolution and the global war it precipitated. The conflict's sheer length and the unprecedented taxation, government expenditure, and mobilization of man- and womanpower made the war's effects virtually inescapable, regardless of age, rank, gender, or geography. But despite its powerful domestic impact, the fighting was conceived far more than it was experienced firsthand. Except for a handful of raids, such as those led by the American John Paul Jones, and the minor sabotage of ports by John the Painter, the violence of the conflict remained distant. The Canadian winter, the East and West Indian heat, Washington's armies, Congress's debates, and American Indian war parties were all worlds away, and, despite a number of scares, even Britain's European enemies generally kept a safe distance from Britain's shores. Yet this war consumed the nation's attention as had no other since the previous century. As a letter from "Britannicus" in the *General Evening Post* concluded in June 1776, "The present conjuncture of affairs between Great-Britain and her American Colonies excites universal attention."[1]

The press brought the Pennsylvania wilderness, Caribbean seas, and Indian plains to life, making these places seem relevant to the national interest and pertinent to Britons' lives. Newspapers and magazines bombarded readers with acute coverage of the conflict, detailing it from political, social, and military angles. The war entered into people's daily routines through the press, making the war-ravaged New York frontier seem closer at times than the next county. Despite being best-known for events that transpired thousands of miles away from Britain and each other, George Washington, Tipu Sultan, and George Augustus Rodney would all become household names as acute coverage made disinterest all but impossible. As a reader of the *Salisbury Journal* remarked in March 1776: "I Believe there is not a person in this kingdom but is more or less interested in the present struggle between us and our American Colonists, and not many so totally divested of all concern for the event, as to take no side in it; but every one seems to have attached himself to one or the other."[2]

The eighteenth-century British press is not a new subject for study; however, its centrality to the present inquiry makes a discussion of its roles and operations necessary. Moreover, the study of the press's coverage of the American Revolution and the wider war it provoked in turn sheds further light on the workings of the press itself. The British press owed its rise in the eighteenth-century to a host of interconnected factors: improved infrastructure, relaxation of printing laws, a century of intermittent warfare, the diminishing authority of the crown and the accompanying growth of party politics, the emergence of a broad middle class, and the rise of a consumer society. Also important was the particular way in which Britain's fiscal-military state developed in the first half of the century: by switching emphasis from land tax to customs and excise taxes, Britain came to rely upon a widespread taxation base that required the complicity of the vast majority of the populace. As John Brewer has argued, this forged a powerful connection between the operations of the state and the ordinary Briton, who increasingly saw himself as invested in the nation's affairs.[3] As an astonished French visitor remarked just before the American Revolution: "public affairs are become the concern of every Englishman: each citizen is a politician."[4]

By the outbreak of war with the American colonies, the British newspaper production had grown from a fledgling industry that catered to the metropolitan political elite into a national medium that infiltrated most households. Some scholars have gone so far as to describe the press as forming "imagined communities" that transcended geographical, class, and gender boundaries in Britain during the century's later decades, and this argument receives qualified support in this study.[5] By the outbreak of the American Revolution, the press had become the nation's pedagogue as well as its forum for discussing national affairs, connecting blacksmiths in Bristol to lawyers' wives in Lincoln. Throughout the war, the press was an established part of Britons' lives, offering access to local, national, and international news, as well as being a forum for debate for just a few pennies. Although professional journalists were few, printers and writers who relied on the press for a substantial portion of their income grew in number as the press prospered. Profits from selling copies and advertising space made newspapers and magazines potentially lucrative business ventures, attracting investors outside of the printing and bookselling trades. The press's appeal was that it offered something for virtually everyone: business news, politics, foreign affairs, travel accounts, scientific discoveries, advice, fashion, gossip, criminal trials, and more. The rise of the press made newspapers and magazines part of a daily or weekly ritual for many Britons, connecting them to the world outside of their local community and enhancing the relevance of such distant events as the conflict with the American colonies.

The history of the eighteenth-century press began in 1695, when Parliament did not renew the Licensing Act, which had previously enabled the Church of England to restrict printing severely. Newspapers, both printed and handcopied, had been available throughout much of the seventeenth century, but expense, the law, and limitations on production had all but prohibited any chance of widespread distribution or substantial economic profit from the ventures. Printers and printing presses were so rare that when William of Orange landed on the south coast in 1688 he had to look as far as York to find the means to print his manifesto. After the lapse of the Licensing Act, the press flourished, particularly in London, which had a pre-existing middling and elite market that had the cash, literacy, and prerequisite interest in the business and political subjects that the press typically covered. And so within a decade of the act's lapse, printers churned out an amazing 2.3 million copies of papers per annum.[6] London was the center of the national press both in terms of news and production throughout the century. Major London weekly newspapers had distributions in the thousands by the 1720s, and the metropolis's major magazines, the *London Magazine* and the *Gentleman's Magazine,* had estimated monthly circulations by the 1730s of 6,000 and 10,000 respectively.[7] By the era of the American Revolution, London boasted at least nineteen newspapers, nine of which appeared daily.

Exact numbers of newspaper copies and readers for the whole of the century are impossible to determine, but the available evidence does allow for reasonable estimates. The government taxed newspapers for most of the century, but only a few years of Treasury records containing detailed figures on newspapers have survived. Nevertheless, these snapshots reveal a meteoric rise. In 1712 the ratio of copies printed that year to adults was roughly 1:2. By mid-century it had increased to 3:2, and by the end of the century it was 3:1.[8] In terms of total copies it meant growth from mere tens of thousands at the end of the seventeenth century to an estimated 7.3 million by mid-century, 9.4 million by 1760, 12.6 million in 1775, and 15.3 million in

1783.[9] This meant an average daily newspaper circulation of nearly 40,000 by the end of the American war. Magazine circulation, which was not included in the tax assessments, would have added at least another 300,000 copies a year to the total. And to this must be added the inestimable number of newspapers that were not taxed either because of exemption privileges invoked by members of the government or because they were traded on a black market.[10] Considering that a handpress could churn out about 250 copies per hour, these numbers translated into at least 62,400 printing hours per annum—a substantial amount of work for printers across the country.

This workload meant that major newspapers during the decades on either side of the American Revolution began to assume organizational structures similar to modern newspapers. Individual papers certainly varied, but the surviving accounts of the successful London daily the *Public Advertiser* for 1765–1771 offer an extraordinarily rare insight into the circulation and business side of a newspaper from this period (see table 1.1).[11] In many ways the *Public Advertiser* was typical of the more prosperous London dailies. It was published, along with eight other morning papers, before 8 a.m., and it circulated throughout the city and then throughout the nation.[12] Advertising space, which consumed as much as one-half of the paper, was typical. Also typical was its content, which consisted of news and commentary on metropolitan, national, imperial, foreign, and business affairs. The *Public Advertiser's* politics were not unusual for the London press in that it provided more criticism than praise of the tory-leaning North government when it came to power in 1770, but the paper was hardly radical. Like the British press as a whole, the *Public Advertiser* suffered low circulation in the post-Seven Years War period, with a mere 1,600 copies circulating daily in early 1765, but during the next few years it benefited enormously from both the political tensions in London fueled by publicity-seeking radicals like John Wilkes and the series of crises with the American colonies. The paper enjoyed a special relationship with anonymous and inflammatory political critic "Junius," often reaping the financial rewards of publishing his popular letters before anyone else.[13] One of these, an inflammatory letter addressed to the king, led to a costly libel trial in 1770, but the expense was worth it as annual circulation had doubled since 1765 to reach over a million copies in 1771. Gross income for the *Public Advertiser* in 1771 had reached £12,815, which, as comparative reference, was equivalent in value to more than four state-of-the-art Arkwright type one-thousand spindle mills.[14] Revenues came from a mixture of copy sales and advertising revenues, with the former outpacing the latter by a ratio of just over 1.6 to 1 for the 1765–1771 period (see table 1.2). Together they yielded profits that exceeded £4,000 in 1770, which would have been divided among the shareholders.

TABLE 1.1 Revenues and profits of the *Public Advertiser*

Year	Copies sold	Percentage increase in copy sales over previous year	Gross income in £s	Est. profit after posted taxes and expenses in £s	Increase in est. profits over previous
1765	510,335	na	7,306	1,963	na
1766	695,400	36	9,108	2,864	47%
1767	721,850	4	9,743	3,047	6%
1768	775,230	7	10,218	3,249	7%
1769	896,821	16	11,546	3,613	11%
1770	977,600	9	12,423	4,051	12%
1771	1,005,400	3	12,815	4,760	18%

Source: "Ledger of the accounts of the *Public Advertiser*," British Library, Add MS. 38169.

The *Public Advertiser* followed the emerging management model of successful British newspapers. At the helm was a seasoned newspaperman, Henry Sampson Woodfall, who came from a printing family and had inherited the printing of the *Public Advertiser* from his father. In previous generations Woodfall might have owned the paper outright or in partnership with a handful of booksellers looking for advertising space, but by mid-century papers such as the *Public Advertiser* were potential moneymakers in their own right that required substantial investment and organization. Libel cases, competition for the most recent news, the labor necessary to produce and distribute daily print runs of several thousand copies, the management of the 14,000 advertisements that appeared in the paper annually, and compliance with government tax regulations was more than one man and some apprentices could handle. In consequence, Woodfall was part of a corporate structure whose investors financed the paper and contracted with him to produce and distribute it. Woodfall, in turn, relied on a team of employees. Typical of this trend, the *Gazetteer,* one of London's newspapers about whose ownership and management more is known (albeit in the decades following the war with America), was owned by a consortium of fourteen major shareholders whose ranks still included some booksellers but also had a myriad of investors from outside the trade in search of profitable returns,

TABLE 1.2   Comparison of revenues from copy sales
and advertising of the *Public Advertiser*

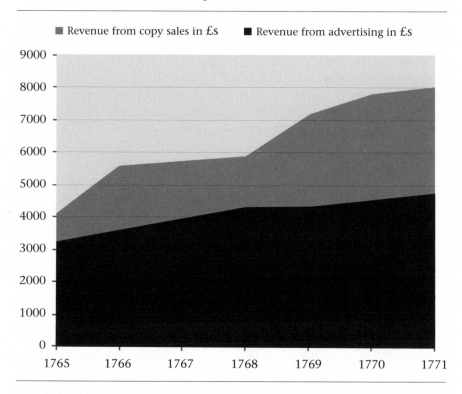

■ Revenue from copy sales in £s   ■ Revenue from advertising in £s

Source: "Ledger of the accounts of the Public Advertiser" British Library, Add MS. 38169

such as John Sotheby (the auctioneer), various merchants, a shipbuilder, and some gentleman investors.[15] The *Gazetteer* had a contracted printer, Mary Say, to handle the physical production of the paper, as well as an editor and staff to formulate its content. Surviving expense reports indicate that by 1792 the paper had a host of staff writers and reporters who covered different beats—Parliament, criminal courts, East India Office, etc.—and were paid middle-class salaries in excess of £100 per annum.[16]

Crucial to the press's rise as a national forum for news and debate was the national distribution of the London-based newspapers and magazines. A number of magazines enjoyed truly national audiences, particularly the best-selling *Gentleman's Magazine* and the leading review magazines the *Monthly Review* and *Critical Review*, which could be found in most large book clubs and circulating libraries.[17] Some London papers benefited from national readerships as early as the 1740s, but by the time of the American Revolution virtually all London papers and magazines claimed circulations that reached well beyond the metropolis.[18] In 1777 The *Morning Post* advertised daily circulation by express post to Bath, Bristol, Portsmouth, Southampton, Brighthelmstone, Margate, and Tunbridge Wells, and the *General Advertiser* claimed that it was sold daily in Bath, Bristol, Portsmouth, Gosport, Oxford, Birmingham, Cambridge, Southampton, Isle of Wight, Winchester, and Brighthelmstone. During the national elections of 1780 a single issue of the *London Courant* carried advertisements from candidates appealing to voters in Essex, Surrey, Buckinghamshire, and Hertford, indicating a regular readership that extended into London's surrounding counties.[19] Newspapers also regularly printed readers' letter purporting to be from locations from across Britain, further implying a nationwide audience. Tri-weekly papers relied particularly heavily on provincial circulation, and papers such as the *General Evening Post* even coordinated its publication with the departure of the post office coaches and paid coachmen to wait for its papers.[20] The General Post Office estimated to the Treasury as early as 1764 that newspapers leaving London weekly in recent years ranged between 15,000 and 21,000 (higher during wartime). By 1782 the estimated figure had risen to 60,000, which would have accounted for roughly one-third of the total number of papers printed in London.[21]

With even fewer surviving records, the development and functioning of the provincial newspaper is sketchier than that of the London press, but a rough idea of distribution during the era of the American Revolution can be pieced together. The general picture that emerges is akin to its metropolitan counterpart: vibrant, extensive, potentially lucrative, and corporate. The biggest problem facing English provincial newspapers during the first half of the eighteenth century was poor infrastructure and an inefficient and corrupt postal service.[22] By the 1750s and 1760s, however, most major towns were linked to London and each other by a frequent, if not daily, postal service. By the late 1760s the post was so regular that the fellows of Corpus Christi College in Oxford could wager their bottles of port on the hour of the coaches' arrival.[23] Improved infrastructure meant provincial printers had regular access to national news and a market eager for it and the London luxuries newspapers advertised. In consequence, English provincial newspapers such as the *Salisbury Journal* went from a paltry circulation of about 200 in the 1730s to 4,000 by the end of the American Revolution.[24] To sell papers, provincial printers, as well as London newsmen, relied on a mixture of horseback carriers and footmen who delivered papers to subscribers and agents in various towns and villages. Many provincial papers enjoyed impressive markets: the *Bristol Journal* claimed 162 locations where it could be bought in 1754; the *Sheffield Advertiser* named agents in twenty-three towns in 1761; the *Newcastle Journal* boasted a circulation area of 600 miles in circumference in 1773; and the *Shrewsbury Chronicle* in 1786 advertized that it could be delivered "to any part of Great Britain at 15 shillings per year."[25] The total number of operations also increased dramatically in the second half of the century from a mere twenty in the 1720s to at least fifty by the outbreak of the revolution, each needing to sell at least 2,000 copies per weekly issue in order to stay afloat.[26]

Central to any provincial newspaper's content was the London news. Local news and advertisements certainly appeared in the provincial press, but this was dwarfed by national news for most of the century. To some extent this may have been laziness on the part of the cut-and-paste provincial printer, but it was just as much a consequence of market demand for national and international news. Provincial printers such as that of the *Derby Mercury* timed its Thursday printing to coincide with the arrival of London newspapers in the post, often holding up printing if the coach was late. It also advertised in 1776 that it could reach readers in nearby villages with its digests of national news before the London post filtered through the provincial hubs, and the paper regularly boasted how many London papers it drew upon.[27] Moreover, provincial editors increasingly acted as local filters, selecting and summarizing the major national issues and giving greater attention to topics of regional interest.[28] As one editor exclaimed, the greatest advantage of relying on a provincial paper was that it sifted through the main news, saving the reader time and expense. "We beg leave, with regret, to observe the great demand among us for the English Magazines," he declared, "when it is obvious, that we enjoy one advantage which should entitle us to a preference; that is, the opportunity of perusing the various English collections of that kind, and culling from them such essays, and fugitive pieces, as are distinguished for their merit."[29]

The English provincial press was also increasingly corporate in structure and profit-oriented in outlook. Like their London counterparts, provincial papers could be major operations with circulations and annual revenues in the thousands, requiring a myriad of investors and workers. Ownership is not clear from the newspaper itself, which often included the name of the printer or editor only and even then kept names of those long-since departed for brand continuity. The *Bristol Journal* and the *Salisbury Journal* were owned by partnerships and run by members of the prominent printing families that established them.[30] Benjamin Collins had made the *Salisbury*

Journal one of the most successful papers in Britain over the course of several decades, raising its worth to an estimated £5,200 in 1773 before selling it to a group of investors who hired him at a massive salary of £400 to run the paper for them. As a comparative reference, an annual family income of forty to fifty pounds was the minimum for a middle-class lifestyle, and a prosperous lawyer might earn £350.[31] The move was a smart one, as the *Journal* yielded annual profits in excess of £800 for them.

The rapid rise of the provincial press in business terms during the second half of the century is most evident in its increase in advertising (see table 1.3). Whereas the London press's advertising more than doubled between 1760 and 1784, the provincial press more than quadrupled. Based on the advertising figures, the Anglo-American troubles were a boon to the provincial press. As premier ports of the Atlantic trade, cities like Bristol and Glasgow often received information from America before the London papers, and because of the dominant social position of the mercantile communities in those cities, editors gave serious attention to anything that might affect trade with the colonies. Advertisements, which came from local and London businesses and included everything from privateer recruiting to tonics, unsurprisingly took advantage of the situation, and by the war's midway point, provincial advertising had nearly caught up with its London equivalent.

TABLE 1.3   Newspaper advertisements—taxes and total numbers

Year ending Aug 2	Advertising tax revenues from London papers in £s	Advertising tax revenues from provincial and Scottish papers in £s	Est. total advertisements*	Percentage increase on the previous listed year
1750	4591	1248	116,780	na
1760	11,239	4567	158,060	35.3
1770	15,642	9505	251,470	59.1
1775	20,656	12,715	333,376	32.6
1777	20,678	14,000	346,780	4.0
1779	19,850	17,406	372,560	7.4
1784	26,639	19,645	370,272	-0.6

* The figure is derived based on the tax rate of 1 shilling per advertisement until 1757, when it was raised to 2 shillings, and 1780, when it was raised to 2 shillings 6 pence.

Source: National Archives, Kew: AO [Audit Office] 3/955-75.

Far less is known about the Scottish newspaper and periodical press, which has not received nearly as much attention as the English press and has been largely ignored or dismissed by historians examining British opinion and the American colonies.[32] Circulation figures are unknown, but the sparse pieces of evidence can be assembled to form a rough picture of the Scottish press during this period. The Scottish press functioned almost identically to the English provincial press. Most newspapers and magazines came from Edinburgh, and with a few largely struggling exceptions the rest were printed in Glasgow. *Ruddiman's Weekly Mercury* [Edinburgh], which receives substantial attention in the present study, typified the leading Scottish newspapers. Like leading English provincial newspapers, it appeared weekly and boasted a similar circulation of 3,000 copies during the American Revolution.[33] Also like the English provincial press, the Scottish press relied heavily on large circulation areas, using a combination of postal carriages, local agents, and walking deliverymen to distribute copies. The Scottish press also served as a conduit for national and international news emanating from London, but, like their English counterparts, editors in Scotland tailored such news for their regional markets by giving greater attention to items that directly affected their readers.

By the outbreak of war with the American colonies, the news network had ceased to resemble a bicycle wheel in which news emanated from the London hub like single spokes to the surrounding provinces. The network instead functioned more like a spider's web in which London served as the dense center of a complicated, multidirectional network. Provincial editors throughout the revolution regularly selected content directly from newspapers around the nation and world, thus bypassing the London filter. For example, the *Derby Mercury* regularly drew from the *Glasgow Journal, Cambridge Chronicle, Oxford Journal,* and *Bristol Journal,* to name but a few provincial papers; on a given day in November 1777 the *Bristol Journal* reprinted news from the *Edinburgh Evening Courant, Birmingham Gazette,* and *Cambridge Chronicle;* and even the *Dundee Weekly Magazine,* which struggled throughout its short-lived existence, drew from as far away as the *Kentish Gazette.*[34] During the second half of the century news regularly flowed both ways between London and the provinces, and metropolitan papers openly drew from the provincial press in dedicated sections, such as the *Lloyd's Evening Post's* "Country News" column. This exchange seems to have intensified from the 1760s as London papers fought with each other to provide the earliest accounts of breaking news from America, which often arrived in provincial ports first. As the credibility of the provincial press increased, provincial papers became a familiar site in

London. Savvy editors, such as those of the *Stamford Mercury* and *Exeter Flying-Post,* printed the locations on their respective mastheads of the numerous London agents who took advertisements and sold copies of their papers. The recently launched *Hampshire Chronicle* in 1779 boasted of seven London locations where it could be bought and advertizing space was sold.[35] Metropolitan subscribers soon included individuals as well as coffeehouses and London editors, and by the war's end, the Post Office estimated, albeit with the caveat that "this is only a guess," that as many newspapers came into London as left.[36] Exact figures aside, it is nevertheless clear that during the American Revolution the British possessed a truly national printed news network.

Even more complicated than the issue of distribution is the problem of readership. Exact figures simply cannot be determined. Yet readership is a subject that has fortunately intrigued book historians, who have cobbled together the scraps of some quantitative and mostly anecdotal evidence from which can be constructed a persuasive case that reading was widespread in terms of geography, class, and gender. Newspaper and magazine reading in particular was public and communal, regularly breaking down many of the usual reading barriers such as illiteracy and economic hardship. By the era of the American Revolution, reading—or listening to someone else read— newspapers and magazines was part of the daily routine of artisans and government ministers alike. Such extensive readership ultimately made the press the nation's main resource for national and overseas news as well as the primary forum for discussing it.

Although the exact number of readers cannot be determined, a fair attempt can be made at estimating it. During the American Revolution the average daily print run for the London press was 25,000 to 30,000. Because most copies found more than one reader, circulation numbers constitute only the start of an estimation of total readership. Many newspaper readers, especially in the crowded London market, would have read more than one newspaper or magazine. Coffeehouses, for example, regularly offered patrons a choice of a dozen or more. In consequence, estimates of the average number of readers per copy from both contemporaries and historians have varied substantially—ranging from as low as five to as high as forty.[37] At the beginning of the eighteenth century Joseph Addison in his *Spectator* claimed there were twenty readers per paper, and later in the century the *Westminster Magazine* declared that the number was closer to thirty.[38] Dennis O'Bryen, a political advisor, claimed in a letter to Edmund Burke that London's newspaper readership was somewhere in the realm of 250,000 (about ten readers per paper), while Burke himself estimated it to be around 400,000 in the 1790s.[39] Given the disparity, almost any ratio would appear arbitrary; however, for the purposes of estimating total readership, a conservative one of 15:1 for the newspapers and magazines that circulated in London is reasonable and takes into account both readers who read multiple papers as well as any spike in readership caused by the American Revolution. After considering the provincial newspapers that circulated in London and subtracting the several million London-printed newspapers that went to provincial locations, this means an average daily London readership during the American Revolution was probably in the realm of 300,000—roughly one-third of Londoners and in line with the contemporary estimates noted above.

Readers-to-newspaper ratio estimates for the press outside of London have received scant attention, with the exception of Hannah Barker's conservative approximation for the English provincial press of 5:1 during the second half of the century.[40] A lower estimate than for London is necessary, because literacy was significantly lower outside of London. Yet even an average middling or elite household could have well over a dozen members, especially if one considers the servants (many of whom read), and many of the papers went to inns, taverns, and coffeehouses, where multiple readers awaited.[41] Moreover, and as discussed in detail below, practices of reading outside of London were communal and included the illiterate. In consequence, a higher ratio of 10:1, while still conservative, seems more reasonable.

Given the similarities between the English provincial and Scottish presses, as well as the absence of detailed examination of Scottish press readership, the same ratio of 10:1 seems reasonable. Arguments for a lower Scottish readership can be made due to poorer infrastructure north of Edinburgh, lower population densities, and a less developed consumer culture; however, a contrary case can be made based on Scotland's superior higher education (four universities to England's two) and the boom in public learning during the Scottish Enlightenment. As the *Edinburgh Magazine* boasted as early as 1758, "We take this opportunity to congratulate our country, on progress that genius, taste, and, every part of the Belles Lettres, are daily making amongst us. Ever since the revival of learning first began to dispel the clouds of Gothic ignorance and barbarism, Caledonia could boast of an intimacy with the muses, little short of, if not equal to, that of Latium itself."[42] Moreover, Scots had a national interest in America that easily matched, if not exceeded, that of the English: Glasgow dominated the tobacco trade, 3 percent of Scotland's population had immigrated to North America in the decade preceding the revolution, and the Scots were disproportionately overrepresented in the British army.[43] Until extensive studies of the Scottish press are conducted, the estimated ratio of 10:1 will have to do. These figures mean that roughly one-fifth of the provincial British population read newspapers on a weekly basis—less than in London but still substantial.[44] As was the case in London, many more Britons had a more sporadic relationship with the press, turning to it in times of national crisis or for matters of personal interest. And the American Revolution produced plenty of crises.

When it comes to the eighteenth-century British press, virtually all numbers are somewhat arbitrary, but, even if one quibbles with the exact figures, the anecdotal evidence is consistently clear: readership of the press was a widespread, staple part of many Britons' routines, and it was increasingly prevalent. Part of the press's appeal was that it offered something for almost everyone. By the American Revolution, the press carried Parliamentary reports, court news, criminal reports, advice columns, extracted travel accounts and histories, theater reviews, book reviews, political and social commentary, the correspondence of key figures, satire, commerce, gossip, and a host of advertisements targeting everyone from artisans to aristocrats. George Crabbe celebrated this in his 1785 poem on newspapers:

> Next, in what rare production shall we trace
> Such various subjects in so small a space?
> As the first ship upon the waters bore
> Incongruous kinds that never met before;
> Or as some curious virtuoso joins,
> In one small room, moths, minerals, and coins,
> Birds, beasts, and fishes; nor refuses place
> To serpents, toads, and all the reptile race:
> So here, compress'd within a single sheet,
> Great things small, the mean and mighty meet.[45]

The press also made expensive books available in extracted form for readers, most of whom might not have been able to justify the expense of a multi-shilling work but could spare a few pennies for a newspaper. The *Derby Mercury* explained in its preface to its series of accounts "of the English Settlements in North America" extracted from a variety of histories and travel accounts, "As many of our Readers have not the Opportunity of consulting Books of Geography, and therefore can know but little of the [geographic] Situation of our English Colonies Abroad; we shall continue (as we have begun) to give some further Accounts of the British Settlements in North America; which will not only give Pleasure in the Reading, but be instructive

and useful."[46] Thus one of the key roles of the press was that of national pedagogue, instructing readers in geography, history, philosophy, and science
through its extraction of stories ranging from the latest discoveries of the
Royal Society to reviews of the latest ideas of human socio-economic development from the philosophers of the Enlightenment.[47]

Newspaper reading was socially widespread throughout Britain during
the second half of the century. As one commentator remarked in 1772,
"The common people, of late years, are become so wonderfully learned
among us, by the vast increase of Diurnals and Nocturnals—Gazettes and
Gazetteers—Papers and Packets—Journals and Ledgers—Mercuries and
Flying-posts-Courants and Chronicles—that you will hardly find the mean-
est peasant, or the sootiest chimney-sweeper so unlettered, as not to be able
to spell a Newspaper."[48] Newspapers themselves regularly claimed a broad
social readership, with the *Morning Chronicle* typically boasting that it was
"read by all ranks of people."[49] The "signatures" of printed letters to the
newspapers regularly paid homage to the social diversity of the readership
with such names as "An Ordinary Briton," "A Common Patriot," "A
Plebian," and "One of the People." When the language of the press became
overly complicated, readers complained. One reader, for example, was baf-
fled by the inclusion of the word "convelescents" in the *London Gazette's*
extract of an official military report from America in 1776. Despite the assistance of his coffeehouse friends, the reader could not determine the
word's meaning until his son arrived home and explained it to him. Irritated, he wrote to the *Saint James's Chronicle:* "I remember, Sir, in the War
before last, all our Generals and Admirals wrote in plain English, that every
Body could understand them."[50]

The extent to which advertisements directly mirrored the readership of a
particular paper is debatable, but when taken as a whole they certainly lend
support to the argument that readership was geographically and socially
broad.[51] As the *Saint James's Chronicle* remarked in response to a possible
increase in stamp tax on newspapers in 1776: "the great Variety of Advertisements which make their daily Appearance, are a Proof of their Utility to
all Ranks of People. The Merchant, the Artist, the Mechanick, have all Re-
course to News-Papers; Commerce is extended, the Liberal Sciences promoted."[52] Some of the advertising targeted the elite—land, merchant ship
embarkations, and port arrivals—but newspapers typically carried a steady
stream of advertisements aimed at the middling ranks, such as the *Bristol
Journal's* advertisements of self-help books for tradesmen, including *Every
Tradesmen his Own Lawyer.*[53] The most frequently appearing advertisements were for other printed materials—magazines, books, maps, and

The Blacksmith lets his Iron grow cold attending to the Taylor's News. ——

FIGURE 1.1. "The Blacksmith lets his Iron grow cold attending to the Taylor's News." *Oxford Magazine*, June 1772. In this satirical print, the artist takes aim at the newspaper-reading artisans, who neglected their work to attend to the affairs of state. BMC 5074, © Copyright the Trustees of the British Museum.

prints—and modestly expensive medicines, but the press also printed advertisements for more affordable small luxuries such as coffee and tea. The
Morning Post and *London Courant* even carried regular advertisements for
employers seeking servants and servants seeking employers, and port cities'
papers often had advertisements for seamen—all suggesting a very socially
broad readership.

The public nature of reading, particularly with regard to the newspaper and periodical press, means that estimated literacy rates have an especially limited relevance in understanding the problem of audience. After all,
the usual criterion for assessing literacy in a pre-industrial society, i.e., signing one's name, is hardly a fair measure of who could or could not read a
newspaper.[54] Based on this standard, most adults appear to have been literate by the middle of the eighteenth century, but this did not represent a
sharp rise in literacy, which, according to Lawrence Stone, leveled out somewhere at the end of the seventeenth century.[55] Printed materials such as
chapbooks were already abundant in the seventeenth century. Charles Tias,
a London Bridge bookseller, had a stock at his death in 1664 of 90,000 chapbooks and another 37,000 ballad sheets.[56] Clearly the newspaper and periodical press's rise in the eighteenth century was attached not to a rapid increase in literacy but to a change in reading practices and interests.[57]
Moreover, illiteracy was not necessarily a barrier when it came to keeping
abreast of the latest printed news and commentary, because literacy was, in
the words of David Vincent, "at once a personal and collective possession"
in which the literate read and wrote for the illiterate.[58] This happened in
homes, shops, and on town and city streets.

The public nature of reading was nowhere more evident than in the coffeehouses that peppered London and other provincial cities, where readers
from a range of social classes took advantage of the free papers and engaged
in debate with fellow patrons. Although the exact number of coffeehouses at
the time of the American Revolution is unknown, Bryant Lillywhite has estimated that there were at least 551 as well as 207 inns and 447 taverns in
London alone by 1739.[59] To these can be added the thousands of book clubs,
circulating libraries, and public reading rooms around the country, which
regularly subscribed to newspapers and magazines and offered venues for
debate.[60] Even barbershops provided spaces for public reading, using newspapers to entice customers. As the *London Magazine* remarked in August
1780, newspapers were central to these businesses' success: "Without newspapers our Coffee-houses, Ale-houses, and Barber shops, would undergo a
change next to depopulation."[61] It was in these places that a single copy of a

FIGURE 1.2. "The Morning News" (1772). The caption reads: "The Rabble gather round the Man of News and listen with their mouths. Some tell, some hear[,] some judge of news[,] some make it." This print highlights the social diversity of readers and the sometimes public nature of newspaper reading. BMC 5086, © Copyright the Trustees of the British Museum.

newspaper found dozens of readers. Although some coffeehouses catered to a specific clientele—Jonathan's and Lloyd's to elite merchants and stockjobbers, the Cocoa Tree to leading tories, and Child's to physicians and members of the Royal Society—many were socially mixed, opening their doors to a diversity of patrons holding a variety of opinions. Lord North and Horace Walpole may have had their favorite coffeehouse haunts, but so too did plenty of other Britons much further down the social scale. While reading at the Chapter Coffee House in London in 1773, Thomas Campbell, a visiting Irishman, was amazed when "a whitesmith [a worker of tin] in his apron & some of his saws under his arms, came in, sat down and called for his glass of punch and the paper, both of which he used with as much ease as a Lord."[62] Although surprising to visitors, such scenes were normal for coffeehouse regulars. As John Trusler informed readers of his London guidebook, coffeehouses generally were places "where certain questions, political, civil and moral, are discussed, and everyone may give his opinion."[63]

Some coffeehouses even offered formal debates with questions advertised in local papers beforehand. For example, the Queen's Arms in Newgate Street, home of the "Society for Free Debate," held a debate on the evening of January 3, 1776, on the question "Which are the most loyal subjects, and best friends to liberty, those who in their Addresses to the King approve or those who in the Petitions condemn, the present proceedings against America?" The *Gazetteer* reported that the question was "ingeniously handed, and some new matter thrown out on both sides," but that it ended with "a very small majority in favour of the petitions [supporting conciliation]."[64] Coffeehouses were not, of course, the only venues for organized debate, and throughout the American Revolution the Coachmakers Hall, Carlisle House, Mitre Tavern, Free Masons Hall, Oratorical Hall in Spring Garden, and the Lyceum Theatre all held formal debates on topics advertised in the press. They were all public, although many charged a small entry fee, and some, such as the Lyceum group, which had been established by young men studying at the inns of court, offered special discounts to women.[65]

Not surprisingly, the press depicted the coffeehouses as representative of the pulse of public opinion. Writers regularly used them as settings for fictitious political dialogues, readers used them as addresses in their letters to editors, and newspapers reported on their latest debates. Coffeehouse goers became subjects of occasional satire, but the ridicule only points to their prevalence. A reader's letter printed in *Town and Country* in 1770 offered a typical complaint about the coffeehouse patrons who had the audacity to comment on public affairs and stir up opinion against the government: "I frequently met with chattering Quidnuncs who pretend to talk decisively about the English nations, though they are very little acquainted with the English language; and make as many false concords as false conclusions."[66] The American Revolution only heightened criticism of government policies and gave larger audiences to armchair generals—much to the irritation of more than one critic. After the news of the British surrender to the Americans at Saratoga reached London in December 1777, a letter to the *General Evening*

Post complained: "It is amusing to hear the coffee-house politicians decide upon the conduct of Gen. Burgoyne, with respect to his late transactions . . . [from] such as have only fought battles in books, or formed attacks upon paper, by a comfortable fire-side."[67] "We every day meet with people," complained another reader, "who in the most peremptory language decide on the conduct of General and Admirals, who never either saw a fleet or an army."[68]

Outside London the press connected people to national and overseas affairs, attaching provincial towns and villages to the national stage. As one contemporary commentator remarked, "The source of information to the gentleman farmer and the flourishing manufacturer, who constitute the great body of the free-holders, especially in this county [Yorkshire], is a provincial newspaper."[69] The newspaper connected communities throughout the country. Typical of many in his social position, south Lancashire

FIGURE 1.3. "A Meeting of the City Politician's" (1779). This satirical print pokes fun at the middling and artisan Britons who debated politics over newspapers in coffeehouses and taverns. The caption reads: "With staring Eye & open Ear/ Each cobling Horned City seer/ Swallows down Politics with Beer/ Neglects his Family & Calling/ To enter into Party Brawling/ Gets Drunk & Swears—the Nation's falling." BMC 5613, © Copyright the Trustees of the British Museum.

FIGURE 1.4. "The Country Politicians" (1784). This print satirizes the country folk who gathered to discuss and debate the news. The caption reads "The Parson, Barber & the Squire, Three Social Souls who News admire." BMC 6730, © Copyright the Trustees of the British Museum.

yeoman farmer Richard Latham shared a newspaper subscription with several neighbors. Thomas Turner, a middling shopkeeper in Sussex, regularly read the local and London papers and excitedly recorded national events in his diary.[70] The editor of the *Salisbury Journal* explained that newspapers were windows on life: "The papers of the day are not only a daily amusement, but a daily lesson in life; every paper is a sort of tragi-comedy that represents the different distresses and pursuits of mankind. . . . [E]ach compiler is a picturesque historian that presents you with something to laugh at, and something to bewail," he continued, "and their compilations, though a chaos of the confused matter promiscuously jumbled together, are aptly expressive of the miseries and follies of mankind."[71]

Places for public reading proliferated outside London to the extent that by the outbreak of war with the American colonies most towns with a population above a few thousand supported at least one coffeehouse and one or more book clubs and libraries. With a population of 3,000, Kanresborough had its own coffeehouse by 1760, the Somerset market town of Taunton boasted four book clubs by the end of the century, one of which was exclusively for women, and as early as 1746 a "Friendly society of neighbors" met in Cambridgeshire to share books, newspapers, and magazines.[72] As in London, many of these places regularly competed for the first and most accurate national news, such as one Birmingham coffeehouse that in 1777 advertised that a special messenger enabled it to offer eleven London newspapers the afternoon following their publication along with an assortment of provincial papers.[73]

Women, in and out of London, were avid participants in the press, both as producers and audiences. Women printers, though not the norm, were not rare. Women in most shopkeeping and artisan families assisted in the business, and the world of print was no exception.[74] Women's names regularly appear on newspapers' lists of locations both within and outside of London for selling the newspapers and taking advertisements, and some women even officially led printing operations. The *Morning Post's* printers were the Griffins, a husband and wife team, and when the paper took its operations elsewhere after the death of her husband in 1776, Mrs. Griffin and other disgruntled former employees set up a spurious *Morning Post.*[75] The Farley family, which partly owned and operated Bristol newspapers for the better part of a century, included numerous women who controlled the family business at various points.[76] Perhaps the most famous female printer was Mary Say, who was a major figure in the London printing trade for much of the second half of the eighteenth century. When Charles Say, her husband, printer, and part owner of a number of publications, died in 1776, she assumed control of his shares and contracted with the other shareholders to continue printing the highly successful *Gazetteer* and *Craftsmen.*[77] Content operations seem to have been handled by someone else, but as the printer she remained legally liable for any libel suits, and in 1779 she was prosecuted and convicted of libel, resulting in six months in prison and a fine of fifty pounds. That Say was truly the force that ran printing operations is evidenced by her twenty-five years of service; and even after remarrying in 1787 she continued to publish the *Gazetteer* under her previous married name for a further three years.

Female readership, although perhaps less socially broad than its male counterpart, was widespread. Newspapers attempted to accommodate female tastes through a range of prescriptive pieces aimed at middling women readers, such as the *Leeds Mercury's* "The Dress of the Month" feature in the 1770s and occasional comments such as the *Ipswich Journal's* warning "for those of the Fair sex" against drinking beverages that were too hot.[78] Comments from "Theophrastus" in a letter to the *Morning Post* in July 1779 typified the remarks that usually surrounded content overtly aimed at women: "As your paper is circulated through most of the polite circles in this kingdom, and as you have many female readers, it has occurred to me that a series of letters in the *Morning Post,* on moral subjects, might prove both entertaining and useful to the Ladies of Great Britain."[79] Despite such prescriptions, women's actual reading practices were hardly so narrow, and there is abundant evidence that women took an active interest in national affairs, including discussions on the American Revolution. Women bought books, read aloud to the illiterate, and subscribed to magazines—the most popular of which for a time was, ironically, the *Gentleman's Magazine.*[80] Middling women belonged to debating societies, circulating libraries, and book clubs throughout the nation, many of which carried newspapers and magazines, and women's book ownership in at least the first decades of the eighteenth century appears to have been equal to that of men.[81]

Although it is impossible to determine the extent to which women focused their reading attentions on the American Revolution and participated in the national forum created by the press, there is plenty of evidence that they did take part. Abigail Gathern, the daughter of a Nottingham grocer, followed the conflict via her father's newspapers, pasting clippings in her diary.[82] Elizabeth Carter, undoubtedly typical of the many British women "who dread[ed] the arrival of every ship," followed the war in the press, anxious for news of male relations and friends who had gone abroad to fight. Writing in the tense atmosphere of October 1777, when the nation anxiously awaited news from the embattled British army under John Burgoyne, Carter observed that "Every body seems very impatient for news from America. . . . I chiefly wish intelligence for the sake of the poor people who are anxious for their friends. Oh that they were all safe in England! It is terrible to be kept in suspence about the event, till another express can cross the Atlantic."[83] Carter was not a passive observer. Probably like most women, she did not hesitate to offer her views when the opportunity arose, such as when she lambasted the nation's politicians for what she perceived to be a dreadful mishandling of the conflict: "What wretched accounts of the state of things in America, and what folly in the measures on all sides, which have involved the nation in such a difficulty! The government by urging an unprofitable right, if a right it be, and the opposition by heightening the refractory spirits of the colonists!"[84]

In May 1775, just before news of the outbreak of war had arrived, the *London Chronicle* carried a fictitious, but plausibly representative, dialogue entitled "The City Patriot; a Breakfast Scene" in which a husband and wife discuss the American crisis over breakfast and newspapers.[85] As the scene opens, the husband, sympathetic to the Americans, is reading a story extracted from the *New York Gazette,* from which he read aloud: "the people in America are so united that they will soon raise a militia to match the very best veterans in Europe." Attempting to provoke his wife—depicted as the rational supporter of the North ministry—he goads her by concluding, "Do you mark that, my dear?" She responds with a simple "Yes; but I don't believe it," which sparks a witty debate in which she attacks the propagandistic nature of the American and British opposition press and pokes fun at those readers, including her husband, who gullibly believe it. The message of the dialogue, espoused by the "common sense" possessing character of the wife is clear: London radicals and their American patriot associates were making things worse with their libelous claims. Although the dialogue is fictitious, its setting, which is portrayed as entirely normal, makes clear that women's participation in the press-fueled discussions of American affairs was not at all unusual.

Like Elizabeth Carter and the fictitious couple debating over breakfast, most Britons were not complacent readers. The proactive nature of Britons was instrumental to the press's role as the national forum for debate during the American Revolution. As *Lloyd's Evening Post* remarked in July 1780, "Without newspapers . . . our Country Villagers, the Curate, and the Blacksmith, would lose the self-satisfaction of being as wise as our First Minister of State."[86] Readers' letters in particular created an image of classless participation in which the lowliest Briton could anonymously critique the greatest minister of state, thus emboldening middling and artisan Britons to take a greater interest in national affairs.[87] As "John Bull" remarked in a letter addressed to the king and printed in the *Public Advertiser* in 1781, "it is the Birth-right of all free Britons to study public affairs, it is their duty to lay the result of their enquiries with candour and impartiality before your Majesty, and even the Public, when their views are laudable to your Royal interest, and the Good of their Fellow citizens."[88]

While celebrated by printers, popular reading was a source of agitation for many critics, who worried that newspapers opened up elite affairs to the unsuitably prepared commoner. As the *Idler* bluntly remarked, the press "enables those to talk who were born to work."[89] A correspondent in a letter to the *Oxford Magazine* woefully admitted: "There is nothing for which our countrymen in general are more remarkable than for the disposition they have always to introduce political subjects into their common discourse."[90] However, the writer continued: "It may certainly be urged with the greatest degree of truth, that the lower and indeed the generality of those whom we now call the middling class of people have little understanding in these matters; —the wheels of government are too intricately contrived for them to apprehend how they are directed, nor is it by any means necessary that they should." The problem, as "Joineriana" perceived it in 1772, was that the newspaper had ceased to be a "brief chronicle of the time—a translator of foreign gazettes, and recorder of domestic occurences." The press instead created popular forums for criticizing and discussing political affairs and elites' conduct:

> Points of all sorts, many of which were formerly accounted difficult and crabbed; are now discussed by all sorts of people, with the utmost ease and perspicuity—whose attention is taken up, not only with government, continental, colony, company, county and corporation affairs—but they have also their neighbours business to mind, as well as their own.[91]

Regardless of such complaints, public opinion had found its rallying point and outlet in the press, in which any humble reader could be equal to any member of Parliament.

Politics and the Press

✳ Central to the press's viability as a national source of
information and forum for debate was its ability to report freely on
national affairs. By the era of the American Revolution, the British
press had largely extricated itself from direct government influence,
emerging instead as a potentially lucrative businesses that responded to market forces. As detailed in the preceding chapter, advertising and readership, not government subsidies, ultimately rendered profits. Entrepreneurs created a national press that protested
government interference and championed the individual. Rather
than packing their papers with political propaganda, by the era of
the American Revolution these men and women instead responded
to market demands with an array of factual information and a wide
spectrum of critical commentary that served to equip readers to
forge their own opinions about national topics.

This is not to suggest that the press was free from corruption or
that only nobly intentioned men and women operated newspapers and magazines, because there are plenty of examples of
bribes, threats, and other varieties of underhandedness. So many
contemporary claims of impropriety exist that earlier studies of
the press have assumed that such corruption dictated content and,
therefore, newspapers were mere party bugles and printers' soap-
boxes.[1] More recent examinations of the press have suggested that
the newspapers and magazines were, for the most part, increasingly independent business ventures during the second half of the
century. This line of thought finds abundant support here. During

the era of the American Revolution, savvy men and women in search of profit rather than political influence or revenge made up the vast majority of owners and operators, and they found the most lucrative revenues by appealing to the wider British reading public. The press helped give middling and artisan Britons a perceived stake in the successes and failures of the national state, but the result was not a euphoric nationalism. What emerged instead was a hypercritical environment in which every move of the nation's politicians and generals underwent close public assessment. The public examination of national affairs was always more intense in times of strife, but the disaster of the protracted American rebellion that grew into a global war saw that scrutiny reach unparalleled heights.

There is little evidence that the British government attempted to control public opinion through the press during this period. The days when Robert Walpole invested £50,000 of secret service money in payments to printers and writers had long since passed.[2] Secret service accounts, from which payments would have been made, are sketchy, but the records that survive from this period suggest that attempts to influence the press were limited at best. Funds for domestic activities were limited by act of Parliament to £10,000 per annum by the end of the war, and out of this came the pensions and payoffs for a host of operations, leaving precious little for direct subsidies to the press.[3] There is no evidence of any provincial English paper being subsidized by the government, and only one Scottish paper appears on any known list, but that was not until 1792.[4] When William Pitt, the Younger took office just after the American Revolution, at least five London papers were receiving subsidies, but none more than £100—an insignificant sum when compared to the annual profits of several thousand pounds that any of the papers enjoyed—and many of the papers were forums for some of the most vociferous critics of the government. At best, such amounts might have persuaded editors to print a handful of stories on a specific domestic bill; it was hardly enough to shape reporting on a controversial, ill-fated, eight-year global war. The government was not shy about spending money to control the political process, but the political elite found better value for their money in electioneering, to which George III regularly funneled his private income. Besides, had the government been able to exert significant control over the press, then surely it would have averted earlier, shorter-lived episodes such as the public campaign to bring down George III's favorite, Lord Bute, or any of those having to do with John Wilkes and his radical London supporters.[5]

Perhaps more important is that even if the government or a political faction had seriously attempted to control the press (and given the lack of surviving documentation, it is possible that they did), they would not have been successful. The organizational structure, profitable nature, and sheer enormity of the British press, as well as the market's expectation of a free press, would have thwarted any significant external attempt to control the press's portrayal and discussion of the American Revolution. As discussed in the previous chapter, newspaper organization in the second half of the eighteenth century was increasingly complex, with a large cast of investors and employees with substantial sums of money at stake. Unlike a generation or two earlier, it was no longer a matter of simply paying off a single, greedy printer, because the printer now was most likely either a subcontractor who merely printed the paper or a minority stakeholder in a partnership involving a dozen or more investors. Although not apolitical, these men and women, whose primary professions were decreasingly connected to the print trade, sought profit, not political gain. Thus any successful control of the paper's content beyond an occasional story would have either required a slew of regular bribes or a corporate takeover.

The minute books of the investors' meetings of the *Saint James's Chronicle,* a moderately successful London tri-weekly, offer a unique and illuminating perspective (see table 2.1).[6] Like many papers, the *Saint James's Chronicle* had been divided into shares—twenty held by about a dozen investors at any given point; thus, no one owned a controlling interest. The investors included various businesspeople and professionals, including David Garrick, the notable actor and theater manager.[7] Henry Baldwin, the original owner and printer, continued to run the business with Nathaniel Thomas, who received a salary and regular performance bonuses. The shareholders were not silent investors. An elected oversight committee met monthly to review the paper's business activities, and all of the shareholders were invited to quarterly meetings held at some of London's finest taverns and coffeehouses. At any given time during this period about half of the shareholders attended. The minutes make clear that the shareholders were most keenly interested in the paper's finances. At each quarterly meeting they voted on the valuation of the shares, approved or declined the sale of a share, and decided the amount of the quarterly dividend.

These were shrewd businessmen. They stockpiled profits in anticipation of legal action, and they regularly bought up any available shares with the newspaper's profits in order to collect higher dividends for themselves or to wait for a desirable partner. They also did not hesitate to command Baldwin in business matters. When advertisers' accounts were in arrears in March 1770, they resolved to cut the debtors off, instructed

TABLE 2.1   Profits of the *Saint James's Chronicle*

Year	Posted total profit in £s	Gross rate of return as percent of shares'* total value	Annual return per individually owned share in £s**	Annual rate of return as a percentage of a single share
1774	1,683	28.1	80	26.6
1775	1,622	27	80	26.6
1776	1,271	21.2	80	26.6
1777	1,184	20	70	23.3
1778	1,112	19.7	60	20
1779	1,352	22.5	65	21.7
1780	1,396	23.3	95	31.67
1781	1,099	18.3	40	13.3
1782	986	16.4	70	23.3
1783	935	15.6	60	20

* Throughout this period the shareholders consistently voted every three months that each of the twenty shares was worth £300, and they sold and redeemed the shares at this price without fail. This means that the total posted value of the investment was £6,000. Because the shareholders carefully controlled trading and fixed the share price, rather than selling to the highest bidder, the paper's real value was probably far higher.

** This includes only the distributed quarterly dividends. Shareholders also took an annual salary of up to £1 for attending quarterly dinners, and profits were often accumulated to buy shares, pay bonuses for staff, and pay legal fees rather than distributed as dividends.

Source: "Saint James's Chronicle, Minute Books," Manuscripts Department, University of North Carolina Library, Chapel Hill, North Carolina.

Baldwin to operate on a cash basis whenever possible, and hired a debt collector who had previously worked for one of the shareholders. When sales, and thus dividends, slumped they offered specific instructions, such as in April 1782 when they instructed the printer to stop delivering papers before the official publication time and to tap into new markets by "try[ing] the Experiment of sending the paper to Bath and Birmingham by the coaches." They also winced at the possibility of libel trials, when the expenses of their prosecuted printer were taken out of the paper's profits. What the shareholders did not appear to do was comment on the politics of the paper. Nothing of the sort ever appears in the minute books that cover the two decades of the American revolutionary era.

Even if the government or a political faction could identify the long list of people it needed to bribe, the expense would have been almost insurmountable. The newspaper business could be extremely profitable, and individual papers were some of the largest and most profitable private enterprises in Britain.[8] This was no more so than during the American Revolution, when advertising revenues increased by 28 percent—despite a 25 percent government tax increase on ads. Circulation also increased, and, combined with advertisement revenues, made the annual newspaper and periodical press market worth about £250,000 during the war.[9] This meant that by the eve of the war, the annual stamp tax on papers and advertisements exceeded the customs duties collected on all of the coffee legally imported into Britain.[10] A successful London paper's value ranged between five and ten thousand pounds, and leading provincial papers such as the *Bath Chronicle* and *Salisbury Journal* were worth £4,000 and £5,200 respectively.[11] The rates of return they yielded for investors lucky or savvy enough to purchase a share were staggering by contemporary standards. The *Salisbury Journal*, for example, yielded an annual return of 15.5 percent for investors in the 1770s, while London papers offered even more, such as the *Gazetteer's* annual return of 18 to 22 percent.[12] In real terms, this translated into average annual dividends of £68 on £300 shares during the war for the holders of the *Saint James Chronicle*—or an average return of 22.7 percent. These rates far exceeded yields on risk-free government debt during the war, which traded at between 3.25 and 5.25 percent, or even the far more precarious African slave trade.[13] As a comparative reference, an annual family income of forty to fifty pounds was the minimum for a middling lifestyle, and incomes above a few thousand would place a family in the most elite tier of the wealthiest Britons.[14] For the vast majority of investors the press was not their sole enterprise, and they spread their wealth across the board in everything from banking to industry. Such profitability meant that the sums necessary to take control of the press had to be colossal—outweighing any long-term loss of profit and the damage done to the reputations of those involved—and there simply is no evidence that any political group was shelling out the necessary cash. Even the government's entire annual domestic secret service fund of £10,000, out of which potential bribes would have come, would have been paltry in comparison to the profits at stake.

By the time of the American Revolution, the newspaper market fully expected the press to be largely free of backdoor political influence and had little tolerance for corrupt newspapers. Editors basked in this role. Pledges such as those from the *Gazetteer*, which assured readers at the height of the war that "It is our duty and wish at all times to lay the best and most authentic information before the public" and "to qualify [news reports] some instances, and to reject them totally in others, when irreconcilable, contradictory, or improbable," appeared regularly.[15] A free press was a source of national pride, as a reader proclaimed in a letter to the *London Chronicle* in 1774: "The Freedom of the Press is considered even by foreigners, as one of the noblest privileges we enjoy."[16] Although not yet heralded as the "fourth branch of government," the press received praise for being a check against government tyranny. In a signed piece for the *London Chronicle*, Oliver Goldsmith declared it "a watchful guardian, capable of uniting the weak against the encroachments of power," and noted, "What concerns the Public most properly admits of a public discussion."[17] Competing publications often policed gross partisanship, publicly shaming violators for any infractions. As the *Gazetteer* remarked, "Among the various useful purposes which a newspaper is calculated to answer, the correction of offenders, by holding them up as objects of the public censure, is not one of the least."[18] Papers hurled plenty of accusations of unacceptable levels of bias, such the *Exeter Flying-Post's* claim that the *London Evening Post's* recent issues were enough to "raise the depressed Spirits of the poor Americans" or the *London Courant's* announcement that it dedicate itself to "exposing" the government-fed lies of the *Morning Post*.[19] For the most part this was merely bravado that readers seem to have dismissed, but when attacks stuck, editors took notice and action. After suffering multiple accusations in rival papers of being a ministerial stooge, the editor of the *Public Advertiser* opened the first issue of 1778 with a lengthy letter to the public pleading his innocence and detailing his sufferings at the hands of the present ministry. All of this meant that bribery made in hopes of influencing content was that much more difficult.

This is not to suggest that the British press was wholly impartial. The pages reek with libel and vehemence that would easily violate modern boundaries of ethical journalism. The British press was notorious throughout Europe for its outspokenness. As Carl Philip Moritz, a German visitor, remarked in 1782: "newspapers are brought out daily in London—some siding with Government, some with the Opposition. It is shocking how they seize every opportunity for personal abuse."[20] But these tactics were not so much about politics as they were about profit. During this period printers regularly paid hefty fines and went to prison for the stories they printed, but these inflammatory pieces were not shipping schedules of vessels bound for America, condemnation of the ministry's handling of the war, or praise for Congress's opposition to Britain, as such topics appeared regularly and without government punishment. Instead, libel cases involving false accusations about the personal habits and opinions of aristocrats and ambassadors were the bane of printers. Yet this was all part of the business. Shareholders set aside funds for legal cases, editors ran their papers from comfortable prison cells, and the newspaper that pushed the envelope furthest, the *Morning Post,* profited the most with a daily print run of 5,000 copies during the American Revolution.[21]

Unlike their colonial American counterparts during the war, who suffered intense pressure and physical violence, British editors and printers were not coerced into becoming propaganda machines of the politically powerful.[22] In consequence, the general balance in the British press's coverage of the conflict contrasted sharply with its colonial American counterpart. More financially vulnerable and isolated than the British press, American newspapers struggled to establish neutrality in reporting. Any gains made by mid-century vanished during the tumultuous years following the Stamp Act crisis in 1765. By the early 1770s, neutrality was impossible, as patriot and loyalist factions alike recognized that a neutral press was far too dangerous an asset to be left untouched, and factions either voluntarily or forcibly enlisted newspapers and their respective causes.[23] As one historian remarked, by the outbreak of the war "Neutrality and press access were no longer practices" as "Each faction accordingly did its best to exclude any good reports from the other side."[24]

Throughout the American Revolutionary era, the British press answered primarily to market forces rather than to elite patrons with political agendas or angry mobs. This is precisely what makes it such a useful tool, albeit not perfectly precise, for examining wider public opinion during the conflict. British printers, editors, and shareholders undoubtedly had plenty of political bias, and they sometimes had favorable relationships with politicians, who sent them advance copies of Parliamentary speeches and inside information; however, unwavering alliances between papers and parties are difficult to find during the American Revolution. Individual papers certainly took editorial stances, at least in the sense that they printed more content in favor of one position or another, but these positions were neither absolute nor static. Taking a specific line on such a confused and protracted subject as the war in America would have been nearly impossible. After all, it lasted eight years, saw three changes in ministries and four different commanders in America, and endured a range of strategies. Moreover, in an effort to satisfy expectations of balance, every paper carried plenty of comments that clashed with any sort of editorial slant the paper may have assumed. The *Saint James's Chronicle,* which was a magnet for fierce opponents of the North ministry, regularly carried letters and commentary that praised the government's American policies. Even the *Annual Register,* for which Edmund Burke regularly wrote, was hesitant to declare a strict stance on American affairs. As its preface for the 1775 volume stated: "The person to whose lot it falls to describe the transactions of domestic hostility, and steps which lead to it, has a painful, and generally unthankful office. . . . It indeed little becomes us to be dogmatical and decided in our opinions in this matter, when the public, even on this side of the water, is so much divided; and when the first names of the country have differed so greatly in their sentiments."[25]

The Rev. Henry Bate (after 1780, Bate Dudley), who was the most notoriously corrupt editor of the day, is something of an exception, but even his story highlights the extent to which newspapers and magazines operated as businesses rather than as party bugles. A man of many talents, Bate became the editor of the new *Morning Post* in 1773, and under his direction it quickly became a scandal sheet (and one of London's most popular newspapers). When gossip was at a lull, Bate obligingly provided some himself. In the summer of 1773, he caused a stir by fighting a duel following an affray with a group of army officers at Vauxhall Gardens over a woman. (Both she and Bate were married but not to each other.) The duel consisted of a boxing match in which Bate, a former pugilist, turned his opponent's face into "a perfect jelly."[26] Rather than resist the public storm caused by the coverage of the story in the *Morning Post's* rivals, Bate embraced it, publishing his own accounts and reveling in the nicknames his rivals gave him, such as "the Fighting Parson" and "the Reverend Bruiser." In the autumn of 1776, North, through an intermediary, offered Bate a substantial bribe to shift the *Morning Post's* editorial stance on the American war. Bate accepted, and literally overnight the paper offered noticeably more praise of the North ministry.[27]

But the North ministry's relationship with Bate and the *Morning Post* was hardly cozy. Despite his support of North, Bate still spent a year in prison (starting June 1781) for libeling Charles Lennox, duke of Richmond, who was an opposition leader in the House of Lords and an outspoken critic of the North ministry and its American policies. The fiasco also ultimately cost Bate both his editorial leadership and his stake in the *Morning Post.*[28] The *Morning Post's* content was hardly that of a party rag. Most of its content was gossip and scandal rather than politics, and its American coverage included plenty of print criticizing the government. While the editorial shift may have been inspired by North's bribe of Bate, it was hardly enough to sustain such a momentous shift. The shift has more markings of a savvy business move from which shareholders profited (doubly profited in Bate's case) than of a rogue editor acting as a government agent. The large number of newspapers made the metropolis something of a niche market, and the *Post* found its niche by printing a preponderance of material that was critical of both the American rebels and Britons who expressed doubts about the war. The majority of Britons most likely believed that the rebellious colonists were at least partly at fault, and the *Morning Post* appealed to that perspective. As "A Constant Reader" remarked in June 1779: "I will confess to you, that I take in your paper preferably to any of the others, because I wish to see what can be thought favourable or hopeful to us in our present embarrassed situation. Now most of the other printers seem not only to rejoice in national, consequently their own misery, but to exaggerate what really exists, and add to it what does not exist."[29]

The *Morning Post* was a highly successful business, not a mere trinket to be deployed and wasted as political elites saw fit. It had a contemporary estimated value of £8,400, with an impressive estimated annual profit of up to £2,000 for its shareholders, whose numbers included the usual array of booksellers, as well as more general investors such as the auctioneer James Christie.[30] It was one of the most valuable and most profitable businesses in the nation. Sales of newspapers and advertising space drove profits, and these revenues towered over the values of any government bribe. When the paper shifted its position on America, it sold more than ever, and shareholders such as Thomas Skinner and Joseph Richardson, who were staunch supporters of the opposition whigs in Parliament, bit their tongues and enjoyed the profits. As much as they disliked Bate—Richardson later fought a duel with him—they kept their shares and Bate as editor until his libelous attack on Richmond made him a financial liability, at which point they withdrew their support from Bate and compelled him to sell his shares in the paper. All the while many of the same investors, as well as the same printer of the *Morning Post,* produced the *English Chronicle,* a paper that consistently attacked the North ministry and its American policies.[31]

Rather than assist the government, the press was expected to aid the populace in policing politicians by reporting on their transactions. The press accomplished this primarily through the reporting of Parliament's debates, which finally became legal on the eve of the war.[32] For the first time the daily operations of the government were open to public scrutiny by Britons, regardless of age, rank, or gender. Horace Mann described how the press enabled the flow of information from the august chambers to the ordinary

Briton in April 1775: "I can easily conceive that the agitation in both Houses of Parliament on the American affairs must be very great. From thence it descends to the coffee-houses and taverns, and then the populace is as violent over a pot of beer."[33] During the American Revolution virtually all newspapers included reports on the debates. Provincial and Scottish papers tailored them for local audiences, extracting reports from the London press that either featured a regional issue or a speech from a local member of Parliament. Some London newspapers, such as William "Memory" Woodfall's *Morning Chronicle,* specialized in reporting the debates. As a reader remarked in that paper in 1780: "It being acknowledged that your paper conveys to the public the Parliamentary Debates in a manner that does no less justice to the speakers than credit to yourself, I rely upon the truth of your representation of that animated speeches in the House of Commons."[34]

Public reliance on the press for information was never higher in the eighteenth century than during the American Revolution, and newspapers pledged to meet public expectations. In typical fashion, the *Exeter Flying-Post* publicly recognized at the start of the fighting that as "the present unhappy Disputes . . . being interesting, some degree or other, to almost every Individual, the most early and authentic Intelligence must doubtless be desirable." To this end, the paper announced that in addition to increasing in size to make room for "every Article, both foreign and domestic" of relevance, "the Proprietor of this Paper . . . duly sensible of the Obligations he is under to the indulgent Public . . . has now, at an additional expence, laid Plan for publishing on Wednesday Evening, with all the material Articles contain'd in the Gazette, and Evening Papers, printed in London on Tuesday Evening."[35]

The extent to which the press actually shaped government policy is impossible to discern. On the American side of the Atlantic, contemporaries credited the press with playing a key role in winning independence, such as David Ramsay's declaration that "the pen and the press" did as much as "the sword."[36] In Britain, the press received substantially less adulation—or blame—from contemporaries for the outcome of major events such as the American Revolution. Quite simply, the breadth of the printed arena and its commitment to providing a diversity of sentiment worked to dilute all causes. Certainly most contemporaries believed, for better or for worse, that the press could place acute public pressure on a ministry over a particular bill, but few held it responsible for deciding the victor in a war.

Nevertheless, politicians themselves came to rely on the press not only as a gauge of public opinion but also, like the ordinary public, as the source for the latest news and information. Thus the press indirectly affected government policy by providing ministers with a greater diversity of information and comment than might otherwise have been had through official channels and, perhaps more critically, more timely information, as the British press coverage almost always preceded the arrival of official dispatches from America. Many members of Parliament did their best to use the press for their own benefit, leaking information to editors and providing advance copies of their speeches. The *Gazetteer* boasted: "We are happy, at all times, to have it in our power to give the best parliamentary informations" even when visitors had been cleared from the galleries, because the paper had a member reporting for it.[37] On one occasion Thomas Luttrell rose in the Commons to thank William Woodfall, who was in the visitors' gallery, for accurately reporting an earlier speech of his—a point Woodfall gladly printed the next day.[38]

Members of Parliament certainly read the papers. North, for example, spent over £11 4s—enough for 1,075 newspapers or roughly three dailies and a tri-weekly—on subscriptions as a rising politician in 1765, and to this must be added the papers he read in the coffeehouses he frequented.[39] Members of Parliament often cited newspapers during debates, such as in November 1776 when an outraged Isaac Barré, a member of the opposition, read aloud extracts from a newspaper as evidence that the American patriots had no intention of surrendering.[40] Thus, when faced with the possibility of an increase in the tax on newspapers, the *London Chronicle* lashed out by declaring that the press was as essential to any member of Parliament as it was to the ordinary Briton:

> the solemn truth is, that to the most of them (some of the first-rate personages in this kingdom, for greatness of fortune and for rank in the State) a News-paper is the very lesson of the day. On many points of the utmost importance to their country they would be reduced to absolute dumbness, in their having nothing to say, through their total incapacity of thinking for themselves, if it was not for the cue they make a habit of stealing from those very papers which they affect to hold [in] such sovereign contempt.[41]

The paper then offered guidance for those with questions: "If any one doubts this, or but thinks it a caricature of the truth, let him . . . [go] to either of the political theatres at Westminster. He may there hear subjects that have indeed been superficially and crudely enough treated in the Newspapers, ten times more horridly handled."

Prolific, largely independent, and sensitive to its readership, the newspaper and periodical press is the best tool for recapturing how contemporary Britons experienced, discussed, and responded to what was perhaps the most contentious national event of the eighteenth century—the war with the American colonies. The growth of the perceived importance of the empire, the continued relaxation of government restrictions on print, and the ideological divisions inherent in any civil war all combined to shred any semblance of national consensus. The stakes were high both on national and—as the war grew to require unprecedented amounts of manpower and resources—personal levels. By the end of the war the tension had risen to an almost unbearable level. The *London Packet* declared as it awaited news of Lord Cornwallis and his trapped army at Yorktown, "Not only England but all of Europe stand in trembling suspense for the result of the contest in America."[42]

To feed the national hunger for news, editors and printers packed their pages with detailed maps, travel accounts, private correspondence from civilians and soldiers, official dispatches and extracts from foreign and American newspapers, along with an abundance of other materials. They printed the proclamations of George Washington, the minutes of Britain's negotiations with the Iroquois, and tables that detailed the name, size, and location of every major ship in the British and foreign navies. The coverage was so acute that knowledge of American affairs was unavoidable. Thus developments in Congress became national news, and the terrain of foreign battle zones became almost as familiar as local landscapes.

The conflict's distance and the strangled, unreliable lines of communication that accompany any war only further intensified the central role of the press. American loyalist refugees and relatives and merchants with ties to America lost most of their regular private lines of communication at one point or another, forcing them to rely on the press. Even a frustrated Horace Walpole, who had one of the most extensive webs of private correspondents, was reduced to depending on newspapers.[43] The government's inability to secure the swiftest lines of communication from the war zone also meant that ministers of state regularly read about war events at the same time as the rest of the newspaper reading public. Because early accounts most often came from the American patriot press either directly to Britain or via France or the Netherlands, the North ministry and its apologists spent a great deal of time defending its commanders and stalling as the official dispatches meandered their way across the Atlantic. As the *Morning Post* observed in November 1777, when the nation eagerly awaited news from its forces in North America, the king and ministry were in a "painful" game of waiting while their opponents attacked them in the press and the rest of the nation fretted. An examination of the press recaptures all of this, reflecting the currents of public opinion and chronicling the experiences of the British populace as they coped and struggled through a momentous period—the main episodes of which for most Britons transpired largely on the printed page.

Part Two

FROM INSURRECTION

TO WORLD WAR

C H A P T E R

Crisis and Conflict before Independence

✳ In July 1774 the *Derby Mercury* painted for its readers the surreal scene of the New York public celebrations of the king's birthday.[1] As usual, the paper explained, there were illuminations of houses and fireworks, but a letter writer from America noted, "the Generality of the Inhabitants . . . were too deeply impressed with the melancholy Situation of all the British colonies, to assume the least Appearance of public Rejoicing." The people, the writer continued, were "perfectly well affected to his Majesty's Person and Family," but they could not rouse themselves to celebrate "while it remains whether we shall remain Freemen by maintaining our Rights, or submit as slaves." Such mixed emotions were not confined to North America. As an examination of the British press reveals, the buildup to war and the early years of the conflict were marked in Britain by public anxiety, speculation, and ambiguity.

Neither the newspapermen and women nor the public they served were naive. By the spring of 1774 commentators from both sides of the Atlantic batted around terms such as "American independency" and "civil war" in the British press with increasing regularity, and so the British public, which continued to accept the colonies' importance to British prosperity, made the colonies their number one topic of conversation. Most rightly predicted that a rebellion would be a full-scale civil war—one that Britain could lose—rather than a disorganized uprising that a handful of disciplined troops could easily crush. Hope for conciliation steadily declined as both sides prepared for war—all under the watchful eyes of the press. When news reached Britain in May 1775 that armed hostilities between colonial militia and British troops had erupted outside of Boston, few Britons admitted astonishment, and virtually no one expressed surprise when Congress's declaration of American independence reached Britain fifteen months later. That the American rebels had hazarded their lives on independence and the British government its soldiers' lives and people's welfare on preventing it was already a fact for the press-reading British nation. The main questions in the press focused on the potential costs of the war, if it could be won, whether it could be contained in North America, and if it was worth fighting.

Because regular lines of communication remained largely open, there was no shortage of information about the American colonies. A newspaper that did not at least mention the subject during this period is difficult to find. For example, a single issue of the *Derby Mercury* from April 1774 included several readers' letters attacking and defending the Americans, an explanation of the "much-talked-of" Boston Port Bill, letters from New York, Parliamentary reports, a description of General William Howe's review of troops before their departure for service in Boston, and comments on the North ministry's plans for dealing with the American crisis.[2] The emphasis in all of these papers was information rather than persuasion. The letters from America, extracts from American newspapers, and reports on government proceedings do not appear to have been cobbled together by crafty editors with discernable political agendas with regard to the conflict. Nor is there any evidence of overt pressure being placed on newspapers by the government or any political faction to tow a particular line on America. Printing presses were not smashed by angry mobs, and editors were not assaulted— actions of which the British had, albeit rarely, demonstrated themselves capable on other occasions. The best evidence of this quasi-neutrality when it came to the American crisis is the newspapers themselves, which carry a remarkably broad range of news and sentiment. Many papers carried more criticism than praise of the government's handling of the affair, but none of the leading London or provincial papers took a hard-line stance favoring either Britain or the American colonies during this period.

While editors' professionalism can account for perhaps some of the prevailing balanced coverage, it was more a result of market forces and a reflection of the uncertainty that prevailed in Britain. The North ministry was hardly proactive and to a great extent stumbled through its pre-war handling of the colonies—much like ministries before it.[3] Orders to the commander in chief in America, Thomas Gage, were vague at best. Ministers were reluctant to send reinforcements to America (despite requests from Gage) and they did not seriously attempt to halt Congress, preferring instead to wait and see what resolutions were passed. The opposition in Parliament was little better, having allowed their own dithering and misjudgments to contribute to the crisis when they were in power. Virtually everyone agreed that war was not the desired outcome, but there was no consensus on how to avert it or to what lengths the government should go.

Outside of Parliament, the situation was not altogether different. Although discussions about the conflict could be heated, personal violence was rare, and, for the most part, neighbors tolerated each other's viewpoints. Adam Smith's description of imperial wars in his *Wealth of Nations,* which first appeared in 1776, best describes the British perspective at the time: "In great empires the people who live in the capital, and in the provinces remote from the scene of action, feel, many of them, scarce any inconveniency from the war; but enjoy at their ease, the amusement of reading in the newspapers the exploits of their own fleet and armies."[4] Britons remained comfortably safe from Boston's mobs, American Indians' scalping knives, and colonial militia musket fire. Hardship for the artisans, middling ranks, and elites who read the papers was but mere conjecture during the war's early years, when higher taxes, economic depression, and military service were distant possibilities rather than actualities or even accepted eventualities. To fight the conflict, the British had a professional army and navy. Should their own forces prove lacking, Britons knew that European rulers stood ready to lease tens of thousands of their troops for British service—a typical solution for British wartime manpower problems during the eighteenth century. In consequence, readers took great liberty in their musing over Congress's proclamations and military strategy. They offered an abundance of predictions and rarely hesitated to make the occasional counterintuitive declaration in favor of the colonial resistance.

By the outbreak of war with the colonies in April 1775, the British had been following and commenting on American news for the better part of a generation. North America became a leading subject of national interest during the Seven Years War, when the press familiarized the nation with the geographies, cultures, and economies of the various colonies as well as the names, strengths, and dispositions of the numerous American Indian peoples who occupied or bordered Britain's territorial claims.[5] With the aid of the press, Britons learned to associate the nation's prosperity with successful rule in America, and they came to see the colonists as "fellow nationals."[6] The unprecedented expense and blood, protraction, and uncertainty of the

Seven Years War fostered a sense of national investment in America, and, as a result, the British continued to read and comment on American affairs via the press even after the war had ended. The post-Seven Years War clashes between the British government and the colonists over issues of imperial authority (particularly taxation) provided plenty to discuss. Boycotts, principles of taxation and representation, and imperial reform became subjects for national scrutiny and debate.

Yet coverage of Anglo-American tensions was not truly sustained until two hundred colonists protesting a British tax dumped three shiploads of East India Company tea into Boston's harbor in December 1773. At that point America moved permanently to the foreground of the nation's attention. Few Britons took the deteriorating situation lightly. As the *London Evening Post* remarked immediately after news of the Boston Tea Party had arrived: "The Affairs of America at present occupy the whole Attention of the Administration; and it is agreed on all Hands to be now the most important Business that has come under Consideration since the Accession of the present King."[7] In Parliament the North ministry and its supporters depicted the Bostonians as radical rabble-rousers rather than as representatives of colonial dissatisfaction, with North himself labeling the Bostonians as "the ringleaders of all the riots in America for seven years past" in a highly publicized House of Commons Speech.[8] Such viewpoints also found representation in traditional opposition corners. Even the *Gazetteer,* whose correspondents and reporters normally lent a sympathetic voice to American complaints, included a letter from a reader suggesting there was a rebellious nature in the Bostonians' actions by comparing them to the Jacobite rebellion of 1745: "Instead of Charles Stuart at the head of Highland Clans, Sam Adams now leads a banditti of hypocrites against Great Britain."[9]

Despite such name-calling, virtually all comments in the press from across the political, social, and geographic spectrums recognized the fundamental issues of governance and authority that lay at the root of the problem. The first response to the Boston Tea Party in the *Glasgow Journal* focused on the "decisive question," which was "Whether the Right of Taxation be here or there?" Disagreement on such a key issue meant little hope of easy resolution: "There is no Medium which can be adopted with Honour or Safety on either Side. No Problem of Expediency can now be started, for the Opposition in America is not to the Sum levied but to the Right of levying it."[10] Regardless of North's claims to the contrary, few in the press expressed doubts that Boston, though perhaps more radical than its neighbors, roughly represented wider colonial opinion. The flood of letters from America that appeared in the press made this abundantly clear to readers from

Exeter to Dundee. As a widely circulated one from New York declared: "All America is in a Flame on Account of the Tea Exportation. The New-Yorkers as well as the Bostonians and Philadelphians are, it seems, determined that no Tea shall be landed."[11]

The North ministry's attempt to quell unrest in America with the heavy-handed Coercive Acts (known as the Intolerable Acts in America) that spring received mixed reviews in the press. The acts substantially curtailed freedoms in Massachusetts by severely limiting colonial self-government and shutting down Boston's port. Although North's substantial majorities and support of the king ensured their smooth passage through Parliament, the acts attracted substantial opposition throughout the press—a discrepancy that was common in topics related to America during this period. Some opponents of the acts took a practical tact, asserting that the original taxes simply were not worth the trouble and expense of forcing the colonists to pay them. As the *Exeter Flying-Post* informed its readers in May, "The Tax upon Tea . . . will not pay the expense of collecting it."[12] Other commentators railed against the overzealousness of the measures. The *London Evening Post* compared General Thomas Gage's new office as governor of Massachusetts to that of a Roman dictator and predicted that tranquility would elude Anglo-American relations for years to come.[13] Underlining the recurring theme that the colonists were partners rather than subordinates, a sympathetic *Derby Mercury* reminded readers of how loyal New Englanders had been in the past, remarking that "while Vengeance is meditating against the People of new England, for the demerit of having destroyed some British tea . . . it is but common Justice to remember, what signal Services they have on various Occasions rendered this country." The paper then proceeded to list all of New England's military contributions since 1690, concluding that "honest Englishmen must recognize such facts prove these People have always been ready and willing to assist our Arms, and therefore deserve Rewards, not punishment."[14]

A minority argued in the press that the Coercive Acts would snuff the enthusiasm of the colonists by exploiting geographic and class divisions. The *Glasgow Journal,* whose pages often vilified the American protesters, called the acts "an unexpected stroke" that would divide the Bostonians, who "after venting their rage, it is supposed the more sensible among them will propose making such concessions as may be expected from the colony." Such comments highlighted the widespread belief that class differences were at work; a concern was voiced in reprinted letters from America that a "rabble" or "mob" of workers, artisans, and lower middling ranks were the root cause of the disturbances.[15] The tough measures introduced by the Coercive Acts, so the argument went, would, as explained by a reader in a letter to the *Derby Mercury*, provoke "a serious reflection on the past outrages" among "those of the faction who are possessed of money" and compel them "to restrain their own miscreants."[16] This was neither the first nor the last time that critics of American resistance in the British press severely overestimated the materialist motives of the colonists.

Speculation about the effectiveness of the Coercive Acts ended in the summer of 1774, when accounts from the colonies that described increased levels of resistance and Britain's deteriorating imperial authority made their way to Britain. The printed accounts came from a variety of sources, including returning sailors and merchants, but most appear to have come directly from colonial American newspapers, whose bias in favor of resistance by this time was predominant.[17] As a "Letter from an Englishman in New York" representatively stated in its warning to the readers of the *Stamford Mercury*, "there is a firmness in the people here to oppose what they hold destructive to their liberties, far beyond what the dependants of Government insinuate, or would wish to have believed."[18]

The image of an outraged American populace stemmed less from British newspaper proprietors' political agendas than it did from a combination of laziness and profiteering. The practice of filling newspapers with information directly lifted or paraphrased from other prints was long established amongst editors and printers; any significant story in one paper was bound to appear verbatim in an array of others the following day. To aid this practice, editors throughout the country made certain they had access to a host of papers, both London and provincial. The American papers they received were added to the resource pile. The American papers from port towns were readily available, thanks to continued commercial ties and, in part, to the machinations of colonists in London who supported the cause of resistance. There is no evidence to suggest that British printers consciously did the bidding of colonial propaganda machines, but savvy colonists, such as Benjamin Franklin and the Lee brothers, who recognized the power of the press and had been providing information to London papers for the better part of a decade helped ensure that the latest patriot prints reached London editors.[19]

Distressing news of American unrest and looming war probably sold more newspapers than stories of harmony (even if they could be found). As a whole, the press flourished during this period marked by Anglo-American tensions and then war. The exact extent to which increases in sales and readership corresponded directly to the conflict is unclear, but certainly the unrest in America was a story line that dominated for well over a decade. As the editor of the *Edinburgh Magazine* remarked at the height of the Seven Years War in America, "Times of war, devastation and bloodshed, tho' the worst to live in, are yet allowed to be the happiest to write in."[20] Waiting for the latest information from America was an experience whose tension newspapers at once created and relieved. Throughout this period Charles Goore, a Liverpool merchant, and his associates, like many Britons, speculated and postulated on American affairs based on what they read in the press. His letters, although invariably focused primarily on other subjects, reveal that the conflict haunted his thoughts, which newspapers fueled and shaped. In January 1775, while he was anxiously awaiting the arrival of the "London papers," he remarked in a letter that "The Coffee houses are now crowded waiting to hear the resolves of Parliament relative to the American affairs."[21] This was neither the first nor the last time Goore found himself in this predicament during the conflict.

Thanks in no small part to the American patriots' dominance of the colonial press by this time, the represented American view in the British press was of a colonial populace in near unanimous resistance. A steady loyalist perspective from the American press did not appear in Britain until the fall of 1776, after the British forces established themselves in strength in New York and New Jersey. In the face of such an overwhelming consensus in the American papers that freely flowed into Britain, most editors and readers accepted this depiction.[22] The British press unhesitatingly informed readers that New Yorkers, often portrayed as the most moderate colonists, had united in their burning of North in effigy in response to the acts and that the House of Burgesses in Virginia had set aside a day for prayer and fasting for the "poor people of Boston," during which time, the *Gazetteer* declared, its delegates planned "to deliberate on ways and means to make Britain feel the consequence of her colonies."[23] Moreover, British readers learned, the colonists had called for an inter-colonial congress in order to act in unison, and throughout the late summer and autumn of 1775 the press overflowed with accounts of colonies electing delegates for the congress; scarcely an issue was printed without mention of that body or the resolutions of some group of colonists in support of it. Through the papers readers learned that one by one the major mainland colonies were throwing their weight behind the impending meeting in Philadelphia. Remarks in the *Public Advertiser* in August typify the seriousness with which the press and the public treated Congress: "The present State of Affairs in America . . . seem to demand the immediate Meeting of a great Assembly, as the Fate of that continent, and the consequent Fate of England, may in a great Measure depend on their Resolves."[24] As the colonists appeared to rally behind the formation of a congress, Britain's authority in America seemed to collapse. Stories of low morale and desertion among the British troops in Boston were rife, starting in late summer and continuing throughout the year. The *London Chronicle* assured readers that "upwards of 300 of the Troops" at Boston had deserted; the *Public Advertiser* claimed that guards had been placed at the entrances of the town to prevent desertion; and the *Saint James's Chronicle* declared that even those guards had abandoned their posts.[25] The *London Evening Post* even reported that the inhabitants of Boston burnt Gage in effigy before his own troops without reprisal.[26]

Anyone regularly reading newspapers or magazines in 1774 would have found it difficult not to conclude the impotency of Gage as accounts of his difficulties from across the colonies bombarded British readers. The colonists' addresses to Gage, which regularly and openly attacked British authority, often appeared in the British press along with Gage's curt but ineffectual replies. The *Bristol Journal* carried a typical example in December 1774, in which the Massachusetts Assembly sent yet another damning address to Gage, whose reply concluded with an obviously futile reminder that he had long since ordered them "to desist from such illegal and unconstitutional proceedings."[27] That Gage did nothing was evident in subsequent issues, which carried further addresses from the "illegitimate assembly" and ineffective warnings from Gage. An irate reader's letter printed in the *Ipswich Journal,* which attacked Gage for being too "fearful" to move against the illegal assembly "a mere three miles from his camp," represented the widespread belief that if he could not halt a nearby gathering, he would never be able to stop an inter-colonial meeting in Philadelphia.[28]

Alongside the exchanges between Gage and the Massachusetts Assembly were the more alarming reports that the colonial militias were being called into service by American opponents to British authority. Gage openly acknowledged the "unusual warlike Preparations throughout the Country" in another one of his widely printed exchanges with the Massachusetts assembly, but, despite his orders for them to disperse, they continued to meet and grow.[29] The *Derby Mercury,* like most papers, reprinted a Boston letter claiming that "Between seven and eight thousand Provincials . . . are now under Arms near Boston, and are exercised every Day in View of Gage and his troops."[30] According to an account in the *Bristol Journal,* Gage could not even persuade Massachusetts workmen to build his barracks, and when he sent a request for assistance to New York, they, too, "all nobly refused."[31] Not surprisingly, many Britons concluded that at least some Americans were in a state of rebellion long before actual armed hostilities erupted the following spring. The author of a widely reprinted letter that first appeared in the *London Evening Post* in October 1774 bluntly stated, "It is but Justice to the People in this Country to apprize them that their Fellow-Subjects in America, particularly in the Massachusetts Province, are in no less than a State of actual Resistance."[32]

Throughout the summer and autumn of 1774 most commentators expected that the first course of action of the American opposition, led by the newly formed Congress, would be continued economic sanctions. The *Public Advertiser* remarked in July "that a Non-importation and Non-exportation will universally take place, sooner or later, is most evident and indisputable."[33] Although boycotts caused some concern, especially among those who warned that manufacturing would take root in the colonies, they were almost routine by 1774, and they had yet to cause the threatened collapse of the British economy. In consequence, many readers and editors openly dismissed their significance. In a letter in the *Ipswich Journal* a reader pointed out that despite the supposed American "non-importation association . . . seventeen ships have been cleared at the [London] Custom House in the course of a fortnight."[34] The *Bristol Journal* assured its readers—many of whom were closely connected to American trade—that "The Non-importation Agreement . . . meets with so many Obstacles [in America] from private Interest, as well as from public Authority, that there is no Occasion for the Mother-Country to give herself any uneasiness about it."[35]

The concern that occupied the most press ink was the possibility of armed conflict. Predictions of a war with the colonies were hardly novel, but the events of 1774 moved the possibility firmly into the forefront of the public discourse. A warning in the *London Evening Post*, which had a tendency to produce some of the most provocative material when it came to Britain's troubled colonies, told of the possibility of war as early as March 1774 and declared that New England could raise an army of 140,000 men "in less than a week."[36] Printed letters from America that appeared during the summer did little to alleviate such concerns, and by autumn other papers had joined the *Post's* predictions of armed conflict. The *Glasgow Journal* summarized the widespread perception of the lamentable possibility, declaring that "It were to be wished that the Colonists would seriously consider their situation, and the necessity of supporting the measures resolved upon by the legislatures." However, and in contrast to the *Post*, the *Journal* offered a confident conclusion: "If their obstinacy should compel the mother country to go to the greatest extremities, dreadful indeed must be the event [for the colonists]."[37] The military buildup in Britain—regiments preparing for service in America, recall of officers on leave, acquisitioning and transporting military supplies, etc.—continued throughout the year and was closely followed in newspapers and magazines across the country. By late autumn, the overwhelming sentiment in the press was that the possibility of war had become a probability. As the *Saint James's Chronicle* predicted, "Government is determined never to relinquish her Right to the Taxation of America, and America is determined not to submit to Taxation; the Consequence is, that a War between the Mother Country and the Colonies will commence."[38]

The British press reveals a public that was acutely aware of the growing likelihood of conflict in America—a conflict that would most likely not be either easily or cheaply resolved. All hope for reconciliation had not been lost, as evidenced by the conciliatory gestures that emanated from the political leaders on both sides of the Atlantic, but comment and reporting in the press was overwhelmingly skeptical of the ability of any of the proposals to avert war. Congress's open letter "to the People of Great Britain" appeared in most newspapers and magazines in December 1774, but it did little to allay public concerns about war. Congress's other resolutions and letters, particularly those written to its constituent colonists and those in Canada, also appeared in the British press, and together they underlined perceptions of Congress's intentions to resist Parliament and to spread that resistance. Forecasts that Congress would flinch at either further ministerial threats or the prospect of war all but disappeared from the press.

That winter members of Parliament made a number of conciliatory proposals, which the press printed but treated with substantial skepticism. North's substantial majority in Parliament following the October elections meant opposition proposals from the likes of Lord Chatham and the Rockingham Whigs never had a real chance of passage; almost all reactions in the press recognized that they served more as naysaying critiques of the ministry's policies than any sort of genuine alternative plan of action.[39] The only peace proposal with a hope of surviving Parliament had to come from North, and he served a king who loathed Congress and was unwilling to allow substantial concessions. As George III made clear in widely printed extracts of his speech for the opening of a new session of Parliament in December 1774, in his mind opponents to British rule were nothing more than criminals: "It gives me much Concern, that I am obliged, at the opening of this Parliament, to inform you, that a most daring Spirit of Resistance and Disobedience to the Law still unhappily prevails in the Province of the Massachusetts Bay, and has, in Parts of it, broke forth in fresh Violences of a very criminal Nature." North's proposal, which appeared in February, not surprisingly yielded little to his American opponents. In it Parliament maintained its supremacy but voluntarily limited its powers of taxation to the regulation of external trade so long as the colonies agreed to tax themselves in order to provide sufficient funds for defense and civil and judicial administration, all of which would be determined and handled at the inter-colonial level. The proposal won quick support from across the political spectrum, including endorsing remarks in London newspapers with such differing political bases as the *General Evening Post, Morning Post,* and *Saint James's Chronicle.*[40] Nevertheless, virtually everyone, including commentators in the newspapers just mentioned, fully expected it to fail.

Meanwhile detailed discussion of the looming war continued in the press. Armchair generals dusted off their maps or consulted new ones from magazines and newspapers in order to calculate the possible operations of a war in America and drill for mock battlefields on coffeehouse tables. Reports in the press of the British military land and naval buildup appeared regularly alongside precise tables estimating British troop and naval forces that gave readers almost as much information as any general or minister. The press coverage offered few illusions that an all-out conflict could be won easily or without some suffering on the domestic front. An estimate of the war's cost that circulated widely in December 1774 was an anxiety-inducing £14 million per annum—a total that substantially exceeded the accepted value of annual trade with the mainland colonies.[41] Impressively accurate, the figure further reveals that the British reading public had a credible sense of what the war would require.[42]

Of particular concern in the press was the vulnerability of Britain's position elsewhere in the world. Britain's diplomatic isolation in Europe had been a source of unease among the ruling elite for some time, but a coming threat of war made it a national public concern.[43] By the summer of 1774 even provincial newspapers were reprinting the troop and naval estimates of France and Spain along with cautions of the French and Spanish desire, in the words the *Derby Mercury,* to "revenge the Disgrace of [their] Arms in the last War."[44] A reader of the *Exeter Flying-Post* admonished the North ministry and warned that if resistance reached open war in America, the courts of Europe would flock to the colonists' assistance, as "independency no doubt would be much to the advantage of every nation in Europe except Great Britain."[45] Widely reprinted tables highlighted Britain's military weakness. Whereas France and Spain boasted estimated standing armies of 150,000 and 120,000 troops respectively, the table calculated Britain's army at a paltry 40,000.[46] Not surprisingly, the *London Evening Post* warned readers that a war would be disastrous for Britain: "Should a Civil War be kindled in America, (as there are too many Grounds for apprehending, the Accounts received from thence, and also from the Royal Proclamation for prohibiting Arms and Ammunition from being sent abroad) it would not only be fatal to Trade and Commerce of this Kingdom, but most probably involve it in a new War with France and Spain."[47]

Little comment in the press did not advocated an all-out war of occupation in America. The military obstacles of such a war would prove difficult at best, most agreed. "A man recently arrived from Boston" offered a typical warning in the *Public Advertiser* that Massachusetts alone would have no trouble raising the necessary "men in arms to defend their liberties."[48] Further reports from America made it clear that resistance was not confined to New England. A letter from Philadelphia, which first appeared in the *Bristol Journal* in March, announced that "We are assured that almost every county in Virginia, Maryland, and the counties of Newcastle, Kent, and Sussex, in Delaware, have chosen their officers, and are learning the military exercise with the greatest diligence."[49] The *Saint James's Chronicle* first printed a widely circulated estimate in April that Virginia already had a pro-Congress militia of 15,000 men formed, and Maryland and Pennsylvania were following suit.[50] Moreover, these men were capable soldiers who, according to the *London Evening Post,* were "all trained to fire at a Mark from their Youth." Such accounts left little doubt that reasserting British authority in America would require a fight. Given the colonists' strength of numbers and America's territorial size, the consensus in the press favored naval blockades with only limited land operations. "Britanicus" representatively dismissed a large land force as "folly" in a letter to the *Saint James's Chronicle* in December 1774, fearing that a sizeable army would only further inflame the Americans and tie the British down in a protracted, bloody war. After all, "Britanicus" astutely foreshadowed, the colonists' "Spirit and Numbers" would have little effect on a British fleet that "can with the greatest ease reduce their best Sea Ports into Heaps of Ashes."[51]

Although the North ministry consistently underestimated both the geographical breadth of colonial support for Congress and the depth of Congress's resolve to resist imperial policies, the vast majority of coverage and comment in the press accepted that Congress represented the majority of American colonists.[52] Having covered nearly a decade of colonial protests, most of the British press accepted colonial unity from the start. The *London Evening Post* rejected any alternative as early as March 1774, arguing, "Some People have suggested an incoherent Idea, that the People of Boston were a partial Faction. Be it known to the Legislature of England, that it is a Falsity—that all the Provinces are united in their Opinion, and are determined to uphold the Cause of America."[53] Like most other papers, the *Stamford Mercury* printed an array of letters from other colonies, describing how their inhabitants had joined the cause of Boston. In one account a colonist from North Carolina reported that after the deputies of North Carolina's assembly "resolved not to drink any more Tea, nor wear any more British cloth, many Ladies of this Province have determined to give a memorable proof of their patriotism." The letter concluded with a call for the English recipient to share the letter in order "to shew your fair countrywomen, how zealously and faithfully American Ladies, follow the laudable example of their Husbands, and what opposition your matchless Ministers may expect to receive from a people, thus firmly united against them."[54]

Such letters seem to have persuaded British commentators of the universality of the resistance. As the *London Packet* declared: "People wish to insinuate, that the Conduct of the People of Boston is not approved of by the other Colonists; be that repeated to them again, with the firm Assurance of Truth, that the Sense of the People of America goes with the People of Boston."[55] A consequence of the abundance of American patriot press material circulating in Britain was that the press generally ignored or downplayed accounts of substantial loyalist sentiment that, while limited, were sometimes available. Taking their cue from the American patriot printers, British papers typically depicted expressions of loyalty as contrived and unrepresentative. For example, the *Derby Mercury* dismissed a Boston loyalist petition with 140 signatures by declaring: "It is said that great Pains were taken throughout Boston, and many other Towns, to procure that Number, which must certainly appear very contemptible, when 'tis considered, that there are full four hundred thousand Inhabitants in that Province."[56]

The appearance of a unified opposition in America provoked concern in the British press. As one reader succinctly concluded in his response to the circulated resolves and addresses of Congress, "We ought, Sir, to be alarmed at this."[57] The apprehension stemmed from two widely held beliefs: first, that American unity presented a significant threat to the British Empire, and, second, that the government was doing too little—either by way of conciliation or coercion—to address it. While awaiting news of Congress's deliberations in early December 1774, a reader of the *Public Advertiser* expressed concern over a united America: "I shall perhaps be asked what can the Province of Massachusetts Bay do by itself? I answer, nothing; but the Province of Virginia, of Pensylvania, &c. &c. &c. united, may form a Power irresistible, when Time, Experience, and external Assistance have had their natural Effects."[58] North, who the press depicted as being inactive at best and in denial at worst, endured the brunt of the nation's frustration-induced public criticism. North had never been popular with the wider reading public, and critics took this opportunity to get personal. In a letter, a reader of

the *Saint James's Chronicle* described North as being "confounded" by the
American situation, and the author of another letter compared him to an
unprepared "School-Boy" who "cons his lesson [when] he cannot get it by
Heart."[59] Another widely reprinted reader's letter lambasted North for
grossly underestimating the Americans. "I thought we had been told that
America was to be chastised," the reader chided, "that the Bostonians must
be forced to fish up the drowned Teas, and swallow them drenched with the
Waters of Bitterness."[60]

By the spring of 1775 the nation had largely resigned itself to a war in
North America. As the *Bristol Journal* informed its readers in late April—
just after the battles of Lexington and Concord had transpired but before
news of them had reached Britain—"the militia of Massachusetts and Connecticut, are actually embodied, have prepared magazines, and are assembled to the number of twelve thousand effective men." In consequence, the
paper accurately predicted, "there is not a doubt, and Ministers themselves
expect it, that the next news will bring an account of an action." Yet support
for the American opposition remained widely palatable, although sometimes controversial, in the press—despite all of the saber rattling and widespread expectation of war. For such groups Congress served as the champion of liberty, not the rabble-rousing destructors of British dominion in
America. As one reader remarked in a frequently reprinted letter to the *Public Advertiser* following the arrival of Congress's first resolutions in December 1774: "The Resolutions of the American Congress are arrived, breathing
the Spirit of English Freemen. Our Ministers have the Impudence to be
amazed; they affect having dared to think that all Englishmen were as servile
as the Slaves at home . . . but American English, who fled from Chains, will
not wear them on the other Side of the Atlantic."[61] London's local politicians
in particular provided a strong example of opposition that appeared in papers nationwide. Long dominated by radicals who took every opportunity to
bash the government, they had found American resistance to be a useful
stick for nearly a decade.[62] In the *Ipswich Journal,* along with a number of
other provincial papers, were the "Proceedings at Guildhall" from October
1774 in which potential candidates for Parliament were presented with a list
of resolutions, including one that unconditionally praised American resistance to the Coercive Acts. According to the report, when a candidate refused to sign his name to the resolution, although he had spoken out against
the acts, the "Livery became very clamorous crying out 'Sign or Decline.'"[63]

Some papers carried commentary that criticized such viewpoints, but
virtually all unabashedly printed it. The *London Chronicle* carried a piece in
September, which subsequently appeared in papers throughout the nation,

concluding boldly that the Americans must oppose the British government: "The Behaviour of the Americans, at this alarming Crisis, will most probably stamp their Characters, and hand them down to Posterity, as a brave Generation of Patriots, or sink them into the Contempt in the Opinion of all future Ages." "Life and Death, or, which are tantamount thereto, Liberty and Slaves are now before them," it concluded, "and it is in their Power to chuse which they please."[64] The *Saint James's Chronicle* even went so far as to link popular opposition to the ministry at home with American resistance abroad in January 1775, observing that "the Question rightly understood, is not Great Britain against America, but the Ministry against both."[65] Partly products of a decade of linking pro-Americanism with English radicalism and Parliamentary reform campaigns in Britain, such sentiments could not be easily shaken off. Not even the eruption of armed hostilities erased them. It took the Declaration of Independence and the entry of France into the war to seriously quiet them.

News of the outbreak of hostilities at Lexington and Concord reached Britain in the last days of May 1775, but it would not have surprised anyone in contact with the press. As the *Stamford Mercury* warned in its issue immediately prior to the arrival of the news, "we expect to hear by the next ships that America is in arms against us." The American patriot version of the battles arrived first, thanks to the maneuvering of Samuel Adams, who ensured that copies of the Massachusetts's *Essex Gazette* and numerous sworn affidavits describing British atrocities reached Britain in record time and well before Gage's account.[66] American supporters in London made sure the accounts reached printers. Arthur Lee, a Virginian in London who had long been involved in placing propaganda in both British and American papers, shrewdly played on his position as sheriff of London to lend a pretended objectivity to the American account. Like the vast majority of papers throughout the country, the *Derby Mercury* followed its reprint from the *Essex Gazette* with extracts from the affidavits prefaced by a letter from Lee, assuring "the public" of the "authenticity of the account."[67] As the public awaited Gage's report, which did not appear for nearly two weeks, the press carried editors' and readers' speculations. Wild accounts of British and American losses circulated, as did claims that Boston had fallen. Descriptions of British brutality also circulated, such as the *London Evening Post's* widely reprinted description of how at Lexington "A poor sick old Man was run through the Body with a Bayonet, and two other sick old persons were shot thro' the Head."[68] Most newspapers readily printed condemnations of the British troops, such as the *Exeter Flying-Post's* remark that "by the last news from America, we have had accounts of the commencing of a Civil War against our Colonies, and of such cruel and inhuman proceedings of our army there, as never before disgraced the character of British soldiery."[69] The incident underlines the divergence between the American and British presses during the conflict. Colonists had identified and successfully molded the newspaper press into an instrument with which to inflame and rally the populace.[70] The colonial newspaper was far more about conveying a message than information, as patriots and loyalists alike usurped the press for their own political agendas. In contrast, the British press maintained a far higher degree of objectivity—afforded at least partly by the luxury of distance from the actual fighting. Mistakenly assuming a similar degree of detachment existed in the American press, most British papers reprinted the heavily biased account without reservation, and most readers seemed to accept it as truth. The *General Evening Post* was among the few papers that offered a defense of the troops by featuring a lengthy letter condemning the American account.[71] Declaring that "Impartiality cannot be expected from Men when they are giving an Account of their own rebellious Proceedings," the author of the account correctly argued that the "Rebels Account of their Skirmish . . . is stuffed with many Falsities." "When the Facts are published," concluded the paper, they will discredit the "rebel Vermin" accusations of British brutality and confirm that the British had dispatched the opposing militia with relative ease. Far more representative, however, was the *Stamford Mercury,* which called the incident a "massacre" of colonists and reported that "horror, consternation, and resentment, were strongly painted on the countenances of every honest man in London yesterday, on receipt of the melancholy news from America."[72] Even Lord George Germain, the war hawk who would soon replace George Legge, earl of Dartmouth as Secretary of State for the American Department and lead Britain's war effort, readily accepted that British troops had instigated the fight. In a private letter written in response to the first newspaper accounts, he conceded that "the Bostonians were in the right to make the Kings troops the aggressors and to claim a victory."[73] The *London Gazette,* the government's official newspaper, did not repudiate the story immediately but instead appealed for calm while it awaited Gage's version of events, which it pledged to print.[74]

The nationwide appearance of Gage's account did not reinstate public confidence in either British authority in America or Gage. Some comment in the press questioned the truthfulness of Gage's rendition. In response to his description of "the Cruelty and Barbarity of the Rebels," who "scalped and cut off the Ears of some of the wounded Men," the *Saint James's Chronicle* accused him of using the more audacious stories as propaganda in

Boston to "reconcile the common Men [of his army] to the Butchery of a Civil War."[75] The most public of his justifications for sending troops to seize military stores in Concord appeared through his leaked, and subsequently widely reprinted, letter pleading his case to the governor of Connecticut. In it Gage insisted that the preemptive strike was designed to avoid a war, not start one: "you must acknowledge that it was my duty, as it was the dictate of humanity, to prevent, if possible, the calamities of civil war, by destroying the magazines."[76] Considering the outcome—hundreds of dead and wounded and Boston besieged by American militia—such statements only further eroded public confidence in Gage. The *Saint James's Chronicle,* among others, accused Gage of having singly ruined any chance of bringing about reconciliation. Although the *Chronicle,* like virtually every other newspaper in the country, had earlier predicted the failure of North's proposal on its own merits, it nevertheless took the opportunity to blame Gage for the disappointment: "By the latest Accounts from Philadelphia we are confidently assured, that Reconciliation would have been the Consequence of Lord North's Propositions of 20th of February, if the Troops under General Gage had not commenced Hostilities before the same could be taken into Consideration."[77] The situation, most commentary in the press concurred, would only get worse.

Channels of communication with the colonies remained entirely open, so reports of preparations for armed resistance flooded into the British press. For example, the *Derby Mercury* reported under its regular section on "American Intelligence" that the "The late unhappy Affair has had the most amazing Effects thro' every Part of America," prompting colonists to take arms in support of Congress.[78] There is nothing to suggest that these accounts appeared as a result of careful plotting on the scale of the Lexington and Concord accounts; rather, British newspapers reflected the overall tenor of printed and private information coming from the colonies, which, thanks to American patriots' grassroots purges of loyalists from key positions and attacks on printers, was decidedly pro-American patriot in tone. At this point British newspapers made little effort to identify the sources for readers, instead either reporting the information without a source or noting only that it came from "a correspondent in ———." That changed as the war progressed and British editors and readers became more wary of the credibility of the American press.

According to the frenzied reporting in the British press, all of America was in arms. The *London Evening Post* reported on June 15th that the Virginians had threatened to remove their governor, John Murray, earl of Dunmore, by force if he did not voluntarily leave.[79] The *Saint James's Chronicle* announced that New Englanders had greeted the arrival of Samuel Johnson's government-supporting pamphlet *Taxation No Tyranny* by burning the author in effigy.[80] Letters from New York printed throughout the British press in June described how the people had armed and appointed a provisional government. "The people of New-York," concluded one widely reprinted account, "have taken the Government into their own hands."[81] Still more letters from the Carolinas, along with reprints of the assemblies' and various associations' resolves, informed readers that armed resistance to British authority had also spread there. The *Ipswich Journal* reported that even the Pennsylvania Quakers, noted pacifists, were taking up arms and "employed in martial exercises even on Sundays" in preparation for war with Britain.[82] The colonists' armed unity seemed complete.

Coverage and discussion in the British press took the situation seriously. The *Oxford Journal* declared in late June, "The unhappy Disputes between Great Britain and her Colonies are now arrived to such an alarming Pitch, that there is hardly an individual in the Kingdom but what trembles at the Consequences."[83] There was no shortage of wagging fingers, as politicians and commentators sought to apportion blame. Thomas Howard, earl of Effingham, an outspoken opponent of the North ministry, offered a critical summary of the situation in a widely reprinted speech in the House of Lords that the *London Evening Post* described as "most affecting."[84] Thanks to the blundering of the ministry, he declared, "here are two Armies in [the] Presence of each other; Armies of Brothers and Countrymen; each dreading the Event, yet each feeling, that it is in the Power of the most trifling Accident, a private Dispute, a drunken Fray in any Public House in Boston, in short—a Nothing—to cause the Sword to be drawn, and to plunge the whole Country into Blood, Flames, and Parricide." A reader in Leeds in Yorkshire wrote a letter printed in the *London Chronicle* that shared Effingham's expressed melancholy over the affair but instead fixed most of the blame on the Americans, who were acting "like a spoilt child."[85] As such, the reader declared, the situation called not for conciliation but a firm hand. Either the Americans or the British would inevitably suffer, and the author had no choice but to prefer it to be the former of the two: "it is the duty of every Englandman to interest himself in the success of his Majesty's arms; and, since the sword is unhappily drawn, not to hesitate whether it should pierce the sides of disobedience and ingratitude, or be turned into the bowels of our country." Only rarely did commentary viciously attack the colonists, such as in a reader's letter in the *Saint James's Chronicle* that described New England as a place where "honest Men and Virgins [were] scarce" and where people "eat like Ploughmen, though they work as lazily as Gentlemen."[86] The *Derby*

Mercury offered a more typically even assessment of blame, declaring that "To Point at any one Man as the Author of these Evils is rather too severe." The colonists, it continued, were guilty of "extravagant Zeal for Liberty . . . without considering that nothing is so essential to the Purpose as a due Obedience to the Government," but the "Government have been equally blameable" for having too much confidence in the power of the strength of arms to bring the Americans to heel.[87]

Over the next few months, the news pouring into Britain confirmed that the fighting at Lexington and Concord was a prelude to a lengthy conflict whose outcome was less than certain. In particular, the arrival in late July of accounts of Bunker Hill confirmed most Britons' perception that the colonists had resolved to fight. Descriptions of the battle filled the press. They came from Gage, private letters from anonymous British officers, and the accounts of American soldiers reprinted from colonial newspapers. The conflict was the talk of the nation. As the great literary figure Samuel Johnson remarked at the time in a letter to Hester Thrale, "America now fills every mouth, and some heads; and a little of it shall come into my letter."[88] The battle sapped the army's fighting strength in America and ultimately resulted in more praise for the Americans.

Although technically a victory for the British, Bunker Hill was widely accepted as an American spiritual triumph on both sides of the Atlantic. Words like "gallantry," "heroism," and "bravery" in reference to the colonial fighters peppered the press's coverage. A widely reprinted extract of a private letter from Boston boasted to an English correspondent that "Before this letter reaches you, you'll have learnt that Americans are not deficient in either Courage or Discipline, and are good Marksmen, as your Officers know very well."[89] The point was not lost on British commentators, as the high level of officer casualties received great attention in the rehashing and analysis of the battle. For example, on August 10 the *Stamford Mercury* printed a table highlighting that more officers were lost at Bunker Hill than at Minden in 1759, when the British and allied forces defeated a French army of some 50,000 men. An unnamed British officer gave personalized testament to the circulating tables and charts in a widely reprinted letter: "This Victory has cost us very dear indeed, as we have lost some of the best Officers in the Service . . . nor do I see that we enjoy one solid Benefit in Return, or are likely to reap from it any one Advantage whatever." He concluded, "We have, indeed, learned one melancholy Truth, which is, that the Americans, if they were equally well commanded, are full as good Soldiers as ours."[90] Johnson agreed. "I do not much like the

BUNKERS HILL
or America's Head Dress

FIGURE 3.1. "Bunkers Hill or America's Head Dress" (1775). This image pokes fun at the enormity and complication of fashionable hairstyles, while simultaneously reflecting the popular interest in American events. Although the scale is exaggerated on the print, the *General Evening Post* for May 9, 1776, described a woman at a London masquerade ball with hair "so enormous as actually to contain both a plan or model of Boston, and the Provincial army on Bunkers Hill, &c. &c." BMC 5330, © Copyright the Trustees of the British Museum.

news," he declared in his letter to Thrale; "our troops have indeed the Superiority, five and twenty hundred have driven five thousand from their entrenchment but the Americans fought skillfully; had coolness enough in the battle to carry off their men; and seem to have retreated orderly for they were not pursued. They want nothing but confidence in their leaders and familiarity with danger."

Some commentators raged against the Americans, as evidenced in a piece in the *Dundee Weekly Magazine* that attacked the Americans' targeting of officers and another in the *Bath Chronicle* that accused the Americans of using buckshot. Yet most publicly expressed observations lamented the fighting in America.[91] Reiterating the common theme that the Americans were fellow nationals, the *Oxford Magazine,* which rarely carried political editorial content, printed a touching two-page editorial "On the Civil War in America."[92] Underlining the tragedy of the whole affair, a number of other newspapers and magazines printed accounts that described the painful, personal anxieties and losses that families on both sides of the Atlantic were suffering. For example, Gage's own loss of a nephew who had fought for the American side was widely reported.[93] One particularly moving account, which appeared in newspapers and magazines across the political spectrum, was the story of "Lieutenant Shea, of the Marines" who died at Bunker Hill. According to the version in the *Derby Mercury,* the brave soldier, who killed "no less than four Provincials after he had received his death Wound," left behind a "disconsolate widow at Plymouth" and nine children, the eldest of whom was also in the army and on his way to America.[94] Shortly after its own abbreviated reprinting of Shea's death, the *London Evening Post* drew attention to the shared suffering, calling the whole affair "so bloody a massacre" for both sides.[95]

The prospect that the enemy would be their own countrymen was the source of the gloom that prevailed in Britain. In a private letter, Lady Sarah Bunbury referred to William Howe's appointment in America as "so vile and fruitless a service, where he may be killed & cannot get any honour."[96] The press made it evident that many soldiers shared her misgivings. A description of a particularly poignant occasion of protest in August 1775 first appeared in the *London Packet:*

> The Detachments from Burgoyne's Elliot's Light Horse, being ordered to march to Plymouth, to be ready for embarking for Boston, put black Crape upon their Swords, and passed in that truly mournful Manner from Kensington to Brentford; and in their Way they met his Majesty, to whom they meant to shew that they disliked and detested the unnatural Service they were going on.[97]

Numerous officers publicly refused to fight in a civil war against the colonists, most notably Major John Cartwright and Lord Effingham—both outspoken opponents of coercive policies.[98] Effingham's resignation of his commission was national news, receiving coverage in most of the London and provincial newspapers. False rumors of other well-known officers' resignations, including those of Jeffrey Amherst and John Burgoyne, also circulated occasionally in the London press.[99] A letter from Charles Lee, a career officer in the British army, to his former commanding officer, John Burgoyne, justifying his decision to join the American cause and imploring Burgoyne not to fight appeared throughout the country. Typical of most papers, the *Derby Mercury* devoted an entire page to a piece on the subject, which consisted of a short biography of Lee followed by his letter.[100] After publication of that article, the newspaper noted that resignations had become so common that "no less than 200 Officers of the Army are struck off the Half Pay List . . . for not offering their Services in the American Civil War."

The American invasion of Canada gave credit to descriptions of American military might and Congressional power, and it further underlined that the reassertion of British authority would require substantial force. The invasion also justified commentary in newspapers that had been critical of the Americans. Supporters of the coercive policies of the North ministry took pleasure in reporting the Canadians' refusal to join the movement against British rule, readily printing such items as Halifax's loyalty address and descriptions of Governor Guy Carleton reviewing regiments of Quebec militia. Representative of the pro-coercion commentary, the *Dundee Weekly Magazine* labeled the Americans as aggressors for "making war" when the Canadians "only desired to observe a neutrality."[101] Nevertheless, few if any Britons expressed surprise publicly when news of Montreal's fall reached Britain via the colonial American press in December. As a testament to the widely held belief that Congress's forces held sway in North America, most Britons also seemed to believe that Quebec—despite its inhabitants' loyalty to Britain—would soon fall as well. As the *Exeter Flying-Post* remarked, the cannon and mortars that the rebels had taken from forts during their march through Canada "will render a siege of Quebec a matter of no difficulty."[102] William Murray, Baron Mansfield, a North ministry supporter, publicly predicted that Quebec would fall in his widely reprinted speech in the House of Lords in December; a few days later the *Saint James's Chronicle* advised the inhabitants of the city to surrender to avoid being plundered; and the *General Evening Post,* which rarely conceded any ground to either the government opposition at home or the colonial resistance in America, readily endorsed a rumor in January that Quebec had fallen.[103] Even when reports of Quebec's successful defense against the Americans' New Year's Eve assault trickled into Britain in February, the public was reluctant to believe the good news.

The despairing projections for Quebec reflected the cloud of pessimism that rolled into Britain in the summer of 1775 and then lingered for over a year. Boston was given up as lost almost as soon as the reports of the battles of Lexington and Concord reached Britain, even though news of the actual evacuation did not arrive for nearly another year. Meanwhile, the British forces in America were depicted as enduring unending hardships and suffering from poor morale. Private correspondence from the troops described the deplorable conditions: in a widely printed letter from a British officer in Boston to his wife, the officer detailed the lack of supplies and rampant disease, concluding that "Many of the sick and wounded found a remedy in Death."[104] Assessments of the war and predictions of the outcome in the press were overwhelmingly dismal. A handful of commentators held out hope that the resistance movement would lose momentum and the colonists would be reconciled to Britain, but such remarks were drowned in a sea of letters from America whose writers expressed the inevitability of a full-fledged war. As a Philadelphian informed his correspondent in a private letter that circulated widely in the press: "I am very sorry to inform you that we have lost all Prospect of Peace, and are preparing to meet the Dangers and Calamities of War with that Degree of Fortitude and Resolution which Justice and a good Cause naturally inspire."[105] During the summer of 1775, virtually every newspaper and magazine carried reports that Congress was amassing a grand army of nearly a hundred thousand men.

Few Britons publicly held out much hope for peace. Congress's Olive Branch Petition, which made a lukewarm effort toward reconciliation and reached Britain in late August 1775, aroused little serious comment in the press. Only a handful of papers even bothered to reprint the entire petition.[106] The king's proclamation, which he had signed the week before and had appeared in virtually every newspaper and magazine in late August and early September, declared the colonists to be in a state of rebellion; this proclamation overshadowed Congress's half-hearted attempt at reconciliation and made it—and any other proposal for peace—mute. His speech at the opening of Parliament in October, which subsequently appeared in various extracted forms throughout the British press, emphasized the government's resolve. After explaining that the agitators in America wanted nothing short of "an independent empire," he detailed the government's plans for increasing Britain's military strength in order to defeat the rebellion. "The object is too important, the spirit of the British is too high, the resources with which God hath blessed her too numerous," he concluded, "to give up so many colonies which she has planted with great industry, nursed with great tenderness."[107] The hundreds of printed tables detailing the augmentation of regiments, the deployment of troops, and the movements of the navy that appeared in the press underlined the king's sincerity and the likelihood of full-scale armed conflict. Thus, despite the best efforts of what one reader of the *Bristol Journal* referred to as "the sensible in both countries" to avert the "horrors of civil war," the reading nation braced itself for what most believed would be a bloody and uncertain conflict.[108]

Only a handful of commentators publicly predicted that any war would be easily won. A reader of the *General Evening Post* made one such boast in March 1776; in a letter to the editor, the reader shortsightedly claimed, "All the business our troops are like to have to do in America will be, to be witness of the submission of the men, kiss the pretty girls, and then— return home." Such confidence was rare.[109] Even the *General Evening Post*, which had taken one of the most consistent lines of the London papers in favor of aggressive coercive policies, freely conceded that a war would be expensive and difficult. Its dominant line, as exemplified in an April 1776 piece, was that the war must be conducted because it was necessary, despite the difficulties it presented. "To permit the Colonies to gain by one rebellion," it declared, "was to sow the seeds of another." Britain was a great power, and, therefore, could not make concessions: "Britain, after having humbled and subdued its rivals in arms and arts, extended its vast and prosperous empire beyond the Atlantic and the Ganges, displayed its victorious ensigns on both elements, must not make inglorious concessions to refractory subjects."[110]

Many Britons during this period openly asserted that the American colonists might prevail. In the wake of Lexington and Concord, the *Saint James's Chronicle* observed that Britain's difficulty maintaining regular supply lines and deploying reinforcements meant that "any war must be on very unequal terms." "A Thousand English Soldiers killed in America," it continued, "must be supplied by a Thousand more from Great Britain; while a Thousand Americans destroyed are supplied by a Thousand more on the spot."[111] Similar comments peppered the press throughout the spring and summer of 1776, such as one from "An Englishman" that called the conquest of America "entirely impracticable," emphasizing its distance, vast size, and substantial population.[112] According to most commentary, Americans also seemed to desire victory more than Britons. In a widely printed letter, a British naval officer in

Boston compared the zeal of "the common People . . . of New England" to Cromwell's supporters in that they were "capable of performing great Things under that Kind of religious Appearance." Combined with such a widespread knowledge of firearms that "every man can be a soldier," this level of commitment made America a nearly impossible conquest.[113]

The dark descriptions in the press of military mobilization in Britain contrasted sharply with the reported fervor in America. During the early years of the war, the North ministry strove to minimize its effects on the home population with such measures as renting foreign troops and augmenting existing regiments rather than raising new ones. The result was that the war's impact on British manpower during the conflict's early years was light compared to 1778 and after.[114] The policy stemmed from a variety of assumptions within the North ministry that the press coverage supported, including the unpopularity in Britain of a war with the colonies and the assumption that a swift strike of overwhelming force, enabled by the rapid acquisition of ready German troops, would nip the revolution in the bud. Nevertheless, the attempt to suppress the rebellion from across an ocean inevitably required a visibly significant effort. News of redeployments, the recall of officers, and recruitment drives regularly appeared in the press throughout the country. Newspapers and magazines printed army lists with precise tables detailing numbers, locations, commanders, and strengths of regiments. Similar tables of Britain's naval strength—complete with the name, commander, location, state of repair, and number of guns of each ship of the line—also appeared regularly. Following its printing of such a lengthy table for the army in February 1776, the *Saint James's Chronicle* estimated that an expeditionary force of 50,000, of which 28,000 would be British and Irish, would be assembled for action that year. Considering that this required the deployment of roughly three-quarters of Britain's peacetime army, the newspaper was right to describe the effort as "stripping [Britain and Ireland] bare."[115]

Drawing so completely on Britain's existing military forces meant that every soldier faced potential deployment to America, thus further making the war a local issue as provincial papers printed the assembly and movement of local regiments. As in all wars, those left behind worried incessantly about their friends and family in uniform. For Lady Bunbury, the deployment of men she knew drew her interest to the war and the press coverage of it. As she remarked in a private letter in July 1775, "I allow of my incapability in politicks, but I'm very anxious about them now partly from a horror of civil war, & chiefly on account of Genl Howe, for whose welfare I am very much concern'd."[116] During this time troops marching through towns and villages on their way to ports were a familiar sight to many Britons, visibly bringing into focus the human cost of war. The press recorded these scenes and brought them to life for those Britons who could not witness them in person. These were not happy occasions, as accounts such as one in the *Saint James's Chronicle* of March 16, 1776, made clear: "Yesterday Morning a Draught from the Guards, of one thousand Men, marched off the Parade in St. James's Park, in three Divisions, for Portsmouth, in order to embark for America. It was computed there were three Females to one Soldier assembled in Tears on this melancholy Occasion." Even the *General Evening Post,* which regularly advocated sending a large expeditionary force to America, remarked after reporting on the embarkation of another group of guards that "their taking leave of their wives, children, and friends, exhibited an affecting scene."[117]

The British press also described growing nationwide concerns about the broader impact of the conflict—particularly how it would affect the economy and the possibility of it widening into a global war. By the outbreak of fighting, the mainland American colonies combined to constitute Britain's largest overseas market. They also provided cereals for the British domestic market and the West Indian sugar colonies, timber for British ships, and tobacco, which satisfied domestic demand and served as a commodity for re-export to continental Europe.[118] Press coverage of the Seven Years War had made the British public acutely aware of America's importance, and the decade of colonial boycotts that followed only reinforced this. Although a handful of observers attempted to devalue the importance of the American trade, such as the *General Evening Post's* claim that "the commerce with North-America has been greatly over-rated," most comment predicted that a catastrophe would soon hit the British economy. Tobacco shortages, which received a great deal of attention in the press, made the economic effects of the conflict felt by the millions of Britons who consumed tobacco regularly.[119] Foreshadowing what would became a regular occurrence in later years, the *Bristol Journal* complained as early as July 1775 about the shortages and how the shop prices had skyrocketed.[120]

Readers and editors increasingly expressed fears that the products and markets of the mainland colonies, either by one or a combination of British coercive policies and Congress's radicalism, would be driven into the arms of Britain's imperial rivals. Although such North-supporting forums as the *General Evening Post* continued to print accounts that the other European states intended to stay clear of America, virtually all other newspapers and magazines printed comment fully accepting that French and Spanish protestations of neutrality were a thin veneer disguising an elaborate effort to promote the rebellion. Accounts of shipments of French, Spanish, and Dutch supplies to America appeared regularly in printed reports emanating from both sides of the Atlantic, and by 1776 reports of engagements between the Royal Navy and European trading vessels attempting to supply the rebels appeared frequently, prompting a number of observers to begin to discuss the inevitability of open foreign intervention. As one commentator remarked in the *Saint James's Chronicle,* the "historical record" indicated that Bourbon powers would strike at Britain at every opportunity, and the rebellion offered the best yet.[121]

Reports of American privateers, hundreds of which scoured the Atlantic, added to the public anxiety. No one questioned that Britannia would continue to rule the Atlantic waves in the American contest, but anyone publicly doubting the power of the Americans to strike a severe blow against British shipping faced ridicule. Although "Friends of the Administration have represented in the Public Papers that there is no danger of the Americans having any considerable Power at sea," the *Derby Mercury* explained, America was not short of ships, sailors, or the manpower and raw materials to build more. As evidence, the paper then proceeded to print "for the Public . . . a list of the Shipping annual built for Sale in the Several Colonies . . . before the present war Broke out," and that list was substantial.[122] The *Bristol Journal,* which primarily served a readership heavily connected to seaborne trade, closely chronicled the attacks, which first trickled into the press during the winter of 1775 and then flowed as the year wore on. Other newspapers that catered to port areas, such as the *Dundee Weekly Magazine* and *Glasgow Journal,* not surprisingly also paid close attention to news of privateers. The London papers, whose immediate readers were involved in the investing, shipping, domestic distribution, and consumption of the overseas goods, also took an interest. Even the insurance status of the captured ships provoked discussion—the policies covered capture by pirates but not rebels—with the *Saint James's Chronicle* grumbling that such discrepancies were "likely to make Work for the Lawyers."[123] When news reached Britain in June that shipping in the West Indies was taking a beating, port newspapers' coverage reached a fever pitch, and even interior newspapers such as the *Bath Chronicle* and the *Oxford Journal* took notice.

Despite the open fighting in North America, privateers' raids on British shipping, and the looming threat of a war with France and Spain, many Britons maintained their opposition to the North ministry's prosecution of the war and used the press to express it. As was the case before the outbreak of fighting, some of this opposition was, no doubt, the opportunistic rumblings of those who already opposed the North ministry. Practical matters—particularly the war's consequences for merchants and the people who would bear the brunt of the fighting—motivated others' opposition, as did ideology. The most highly publicized opponents continued to be the London radicals who dominated local metropolitan politics. At a meeting in the late summer of 1775 at Guildhall that included the Lord Mayor of London, those in attendance "resolved that thanks be presented to [the] Earl of Effingham for having refused service [in America]."[124] When the king's heralds entered the City of London, the Lord Mayor, a longtime vocal opponent of George III and the North ministry and a famed supporter of the American cause, refused to endorse the king's August 1775 proclamation that the colonists were in a state of rebellion. A nationally reprinted report from the *General Evening Post* explained: "It has always been usual for the Common-Cryer of the City of London to attend on Horseback, with the City Mace; he attended this Day on Foot, and without the Mace; which, it is said, was owing to the Lord Mayor's not choosing the City Regalia should be used on the Occasion." In its own description of events, the *London Evening Post* added that "After it [the reading of the king's proclamation] was ended, there was a general Hiss."[125] The numerous petitions from the Lord Mayor and aldermen of the City of London, which appeared nationally, publicly underlined their continued opposition to the war lest anyone forget. One from the "Lord Mayor, Aldermen, and Livery of the City of London in Common Hall assembled" addressed and presented to the king on July 5, and subsequently printed in newspapers throughout the country, clearly stated that they could not support a war against the colonists: "As we would not suffer any man, or body of men to establish arbitrary power over us, we cannot acquiesce in any attempt to force it upon any part of our fellow-subjects." As a result, the petition called the king's ministers "evil counsellors" and beseeched their sovereign to "dismiss your present ministers and advisers from your person and counsels for ever." In March 1776 another petition even went so far as to describe the colonists as being "driven to open Hostilities in their own Defense."[126]

The number of Britons who had reservations about the war and the ministry's prosecution of it cannot be estimated with exact certainty but a reading of the press suggests both were substantial and widespread. It was certainly vocal. The public behavior of the London radicals was extreme, but its opposition still touched a national nerve. The *Saint James's Chronicle* carried a report in April 1776 arguing that if a "national poll" was "taken on who sides with whom in the present Contest between the Ministry at home, and the Congress at Philadelphia" the ministry would lose.[127] Key leaders of the Parliamentary opposition publicly blamed the ministry for pushing the Americans into a state of rebellion. In just one reported Commons debate in May 1776, Isaac Barré accused the ministry of "shamefully" misleading the nation with false reports in the *London Gazette;* David Hartley declared that the abuses of the ministry had "forced" independence upon the colonists; and Edmund Burke satirically commented that had he not known better, "he would suppose the ministry to be secret friends" of the American rebels, as it could not have facilitated their ambitions of independence in any better way.[128] Such comments clearly angered a number of commentators, including one of Burke's own Bristol constituents, who after overhearing him at a local coffeehouse wrote to the *Bristol Journal* to complain that "Those who at this critical juncture, feel the unnatural inclination to whish success to the American arms, must not be offended with us if we as Britons disclaim them. Let them pack up their seditious principles and retire to America; we had rather meet them in the field, as open enemies."[129] Nevertheless such constant picks at North's handling of the situation had the potential for broad appeal, because virtually no one wanted war. A widely reprinted letter from "Britannicus" summarized the situation in representative fashion in the *General Evening Post.* Although at the conclusion of a lengthy tirade against the "self-created senate [Congress]," Britannicus nevertheless proclaimed, "May the sword of vengeance be sheathed, and the olive branch of peace flourish in the land."[130]

Popular petitions to the king that advised conciliatory measures continued to flow to him, despite his highly publicized objection to both conciliation and the petitions. Provincial petitions in favor of conciliation tended to be far more respectful than those emanating from the City, but the position of its signers was never left in doubt. Newspapers and magazines reprinted them regularly—usually in extracted form but sometimes complete with the names of the signers—and often commented upon them. The pages of the *London Gazette,* the government's official paper, were packed with loyalty petitions around the country, but readers of other papers realized that this was a skewed representation of national sentiment and shamed the *Gazette* for is bias. For example, in a letter to the *London Chronicle,* a Manchester native complained that the *London Gazette* had falsely "represented [Manchester] as inimical to the Americans, by means of [printing] an Address sent up to the King. . . . Be assured Sir," he countered, "that this Address does not give the true Sense of the Town in general." He explained that the address had been "smuggled" into Manchester with only a day's notice so as to ensure that "the Address is signed by very few, excepting High Churchmen and Men of Jacobite Principles."[131] The *Saint James's Chronicle* policed the situation by keeping running tallies of the total names of signatures when opposing petitions came from the same place. Following the presentation of Colchester's pro-conciliation petition to the king on January 29, the newspaper cheerfully noted that the numbers of signatures on this petition topped 500, whereas the pro-coercion petition the *London Gazette* printed earlier had only 125.[132]

Provincial newspapers often followed the fortunes of local petitions with great interest. In the fall of 1775 the *Bristol Journal* traced the progress of a petition from "the Merchants, Traders, Manufacturers, and Others, Citizens of Bristol to the King." The petition called for conciliation on the grounds that the war would harm trade, that "our fellow-subjects in that part of the world [America] are very far from having lost their ancient affection and regard to their mother country," and that force, however justified it may be, would only push the colonists further away from Britain. The newspaper first printed extracts from it as the petition circulated around the city attracting signatures. This was followed some weeks later by a letter from Edmund Burke, one of the city's members of Parliament, describing his personal presentation of the petition to the king. Then on October 14 the paper dedicated almost an entire issue to reprinting the petition in full, concluding its report with the names of all 901 signers. Clearly opposition to the conflict, or at least the desire to explore peaceful alternatives further, was substantial; the press helped ensure that it was nationwide and publicly considered.

The arrival of the Declaration of Independence in mid August 1776 seems to have surprised no one. After well over a year of intense press coverage of war preparations and close reporting of the increasingly radical resolutions of American political bodies, the Declaration's formalization of the two sides and the signers' goal of full independence was hardly a bold move as far as the discussion in the British press was concerned. Serious speculation of a formal declaration of independence had circulated since the autumn of 1775, and the following spring it became particularly intense. During the summer months printed news on colonies' individual conventions included the explicit instructions they gave to their congressional delegates to endorse what the Virginian assembly meeting in Williamsburg described as "declaring the united Colonies free and independent States, absolutely from all Allegiance to, or Dependence upon the Crown or Parliament of Great Britain."[133]

In consequence, when the Declaration arrived and shortly thereafter appeared in virtually every newspaper and relevant magazine by the end of August, it aroused little public debate. Typical of most newspapers, the *Bristol Journal* merely prefaced its printing with the following anticlimactic statement: "Advice is received, that the Congress resolved upon independence the 4th of July, and, it is said have declared war against Great-Britain in form."[134] Some commentators, including those at the *Gentleman's Magazine*, openly dismissed any value in analyzing it: "Whether those grievances [in the Declaration of Independence] were real or imaginary, or whether they did or did not deserve a parliamentary enquiry, we will not presume to decide. The ball is now struck, and time only can show where it will rest."[135] Meanwhile, frequent reports of the massive British expeditionary force embarking for New York appeared in the press, making clear, in the words of one reader, that someone would soon have to "pay the piper."[136]

The American War

✳ The months between the circulation of the Declaration of Independence in the late summer of 1776 and news of
a formal Franco-American alliance in the early spring of 1778
constituted a distinct period in the wartime British press. The
war dominated the press just as it had previously and would until the war's conclusion, but the coverage remained almost exclusively focused on the American colonies—the last time it
would do so. Moreover, the discussion in the press still bore
many hallmarks of a society engaged in an internal conflict—
features that would shrink or disappear once France's entry entirely transformed the nature of the conflict for the British.
Sympathy for the American cause endured—although it was
less pronounced than earlier—as did venomous hostility for
those who publicly professed it. Nonpartisan charities sprung
up to support those who suffered as a result of the war on both
sides of the Atlantic. One particularly successful charity that
garnered substantial public support even directly aided American prisoners of war being held in Britain. As the charity's
committee explained in a newspaper advertisement for the
drive, this was not intended to be about politics. The recipients
may have rejected Britain, the committee explained in one of
its press releases, but the charity would show that "the bulk of
[Britain's] inhabitants have not withdrawn all national affection from them."[1]

Hopes for victory were at their highest following the news in August 1776 of the arrival of the British expeditionary force at New York under the Howe brothers. Worries about supply lines, the superior valor of the American militia, and unified American support for Congress and the revolution all faded as Britain's disciplined troops seemingly marched over all resistance, and formerly silenced loyalists spoke out in favor of British rule. Confidence in Britain's institutions and governance revived as the image of Congress became tarnished. As a reader remarked in a letter in *Lloyd's Evening Post* in January 1777, sympathy for the American cause had lost much of its luster in Britain: "with great pleasure I have observed the opinions of many people to have changed, and that they think very differently of the conduct of the Americans to what they did some time since."[2] As the British press generally depicted the scene, within a few short months of the Howes' arrival the thunderous rebellion that had caused so much consternation in Britain appeared to have been reduced to a mere whimper. Washington and his grand army of citizen soldiers had been smashed, and Congress's authority was disintegrating. All that remained was a series of mop-up operations. Worries of possible French intervention and the global war that would accompany it were made mute in the belief that the war would be over long before the French could mobilize. By the winter of 1776, overconfident commentators in the press were already discussing how the colonies should be ruled after the war. Indeed, the American war, at least for some, had become old news. As one reader remarked in the *Morning Post:* "The public . . . are so sick of politics, and American affairs, that some genius needs but start, and fix their attention on another subject, to give literature and reading quite a new turn."[3]

This new confidence, however, came crashing down in late 1777. The overwhelming successes of the British forces at New York had led the public to create an impossible timetable. The nation became critical of Sir William Howe and his generals' inability to deal a death blow to Washington's army and Lord Howe's failure to blockade the colonies fully or stop American privateers. Adding to the anxiety was that by late autumn of 1777, the looming possibility of a formal French alliance seemed to be a likelihood. As "Old England" warned in a letter addressed to Lord North in the *General Evening Post* in September, France and Spain "wanted only time" in allying themselves with Congress. In consequence, the British public discussion was increasingly marked by impatience. Victories meant little unless they were on schedule, and when faced with the setbacks the public mood as expressed in the press turned swiftly to defeatism and exposed the fragility of its former confidence.

The battles for control of New York and its hinterland marked a high point in the public expectations for victory in Britain. After more than a year of printing predominately gloomy reports and commentary, the press as a whole shifted into a much more optimistic mode in August and September 1776, when the British military buildup on Staten Island came to dominate the war news. The Howes first successfully conducted what would be the largest British amphibious landing until the twentieth century, involving 40,000 men and over 300 ships, and from there operations proceeded smoothly. The Howes did carry a weak proposal of accommodation to the rebels, but hardly any commentary in the press held out hope for success. Full-scale war had begun. As the *General Evening Post* remarked, "all hopes of Accommodation are now at an End."[4] The nation had accepted that Anglo-American differences would be resolved through war, and, as described in a letter to the *Exeter Flying-Post*, braced itself for "a war on the success of which the honour, the interest, and consequence of the British empire ultimately depends."[5]

There was no shortage of information upon which the British newspapers could draw and comment. Most notably, the information arriving from America was remarkably more balanced than in the previous eighteen months. Patriot newspapers and private letters continued to reach Britain in droves, but the arrival of the British army offered security to numerous loyalists and moderates in New York whose dissenting voices had been quieted by Congress's supporters in America. News from America flooded into Britain that autumn, with the *Saint James's Chronicle* reporting in October that over 2,000 letters from New York alone had just arrived at the General Post Office.[6] Alongside colonists' letters came both official dispatches and private letters of British soldiers, whose remarks generally were less extreme or politically entrenched than those of the colonists. To all of this editors added extracts from old travel accounts describing the geography, climate, and culture of the regions at stake. The comment and analysis of readers, politicians, and editors was never lacking, as the whole nation seemed ready to offer an opinion. The result was a host of viewpoints in the press from throughout the British Atlantic. Nevertheless, a broad examination of the London and provincial press reveals that the publicly expressed consensus was decidedly optimistic at the prospect of a quick and easy war. Dire predictions reduced dramatically in number as did respect for the military capacity and political hegemony of Congress and its American followers.

The press took Washington's forces seriously before the New York and New Jersey campaign. Memories of the bloody nose the veteran British troops received on the return from Concord and at the Battle of Bunker Hill had not dissipated, and the press and its readers remained cautious in its expectations of an easy victory. In their letters home, British officers generally depicted the colonists as prepared and, more worryingly, well fortified. Even the *General Evening Post,* which in the previous year had tended to downplay the Americans' ability to resist, carried a widely reprinted British officer's letter, which declared that: "strong Intrenchments as the Rebels have thrown up at New-York were never seen in an Enemy's country; according to the best Information, they extend Miles together, are at considerable Height, and have near 30,000 men to defend them."[7] Not surprisingly, the press universally warned its readers to expect heavy casualties, such as the prediction in *Ipswich Journal* of the likely "general carnage" a battle would entail and how "the lives of thousands of his Majesty's British and American subjects" were at risk.[8]

At least partly in consequence of such warnings, the press universally portrayed the British victories at New York and in New Jersey as nothing short of a total rout of the formerly admired colonial forces. The ease of the successes was a cause for national celebration. Bonfires were lit around the country, and church bells rang. No one publicly gloried in the deaths of the colonists; rather, the elation was more a mix of expectation of the war's end and relief that far fewer men had died than expected. A special issue of the government's *London Gazette* on October 10 devoted itself to coverage of Britain's resounding victory at Long Island, and a week later it had circulated around the nation and appeared in extracted form in virtually every newspaper. In what was to become a familiar occurrence, the coverage included extracts of the official dispatches from General Howe and his officers, which were meticulously constructed with blow-by-blow battle accounts, lists of units involved, and numbers and lists of dead and wounded. Private letters from British officers also circulated. One, which the *Bristol Journal* attributed to Charles, Earl Cornwallis, overflowed with elation. "Such was the extreme judgment, the cool bravery, the recollection, and the humanity of those gallant brothers," it declared, "that if this action was to be repeated, no part of their conduct would admit of emendation; the whole being a perfect master-piece of Military Greatness."[9]

Some commentators remained wary, but most Britons seemed to bask in the uncommonly good news from America. The *Saint James's Chronicle* printed several warnings from readers that the American rebels should not be discounted after a single campaign, because Washington's army had

FIGURE 4.1. "News from America, or the Patriots in the Dumps," *London Magazine*, November 1776. In the scene, Lord North and his supporters hold out the news of the British triumph at New York. To the left, the "Patriots" (the term used to describe the Parliamentary opposition) are dejected by the news, underlining the view that they do not truly want the best for their country. BMC 5340, © Copyright the Trustees of the British Museum.

survived.[10] Other readers worried that the Americans showed more discipline than at Lexington and Concord by building impressive entrenchments and retreating in an organized fashion. True, several admitted, most colonists ran at the sight of veterans, but soon the rebel army too would consist of veterans. Such remarks, however, were drowned out by the predominately positive coverage. The autumn of 1776 belonged to the Howe brothers. According to the overwhelming consensus of the press coverage, which included plenty of material purporting to have come from American patriots, the British not only defeated the rebels, they appeared to have crushed them.[11] The Howes occupied New York, and then their subordinate commanders, Henry Clinton and Lord Cornwallis, proceeded to chase the rebels through New Jersey and effortlessly take Rhode Island. The Howes' proclamation, which was widely reprinted in the British press, announcing pardons for all rebels who reaffirmed their allegiance to the king was followed by numerous accounts of would-be rebels flocking to the British for forgiveness.[12] The war seemed as if it would conclude soon and that the small minority of commentators who had publicly proclaimed the fragility of the rebel cause had been right all along. Not surprisingly, the press was full of praise. News of General William Howe's aristocratic elevation to the Order of the Bath appeared in the same issue of the *London Gazette* that carried reports of his Long Island victory. The brothers' mother, the Dowager Viscountess Charlotte Howe, was received by the king and queen at court with the "most gracious reception." "This worthy Lady," the *General Evening Post* remarked, "had had the singular happiness of seeing three of her sons head the British armaments against the common enemy" and likened her to a "Roman matron, in the virtuous times of the republic."[13]

A result of these successes was a newfound public confidence. As a widely reprinted petition from the citizens of York declared, "[We] acknowledged the Justice of coercive Measures," and "by the wisdom of your Majesty's councils, and the terror of your arms, the authors of this unnatural rebellion will speedily be subdued."[14] Accompanying the repairs to Britons' confidence in the military was a restored faith in the justice of the war's prosecution. North and his ministers were never widely lauded in the press during the war—even for the brief periods that some of the generals enjoyed—but public criticism abated during the period between Long Island's fall and the British surrender at Saratoga. Much of the venom was gone. Although printed in a handful of newspapers, Charles James Fox's description of the Americans at New York as "gallant Men, who stood forth undisciplined, to defend and protect the common Rights of Mankind" received few echoes in the press outside of the Parliamentary reports.[15] As a widely reprinted reader's letter in December 1776 explained, Congress's Declaration of Independence had forced would-be sympathizers to choose, and they chose their own country:

> There never surely was a more sudden Change effected in the Minds of Men, than has been occasioned by the Americans declaring for Independency. Before that fatal Error of the Congress, in every mixed Company, America has as many Advocates as Government; now every Man feels his Interest inseparably involved in the Success or Failure of the Mother Country, therefore every Man naturally wishes to hear that he is not likely to be a loser.[16]

Publicly expressed support for American resistance had declined markedly. This is not to suggest there was great enthusiasm for the war or that American supporters had disappeared. Although the war prompted much heated debate in Britain, it paled in comparison to the divisiveness in the American colonies. For example, the government's calls for public fasts and days of prayer in support "of his Majesty's arms" were, according to press reports, largely ignored (one commentator wryly remarked that "the People of Great Britain seem to have but little stomach for fasting").[17] The experience of John Marsh, a young Salisbury lawyer and musician, on the national fast day of December 13 was probably more typical than not.[18] A subscriber to the *Salisbury Journal* and *Gentleman's Magazine* and a regular coffeehouse patron, Marsh had followed the war in the press. He had two brothers in the Royal Navy in service in America (both would eventually become prisoners of war), but opinions about the war did not dictate his social interactions. Marsh attended the special church service in observance of the fast, but a friend, "who would not go to church, saying it was an unjust war . . . chose not to go." Marsh also declined to attend another friend's musical party, wanting to maintain a reverence for the occasion, but within a few days he was happily meeting and conversing with both, and there is nothing in Marsh's meticulously kept diaries to suggest that either he or anyone else harbored any ill will. Disagreement, its seems, was largely tolerated.

While public criticism of the North ministry had lessened considerably in the wake of the British victories, it had not disappeared. The ministers' handling of the war continued to attract plenty of disapproval from both original opponents and commentators who professed the necessity of the war.[19] The abundance of information in the press, which included such pertinent information as troop placements on battlefields, lists of regimental strengths, and descriptions of local geography, enabled readers to transform themselves from mere spectators into self-proclaimed counselors. These armchair advisors were impatient, having convinced themselves that the war should have ended and that the real obstacles were British rather than American. As a reader remarked in a letter to the *Gazetteer*, a longtime forum for anti-North commentary: "however just and right the war may be on our side; certainly nothing can be worse conducted than it has hitherto been by our ministers."[20] Such commentators had little public reverence for their leaders. In typical fashion, readers of the *Saint James's Chronicle* slurred ministers' characters, accusing them of prolonging the war for personal profit. Even the lauded Howes were not immune. For example, the predominately pro-war *Morning Post* nitpicked William Howe, whose popularity did not last long into the new year, for letting Washington and his army escape for the winter into warmer New Jersey rather than the colder New England.[21] Subsequent letters and news paragraphs throughout the press in the spring of 1777 harangued his brother for allowing the American privateers to hit British shipping and thus drive up the price of goods.

Personal attacks in the press continued, too. A favorite target for public ridicule was Lord Germain, who, with North's support, was appointed by the king as Secretary of State in the summer of 1775 with the expectation that he would administer Britain's war effort. Germain had been a career army officer who had reached the rank of lieutenant general, but during the Seven Years War at the battle of Minden (1759) he cost the British and their allies a decisive victory by disobeying a direct order to advance the British cavalry against the retreating French. Germain, it seems, was jealous of the allied commander and did not want him to gain credit for a great victory. The court-martial that followed was public and particularly damning in its sentencing of a guilty verdict. The ruling that Germain was "unfit to serve his Majesty in any military capacity whatsoever" was ordered to be entered into every orderly book of every regiment in the British army.[22] But that was during the era of George II, and the American Revolution transpired under the watch of his grandson, who redeemed Germain. The court of public opinion, however, was not so amicable. Dubbed "Lord Minden" by his opponents in the press, Germain's critics mocked him for sending brave troops into battle when he himself had shunned it. One widely reprinted piece joked that he had written a military treatise to be distributed to all officers embarking for America, in which "he has laid down as a fixed Rule, that they should never (particularly in Action) be in a Hurry to execute any order they may receive from the superior Officers." Moreover, the story continued, "each of the

Hessian Generals"—it was the Hessian infantry that Germain had failed to support at Minden—was to be "complimented with a Copy of this valuable Work before they set out for America."[23]

Far more common than attacks on the ministry in terms of both the frequency and the diversity of newspapers printing them, however, were the assaults against the war's opponents and lukewarm supporters. Dissent, once cherished and widespread, came increasingly under siege in the press. To some extent this can be attributed to the arrival of the Declaration of Independence in Britain in August, but far more significant was the series of sweeping British victories under the Howes, during the coverage of which comment and reporting in the press portrayed the public as a whole as accepting the war as winnable for the first time. Within this newfound consensus, attacks against the remaining visible naysayers became bolder and more frequent. The *General Evening Post,* a longtime haven for critics of American sympathizers, printed especially venomous letters and news stories in the wake of the battle of Long Island. In the same issue that detailed Howe's victory, a letter from "Pacificus" referred to British opponents of the war as "abettors of rebellion," whose "object is the gratification of ambition, republican fanaticism, the pursuit of wealth by private plunder, public devastation."[24] Although such attacks may have been more frequent in such pro-war beacons as the *General Evening Post* and *Morning Post,* they were not confined to those papers. The change is much more evident when one considers that newspapers that had and continued to host antiwar sentiment increasingly included commentary that railed against American sympathizers, such as a piece in the *Saint James's Chronicle* that accused them of "yearning for only ill news" from America.[25]

Britain's rebounding public confidence in its military coincided with a sharp decline in the perceived legitimacy of Congress. Congress, which enjoyed widespread acclaim as the embodiment of English liberties as late as the summer of 1776, suffered a barrage of criticism following the news of the Declaration of Independence and the arrival of the British force under the Howes at New York. Never again would Congress enjoy acceptance in Britain anywhere on a par with what it had during its first two years. Accounts from the colonies, British officers, and commentators in Britain tarnished Congress's once-gleaming image with accusations of tyranny, greed, and abuse. Questions about Congress's ability to wage war, prompted by the British military's surprisingly easy defeat of American resistance at Long Island, accompanied the assault on its reputation. Even Washington's success at Trenton on Christmas Day 1776, which has been so celebrated in American lore, hardly made a dent in the seemingly universal expectations in the British public sphere that the rebellion's demise could be measured in a matter of months.

American loyalists who found refuge in British-occupied New York significantly aided the rediscovered confidence on the British home front. New York was a magnet and headquarters for loyalists for nearly the entire war. Its newspapers, and those from Charlestown after its capture in May 1780, produced a steady stream of reports supposedly from throughout North America that grossly exaggerated both the strength of the loyalists and the abuses carried out against them by Congress-led Americans. The New York papers served as anthologies of accounts of loyalists' sufferings throughout North America with seldom an issue going to press without some tale of an abused loyalist in it. Assault, murder, and plunder became regular themes as refugees poured into New York and recounted their tales of the purges and persecutions meted out under the guise of Congress's 1774 Association Act, which, although officially designed to encourage compliance with economic boycotts, became the justification for removing and punishing suspected loyalists in positions of local power. These newspapers, particularly James Rivington's *Royal Gazette,* appeared regularly in Britain and became cited sources for American news in the British press. Tarring and feathering, never widely practiced in Britain, became part of the national vocabulary. Although some newspapers occasionally printed readers' attacks on the credibility of the loyalist press, this did not seem to prohibit anyone from mining it for information; however, and in contrast to the previous unqualified printing of extracts from American patriot papers, most British publishers were often noticeably wary of wholly backing the loyalist accounts. Papers decreasingly offered endorsing comments and increasingly cited the loyalist newspaper source above the printed extract, leaving readers to decide on the report's credibility. This was a tactic editors had traditionally used when the information was dubious. As described in later chapters, as the war continued this suspicion turned to disbelief among editors and readers alike, and they eventually began to challenge the accounts more directly.

Despite British editors' occasional caution in dealing with American press sources, news from the colonies describing the tyrannous actions (often false but sometimes true) of Congress and its supporters against loyalists damaged its credibility in the British public sphere. It fell to opponents of Congress to balance the picture. Letters from colonists and British officers describing Congress-supported seizures of property and imprisonment of suspected loyalists abounded in the press after the arrival of the British force under the Howes and their successful occupation of New York and New Jersey. A

British officer at Staten Island remarked in a widely reprinted letter that "Congress have for some Time turned perfect Tyrants"; another described the experience of the "friends to Government" in America as "suffering almost Egyptian bondage."[26] The *Derby Mercury* informed its readers as early as September that "Congress have issued a Proclamation" stating that anyone fleeing their homes would have "all their Property confiscated and sold" to support the war—a complaint that would resurface in almost every newspaper and magazine in Britain in at least a hundred different forms during the war. The *Stamford Mercury* reported that the "Liberty of the Press was entirely destroyed in America" in that any printer producing comment contrary to "the wishes of their new Governors" was "imprisoned, and his property destroyed, without hearing or trial."[27] This climate of censorship and fear was so awful, claimed the *Exeter Flying-Post* in an effort to "shew the public in general . . . what sort of subjects the good folks over the water are," that even praying for the king's health had become a jailable offense.[28]

The Quakers, well known in Britain for their peaceable ways, became a particularly pitied group in the British press from late 1776 on, as claims of Congress's imprisonment of them for refusing to swear allegiance to the rebellion began to appear with some regularity. The *Oxford Journal* printed in December 1776 that the Philadelphia Quakers appealed to General Howe in New York to rescue them "from the Tyranny of Congress," but, according to the *Journal* and a host of other papers, their fate was to flee or languish in jail with the throngs of other victims of congressional tyranny—a population *Lloyd's Evening Post* estimated in March 1777 to exceed an impossible 20,000.[29] Moreover, as the *General Evening Post* reported, the rebels treated their prisoners "in the most barbarous manner; Some are chained on their backs to the floor, and others so loaded with irons, that they can hardly walk."[30] The mere suspicion of traveling to a British-held city risked a death sentence, complained a colonial tradesmen in a letter to the Reverend John Wesley printed in the *London Chronicle:* "A number of rebels . . . watch the motion of travelling people; and on suspicion of their intending for New York, shoot them without inquiry."[31] These accounts did not galvanize erstwhile American rebel apologists or sympathizers; instead, such reports largely hushed them, or, as the *Morning Post* observed in the early spring of 1777, the "villainous designs" of Congress had "at length sealed the lips of every republican on this side of the water."[32]

Congress's hypocritical swindling of Americans' freedom behind a facade of protests against British tyranny became a regular theme in the British press. The North ministry and its supporters certainly favored this line of argument. Even George III publicly referred to "the Blessings of Law and Liberty" that some of his colonists had "fatally and desperately exchanged for the Calamities of War, and the Tyranny of their Chiefs" in his widely circulated speech at the opening of Parliament in November 1776.[33] Attacks against the characters of individual members of Congress also became prevalent as the press's intense coverage made America's leaders household names. The *General Evening Post* carried a letter from a Lancashire reader who charged that "the wealth, the opulence, the power of [that] rank of men, who derive their rights, not from the election of any body of men, but from the Crown, or hereditary descent" had aroused the petty "envy of a Mr. Hancock and a Mr. Adams," who sought titles for themselves.[34] Even the *Bristol Journal*, which had endorsed the city's petition in favor of conciliation and served a population that in the last election had selected well-known American sympathizers Edmund Burke and Henry Cruger (who was American born) as its only two members of Parliament, referred to Congress as the "tyrannical . . . government under which the deluded Americans have vainly fought for security of their freedom."[35] Clearly Congress had fallen from the pedestal upon which much of the earlier commentary in the press had placed it.

A consequence of reports of Congressional tyranny was that some in the press pitched the case for prosecuting the war as a rescue operation, which Britain had a moral obligation to conduct. Loyalists taking refuge in Britain endorsed and promoted this view, but the extent to which they, like their American patriot counterparts before them, were able to influence the national discourse in the press is impossible to determine. The seven thousand or more loyalist refugees who fled to Britain during the course of the war and its aftermath typically were wealthy and unemployed, which meant they were literate and had plenty of time to gather in coffeehouses and read newspapers.[36] For example, Samuel Curwen, a Massachusetts refugee who arrived in London in summer of 1775 and chronicled his experience, passed much of the war in coffeehouses in London and the south of England, where he met fellow Americans and scoured the papers for news.[37] Based on some of the private correspondence from America that appeared in the press, loyalist refugees and their friends seem to have been ready to supply editors with sources of information, but, despite their numbers, the refugees appear to have been too disorganized and divided to construct an elaborate agenda backed by a propaganda machine. They did not even manage to form an official association until 1779. Nevertheless, loyalists in the public eye regularly took the opportunity to emphasize the view that loyalty remained strong in the colonies and that these dutiful subjects were being mistreated by their fellow colonists. Such was the case of Myles Cooper, president of

King's College in New York (later Columbia University), who declared in a widely extracted and reprinted sermon delivered in England that the protection of loyalists made the war a just one. "One important object of this war ... and which proved it to be a just one," he railed, "is to protect those Loyalists, who have been thus persecuted for adhering to their allegiance. . . . For these purposes the sword is unsheathed, and the battle set in array."[38] Depictions of the British as liberators became increasingly frequent. As a British officer embarking for America proclaimed through a poem that appeared throughout the press, the British, not the American rebels, were the protectors of liberty:

> Sent by our Sovereign's mild, but firm command,
> To quell the tumults of a mad'ning land,
> To win to order, or force to peace,
> To crush the factions, the compell'd release,
> To give sweet Liberty her wonted sway. . . .
>
> O'er winter seas with arms prepar'd, we go
> To meet a brother, or—disarm a foe.
> Impell'd to action for the common weal,
> We'll strike like Britons, but—like Britons feel. . . .
>
> Receive with ready arms the men reclaim'd
> At Rebels arm'd the only blows are aim'd.
> The cities, lands, from fire, from ruin save,
> O'er anxious provinces our banners wave,
> And shield those blessings God and nature gave.[39]

Moreover, according to reports in the British press, the loyalists appeared ready to fight for their own freedom. News of loyalist regiments forming in the colonies appeared regularly, with such papers as the *Derby Mercury* informing its readers via a loyalist's letter that 10,000 colonists had joined Howe even before his victory at Long Island.[40] Following the British occupation of New York, these estimates grew remarkably and out of all proportion with reality. The *Saint James's Chronicle* reported in December that William Tryon, the former royal governor of New York, had alone raised a loyalist militia of 13,000 men; the *Dundee Weekly Magazine* estimated loyalist regiments ready for campaigning in 1777 would include more than 20,000 men.[41] All of these figures exceeded any of those offered in the same papers for the strength of Washington's army. In consequence, someone reading the press with any regularity between the autumn of 1776 and that of 1777 would have been hard-pressed not to conclude that the loyalists were in the majority and ready to fight Congress's disintegrating army, which the *Stamford Mercury* typically described as being "in so wretched condition as to cloathing and accoutrements I believe no nation ever saw such a set of Tatter-de-mallions."[42]

In addition to attacks on Congress's legitimacy, the American cause of independence also suffered a steady barrage of reports and commentary challenging that body's practical authority over the American colonists and its ability to conduct a war. Before the autumn of 1776, the vast majority of press coverage emphasized the widespread popularity of a unified Congress and the colonists' military strength. This changed dramatically and immediately after the Howes arrived in New York. In the same issue that announced the army's disembarkation at Staten Island, the *Oxford Journal* reported that many notable revolutionaries, including John Hancock, had "of late wavered very much in their sentiments," and it predicted that Congress would soon collapse under the weight of an ill-conceived claim of independence and the arrival of a sizeable British military force.[43] A week later the *Derby Mercury* printed a letter from Philadelphia announcing that "one third of the Delegates have entirely withdrawn."[44] Lack of commitment, according to many readers and reports, lay at the heart of the rebellion's woes. In sharp contrast to years of coverage that depicted the colonists as steadfast supporters of liberty ready to sacrifice their lives in a common cause led by virtuous leaders, Americans appeared lukewarm supporters of revolution at best and corrupt men motivated by opportunism at worst. The *Morning Post* claimed in its first issue of 1777 that members of Congress had abandoned the quest for independence and fled to France "with the most valuable of their effects."[45] *Lloyd's Evening Post* corroborated the claim two days later, reporting: "several Members of the Congress have turned as many of their bills as possible into hard cash, and by that means . . . have raised considerable sums, with which some have already decamped, and other are preparing to follow."[46]

From late summer 1776 the press generally depicted Congress as hanging on by a thread. Its army, once widely feared in Britain, appeared to be in a state of collapse. The desertions and recruiting problems that plagued Congress's troops were well known in Britain. Magazines and newspapers carried numerous reports that would-be recruits on their way to join Congress's army returned home after learning of the British victory at Long Island. Accounts of Washington's supply problems filled the press, too, and the image of the American soldier went from robust farmer to decaying pauper. The American army's lack of munitions, food, and horses were detailed regularly, but most commonly reported was the lack of clothing. As the *Glasgow Journal* stated in a typical description, Washington's troops were "not only without coats and waistcoats, but very many regiments [were] without half a dozen pair of breeches or stockings among them."[47] Accounts that described the army in a state of dissolution were common, such as the widely reprinted announcement in *Lloyd's Evening Post* in January that "There are small or no hopes of another [Congress] army being raised, the eyes of the common people generally being open to their situation; a sovereign contempt for their Officers prevails universally."[48] The military commentators concurred, with the *Morning Post* quoting Jeffery Amherst, Baron Amherst, commander in chief of British forces in North America during the Seven Years War and now a chief military advisor to the king, as informing George III that in terms of Congress's army, by the spring of 1777 "there would be none."[49] Congress and its cause seemed finished.

Not surprisingly, the press depicted morale in Congress's forces as poor. News of the swift fall of Fort Washington, the supposedly impregnable fortress on Manhattan Island that held a sizeable chunk of the army's munitions and cannon, on November 16 included numerous claims of American cowardice and defeatism. After a brief engagement that left about fifty Americans dead, the remaining force of 2,722 surrendered, earning the scorn of British soldiers. The *Morning Post* printed claims that the fort could have held out for weeks against 40,000 men, "if bravely defended." The report continued, "the British soldiery look upon the Provincial forces [American forces supporting the rebellion] in the most contemptible light imaginable."[50] For further evidence, the British papers relied heavily on the circulating false testimony from well-known British officers then in the service of Congress. "The cowardly disposition of the provincial troops is strongly painted by the rebel General Montgomery," asserted the *Morning Post* in the wake of the fall of Fort Washington, "who says . . . that the people he commanded were a set of wretches that trembled at the very thoughts of danger; that he had been accustomed to fight with British troops, who, when they came to the field, looked for the enemy, and fought like heroes." The Americans, however, "instead of seeking the enemy, ran for shelter."[51] A widely reprinted report in the *Bristol Journal* confirmed Montgomery's supposed assessment of American troops with a report that Charles Lee, the British army career officer turned rebel whose correspondence with Burgoyne imploring him to refuse service in America had previously been printed throughout the press, was now "dubious of the Provincial troops, whose courage he is doubtful of."[52]

Washington's victory at Trenton in December did little to dispel this image. Although central to the American national memory, Washington's now famous crossing of the Delaware and surprise attack on the Hessian garrison received scant coverage in the British press. Even the *Gazetteer,* which was a haven for critics of the North ministry's military strategy, paid little attention to the victory. Most provincial papers barely even mentioned it. For example, the *Bristol Journal* gave the event only a few lines of print, and the *Dundee Weekly Magazine* dismissed it as a mere skirmish.[53] The only small point of debate focused on whether or not the defeat of the Hessians—all papers were quick to point out that British troops had not been involved— indicated poor quality in all of the German troops in British pay. Most readers probably would have seen such discussion as academic, however, because they had every reason to expect the war to be over in the next campaign.

The press brimmed with public confidence when campaigning opened in 1777. News from America arrived steadily throughout the winter and spring, keeping the reading public better and more regularly informed of the details of the conflict than ever before. Long before the campaigning began, the press correctly detailed the strategy: William Howe would take Philadelphia, the seat of Congress, and John Burgoyne would lead a motley army of British regulars, German auxiliaries, loyalists, and American Indians from Canada through New York, slicing New England—the perceived head and source of instigation of the rebellion—from the rest of the colonies. At first, the news was overwhelmingly favorable. Accounts of the previous autumn's successes at White Plains, Fort Washington, and Rhode Island reached and circulated throughout Britain in January, further underlining the publicly professed faith in the superiority of British arms that had been established at New York. By the following autumn, however, the mood had changed remarkably. The slowness of the campaigning and the capture of Burgoyne and his army at Saratoga revealed the fragility of the nation's confidence and shattered it. By winter the consensus of opinion in newspapers and magazines throughout the country was that the colonies had been lost, and Britain must withdraw from the war.

At the start of 1777, the North ministry enjoyed more support in the press than it had since fighting began, and its members and supporters brimmed with public confidence. As the *Morning Post* remarked in early January, "Since the Howes letter came, the Court has been full of congratulations, and felicitation; the king never was in higher spirits; Administration plume themselves on the success of their measures."[54] The next campaigns, supporters claimed, would end the war, and, based on the most recent results, they had every reason to be positive. The *Dundee Weekly Magazine* offered a typical assessment of comparative strengths for its readers, estimating that Congress had less than 7,000 men in its army while the British army in America boasted 39,000.[55] Moreover, according to endorsed reports in the press, tens of thousands of loyalists had joined the British side and tens of thousands more British and German troops were on their way. Philadelphia, Congress's home and the widely assumed next stop for Howe's army, was expected to be an easy conquest. Typical of the confidence to be found in British prints, a broadly circulated officer's letter from New York boasted that the British would take it "without so much as striking a blow."[56] Comment from home in the press concurred, witnessed by typical remarks such as the *Exeter Flying-Post's* claim that it would be an "easy conquest."[57] Such a blow against a cause already suffering from "low esteem," estimated the *Lloyd's Evening Post,* could "bring about a speedy resolution" of the conflict "in favour of his Majesty's Government."[58] Few refuted such predictions. Although some commentators expressed pessimism about the 1777 campaigns, these were, more often than not, tepid warnings about being overly optimistic rather than any real warnings of looming failure.[59]

The British nation seemed ready to fight as the time for action drew nearer, or at least it told itself this in the press. As a *Morning Post* reader exclaimed in April, "let the present operations thro' America declare!—She [Britain] has, or by June next will have, an armament in that quarter of the globe, sufficient to ensure the conquest not only of North—but if necessary, all of South America likewise."[60] The government's public declarations left little doubt as to the expected outcome. The king, the *Ipswich Journal* informed its readers, was ready to lead and was committed to "hazard the last jewel in his crown, rather than leave the infamous Rebels of America to their independency."[61] In its coverage of North's widely reported national budget speech in May, the *Bristol Journal* informed its readers that the Prime Minister "delivered himself with great clearness and candour, giving the House [Commons] assurances that government had every reason to expect that the ensuing campaign would terminate in a happy conclusion of our differences with America."[62] The egregiousness of his assessment would soon be evident.

Although the buildup had created an expectation of rapid success, the actual campaigning proved to be frustratingly slow. Throughout the summer, Britons closely followed the lumbering progress of Howe and Burgoyne in the press as they seemingly snailed their way to their respective targets in Pennsylvania and New York. No detail was too mundane to escape the press and its anxious readers; this was the main news story of the summer. Confirmable information from both commanders, however, arrived sporadically and infrequently, resulting in a steady stream of readers' complaints. Nevertheless, the public mood remained confident. As the *Exeter Flying-Post* declared, "From the present admirable disposition of the King's forces in America, it should seem evident that the rebellious game of the Provincials is nearly over."[63] Serious rumors that Burgoyne and his army were in danger did not circulate until late September, and even those came via France, which meant that the press treated them cautiously.[64] Not until news of the battle of Bennington reached Britain in the final days of October did newspapers such as the *London Evening Post* warn that Burgoyne's army was in serious danger.[65] Meanwhile, the *Morning Post* and *General Evening Post*, magnets for the ministry's self-appointed apologists, continued to print news and commentary that emphasized Burgoyne's likely success.[66] But then even the *Gazetteer*, whose readers and regular commentators took every opportunity to point out flaws in the ministry's war strategy, did not conclusively announce Burgoyne's surrender until early December.[67]

The news of Burgoyne's surrender of his entire army at Saratoga was devastating. Casting a dark shadow on the public discussions of any bright accounts from Howe's forces and their successful capture of Philadelphia, descriptions of the shock in Britain bordered on the melodramatic. The *Edinburgh Advertiser* used the following language to describe for its readers the scene of the House of Commons when Lord Germain announced that Burgoyne had surrendered: "His Lordship's speech struck the house with astonishment; and such a gloom appeared on the countenance of every member, as might be supposed to have been settled on the face of every Roman senator, when the defeat at Cannae was announced in the senate."[68] That Howe had taken Congress's seat at Philadelphia made little difference to popular discussions. Most papers seem to have accepted Howe's victory by early November, but the slow arrival of his dispatches meant that the government's *London Gazette* did not print them, and thus officially announce the victory, until December 12. The gap meant a month of further speculation at a time when news of Burgoyne's troubles was arriving in Britain. The *Morning Post* called the waiting game "painful" and railed against the handful of "libelous" commentators who pretended that Howe's victory was a fiction. Although the dispatches had surely been "unavoidably delayed," the *Post* assured its readers, "men of sober tempers, and capable of rational information, interpret nothing from this delay favourable to the cause of rebellion."[69] The *Bristol Journal* dealt with the delay in a fashion similar to most newspapers by printing a series of extracts from the available American newspapers and explaining to readers that these papers' accounts typically preceded any official dispatches.[70] When the *London Gazette* finally declared the victory with the printing of extracts of Howe's report, any luster had been lost. The month's wait meant that it was old news; the current story was Burgoyne's surrender at Saratoga. As a reader of the *Morning Post* lamented, "the joy of General Howe's success, has been so soon followed by the mortifying news of the brave General Burgoyne."[71] In many provincial papers Howe's dispatches appeared in the same or following issue as Burgoyne's terms of surrender.[72]

The months that followed Burgoyne's surrender comprised a low point for the British at home, as the nation's high hopes plummeted rapidly into despair. As a reader of the *London Chronicle* reflected: "No occurrence, in the course of the war, seems to have made so unfavourable an impression on the minds of the people in general, or to have caused so many to doubt of final success, as the army under general Burgoyne having been reduced to the necessity of laying down their arms."[73] Some Britons had difficulty absorbing the shock. A slew of letters from readers appeared in the *Morning Post* denying the defeat until the official dispatches appeared in the *London Gazette* of December 15—despite an abundance of evidence to the contrary in the press, including in the *Morning Post* itself.[74] The vast majority of readers, however, predicted total defeat would follow. The *Gazetteer* warned that the unsuspecting Howe would soon feel the full brunt of the rebels and suffer the same fate as Burgoyne.[75] The *London Packet* and *Ipswich Journal*, along with a host of other newspapers from around the country concurred, predicting that the newly conquered Philadelphia would soon be surrounded.[76] The *Public Advertiser* predicted that New York, too, would fall in a short time once Horatio Gates, the victor of Saratoga, and his superior force turned their attention to the remnant force that Howe had left to guard it. The following week the same paper reported that it expected the news of New York's surrender to arrive at "any hour."[77] The mood as presented in the press could not have contrasted more with that of six months earlier, and the shift highlights that the public confidence in victory, despite the bravado, was ultimately shallow.

Once readers realized that the worst of the predictions would not come true—at least not immediately—they began to debate what went wrong and, more importantly, who should be blamed. A handful of commentators tried to downplay the incident, such as a *Morning Post* reader's reference to the defeat as "the temporary miscarriage of Mr. Burgoyne's enterprize," but most accepted it as a disaster. Virtually all public comment initially extolled the bravery of the British troops, but their commander soon became the focus of ridicule, which peaked when he returned to Britain on parole in May. A reader from Birmingham described Burgoyne's arrival in that town for the *London*

Chronicle: "the spectators were become very numerous, both in the street, and at the windows of the houses therein, who all discovered an uncommon propensity to see this unfortunate commander, whose conduct in America, had been the subject of universal conversation in the political world."[78] As further discussed in Chapter 7, Howe also suffered increased scrutiny—both in public and the ministry's closeted circles—and was recalled in May.

Readers' calls for an aggressive continued prosecution of the war were not absent from the public discussion, but they were rarely and almost entirely confined to newspapers that had long attracted hawkish commentary. A letter from a "British Coffee-House" in the *Morning Post* called on the nation to "once more rouse itself to that magnanimity, and resolution, which have for ages rendered this country, the envy, and glory of all of Europe."[79] In a similar vein, a reader of the *General Evening Post* asked, "Has courage forsaken the British Isle?" "It is a bad sign," he continued, "when Britons seem to faint under a stroke of adversity." However, such calls for redoubled efforts were particularly rare outside of the London press, thus further indicating the pervasiveness of the war-weariness.

Most public criticism that winter fell on the North ministry. In contrast to the usual pro-North sentiment expressed in its pages, and further underlining the editorial independence of the British press, the *Morning Post* printed a reader's lengthy letter that viciously attacked the ministry. Although "no friend of America," the reader's letter seethed with anger at the betrayal of trust. The British people, the letter declared, had been "so grossly misled" by the ministry so as to believe that both the ministry's strategy and Burgoyne's execution of it would easily work. Now was the time, he concluded, to "find out where such an ill-contrived shoe has so sorely pinched this crippled country."[80] Most readers appeared to blame North and Germain personally. In a rare moment of harmony, rival papers such as the *Gazetteer, General Evening Post, Morning Post,* and *Public Advertiser* took lines that frowned upon the ministry. All of these papers printed a host of letters from readers who professed support for the war but viciously attacked the ministry's handling of it. A reader of the *Gazetteer* declared that regardless of what one thought about the grounds "for commencing the present contest"—he professed support for the war—all must agree that "certainly nothing can be worse conducted that it has hither to been by our Ministers."[81] The mood during the winter of 1777/8 had become decidedly defeatist. As the *General Advertiser* complained, "at the end of every campaign we are worse off than we were at the beginning."[82] A reader of the *Public Advertiser* captured the public sense of futility in the dark humor of a poem:

First General Gage commenc'd the War in vain;
Next General Howe continued the Campaign;
Then General Burgoyne took the Field; and last,
Our forlorn Hope depends on a General Fast.[83]

Essential to note is that almost all of these calls for ending the war professed practical motivations, rather than any admission of the righteousness
of the rebel cause. The difficulties met by British forces in America were
signs of mismanagement, so the argument went, not moral inferiority. As a
reader of the *Morning Post* explained, "the question now is not whether the
war originated from principles of injustice, and oppression on the side of the
Mother Country, or whether or not it took its rise from the ingratitude, and
long nourished principles of dependency on the side of America." What
mattered now, the reader concluded, was the war's cost and whether it could
be won.[84] Most commentary came down decidedly in favor of Britain cutting its losses in America. Sending more troops would simply create more
Saratogas, because, as a reader of the *London Chronicle* concluded, the
British troops could not cope with the irregularities of American warfare.
"Our ministers speak of discipline, as if there were some magic in it," the
reader argued, "but the Americans, who fight for every thing that is dear to
freemen, stand in no need of so rigid a subordination; all that is requisite for
them, is such confidence as many induce them to follow their directions; enthusiasm does more than supply the rest."[85] Besides, as "Philopoemen" remarked in a widely reprinted piece that first appeared in the *Public Advertiser,* pretending any longer that Congress represented a minority was
"ridiculous." Tyrannical or not, "Philopoemen" continued, Congress had
proven that it commanded the bulk of colonial loyalty by its total defeat of
the British at Saratoga.[86]

The overwhelming sentiment throughout the British press was that the war
in America should be brought to a close and the rebels accommodated. Peace
through conciliation now was far better than a peace imposed by further defeats on the battlefield later. A widely reprinted letter from "A Friend of Reconciliation" made the common argument that peace now might even be the
best way to secure long-term victory. "So long as we keep the Americans . . . by
retaining even a latent Claim of Authority over them, so long will they unite
together against us," the letter argued. However, it continued, "Quit that Claim
. . . and they may then differ with one another, and some of them may come, in
Time, to think that they were better off, when they were united with England;
and offer to return . . . so the only Chance we have of recovering some, is to
give up them all."[87] As discussed in greater detail later, concerns that a lengthy

war in the colonies would ultimately attract France and Spain became the most cited reasons for concluding the war as soon as possible. As a nationally circulated letter signed "Common Sense" argued, the costs of a global war with France far exceeded those of the loss of sovereignty over the rebelling colonies. Thus, he concluded, Britain had no choice but to withdraw its forces from America in hopes of "putting an end to this ruinous war."[88]

Perhaps most surprising is that, despite over two years of intense armed conflict, many Britons continued to harbor lingering familial obligations toward the colonists. Nowhere was this more evident than in the charity campaign for the thousands of American prisoners of war held in Britain.

FIGURE 4.2. "A Picturesque View of the State of the Nation for February 1778," *Westminster Magazine*, February 1778. This print attacks the abysmal state of affairs in early 1778, following the disastrous surrender at Saratoga and the likelihood of a Franco-American alliance. The cow represents British commerce, which an American Indian [representing the colonists], a Dutchman, a Frenchman, and a Spaniard are dismantling and milking. North looks on in horror, while the British lion, representing the armed forces, sleeps as a dog urinates on him. In the background, the British forces in America sit drunk and idle in Philadelphia. BMC 5472, © Copyright the Trustees of the British Museum.

Predominately sailors, these men endured the typically unsavory life of a prisoner of war but with the added difficulty of having fought for a government that was effectively bankrupt and unable to extend to its captured men the benefits of additional clothing and domestic supplies as was the practice in European warfare.[89] The combination of social status and access to family funds usually saved wealthy American officers from this plight, and loyalists living in Britain no doubt aided former neighbors and friends. For the rest, conditions were sufficiently intolerable that prisoners petitioned members of Parliament for relief in 1777.[90] The national response from late that year to the end of the war was a series of private charity drives. The most successful was a campaign started in December 1777, following a meeting at the King's Arms Tavern in London. According to the extensive press coverage, those present "unanimously resolved, that the American prisoners now confined in this country are in great distress" and decided to start a national subscription "for the purpose of furnishing the American prisoners with cloths and other necessaries."[91]

The charity received close press coverage for the next few months and then sporadically for the next few years as it made further appeals, took out advertisements in papers across the country, and began spending the money. Fundraising for causes ranging from assembly rooms to animal welfare was a standard feature of eighteenth-century life, and charities had grown sufficiently savvy by mid-century to make regular use of the press. For example, the Society for the Propagation of the Gospel, the Church of England's missionary wing, spent £237 18s 9d on publicity for a campaign for the relief of its persecuted clergy in the American colonies during the war, which included weeks' worth of daily advertisements in newspapers across the country.[92] Although perhaps not as centralized and organized as the professionally administered drive by the Society for the Propagation of the Gospel, the campaign for the American prisoners proved successful, creating enough buzz for Oxford dons to wager bottles of port on which of their colleagues had subscribed and raising £4,657 9s 6d by the end of 1778 alone.[93] By contemporary standards this was no small sum; it was substantial enough to make a genuine difference in the quality of the prisoners' lives. For example, it could have bought over six tons of tea, sixteen tons of twist tobacco, or ten thousand wool blankets.

The charity took an overtly apolitical posture, printing in its advertisement letters from the Admiralty praising the "humane motives of the subscription" and noting that the charity "did not want to interfere with government regulation."[94] However, from the two-column list of major donors printed in the *Gazetteer* in January 1778, the appeal of it to American sympathizers and the North ministry's opponents is evident.[95] Two of the principal opposition leaders in Parliament, Lords Rockingham and Shelburne, both of whom would serve as replacements for North as prime minister before the end of the war, donated one hundred pounds each. However, the list of several hundred names also included plenty of men and women who were not politicians, including merchants, clergymen, and even a Mr. Robert Goodwin, who "out of gratitude for the very generous and kind manner in which he was treated when a prisoner among the Americans" contributed fifty pounds. Not surprisingly, the charity aroused the ire of a handful of commentators. Several, including a reader of the *Exeter Flying-Post*, complained that the whole affair had been schemed for no other "end than merely to serve the Purposes of Faction" and that the charity's administrators would line opposition politicians' pockets with the proceeds. Another questioned the point of showing generosity to the American prisoners when "English seamen who were prisoners at Philadelphia . . . had neither shoes nor stockings to wear, and very little victuals, but not a soul there thought it proper to subscribe even a paper dollar to relieve their distresses."[96] But even most critics recognized that attacking the charity would appear inhuman and unpopular. As one confessed in the opening lines of a letter to the *London Chronicle* criticizing the charity, "Here many . . . will perhaps cry out against my arguments without reading further, and brand me with the name of cruel, and deny me the honourable appellation of an Englishman."[97]

The success of the charity ultimately underlines that, in the eyes of many Britons, the Americans remained different from other enemies, despite the rebellion and the lost lives. Plenty of Britons, it seems, accepted the fundraising committee's expressed hope that the charity "will afford an opportunity of placing the character of the nation, and of individuals, in its most honourable light, by proving that humanity is not the capricious or fashionable exertion of the moment, but a constant impulse, and the deliberate result of their reason."[98] Some Britons publicly questioned the move, such as a reader of the *Exeter Flying-Post*, who wondered why "an American Prisoner should have greater Claim to Indulgence than a French one, though all Circumstances considered he ought to have less."[99] But the answer in 1778 was not altogether different from those given during the decade before the war: the American colonists were culturally, if not necessarily any longer politically, part of the wider British family. This was a view that virtually all perspectives of the Anglo-American crisis and conflict could embrace—even those who had no sympathy for the colonists' grievances. Thus even in its attack on the colonists, a letter in the *General Evening*

Post—like so many others during the conflict—submitted that the rebels were fellow nationals: "The Yankies, or rebellious Colonists, are originally of Old England . . . and are naturally fellow-subjects with the people of Old England; their being on this or that side of the Atlantic making no more difference in original rights, than would their being of the North or South side of the Trent, or Severn."[100]

Congress endured its share of public censure, but as much, if not more, hostility in the press was reserved for its British supporters and critics of the war. The term "patriot" in the eighteenth century had traditionally included in its usage the reigning government's opponents who, although sometimes highly critical, remained loyal to the king and constitution. During the 1760s the London radicals stretched the rhetoric to its fullest extent and often earned the ire of commentators who professed that the self-proclaimed patriots abused the rhetoric for their own ends.[101] Samuel Johnson had such characters in mind when in 1775 he famously referred to "patriotism" as "the last refuge of the scoundrel."[102] As the Anglo-American tensions turned into armed conflict, public comment became increasingly impatient with critics of the government and American sympathizers who wrapped their critiques in the language of patriotism. Affixing such labels as "mock patriots," "pretended patriots," and "false patriots" to them, commentators in the press made a strong bid to narrow the accepted usage of "patriotism" to exclude critics of the war. For example, calling himself a patriot "in the old sense of the phrase," "Philo Patriae" slammed the Parliamentary opposition for "false patriotism" and disingenuousness in a letter in the *Morning Post*.[103] Those devoted to their country did not offer public criticism that might aid or comfort the enemy. As a letter signed "A True Briton" argued in the opening line of a lengthy attack on "mock patriots," "[a]t a time when faction is straining every nerve to overturn our glorious constitution, it becomes the duty of every true lover of this country to contribute all in his power to the support thereof."[104] Therefore, this letter—and hundreds like it—concluded, those who opposed the war on whatever grounds and did not give their full effort to prosecuting it, whether it be with the pen or the sword, must not truly love their country.

The discourse in the press during this period was perhaps the most politically factional of the entire war. Outspoken members of the opposition in Parliament who had at one time expressed sympathy for the Americans, such as the earl of Chatham (William Pitt the Elder) and Edmund Burke, were singled out for particularly noxious abuse. As a letter in the *Saint James's Chronicle* remarked after identifying Chatham as one of the guilty,

"Those false Patriots who have the barefaced Impudence to defend the American Rebellion . . . are the most driveling Fools for endeavouring to impose on our Understanding, and the most arrant Knaves for defending so black a Crime against the Authority of the Nation and the Interest of the People."[105] Such men and women, a host of commentators asserted, were not even true to their own professed cause. Instead, they were mere sophists using the American war for personal gain. The *General Evening Post,* which printed a great deal of commentary critical of the so-called mock patriots, provided the following satirical "Creed of a Modern British Patriot":

> I Believe that self-interest is the deity which I ought to worship. That to get the present Ministry removed, and secure to myself a place or pension, all means are lawful. That the good of my fellow-subjects ought not to influence me in the least. That if some few thousands of them are slaughtered in a civil war, it is of no consequence at all, provided I can thereby obtain what I desire. The advantage of keeping America in subordination to the legislature of this country, is a mere trifle, compared with a neat income of two thousand a year to myself. . . .[106]

In a similar vein, a multitude of letters and articles declared that these self-serving men and women yearned for the defeats that might sweep them into power: "These worthy patriots are upon the wing of expectations, to rejoice at what, with a malicious sneer, they call bad news from America," a letter in the *General Evening Post* declared, "and basely anticipate the pleasing accounts of the destruction of the British armies by pestilence, fire, and the sword."[107]

Despite the ruckus described above, few people either in Parliament or the press unreservedly backed Congress by 1777, including almost all members of the opposition who were being singled out by name.[108] Yet their detractors attempted to tar them with the brush of treason and in the process produced something of a straw man on which they could visit their frustration and draw attention away from the quagmire that had been developing in America. The only response of the war's critics in the press and Parliamentary debate was either to continue to preface their claims of loving the nation but not the war or to preface their comments with statements of support for the idea of the war but not its handling. However, neither of these caveats seem to have disrupted the tenor of the faction-driven discourse.

When the tide of war began to turn against Britain, the venom and accusations increased dramatically. Beforehand, this line of argument largely stayed in those London papers that had traditionally been critical of sympathizers, but by the late autumn of 1777, when news of the disaster at

Saratoga began to arrive, the attacks began to appear, usually as reprints of the London press, in almost every paper and magazine in the country. The *Stamford Mercury* reprinted a piece that asserted, in typical fashion, that upon learning about Saratoga the opposition politicians, which it referred to as "the Sons of Sedition," "have been flocking to London last week from all parts, and are laying their heads together for the laudable purposes of distressing their country, and serving themselves."[109] Even the *Public Advertiser*, a one-time magnet for commentary that unabashedly championed Congress, printed a letter from a reader who referred to American sympathizers as "secret Enemies of this Country."[110]

Some of the most vehement commentary went so far as to hold American sympathizers responsible for both the rebellion and the deteriorating state of affairs. As one reader remarked in a letter to the *Morning Post*, the "tongues at home" had been "more fatal to their mother country" than "swords abroad."[111] Such labels as "Abettors of rebellion," "domestic rebels," and "Encouragers of rebellion" became familiar phrases in the *General Evening Post* and *Morning Post* and in the array of provincial papers that extracted their contents. A letter to the *General Evening Post* declared, "A too credulous public, Mr. Editor, may be deceived, but it is beyond doubt that those in opposition at home have fomented the divisions in our colonies abroad; and, like sly incendiaries, have kindled the fire with the dreadful ravages of which they now perpetually alarm us, and at which they affect to be so much concerned."[112] Public criticism of the war and descriptions of the American rebels as victims, so the argument usually went, had planted seeds of doubts in the minds of ordinary Britons and sapped the nation's fighting strength. A reader of the *Morning Post* identified opposition leaders by name in a widely reprinted letter and took aim at both the "mock patriots" and their supporters: "It was for some time a doubt with me, whether the hostile leaders of rebellion on the continent of America, or their oratorical, and paragraphical friends at home were the greater or mere dangerous villains."[113] The public criticism had also made Britain appear weak before its European enemies, claimed a letter in the *Public Advertiser* attacking "our Pseudo Patriots," and had encouraged them to strike.[114] Therefore, it deduced, the global war that would ensue would also be on their heads.

The extent to which these attacks succeeded in silencing critics and rallying support for the war and North ministry cannot be definitively determined. But the attacks did not draw significant attention away from the difficult situation the British faced in America, as virtually every newspaper continued to prioritize reports from America over squabbles at home. Moreover, general criticism of the war did not ebb during this period, and at

FIGURE 4.3. "The Parricide. A Sketch of Modern Patriotism," *Westminster Magazine*, May 1776. In this print, Britannia, the personification of Britain, is about to be murdered by an American Indian (representing the rebel colonists). The image also attacks the political opponents of the North ministry for their lack of support for the war effort by depicting them as leading members assisting in the murder. John Wilkes, Lord Camden, Lord Chatham, Charles James Fox, and Edmund Burke are all among the background figures encouraging America and preventing the British lion from protecting Britannia. BMC 5334. © Copyright the Trustees of the British Museum.

times it increased—even in the very papers that served as the primary bases of the attacks. Unreserved support of the American cause of independence diminished significantly during this period, but that was probably far more a result of other factors that had received close attention in the press, including the Americans' formal declaration of independence, reported abuses of Congress, and the highly publicized attempts of Congress to bring Britain's ancient enemies, France and Spain, into the war. The reputations of politicians singled out for attack were not permanently sullied. After all, Burke, Fox, and Chatham's successor, Shelburne, all took up key cabinet positions after North fell. The smear campaign may even have added to their public credibility as having a finger on the American pulse—increasing their appeal as leaders of the peace negotiations.

The largest immediate impact of the debate was that it provided some publicly stated semblance of dividing lines on the war that could be reflected in contemporary political divisions. The "mock" patriots, quite simply, were all the members of the opposition lumped together—everyone from the London radicals, who openly sympathized with the ideological cause of the Americans, to those moderate members of Parliament who agreed with the North ministry's cause but questioned the practicalities of the prosecution. The war's supporters grew weary of the public criticism and hoped to stifle it by grossly exaggerating criticism so as to make it appear fanatical and unpalatable to ordinary readers. Some commentators even went so far as to demand restrictions on the freedoms of speech and printing in order to stifle opinions that dissented from their own. As a letter to the *Morning Post* signed "A Citizen" proclaimed, "Sir, I am an advocate for the freedom of debate, but an enemy to the licentiousness of it . . . when I see the members of a disputing society . . . sow sedition among their auditors, and to traduce the most respectable characters in this country,—in my idea the meeting becomes illegal, and calls aloud for suppression."[115] Ultimately such hard talk proved to be impotent bluster. The government did not crack down on the press. Moreover, even those newspapers that served as the primary hosts for such commentary were hardly its champions. After all, they printed plenty of so-called "mock patriot" commentary—no doubt sometimes to fuel further reader outrage and increase sales.

By the spring of 1778 the nation had grown tired of war, and many Britons openly accepted the loss of America if it could be exchanged for peace. As Horace Walpole remarked, "I am persuaded in the present apathy that the nation would be perfectly pleased, let the terms be what they would."[116] The disaster at Saratoga had amply persuaded large swathes of the British public that the war would probably not be won—at least not on the terms and within a time frame they would accept. Samuel Curwen, a loyalist refugee, wrote in his diary after reading the terms of Burgoyne's surrender in a newspaper that American independence was inevitable.[117] The overwhelming consensus in the press concurred, and an increasing number of reports, editorial commentary, and readers' letters called for a settlement with America in order to avoid, or to concentrate on, a renewed war with France.

The Carlisle commission was the North ministry's, and Britain's, last-ditch effort to prevent the war from expanding, but virtually all commentary in the press fully expected it to fail. The commissioners, led by Frederick

Howard, earl of Carlisle, carried North's peace proposal, which the prime minister had navigated through Parliament in February. The terms effectively offered everything Congress had demanded before 1776; or, as Walpole described the proposal after following it in the press: "[it] solicits peace with the states of America; it haggles on no terms, it acknowledges the Congress, or anybody it pleases to treat; it confesses errors, misinformation, ill success, and impossibility of conquest; it disclaims taxation, desires commerce, hopes for assistance, allows for the independence of America, not verbally, yet virtually, and suspends hostilities."[118] No one expressed concern about its passage through Parliament or winning public support. North and his supporters, not the opposition, had been the main obstacle to conciliation, and, as the *Public Advertiser* stated, "what was agreed on by all Parties in the House of Commons on Tuesday was [already] settled in the Alehouses . . . and for a pint of Beer, or a Glass of Brandy, our Ministers might have learnt the heads of the Conciliatory Plan, such, at least, as are wished by the People."[119]

Congress was the primary roadblock, however, and few commenting in the press expected it to accept any terms short of total independence. It was a case of too little, too late. Congress had tasted victory and, with the signing of the Treaty of Amity and Commerce with France two weeks before the passage of North's proposal, it had the advantage. The *Gazetteer,* like many newspapers and magazines, lamented that the same proposal would have ended the conflict two years earlier.[120] Even the usually optimistic *Morning Post* printed letters doubting its success.[121] Nevertheless, the ill-fated commission lumbered forward. The king gave his reluctant approval in early March, and Carlisle and his cohort sailed in mid April. In June, however, the press informed the nation that Congress had rejected the terms outright, refusing even formally to receive the commissioners. By then the Carlisle commission had been demoted to second-rate news, meriting only an odd paragraph or two in most papers, because when the reports arrived, the global war that the proposal had been designed to avert had just started.[122]

5

The Global War

✳ France's entry into the American Revolution in 1778 on the side of American independence redefined the war for the British. Instead of a costly but confined colonial war, the British faced a global war on an epic scale. The numerically superior armed forces of France and Spain, which joined the fight on the side of its old ally in 1779, jeopardized British possessions on no less than five continents. The lucrative trades in sugar, slaves, cotton, tea, and spices were now under threat along with the massive tax revenues the East India Company collected in Bengal. Such considerations together dwarfed the press coverage of the thirteen rebelling North American colonies. Although North America continued to receive considerable attention in the press, it had clearly been relegated to secondary news. The general mood in the press was decidedly pessimistic, if not fatalistic. Still not quite comfortable with their post-Seven Years War status as the leading European imperial power, the British reading public regularly assumed the worst when it came to overseas news. At any given time in the next few years, the consensus of opinion in the press was resigned to the loss of the West Indies, the conquest of the majority of Britain's possessions in Asia, an invasion of southern England, and the loss of the colonies in rebellion—yet only the last eventually happened.

Although increasingly frustrated and war-weary, the reading public, at least as far as it can be measured by the content of the press, was more interested in the war than ever. In this new climate of global war, the press took a greater interest in naval affairs, printing innumerable naval tables, descriptions of major and minor engagements around the world, and copious commentary to accompany it all. The coverage offered a few glimmers of hope, but the bad news decidedly outweighed the good. The West Indies, the British Empire in Asia, supremacy over the oceans, naval control of the Mediterranean and English Channel, and southern England itself all came under threat. In North America the situation improved remarkably as the British campaigned in the southern colonies in earnest, but, despite British victories and continued portrayals of a collapsing Congress, Britain seemed as far away from re-establishing control over the rebelling colonies as ever. Yet until news arrived of the British surrender at Yorktown in the autumn of 1781, none of this struck the public as catastrophically war-ending. Each year the British survived, although a little more battered and bruised, to fight again in the next. With no one nation able to achieve a series of decisive victories around the globe, the war, it seemed, would last forever.

The global war was a distinct phase in the British public's engagement with the conflict as facilitated by and depicted in the press. This was partly because the international struggle had a larger immediate impact on the British at home. Unlike the first three years of the conflict, which was a distant affair fought predominately with existing or hired foreign troops, the next five years were marked by the calling up of the militia to address threatened invasions, massive recruiting into the armed forces, and the creation of new regiments. This phase was, in many ways, a dress rehearsal for the total mobilization that would be required in the French Revolutionary and Napoleonic Wars.[1] In consequence, the war directly affected far more families, friendships, and communities than when it was a rebellion on the edge of the empire. The global war also proved more palatable than the American war. Fought predominately against its traditional European rivals of France and Spain, this war fit more neatly into the national rhetoric that the English (and, after the 1707 Act of Union of England and Scotland, Britons) had been espousing for centuries.[2] Once again surrounded by Catholic enemies, Britain could assume the role of champion of Protestantism and liberty—a mantle that had been difficult to wear when the war had been primarily with the Protestant and liberty-espousing American colonists.

The war after 1778 and the press's coverage of it can be roughly divided into three periods. The first is the introductory period consisting of 1778 and 1779, when the press and public adjusted to the return of war with France and Spain and then braced for defeat around the world and at home. During the following two years the global war seemingly reached a kind of stasis according to the press coverage, as readers settled down for what they anticipated would be a lengthy and expensive war when it became apparent that Britain's enemies would be unable to deliver the originally anticipated series of quick and decisive blows. This phase ended with the arrival in late autumn 1781 of news of the surrender of Yorktown. Although not necessarily strategically crippling, it dealt a decisive blow to British morale and pushed the remaining pro-war commentators in the press to accept the need to seek peace terms with Britain's enemies, even though it would mean territorial concessions and American independence. The final phase of the global war, which is discussed in the following chapter, spanned the aftermath of Yorktown to the conclusion of the terms of peace in 1783. In this period victories at sea and on land over Britain's European enemies redeemed the nation in the eyes of the reading public, enabling the British to claim a comforting partial victory in one of the least successful wars of its history.

The press coverage of the war after 1778 ultimately sheds light on how the British public's imperial outlook had obtained a global focus, but it also emphasizes that powerful elements of the old Euro-centric outlook remained. Throughout this period the press provided and assumed an extensive knowledge and interest in the worldwide possessions of the empire. North America had dominated the public discourse on empire for more than a decade, but, as the press coverage reveals, America had not snuffed out the popular interest in other parts of the empire that emerged during the Seven Years War and would dominate long after the American Revolution ended.[3] Yet for all the post-1778 war's global aspects, the conflict as depicted in the press was still largely defined in terms of old European rivalries. First France and then Spain were criticized and parodied in the press along lines that would have been familiar to the readership from previous wars with the Bourbon powers. Moreover, editors and readers regularly tapped into popular notions of national identity as being defined by Anglo-European (particularly Anglo-French) conflicts, regularly recounting ancient and more recent victories alike as a way to familiarize the present war.

Britain's experience of the American Revolution never focused entirely on Anglo-American affairs. Concerns about European rivals, particularly France, lurked in the background of the national discussions in the press from the start. After Congress's Declaration of Independence, these worries moved to the foreground, where they remained until after the conflict. The significance of Anglo-French rivalry in the eighteenth century is difficult to exaggerate. These "natural and necessary enemies" dominated European foreign relations for the better part of a century, and French military strength, both in North America and abroad, played a crucial role in ensuring an outcome of American independence.[4] Although French forces in North America accumulated slowly—the Caribbean was the French focus—and never reached the numbers hoped for by Congress, their ability to stretch British forces thin across the globe was essential, and the timing at Yorktown was impeccable. That France would play a role in the conflict would not have surprised many Britons at the time, nor would many have been stunned by the impact France ultimately had. If predictions in the press are any reflection of privately held expectations, most Britons in and out of government imagined France's entrance to be far more devastating than it proved to be.

European aid, which flowed to the colonies almost as soon as the fighting erupted, was widely known in Britain thanks to the press. Through the direction of Charles Gravier, comte de Vergennes, Louis XVI's secretary for foreign affairs, France played the largest role. Under the guise of the fictitious trading company Rodrigue Hortalez et Cie, France and Spain funneled millions of livres' worth of weapons, cash, and supplies to the rebels.[5] Although the exact details of the scheme escaped British editors, they were informed of the gist of operations. Rumors of French arms shipments had circulated since 1774, but after the fictitious trading company was established in August 1776 the reports stemmed from eyewitness accounts, such as the *Saint James's Chronicle's* widely reprinted description in August from a merchant recently returned from France of six French vessels being loaded with arms for the rebels and the *Derby Mercury's* printed letter from an Edinburgh merchant in Hamburg to his father describing two American ships loading war supplies bought with French funds.[6]

The Dutch and French ports also became well-known havens for American privateers, who sold their booty and refitted their ships safe from Britain's navy. The *Dundee Weekly Magazine,* like many other periodicals, detailed the system for its readers, explaining that in many instances the privateers operated as Euro-American partnerships. The ships sailed under American flags, but they were owned and often crewed by a mixture of Americans and Europeans, and their home ports were in France and the United Provinces (or Dutch Republic).[7] Such a dilemma provoked the *Morning Post* to cry out: "we are likely to have half the naval strength of France to contend with under the name America!"[8] As American privateers launched attacks against British shipping in the Caribbean and Africa, reports also appeared from French colonies describing similar partnerships and arrangements of aid. As a reader from Martinique bluntly stated in a letter to *Ruddiman's Weekly Mercury* of Edinburgh, "This port is full of

American privateers."[9] Britain's European rivals, especially France, would seem to stop at nothing to take advantage of the British predicament. Frustration in the press mounted. As the *Exeter Flying-Post* remarked, France's "present treacherous conduct . . . [has] given her all the advantages of a war without any of the dangers and losses."[10] Reports of French underhandedness and angry commentary reached such a frenzy that the *Gazetteer* printed a reader's apparently well-intentioned claim that the French government had even concocted a plan to sap Britain's military strength by sending "near two hundred ladies of pleasure, with constitutions replete with the most fashionable diseases" across the English Channel in order to "operate on our youth as destructively as a general plague."[11]

Any deniability of French involvement in the war—a position taken both by French officials and North ministry backers in the press who wanted to downplay the threat of war—evaporated in late 1777, when the October 27 edition of the *Boston Gazette* reached Britain carrying a Congressional resolution dealing with loan repayments to France and Spain. Extracts circulated throughout the British press. "It has long been notorious that the Courts of France and Spain have supplied the Colonies with arms, ammunition, artillery, clothing, &c.," the *General Evening Post* declared in response to the news, but "the extraordinary resolution of Congress demonstrates, that the Colonies are subsidized by these Courts; and that being thus secure of having the interest of their public debt discharged in Europe, they can want no other assistance for the establishment of their independence, and the solidity of their national credit."[12]

As outrageous as France's actions were, the public was well aware that the North ministry had few diplomatic tools available to deal with the problem. Short of declaring war against Congress's European suppliers, which Britons of virtually all opinions in and out of public office keenly wanted to avoid, there was little that could be done. In consequence, the press was uncharacteristically patient with North. Britain simply was too ill-equipped to fight a global war, and ministers and readers alike knew it. Unlike in previous wars with France, Britain had little hope of gaining a major continental ally, as its potential candidates—Russia, Prussia, and Austria—were busy carving up Eastern Europe and thus had little to gain by taking sides in another Anglo-French war.[13] On land, the comparison of forces was demoralizing, with press estimates of combined French and Spanish forces outnumbering Britain's meager army by five or more to one. At sea this situation was better but still unfavorable. The French and Spanish fleets combined outnumbered the British navy, as made evident to readers in the numerous charts and tables that appeared in virtually every newspaper and magazine from 1777 onward. Britain's navy was already overstretched, which a steady stream of complaints about the navy's inability to shut down American privateering or effectively blockade the American coast during this period made clear to the reading public.[14]

Virtually all public commentary assumed Britain would lose an all-out war. Even North wrote to the king on March 25, 1778, that Britain was "totally unequal to a war with Spain, France and America."[15] The general consensus in the press believed that Spain would easily retake the Floridas; France and Spain would assert control over the Atlantic and Caribbean; and the British Empire in Asia would collapse under the combined pressure of its native and European enemies. A widely reprinted reader's letter in the *Saint James's Chronicle* thus concluded in December 1777, "The Answer then . . . is, make the best Peace you can with America" as it "is better than [Britain's] Subjection to France and Spain." After all, the reader remarked, "It is not now a Question what we would wish to do, but what we can we do? We cannot conquer America and defend ourselves."[16] This was a point upon which few Britons, regardless of their position on the war, disagreed. For example, the *Morning Post* freely admitted that a global war would ruin the economy; and the *Public Advertiser* went even further, warning that French victory would result in French control of American trade, meaning "that in a few years . . . she will be the most potent and opulent Power on the Globe."[17] In consequence, this was not a war for which any major interest group or slice of British society openly clamored—despite an intense national loathing for France and disgust at its thinly veiled support for the American rebels.

The only significant debate on the subject of French assistance was whether or not France would be able to pursue another global war with Britain. The poor state of French finances, which rightly worried the minister of finances, Anne Robert Jacques Turgot, were well known to British readers, and merchants who relied on overseas trade and government apologists publicly latched onto this glimmer of hope. A particularly buoyant letter in the *Bristol Journal,* which drew a substantial audience from merchants who had been hit hard by the American Revolution and winced at the idea of extending it, argued as late at April 1778 that because "French finances are, if possible, in a worse state than the English," France might avoid war and allow the "very gloomy" state of affairs to "blow over."[18] The *Morning Post,* still serving as a forum for the apologists for the North ministry, regularly carried articles and letters that attempted to assure the nation that open war would not erupt. One letter went so far as to assert that France had not yet begun to mobilize its forces and that "there is every reason to believe that she has no more idea of attacking us, than of marching armies to the moon."[19] Another report pretended that Louis XVI personally detested the rebellion and "has frequently spoken of American perfidy."[20] Another letter asserted in a fashion that became the mantra of many *Post* readers: "the system embraced by the French Ministry is to go every length in supporting the Colonies without engaging in a war."[21] Yet such claims would have appeared increasingly hollow in the context of the abundance of reporting and commentary that reluctantly saw war as inevitable. Privately, both governments recognized that war was highly likely by the summer of 1777 and began to prepare. At the behest of North, George III omitted his usual lines about the preservation of peace in Europe in his speech closing the Parliament session in May 1777, and in June the government ordered the navy to stop and search any French ships near the mainland colonies.[22]

Defeat at Saratoga persuaded all but a handful of diehards that war with France was inevitable. Stocks fell two percent in the weeks that followed—a drop that the *Bristol Journal,* like most papers, directly attributed to the now "unavoidable" war with France.[23] The *General Evening Post,* one of the last holdouts for commentators denying an impending breach with France, accepted the reality of the situation in February 1778 and described the undeniable logic to its readers:

> A French minister must infallibly consider the present crisis as an opportunity too valuable to be missed;—they never could desire, or wish a moment, in which that great aggregate of distant force united in the last war, almost to their destruction, was so divided as at present. North American privateers in that war tore their Newfoundland, their West Indian, and American trades to pieces; North America paid, and supported near 40,000 men against them by land, and 20,000 by sea;—but North America now would be united with themselves:—such a moment would be tempting to a wise Bourbon Minister; —it is irresistible to an ordinary one.[24]

Changes in gambling odds, which papers regularly treated as reliable diviners, certainly suggest that betting men and women believed war would erupt within the year. The *Public Advertiser* announced on January 2 that bets could be made at coffeehouses for 6 to 1 against war being declared by March or 4 to 1 against war being declared by June. News of the gambling went national the following week, with such papers as the *Bristol Journal, Oxford Journal, Ipswich Journal,* and *Glasgow Journal* all printing similar odds. These advertised odds corresponded to those that could be procured by George Grant, a London-based marine insurance broker who catered primarily to Scottish clients. The best he could offer a client in Leith, who like many merchants wanted to be able to soften the blow if war was suddenly declared, was 7 to 1 with a maximum payout of £300 on a two month policy only.[25] Enough people had taken wagers or policies that the *Morning Post* thought it necessary to announce at one point that the betting had been thrown into confusion by the news that a French ship had captured a British merchant vessel, causing potential losers to cry out that the war had to be declared formally.[26] Apparently no one would offer odds beyond six months.

The two years following the news of Saratoga marked Britain's nadir in the war. The public discussion in the press wallowed in the misery of presumed defeat and ruin with only a handful of vocal commentators attempting to rally the nation's spirits. Although only the first major British defeat, the loss of Burgoyne's army was enough to shake the resolve of the already wavering public for an all-out war of conquest in America. As discussed in the previous chapter, the North ministry's peace proposal and appointment of the Carlisle commission in early 1778 was accepted by most as being the government's admission that Britain could not feasibly win the sort of victory that would establish a lasting British supremacy in North America—at least not before the Bourbon powers entered the war. Few in the press challenged the proposal's logic, although almost all commentators assumed it would not succeed. They were right.

When the war went global with France's official entry that June, the national mood in the press was slow to rally. But when the gloomy forecast of Britain's swift demise proved untrue, and Britain won a few small victories, morale as measured by the press began to improve slightly. Virtually no one publicly expressed an expectation of victory, but the reading public seemed to accept war as an unavoidable state and willingly, though not gleefully, trudged forward. As the *Annual Review* for 1779 remarked in the opening lines of its preface: "The Year of which we treat, presented the most awful appearance of public affairs, which this country has perhaps beheld for many ages." It continued, stating that the world had turned upside down not only in America but in Europe as well: "All ancient systems of policy, relative to any scheme of equality or balance of power, seemed forgotten in Europe. . . .[M]ankind seemed to wait, with an aspect which at best bespoke indifference, for the event of that ruin which was expected to burst upon us." Britain's transformation from confident imperial power to isolated and vulnerable target seemed complete in the public mind.

The only consistently upbeat news came from British privateers, for whom business was booming. Individual reports of ships being captured abounded, as did monthly, quarterly, and annual tallies based on those accounts. From this information, the *General Evening Post* boasted in September that in 1778 the British had captured or destroyed 222 American ships in the West Indies alone. The *Oxford Journal* estimated in October that at least forty French merchant vessels valued in excess of £600,000 had been captured by British privateers that in the summer alone.[27] Newspapers that served port areas, such as the *Bristol Journal* and *Exeter Flying-Post*, carried a host of advertisements recruiting seamen, surgeons, officers, interpreters, and even ships for privateer expeditions. The *Exeter Flying-Post's* issue for November 13 carried four such advertisements. Announcements of auctions for the goods taken were even more plentiful. Inland towns took an interest, too. The local paper of Stamford in Lincolnshire printed a large table estimating the total number of British privateers in service (280), the number of men involved (22,400 based on an estimate of each ship having eighty crew), and gave a breakdown of the distribution of privateer ships by port.[28] Although the war in virtually every other theater only got worse for the British, privateering continued to prosper.

Having stripped France of much of its empire in the Seven Years War, the British had a great deal more to lose than just thirteen of their mainland North American colonies. First and foremost in the press discussion was the West Indies, which were widely regarded as lynchpins of the British Empire. These colonies bought the vast majority of British slavers' cargoes and enormous amounts of American grain, and in return they produced, along with other products, the largest and most valuable product that the British Isles imported in the eighteenth century—sugar. Sugar consumption in Britain had increased nearly 2,500 percent in the previous century, and the annual customs duty alone on sugar in the 1760s was roughly equivalent to the cost of maintaining all the ships in the British navy.[29] West Indian planters also enjoyed a much closer relationship with metropolitan society than the mainland colonies ever had. Absentee planters had lived in Britain for generations, and those leading families who stayed in the West Indies were far more likely to put their daughters on the London marriage market and send their sons to a British school or university than mainland colonists ever did. By mid-century the West Indian interest had a powerful lobby and faction in Parliament made up of planting families and merchants closely connected to the Caribbean economy.[30] Not surprisingly, these men and women would have taken great interest in Caribbean news, and, like virtually all interest groups, ensured that reports and letters reached the press in a timely fashion.

Throughout the first two years of the global war, news about the Caribbean and the spread of the war there filled the press. The situation it depicted was not good. While Britain's defenses had been drained by the

American war, France had been able to stockpile troops and supplies and ready its navy.[31] Detailed estimates of military strengths that appeared throughout the spring and summer of 1778 graphed the enormous French advantages in terms of troop numbers and ability to concentrate its naval strength. Reports on the ground confirmed worries at home, such as a slew of letters from Jamaica that appeared throughout the press in October 1778 describing sightings of French troopships and troops massing at French ports. As a writer of a letter that appeared in the *Stamford Mercury* declared, "we are very much alarmed."[32] The general outlook was not good, as almost no one went on public record stating that Britain would mount a capable defense. A reader's letter in the *Public Advertiser* that predicted the imminent loss of all the West Indies in July was extreme, but virtually all comment in the press expected a fairly good drubbing at the hands of the French and, eventually, the Spanish.[33]

Although the extent of the influence of the press reporting on the government's actions is impossible to determine, the North ministry at least concurred with it and in 1778 began redeploying Britain's land and naval forces from the American mainland to the Caribbean.[34] While the land commitment was substantial—redeploying some 5,000 troops from the North American mainland in 1778 and then absorbing a further sixteen British infantry battalions before the war's end—the naval shift was dramatic.[35] Most opinions expressed in the press recognized that naval superiority was the key to the West Indian colonies' survival. The *General Evening Post* complained that "if these islands cannot be protected by a superior fleet, it will be in vain to attempt any conquest, or even stand upon the defensive, in that part of the world where the French can transport fifty men to our one."[36] The ministry agreed and redistributed Britain's navy in favor of the West Indies. North America's proportion of the total number of British capital ships declined from 41 percent to 9 percent in the year following July 1778 and would not rise above 13 percent for the remainder of the war, whereas the proportion of the navy in the West Indies grew from 9 to 48 percent.

Despite such a commitment, British public sentiment remained far from hopeful during the first two years of the global phase of the war. Accounts of troops massing in France or various islands for service in the Caribbean appeared regularly in newspapers and magazines throughout the country. The first island to fall had been Dominica, formerly a French possession, in September 1778, causing "inconceivable distress," according to the *Gazetteer,* in the merchant community.[37] The British countered by taking St. Lucia in December, which included a dramatic repulse of a French counterattack. Accounts of the victory and counterattack appeared in virtually every newspaper

in the early months of 1779, with such papers as the *Bristol Journal* highlighting them for particular praise.[38] However, the events of subsequent
months dashed any renewed hope. St. Vincent's fell in June, when the British
navy failed to intercept the French war fleet on its way from Europe—a point
on which North was harangued both in Parliament and in the press. The loss
of St. Vincent's itself did not cause a great deal of anxiety in the press, and
most printed opinion concurred with the *Glasgow Journal's* assessment that
"the loss of itself is no way considerable . . . it is so small, and the natives are
so turbulent and refractory, that little solid advantage can be reaped from it
by us."[39] The problem, commentators throughout the press agreed, was that
the fall of the island reflected the poor state of British defenses in the region
and foreshadowed the capitulation of Grenada, St. Kitts, and the rest of the
islands. Grenada duly fell in July, and accounts of the French fleet appearing
near St. Kitts soon appeared in the press, such as this widely circulated description of the island population's reaction to seeing it: "The cries and distresses of women of all ranks . . . was one of the most high finished scenes,
that nature and the soft affections, void of art, ever exhibited."[40]

By the end of the year the betting odds at the Royal Exchange were more
than 2.5 to 1 that Jamaica—Britain's largest and most populous possession in
the West Indies—would fall within a year. Rumors that it had already fallen
were beginning to circulate in the London press, and merchants connected to
Jamaica delivered a memorial to the First Lord of the Admiralty "praying [for]
for a naval force for the protection of that island," which subsequently appeared
in newspapers throughout the country.[41] In response to these reports, the London and provincial papers printed an array of letters from readers across the
nation. Such widespread reporting reveals that although the initial coverage of
the Caribbean may very well have been aided, if not influenced, by the absentee
planters and merchants connected to the trade, by this point it had become a
subject of national concern. Unfortunately, the news was not good. A reader
from Witney, a market town in landlocked Oxfordshire, best characterized the
anxious public mood by calling it the "hour of our national distress."[42]

The situation in Europe during the first two years of the global war
was not much better. American privateers became even bolder in British waters, the entry of France highlighted Britain's vulnerability on sea and land,
Spain entered the war, and the Irish took advantage of the situation to press
for long sought (and hitherto denied) concessions. The British press covered
it all so that anyone in regular contact with the press would have found it
difficult to escape the anxiety that seeped through the pages. Everything
seemed to be going terribly wrong.

At sea Britannia no longer seemed to rule even those waves closest to home. American privateers had been the bane of British shipping since the start of the war, but the highly publicized exploits of John Paul Jones and other American captains brought many Britons to question publicly the ability of the navy to defend Britain's shores. In April 1778 Jones became a household name following a raid on Whitehaven, where he landed two boats of men, attacked two forts, and set fire to the harbor. The *Whitehaven Packet* printed a special issue for April 23 dedicated to covering the attack, which depicted Jones as ruthless and highlighted the vulnerability of Britain's ports. According to the leading account, which subsequently appeared in virtually every newspaper across the country, "The scene was too horrible to admit of any further description . . . only by an uncommon exertion, the fire was extinguished before reaching the rigging of the ships, and thus in a providential manner prevented all the dreadful consequences which might have ensued." Although the predicted rash of subsequent raids never transpired, Jones nevertheless became a lasting symbol of Britain's naval weakness as he continued his campaigns around the British Isles.[43] As a reader's letter addressed to North in the *London Courant* railed eighteen months after Whitehaven: "[Jones] hath stripped you naked, and driven you from every subterfuge, and exposed your negligence and incapacity, more generally, if possible, than they were before exposed." If North could not protect "our coasts from the long-continued depredations of a daring free-booter," the letter concluded, how could he possibly "be fit to direct the naval force of this nation against the united efforts of the House of Bourbon!"[44]

Even more devastating to public morale in the press was the indecisive outcome of the First Battle of Ushant in July 1778 and the political aftermath that reverberated well into the next year. When France entered the war, the press depicted a major naval engagement for control of the English Channel as imminent. Leading the British forces was Admiral Augustus Keppel, who became the darling of opponents of the war when the press highly publicized his refusal to serve against the American colonists at the outbreak of the rebellion. Keppel remained active in Parliament, where he continued his association with the opposition and vehemently criticized North and the First Lord of the Admiralty, John Montagu, earl of Sandwich. The entry of France into the war enabled Keppel to maintain his opposition and serve his country, and so he took command of the fleet responsible for protecting the English Channel. Keppel's cousin and opposition leader, Charles Lennox, duke of Richmond, warned him that the appointment was a setup by Sandwich, who was putting Keppel in command of a poorly equipped fleet so that he would suffer the blame for any defeat.[45] Opposition commentators, however, rejoiced at the news. As the *Gazetteer* declared in June, "Britain may once more . . . regain her former character abroad, and punish the perfidy of her enemies if Keppel, and such men as Keppel, are permitted to continue to command our fleets."[46] The outcome of the battle a month later crushed such testimonies of optimism.

The tables, charts, lists, and comments in the press for years had consistently assured the British of their naval superiority over any European rival. When the news from North America soured and accounts of privateers hitting British merchant vessels rolled in, the public seemed to latch onto the one truism that Britain could defeat France in a major battle at sea. When Keppel sailed confidently with a superior force that included thirty ships of the line against the French fleet at the Western edge of the English Channel, the nation may have held its collective breath considering what was at stake, but all public commentary predicted a decidedly positive outcome. Unfortunately for Britain, a combination of bad weather, disorganization, and poor luck led to a rather lackluster battle and a less-than-satisfactory result. The British were not defeated by any stretch of the imagination, but the French fleet escaped largely unscathed, which left it fully capable of escorting a French invasion of Britain. The consensus of public opinion expressed in the press agreed that such a result following high public expectations was nothing short of a national humiliation.

During the next year Keppel, his officers, and the ministry were tried in the court of public opinion as convened by the press. In anticipation of the battle, the *Stamford Mercury,* like most papers, printed a huge table providing the names, guns, commanders, and locations of all ships in the British fleet that could participate; they provided the same for the French fleet and a detailed explanation of the British rules of which size ships must engage enemy ships of a certain size. In the aftermath of the battle, the *Mercury* and virtually every other paper across the country filled its pages with officers' accounts, further tables, and maps. Average readers had almost as much information at their fingertips as ministers of state, and these armchair admirals relentlessly criticized everyone involved in the affair during the months that followed. Privately, Keppel blamed Sir Hugh Palliser, who commanded the rear of Keppel's fleet and failed to follow Keppel's order to re-form the battle line, thus enabling the French to escape. Keppel's supporters denounced Palliser publicly in the press. An outraged Palliser, who was a career naval officer and most likely did not intentionally disregard Keppel's order, demanded that Keppel sign a public statement exonerating him. Keppel refused. Palliser wrote his own public defense, printed initially in forums sympathetic to the ministry, such as the *Morning Post,* but eventually in various extracted forms in newspapers across the country.[47] Unfortunately for Palliser, he made the perfect scapegoat for Keppel's supporters. Palliser was both a member of Parliament firmly aligned with the North ministry and a member of Sandwich's Admiralty Board. In consequence, many commentators depicted him as little more than a ministerial stooge.

Formal court martials for Keppel and Palliser ensued, which added further fuel to the public debate. The trials were a disaster for the ministry from the start. Twelve admirals signed a statement to the king denouncing the prosecution of Keppel, which appeared throughout the press on the eve of the trial.[48] One of the admirals, Lord Edward Hawke, is credited with declaring that he "would sooner cut off his hand than be accessory to such a trial."[49] On account of Keppel's poor health, his trial that winter was held on land, which meant that the government was unable to maintain any control over the flow of information to the press. For twenty-seven days, the trial appeared in serial form in almost every newspaper in the country. The *General Evening Post* even printed a diagram of the room, which promptly appeared in a number of its competitors so that its readers could visualize the proceedings.[50] Though the press did its best to emphasize the drama of the affair, Keppel's acquittal was hardly in doubt. Coffeehouse gamblers refused to take any more bets on his acquittal at any odds by late January; towns in the country pre-ordered ribbons, stockpiled luminaries, and planned parades to celebrate his acquittal well before the trial even ended.[51] Although Palliser, too, was later acquitted, Keppel's acquittal was a boon to popular opposition to the North ministry, and, to a lesser extent, to the continuation of the war in America.[52] With so much time to plan, celebrations took place throughout the country. At Dartmouth 10,000 yards of blue ribbon were purchased for garlands and cockades, Bath lined the famous Crescent with luminaries, and Plymouth featured a parade of over 2,000 shipwrights and rope makers, who carried with them a model of Keppel's flagship before a crowd of more than 10,000 spectators.[53] In London thousands of supporters formed in celebrations that featured the burning of Palliser's effigy at several locations and ended with rioting, in which the rioters attacked the houses of Palliser and his perceived backers, including North's house. Although Keppel appeared reluctant to be used as an anti-war icon—he refused a host of public appearances after the trial and did not make statements in the press—a number of his supporters took advantage of the situation, such as at Newcastle, where a petition for ending the war was launched, and celebrating crowds burned Sandwich and Germain in effigy as "abettors of the American war."[54]

By mid-1778, the press largely depicted Spain's entry into the war on the side of its ally, France, as inevitable. The *General Evening Post* printed occasional commentaries arguing against the likelihood of Spanish entry— just as it had for France just before it formally declared war—but the paper was a lone voice whose message ran against the grain of most expressed sentiment.[55] Reports of Spain's war preparations, which appeared in detail throughout the press in the summer and autumn of 1778, underlined the reality of the situation. Given the size of Spain's naval and land forces, its ambitions in the Americas, and its desire to regain Gibraltar, most Britons braced themselves for a slew of defeats at the hands of the united Bourbon powers. The gloom of a report in the *Gazetteer* was typical. In the last war, it explained, Spain joined the fight when France's navy had been ruined by Britain and its land forces severely bloodied in Germany. This time, how- ever, French military strength was "untouched." In consequence, the paper concluded, Britain's past success would not be a predictor of the future: "In such circumstances, it is absurd to argue from our former success (a success at which we ourselves, as well as the whole world, were astonished) to what it will be in the present contest, when we must labour under so many disadvantages."[56]

Meanwhile, Ireland, which had served as the starting point of English im- perialism and remained the practicing ground for many of its purveyors, rumbled. Ireland had long received the attention of the British press, which regularly reported major transactions in its parliament and the ruling legis- lation and proclamations that Britain sent across the Irish Sea. Informed Britons would have been well aware of the various factions within Ireland that vied for power and the major grievances they had against British rule. Difficulties between Britain and Ireland were hardly new. In the previous centuries and the centuries that followed, Anglo-Irish relations can be char- acterized as having cultivated hostilities between virtually every ethnic and religious group on both sides of the Irish Sea at one time or another. At the time of the American Revolution, it was the turn of the Irish Protestants.[57] The Dissenting Protestants were particularly vocal. Constituting a large slice of Protestant Ireland, but technically excluded from voting and holding public office by the Irish Test Act of 1704, the Dissenters fell somewhere be- tween the completely marginalized Catholics and the enfranchised Angli- cans.[58] Like their fellow Dissenters in Britain, the well-educated Irish Dis- senters expressed a great deal of sympathy for the American colonists' cries of "no taxation without representation" during the 1760s and 1770s, and when war erupted many maintained public sympathy for the American cause and shied away from service in the British army.

The underlying threat behind virtually all Irish demands during this period was that Britain's failure to offer concessions risked sabotage, work stoppages, and possibly open rebellion. That demands came over from Ireland would have surprised few readers, but the reading public was also well aware that there was little Britain could do in the way of force to deter them. Britain's highly publicized manpower problems at the start of the war meant than by 1778 Ireland had been stripped bare of troops for service elsewhere. The Protestant Irish response was to form "volunteer" companies under the auspices that Ireland had no militia and that the Protestants potentially faced both a Catholic uprising and an invasion from France and Spain. Although the volunteers received arms and supplies from the British government, the 60,000 men who comprised these units were not under the direct control of either the British government or its representatives at Dublin Castle, which accepted the force as a necessary evil in the face of the uprising and invasion alternatives. In such an advantageous position, Protestants in favor of increased Irish autonomy began to make demands on the North administration.

By late 1779 the issue on the table was trade. At the time, Ireland, like any other colony under British rule, was prohibited from trading directly with other colonies, except in circumstances specified by the British government. North successfully introduced legislation repealing these restrictions, which was a boon for the Irish woolen trade. The debates in the Irish and British parliaments were covered fairly closely in the London press but somewhat more sparingly in the provincial press in the autumn and winter. Commentary generally focused on two issues: whether or not such concessions would irrevocably hurt British trade and whether or not the concessions would be sufficient to keep Ireland loyal. No consensus in the press was reached on the first question. On the second, most expressed sentiment seemed generally satisfied with North's trade concessions. Some commentators were dramatic, as is evidenced by the *London Courant's* assertion that "the present hours seems to furnish the most important suspense that ever agitated any nation. Armed with spirit and resolution to turn the fate of an empire, Ireland awaits the answer to the English Parliament."[59] Yet the overall tenor of commentary in the press, whether provincial or metropolitan, anti- or pro-North, was decidedly calm. As alarming as the Irish situation might have been, it received far less attention than the rift with America, the West Indies, or the outbreak of war with France and then Spain. Care should be taken not to rush to an interpretation that the British public, at least as reflected in the press, assumed the security of British rule in Ireland. Nevertheless the comparative lack of gloom at a time when readers across the nation bemoaned the steady loss of British imperial power elsewhere suggests that the reading public was more confident about Ireland than almost anywhere else in the empire.

By mid-December 1779, the majority of public commentary agreed that the situation with Ireland had been successfully diffused. The *General Evening Post* announced: "We have the pleasure to assure our readers, that the information is received from the leading men in Ireland, that the proposals made by Lord North will be highly satisfactory to that country."[60] Shortly afterward, the *Morning Chronicle* gave some of its rare praise to North for his handling of the situation, describing him as having "acted with a degree of candour, explicitness and liberality, which has not only endeared him to the Irish, but opened the eyes of his own countrymen, and, by dissipating the mists artfully raised by faction, enabled the people without doors to judge of his true character, and to see . . . that the First Lord of the Treasury is by no means an enemy to freedom."[61] For now at least, the difficulty with Ireland seemed resolved.

The threat of French invasion caused the most alarm in the press during the first two years of the global war. Invasion brought the war home for ordinary Britons, who beforehand had enjoyed the luxury of merely having to image the battles that raged overseas. The threat placed men who were ordinarily civilians (and often newspaper readers) in arms as the government attempted to rapidly augment its regular forces with part-timers and new recruits. Worries had surfaced since France's entry became likely, but invasion anxiety seemed to consume the nation after Ushant. In reality, the French government never planned to mount an invasion capable of occupying London and removing George III; however, it did hope that massing tens of thousands of troops, which might conduct raids on the southern English coast, would distract British resources from other theaters and demoralize the populace.[62] Although some commentators correctly identified the French movements as something of a ruse, the vast majority of press coverage took the situation very seriously.

The British government's strategy, although perfectly valid, did little to instill public confidence. By 1779 France enjoyed naval superiority in the English Channel, but its advantage was moderate, and its ability to protect an invasion force adequately from the British fleet was questionable. Therefore, knowing its very existence was a deterrent, the British navy avoided confrontation—thus temporarily ceding the Channel to French warships but ensuring that the thousands of vulnerable, troop-laden, flat-bottom boats would not attempt a crossing. Although several commentators explained the plan in the press, such calm applications could not compete with the highly publicized panic in the coastal areas when the inhabitants looked out to see French ships sailing within sight. As a reader in Plymouth, one of the ports most likely to be attacked, explained in a letter to the *General Evening Post* in the late summer, "the appearance of the enemy's fleet on this coast, and the public exertions of this country, are now the general topics of conversation."[63]

To thwart the invasion after years of stripping itself of regular troops for service elsewhere in the empire, the British government turned to its citizens by calling out the militia and supporting temporary volunteer units. Such a move directly tied more households than ever to the conflict, and, not surprisingly, the press reacted with intense coverage. The public response to the government's call was impressive: by the war's conclusion some 46,000 Britons had served in official militia units along with another 30,000 in less formal volunteer units.[64] Many of the men who constituted the militia and the volunteer companies were precisely the sorts of people who read newspapers. Far more literate than the rank and file of the British army, many of these men were artisans, shopkeepers, farmers, and the local gentry in civilian life. Thus the threat of invasion turned many newspaper readers and commentators into part-time soldiers, taking them out of the coffeehouses—at least for the summers in which they were called out—and putting them on the perceived front lines. This was in addition to ongoing massive recruitment drives that brought an additional 60,000 men to the regular army and Royal Navy between 1778 and 1779. Such a massive effort meant that news of local recruiting drives, warnings of press-gangs, and advertisements announcing the formation of the militia appeared with some regularity in every newspaper. Even the *Stamford Mercury*, whose predominately Lincolnshire readers were safely tucked away from the immediate threat, kept tabs on the movements of the French fleet along the Southern coast. In June, militia units in its circulation area began marching to Bristol, prompting further press coverage, and in July the paper, like many others, began a "Camp Intelligence" column for keeping local readers abreast of their husbands', sons', and brothers' activities in the major camps where anti-invasion forces were congregating.

A direct consequence of the combination of a shift in primary enemies, the threat of invasion, and a national call to arms was that the language in the press, both from editors and readers, became decidedly more nationalistic in tone. As a letter to the *Morning Post* explained,

"When a country is verging upon destruction . . . it becomes the duty of every citizen to take up arms for his country's defence."[65] A reader's letter in the *Morning Post's* longtime rival, the *Gazetteer,* fully concurred. A stout opponent of the North ministry, the author "[did] not mean to write in praise of Ministers," but he could not help but support the government on at least one vital issue: "no service is equal to that of free men acting with their own good will. . . . On these principles I profess myself to be greatly pleased with the scheme of raising volunteer corps to reinforce our national militia."[66]

War with the Catholic Bourbon powers made sense in the cosmology of the eighteenth-century British press; after all, such wars had shaped British domestic and foreign affairs alike for the better part of a century.[67] For the first time since long before the war began, newspapers throughout the nation took a common stance. To be sure, opponents of North continued to rely upon such papers as the *Gazetteer* and *Public Advertiser* to provide venues for their criticisms of the conduct of the war, but then long-standing forums for North's public apologists also increasingly printed impatient commentators' attacks on tactics and commanders. "Pro Rege et Patria," in a lengthy letter written to the *General Evening Post* in October, went so far as to call on the king to sack North and the rest of the "unskillful Ministry" before "destruction preys upon the vitals of this once happy [nation]." Exceedingly little printed commentary, however, challenged the necessity or righteousness of the war as a whole. The *London Courant* might print the odd piece that referred to Britain's actions in America as "crimes," but virtually no one publicly challenged the now overshadowing, vastly more important (at least as contemporaries depicted it) struggle against France and Spain.

National morale as reflected in the press cannot be described as jubilant, but it was improving noticeably by the summer of 1779 as the American debacle shifted further into the background. Such a shift is best reflected in the reaction to Spain's entry into the war. In sharp contrast to the fretting over the likelihood a year earlier, the positive public response when war with Spain finally came was more akin to the confident boasting that had been observed late in the Seven Years War. The king's widely reprinted—and supposedly private—response to Spain's war manifesto, also extensively reprinted, in which he referred to it as "the most impudent piece of writing ever penned by one state to another," appealed to national pride.[68] After more than a year of anticipation, the public seemed relieved at the outbreak of war. The *General Evening Post* reported that the nation was anxious "to correct the insolence of the Court of Spain."[69] The *Morning Post* reported that "The news has been received at every seaport in this kingdom with unbound joy," because the Spanish mercantile shipping provided more lucrative targets for privateers than the French.[70] "[T]housands of brave seamen, who had hitherto withdrawn themselves from the service under the idea that but little was to be got by a French war," the report continued, "now stock from all quarters with the laudable views of punishing the perfidious Dons, and pocketing their hard dollars!" The *Ipswich Journal* concurred in its report on war preparations a few days later, noting that although the new war "alarmed many people, many more are glad of it, especially those who want to enter into privateering, as there is more to be got by a war with the Spaniards than the French." So great was the British bravado toward Spain that half a year later the *Stamford Mercury* printed a letter thanking France for enticing Spain into the war. "The French have made us some amends for their mean perfidy and promoting rebellion in North America, by drawing King Midas of Spain," it brazenly declared, "for we have great reason to hope from what has passed, and from the present prospect, that Spain will not only furnish this country with money for carrying on the war, but with ships for maintaining the Sovereignty of the sea."[71]

Much of the supporting rhetoric was of the familiar anti-Catholic genre that had laced English-Continental European conflicts for over two centuries. As the widely reprinted opening verse of song signed "A Cobbler of Cambridge" reflected:

> Good neighbours, attend
> To the voice of Friend,
> Who feels for Old England's Cause,
> Now the mad House of Bourbon,
> By ambition spurr'd on,
> Would down with our Freedome and Laws.[72]

Rather than focus on the "unnatural civil war" in America, recruiting advertisements concentrated almost exclusively on France and Spain as more palatable enemies. A typical ad appeared in the September 2 issue of the *Stamford Mercury*. Calling for volunteers to serve for three years in a local regiment, the ad features a soldier holding a flag emblazoned with the word "Honour" and opens with the words "To Chastise the Insolence of France and Spain." America is conspicuously absent.

FIGURE 5.1. Recruiting advertisement in the *Stamford Mercury,* September 2, 1779.

The outbreak of war with Britain's European rivals demoted the conflict with the American colonies to a secondary concern in the British press's
coverage of the war. Not only did American news have less of a presence,
but the stories themselves were shorter and provoked fewer printed responses. The reduction was a direct consequence of competition from other

theaters, particularly the West Indies and Europe, and the general consensus in the public sphere that North America, or at least the thirteen colonies, had largely been written off as lost in the wake of Saratoga. Few in the press saw full independence as satisfactory, but fewer still were willing to argue that Britain would ever again have anything akin to its pre-war authority over the American colonies. As discussed in the previous chapter, when France allied with the United States and Congress refused to meet with the Carlisle commission, most commentary in the press accepted that the war would trudge forward, albeit rather fruitlessly and pointlessly.

Despite a lack of expressed ambition for America, the printed reports from 1778 and 1779 were increasingly favorable. Thanks in part to the loyalist press, particularly in New York, news of Congressional squabbles and predictions of the eminent collapse of its armed forces due to lack of pay and supplies appeared regularly in most newspapers around the country. Even the alliance with France appeared to be under strain, thanks to false and exaggerated claims that abounded.[73] The *Morning Post* carried reports in May of Philadelphians hunting down French representatives and burning the French king in effigy. Such "a general discontent prevailed through all ranks of people," the paper declared, "that Pennsylvania and the Jerseys were on the point of submitting to the British government."[74] The *Gazetteer* printed the ludicrous claim that sixty Frenchmen in Boston had been murdered and thrown into the harbor.[75]

The extent to which either editors or readers accepted as credible the accounts that came from obviously loyalist sources is not known. Although no definitive hierarchy of credibility existed, reports in the *London Gazette*, which usually appeared in the form of extracts from commanding officers, were taken as fact in every virtually every newspaper across the country; next were letters from British officers, followed by colonial and foreign newspapers; and anonymous private letters were usually given the least weight. The problem was that the *London Gazette* almost invariably appeared last. The British press regularly printed extracts from loyalist papers, which were widely available to editors, and, judging by the content and timing, provincial editors had access to these sources on a par with their metropolitan counterparts. Some, such as the *Stamford Mercury* and *Ruddiman's [Edinburgh] Weekly Mercury,* unabashedly relied almost solely on loyalist newspapers for its American news during this period, treating their pages as wholly reliable. Most papers by 1778 were far more careful, and particularly in cases of the most improbable claims, they typically distanced themselves from the report by noting the loyalist newspaper from which it had been taken. These sorts of stories rarely provoked printed commentary from readers, which suggests that most readers did not take the loyalist reports too seriously. Moreover even a cursory reading of the loyalist press reveals that British editors discarded the vast majority of the content of the loyalist newspapers to which they had access. In some instances, however, papers clearly intended the accounts to be taken as trustworthy news: when editors reprinted some of these stories from other British papers, they either did not note the American source, thus taking credit for it, or instead gave it as the British paper from which they had extracted it. Thus a report identified as a loyalist newspaper account in the *General Evening Post* might be depicted as an account from the *Post* in the *Ispwich Journal* or as the *Journal*'s own information. However, these endorsed reports almost always could have been verified with one of the host of other sources available to editors—including Congress-supporting American newspapers, private letters from Americans, letters from British soldiers, or reports of debates in Parliament. But, of course, these are all generalities about a press that churned out roughly two hundred distinct issues per week, which had to be filled by men and women whose job it was to find fresh information that readers wanted. In order to meet this demand, particularly when news on the war was scarce, editors were more flexible in what they were willing to print.

Most America-related coverage focused on the strategic shift to the southern colonies, which until then had received little attention in the press. A small force from the main British army in New York landed in Georgia in late December 1778, quickly defeating the local resistance and taking Augusta and Savannah with little hassle. When news of the victories first circulated in Britain in late March and April of the following year, the initial reports arrived via loyalist newspapers and private letters, leading papers such as the *General Evening Post,* which was more willing than most to endorse any news that favored the government's course of action, to claim almost immediately that Georgia had been subdued.[76] Such reports proved to be exaggerations that subsequent issues corrected, but the news in the British press remained steadily favorable. Reports of southern loyalists flocking to the British side appeared regularly and went unchallenged throughout the press, and by summer the more optimistic commentators began predicting that Charlestown, South Carolina—the preeminent city in the southern colonies—would fall in a matter of months. The combined French-American forces' bloody failure to retake Savannah in the early autumn— they attempted a hasty assault that resulted in a 20 percent casualty rate— was met with rejoicing in the British press. The news, which reached Britain in November and December, prompted a reinvigorated reader of the *Morning Post* to rub the naysayers' noses in the victory. The doubters had thought

Georgia lost when news arrived that "the united forces of the French King, and the American Congress" had landed, but instead it was the "belligerent power who would soon seek accommodation."[77]

Despite the apparent improvement in fortunes in America, pessimism still defined the public's mood as reflected in the press. Like Burgoyne the prior year, General Howe spent much of May being quizzed in the House of Commons. The highly publicized extracts of his testimony emphasized Britain's ability to win battles but not the war in America. In consequence, initial reaction in many papers to the successes in Georgia was that the army was overstretched and, as in the ill-fated campaign in 1777, extremely vulnerable. Calling the news of Savannah's capture "very unfavorable," the *Gazetteer* declared that the problem was to "either extend their conquest, or protect what they had already conquered. . . . This has been, and it is to be feared will always be, the case with this ill-fated American war," it concluded, "where the people are almost unanimously against us."[78] In this instance a letter from a reader in the *General Evening Post* concurred with the rival *Gazetteer*. Describing the "melancholy prospect of conquering America," the reader raged against the "madness" of continuing the war. "[W]e are no nearer accomplishing the great object of our armaments than we were on the fatal and unfortunate day of Bunker's Hill . . . ," the reader concluded, adding, "we have been upon the tip-toe of expectation, for these five years, that every western wind would bring up peace, reconciliation, or victory, from America: but every campaign ends with the disgust of our Generals and Officers by sea and land, and a change of men brings not change of measures, or means of terminating a destructive war."[79]

Letters from other self-described former North supporters appeared in droves throughout the press, including normally supportive venues, and represent a genuine shift in public opinion regarding the war in America. Professing to be, like most readers of the *General Evening Post,* a longtime supporter of the ministry and the war, the author of a typical letter of this type explained that it was time to admit defeat: "It is the voice of the army, from the General in Chief to the common soldier, that our attempts our fruitless."[80] Confirmation of news of Britain's victories over the Franco-American forces in Georgia boosted the morale of some, but against such a backdrop of negativity the impact was temporary. As a reader's letter in the *London Courant* observed in its last issue of 1779, any victory in America was hollow, because a conquered America would be useless to Britain. So long as the colonists wanted independence, they would undermine and work against British authority. Thus, the letter concluded, "we find American independency is founded on necessity."[81]

Throughout 1780 and until Britain's disastrous defeat at Yorktown in October 1781, the global war effort appeared to many readers to be in a state of limbo. After the initial adjustment to a global war, the British public hunkered down for what it expected to be a long, largely unproductive conflict. As one reader remarked with frustration in the *Stamford Mercury* in September 1780: "Our conduct of the war, as well as that of our enemies seems to be merely the Chapter of Accidents, without any digested plan of offence on either side."[82] Even defeat was not longer feared, because, as the *Salisbury Journal* asserted, "in the worst [it] even must be attended with a general peace."[83] Predictions of a Bourbon conquest of the British Empire had proven false, but so too did hopes that Britain might deflect the assault and either quell or negotiate away the rebellion. In Europe, the British again endured the now annual routine of calling out the militia in the spring and forming massive camps of troops who waited to repel an invasion that many expected but never arrived. Spain failed to tip the balance but continually threatened British possessions in the West Indies and Mediterranean. The entry of the United Provinces into the war in 1780 changed even less. Dutch outposts in Asia became soft targets for the British, but this was offset on land by Haidar Ali, the ruler of Mysore, and his son, Tipu Sultan, who were nominally allied with France and dealt severe blows to the British forces. In the West Indies, the stasis seemed most firmly established, as the outnumbered British made some gains, particularly against the Dutch, but ultimately lost ground to the Bourbon coalition.

The situation in North America, as the British press depicted it, was little better, and it remained wholly overshadowed by the rest of the war. The *Salisbury Journal* went so far as to remark in May 1780 that failure in America that season would have a definite silver lining, "as it will enable us, by leaving us more at leisure, to pay greater attention to our enemies in Europe."[84] A year later in its lengthy "Seasonal Reflections on the Present Posture of Affairs, Foreign and Domestic"—although at a time when the situation in America looked better than at any time since Saratoga—the *Gazetteer* devoted only a scant few lines to America.[85] The loyalist press continued to churn out propaganda that proclaimed the imminent downfall of Congress, but, even for those readers who accepted the reports, Congress's disarray seemed to make little difference, because Washington's forces and their French allies endured and kept the main British forces in check at New York. Cornwallis's drive through the South received substantial attention, but the British public was much more wary of claims of success than it had been before Saratoga. Some expressed hope that either Congress's difficulties or Cornwallis's victories might force some sort of negotiated settlement that would not end in absolute American independence. Most readers and editors, however, expressed deep suspicion of assertions that that campaign would significantly alter the war in America. The *London Courant,* like most printed commentary, dismissed the effects of the late successes in America, declaring that the "trivial gleam of success that has lately dawned upon us, though it may have raised ministerial spirits to the highest degree of [the] administration's thermometer, has not had a proportionate influence upon the Free Briton."[86]

The reading public may have been growing tired of the war, but they were as ready to comment on it as ever. Military advice was never in short supply from readers who fancied themselves as armchair ministers of state, generals, and admirals. As a reader of the *General Evening Post* remarked, the "coffee-house politician . . . thinks himself qualified to command the fleet that is to watch the ports of the enemy; and, because he has seen the evolution of a squadron of dragoons, thinks he is entitled to Judge the maneuvers of a squadron of ships. . . . Such are the people who are now busily arraigning the conduct of a General in one quarter of the world, and an Admiral in the other," the reader continued, "and do not hesitate to pronounce both the one and the other guilty."[87] Fueling these commentators was the abundance of information presented in the press. Most newspapers dutifully followed the anti-invasion military camps' developments in special sections detailing which regiments were where and under whose command, such as the *Stamford Mercury's* full page "Camps and Quarters of his Majesty's Forces in South-Britain" in May 1781. Official reports from commanders abroad continued to appear first in the *London Gazette* and then in various forms in almost every newspaper and most magazines within the next two weeks. Articles of capitulation, with the British side usually doing the surrendering, followed the same pattern. Tables listing the strengths and locations of various regiments sent abroad peppered the press, as did the usual array of letters from their officers. Private letters from colonists and colonial newspapers from throughout the empire also remained a staple source of information for the British press.

Naval tables received the most scrutiny. As in all of the island-nation's major eighteenth-century conflicts, the navy was perceived as paramount, and the press's attention both highlighted and fueled the reading public's awareness of this. Its wooden walls protected the home country, secured the empire's trade supply lines, and transported its armies, and so the upper-artisan and middling ranks, who ran British overseas trade, consumed most of its products, and constituted the bulk of the reading public, all had an

APOTHEC.ARIES__ TAYLORS, &c. Conquering FRANCE and SPAIN.

FIGURE 5.2. "Apothecaries__Taylors, &c. Conquering France and Spain" (1779). Probably by James Gillray, the scene depicts members of the lower-middling ranks armed with newspapers and playing armchair generals and cabinet ministers in a violent debate on how to conduct the war. BMC 5614. © Copyright the Trustees of the British Museum.

understandable interest in the navy.[88] They typically provided ship names, numbers of guns, sizes of crews, ship locations, and commanders' names, which appeared in virtually every newspaper in the country. Papers also printed similarly detailed tables of opposing European fleets. An analysis often followed the tables, which weighed the merits of various fleets and navies. The *General Evening Post,* after filling the entire first page of its March 18, 1780, issue with intricate tables, confessed that the enemy outnumbered the British but gave a slight edge to the home side, noting the superiority of British sailors and the advantage of being under one command structure rather than a coalition of countries. Although most commentators agreed that the British could produce ships at a faster rate, others, such as the *Glasgow Journal,* warned that "the French have made greater exertions in the naval line this year than during any former period."[89] Everything taken into consideration, no one gave either side a decisive edge; victory, therefore, would result from strategic deployment and commanders' abilities.

The stasis of 1780–1781 only increased expressions of war weariness and frustration with British leaders. The mainstream opposition and many former proponents of the war continued to question the North ministry's strategy and clamored for a limited withdrawal from America—or at least an end to further offensive action. Complaints about the war's costs and the corruption associated with it were rife in the press. The *Morning Chronicle* accused Howe in particular of pocketing in excess of £30,000.[90] Germain, as usual, was a lightning rod for criticism, and papers such as the *Bath Chronicle* referred to him as that "proud, conceited, and supercilious man, fully convinced of his own importance." Besides the ongoing war, the North ministry had to contend with increasing domestic unrest caused by the Protestant Association movement, which spewed petition after petition criticizing the ministry predominately for passing the 1778 Catholic Relief Act but also for corruption, high taxes, and continued war expenditures. The movement culminated in a march of tens of thousands of protesters on Parliament in June, which ended in the Gordon Riots—several days of some of the century's worst looting and destruction resulting in the deaths of several hundred Britons, twenty-five of them by execution. North himself barely escaped the mob—literally losing his hat, which rioters treated like a trophy.[91]

North was also the subject of increased personal abuse in newspapers and magazines throughout the country. Calling the war "the daily waste of blood and treasure," a widely reprinted letter in the *London Courant,* rarely a venue for North's friends, railed against him and the British electorate for not removing him from office. The alternative was the status quo, which the letter described gloomily as: "The daily increasing burthens of the state, our colonies revolted, and leagued with our natural enemies, our most valuable West-India possessions wrested from us by force of arms, commerce expiring, trade and manufacturers rapidly declining, lands sinking in value, taxes and impositions, unknown to our ancestors, accumulating on the people, without a prospect of relief."[92]

Hardly anyone in the press overtly came to North's defense by specifically supporting his actions. Instead, apologists deployed the tactic of attacking the naysayers for being critical of the government in a time of national distress. As described in detail in the previous chapter, apologists continued to accuse critics of being "false patriots" who reveled in British defeats. Their motivation, so the argument went, was to seize power for themselves even if it meant Britain losing the war. As a letter in the *General Evening Post*, a long-time magnet for such viewpoints, declared in May 1780: "To see Englishmen vilifying their country . . . instead of rousing her to arms and victory, is a horrid spectacle."[93]

During the stasis of 1780–1781, the military situation in Europe and the press's reporting of it changed little. Recruiting in Britain continued at its rapid post-Saratoga pace; by 1782 the army and navy had about 100,000 men each—twice the size of the army and six times that of the navy at the start of the war.[94] Added to the 76,000 or more militia and volunteers, this was the most militarized Britain had ever been. Recruiting advertisements in the press continued to emphasize France and Spain, while ignoring North America, thus further underlining that the national perception of the war had shifted away from the localized colonial affair that had precipitated it. The threat of a French invasion also continued compelling militia and volunteer units to turn out every spring.

Although apprehensive, public spirit was full of bravado when commenting on the ancient foes. As a letter from a reader recently returned from coastal Kent happily reported, "There is nothing else talked of at those places . . . but the exercise, and use of arms. Should the insulting foe dare invade this country, those worthies view with each other who shall be the most expert in the use of them, to oppose those vain boasters."[95] Other readers recalled England's legendary successes over its ancient enemies. The 1415 battle of Agincourt, in particular, became a regular theme, as commentators used popular memories of it to make Britain's current state of affairs—isolated and outnumbered—seem familiar and manageable. "At the battle of Agincourt," a letter in the *Bath Chronicle* recalled, "when the brave English General was told, that the French was thirty thousand, and the English were only ten thousand, he coolly answered, 'Then there will be ten thousand to be killed, ten thousand to be taken prisoners, and ten thousand to run away.' The event fulfilled the prediction, and a handful of Englishmen trampled over the whole power of France." The letter concluded: "That same patriotic enthusiasm which inspired our ancestors is still lodged in the breasts of our fellow subjects . . . [and] England has always risen triumphant in consequence of the greatest dangers."[96]

The eruption of war with the United Provinces had little impact on the public discussion in the press. Ultimately a disaster for the Dutch, the conflict resulted in little fighting in Europe and aroused even less concern in the British press, which had carried predictions and news of war preparations for the better part of a year.[97] Although the nation was not publicly eager to fight with their former allies, the best complaints that long-standing opponents of the North ministry and the war-weary could muster were occasional lukewarm protests that the war was unnecessary. Remarks from commentators salivating at the prospect of seizing poorly protected Dutch merchant vessels and colonies were far more common. This would be payback for the Dutch, who had spent the past five years supplying Britain's enemies around the world. As a reader of the *General Evening Post* remarked, the "king's manifesto outlining the causes for war," which appeared in virtually every newspaper in December 1780, "has given almost universal satisfaction." The reader continued: "Not a man has read it . . . but has commended it for its firmness of tone, and declared that, with such repeated provocations, had his Majesty said less, he would have betrayed a dress of pusillanimity that must eternally have disgraced himself and his people."[98] This was the one aspect of the global war to which few Britons objected.

There were other bright spots, as Britain gained its first nationally celebrated heroes of the war. In January 1780 Admiral Sir George Rodney, whose reputation continued to grow, gave the British a major victory over the Spanish by soundly defeating an enemy squadron and re-supplying Gibraltar. This prompted a brief round of adulation—such as the *Bristol Journal's* typical declaration that "perhaps we have no such instance in the annals of our country, as the present Admiral Rodney."[99] A year later Major Francis Peirson died successfully thwarting a French attempt to capture the island of Jersey, prompting another round of praise. The nation at last seemed to have some heroes. Yet these victories ultimately did little to alter what the *London Packet* described as the prevailing "gloomy apprehensions in the breasts of most people."[100] After all, they did not change the state of affairs in which, as a reader of the *Gazetteer* explained, "we have all of Europe against us."[101] Britain's Mediterranean bases were still under siege, Jersey and southern England lay vulnerable to invasion, and Britain remained unable to assert decisive naval superiority.

During this period Asia moved increasingly into the national printed coverage and discourse on the war. Concerns about the spread of the war to Asia had appeared sporadically in the London press since 1775, but the provincial press barely covered the subject until 1778. Considering that over half of the East India Company stockholders posted London addresses from the mid-1760s onward, greater metropolitan press interest in Asian activities is hardly surprising.[102] More telling is that the provincial press ultimately took such an interest. Asia never rivaled European, Caribbean, or American events in terms of printed attention, but the national interest it garnered suggests that Britons throughout the country regarded India in particular as part of the empire worth fretting over. The public concern stemmed partly from the same mid-century imperial awakening of the British public that brought America onto center stage, but more immediately influential was the intense press coverage in 1772 and 1773 of North's Regulating Act of 1773, which brought the state of the empire in India into the public discourse far more than was the case during the mid-century wars. The act was a response to the financial peril that mismanagement and rapid territorial growth had placed the East India Company in and was a major step in the assertion of government control over the empire in India. Public debates surrounding the act received close coverage in the British press, educating readers on the complexities and tenuousness of British rule in India.[103]

Most of the early war news from Asia was initially positive. The East India Company, already on a war footing due to its conflict with the Maratha Confederacy, quickly mopped up the remaining French outposts in India in 1778 and 1779. The series of victories received substantial coverage, often appearing as the lead story and taking up several columns of print. For example, when news of the fall of Pondicherry—the largest French possession, in India, which surrendered after a seventy-seven day siege—reached Britain in March 1779, the *Stamford Mercury* devoted the entire first page of its March 25 issue to commanders' letters and the articles of capitulation.[104] Throughout 1780, British forces in Asia continued to attack the soft targets of European outposts, particularly those of the Dutch, but the tenor of the national discussion became increasingly apprehensive. Whereas beforehand newspapers were content with printing only official accounts of battles, coverage in 1780 increasingly included and provoked reader comment. This was largely precipitated by the eruption of war with the French-allied ruler of Mysore, Haidar Ali, a formidable opponent whose force invaded the British-allied Carnatic in July 1780 with 80,000 men—a far cry from the French and Dutch outposts that the British had faced. Their advance on British-controlled Madras put Britain on the defensive. When a British force set out to check their advance, poor communication and mismanagement resulted in the total elimination of one wing consisting of 4,000 men and a panicked, baggage-abandoning retreat of the other. News of the fiasco at Polilur arrived in Britain in April 1781, via an issue of the *Bengal Gazette,* and for a couple of weeks it dominated the war coverage throughout Britain. Newspapers from Exeter to Edinburgh devoted several pages to reprinting the issue in full and recording the bewildered reaction of commentators. Like the *Glasgow Journal,* most accepted the defeat as "a disaster," and were ashamed by the humiliating retreat of Sir Hector Munro, a longtime source of military success in India.[105]

Newspaper reports that Sir Eyre Coote was on his way to Madras with a substantial force from Bengal seemed to relieve readers, but most commentary expressed concern that the balance of power in India now favored Britain's enemies. The *Gazetteer* explained that "as the French have no possessions to defend in India, their whole force is left at liberty for offensive operations," whereas the British were forced to protect their own vast territories —as well as those of their allies—from the marauding forces of "Hyder Ally, or any other adventurer who will disturb our settlements in that quarter."[106] The *Glasgow Journal* concurred, lamenting that British possessions had become the new soft targets of Asia and that "All the European powers are sending out reinforcements to their settlements in the East-Indies; a disposition having been discovered in the inhabitants to make a general war upon [us]."[107] By the end of 1781, British power in India seemed no more secure than anywhere else on the globe.

Despite increased interest in India, the war remained a predominately Atlantic conflict in the reporting and commentary in the British press. Throughout the stasis of 1780 and 1781, the West Indian theater maintained a strong presence in the printed war coverage and corresponding commentary. The navies of France and Spain, which together were numerically superior and less geographically stretched than Britain's navy, were on the offensive, and the West Indies is where they concentrated their efforts. The result in the British press was intermittent waves of panic spurred on by private correspondence from the region and reprinted extracts of colonial newspapers—items that likely reached the press via merchants and absentee planters, whose powerful lobby pressured the government to increase its troop levels and naval presence in the Caribbean.[108] The *London Evening Post* concluded in August 1780 that there was "no security" anywhere in the region.[109] An extensively reprinted letter to the printer of the *Gazetteer* concurred, remarking, "I [cannot] think of that Naval Superiority which the French and Spaniards have over us in the West-Indies, without suspecting that they will soon take from us ALL . . . that is left of our vast Dominion in America."[110] Most correctly expected Jamaica to be the primary target, and private letters and newspaper extracts from the island described the population as bracing for the attack. Although the incorrigible optimists praised the islanders' spirited preparations, most commentary dismissed them as futile; however, like the feared invasion of England's southern shores, the conquest never came. Instead, two hurricanes ravaged the Caribbean in October, flattening towns, killing tens of thousands of people, and causing greater devastation there than the war ever would.[111]

The press coverage and commentary regarding the West Indies was decidedly more commercial in tone than was the case with either the European or North American theaters. This is most evident in the intense interest in privateering in the region, which had taken a heavy toll on shipping and driven up the cost of doing business. As privateers from France, Spain, and the United Provinces officially joined the Americans in the lucrative Caribbean waters, which were packed full of merchants vessels and littered with hiding places and protective ports, marine insurance rose considerably for anyone involved in trade there. George Grant's Scottish clients paid premiums as high as 20 percent of the declared value of the ship and goods for ventures in the African-Caribbean slave and ivory trade.[112] This suggests an expectation of roughly one in five ships not completing the voyage. Policies also regularly carried specific conditions that ships travel in convoys along with definitions of what convoys constituted. With such interest, news of even minor engagements between warships and privateers appeared daily in the British press. Whereas commentators primarily—albeit with many exceptions—bemoaned the loss of subjects in North America, they measured losses in the Caribbean in terms of prices and commodities. Most papers printed regular lists of merchants' ships taken or lost in the West Indian trade, and, some, such as the *London Courant*'s issue for March 27, 1780, offered readers elaborate tables breaking down which ship captured which.

The distinct commercial tone of the press's discussion and coverage can largely be attributed to the power of the nature of the West Indian lobby and the nature of the trade. The elite planters and merchants who led the West Indian lobby typically perceived themselves as Britons rather than West Indians.[113] Like governors, soldiers, and sailors, planters and merchants typically saw the eighteenth-century Caribbean as the place they might make their fortune so that they could return to Britain and live in comfort. In consequence, they generally did not perceive or present the West Indies in nostalgic terms. It was money that largely drove their interest, and it was in commercial terms that they sought to persuade the British people and government of the colonies' importance. The press followed along for the most part, readily printing stories that emphasized the importance of the West Indian trade and thereby shaping the views of the broader reading audience. To be fair though, this was hardly propaganda as such depictions would have fit with the interests of most readers, who had long perceived the West Indies as a place of fortune-making commodities. Sugar was a more common staple than meat, even reaching the poorest households, and the vast majority of the coffee that middling and elite readers consumed while perusing a newspaper came from West Indian plantations by this time.[114] That readers in the second half of the century knew the origins of these products is evident in the literature, advertisements, and, shortly after the American Revolution, commercial boycotts.[115] British investment in the West Indian trade was uncommonly diffuse among the British populace. British grocers who relied on sales of sugar and coffee numbered well into the tens of thousands, thus connecting at least that many middling households to the trade—not to mention the refiners, brokers, and distributors who moved the product from dock to shop shelf.[116] The African slave trade, too, had evolved into an enterprise that spread risk broadly across an array of mostly middle-class investors.[117] For example, any one of the voyages from Britain to West Africa to the Caribbean would typically have involved five or six primary backers, one or more of whom would divide his share and sell it to numerous smaller investors. Insurance policies were also group affairs in which a dozen or more individual underwriters took on portions of the risk at varying rates, which brokers such as Grant cobbled together to form a single policy. Important to note is that few of these people dealt exclusively in the slave trade, which was typically deemed too risky for total investment. Thus each voyage and each insurance policy was a distinct enterprise that dissolved after the termination of the voyage. A privateer who took one of these ships therefore affected a host of the very sort of people who constituted the core of newspaper readership.

In early 1781 war accounts seemed to favor the British side. As in Asia, Britain acted quickly against the ill-prepared Dutch Empire and, under the leadership of Rodney, took St. Eustatia. Throughout the war, the island had served as a crucial point for privateers as well as Americans exchanging their tobacco and other goods for war materials, and from 1778 St. Eustatia had also used its neutral status to supply French Martinique and Guadeloupe. Rodney loathed the Dutch and foreign merchants at St. Eustatia, blaming them for the American rebels' ability to continue the war and thus drag Britain into a global conflict, and he took Britain's revenge by plundering the island and brutalizing the populace.[118] Merchant houses and shops alike were closed for twenty days, forcing the populace to the brink of starvation, as the British pillaged their stocks. Even the governor's house was emptied of its valuable contents. Greed was perhaps an even greater factor than revenge. By the rules of war, Rodney and his commanders were entitled to one-eighth of the proceeds of the sales, and it was then that the man who had once fled to France to escape his debts made his fortune. The Parliamentary opposition attempted to make a public issue of it and even succeeded in having him recalled the following year. Privately, ministers and military commanders alike were appalled.

The British press, however, was not interested. A handful of scathing accounts appeared in newspapers that tended to favor the Parliamentary opposition, but even these prints' preponderance of coverage embraced Rodney as a hero. Reflecting the overwhelming majority of public sentiment, a delighted *Stamford Mercury* reported in May that the war against the Dutch was going splendidly: "It is now near four months since the commencement of hostilities against the Dutch, in which time more than three hundred vessels have been taken from them in different parts of the globe, without our having lost a single ship of any consequence."[119] Rodney's heroic stock rose even further when he took time away from his busy fighting schedule to aid hurricane victims in Barbados. Letters of adulation poured in from the island, where the people reportedly offered to rename town squares in honor of the great man (who was said to have modestly refused, thus winning even further acclaim). As one admiring reader in Britain summarized, "the gallant and humane Rodney already sufficiently revered and beloved for his valour, is now extolled for his humanity."[120]

The situation soon took a turn for the worse, however, when the French arrived in the spring with a fleet, giving them decisive superiority. Many commentators, particular those in the more optimistic *General Evening Post* and *Morning Post,* pretended that Rodney was on the tails of the elusive enemy fleets, while others depicted him as being pinned down by a superior French force. Historians have argued that greed led him to prioritize the plundering of St. Eustatia and then secure transfer of the booty to Britain—a decision that contributed to the poor strategic decisions that partly enabled the disasters that followed. Some papers printed snippets that concurred with this view, but readers rejected outright any criticism of their national hero. Regardless of where blame lay, the French navy proceeded to take Tobago in June, bottle up Cornwallis and his army at Yorktown in October, and then return to the Caribbean in November to take the Dutch islands that had capitulated to Rodney earlier that year. The situation soon appeared as terrible as ever to readers at home.

During the 1780–1781 stasis, news from North American initially was by far the most palatable of any of the major theaters of operation, but ultimately it, too, went sour. Following news of the successful repulsing of the combined Franco-American assault on Savannah, reports from soldiers and loyalist civilians in Georgia flowed into Britain and saturated the press. The subsequent renewal of hope was akin to the surge following the British arrival in, and subsequent capture of, New York in 1776—albeit on a much smaller scale given the prevailing war-weariness and reduced position that

North America now occupied in the British press. According to the *London Chronicle*, in January 1780, 20,000 American colonists had flocked to the British standard to take an oath of allegiance in the past month alone. The press closely followed the British advance northward, and readers marveled at the quick capitulation of Charlestown, news of which arrived in June 1780. Reprints of loyalty addresses from the citizens of Charlestown and descriptions of former rebels taking oaths of allegiance dominated the news coverage of America, affirming the perception of British mastery over the southernmost rebelling colonies. Everything seemed to be going splendidly. Even the usually pessimistic *Gazetteer* euphorically declared in July, "The last dispatches from Sir Henry Clinton are so flattering a complexion, that every Englishman and well-wisher to this country ought to rejoice at the happy tidings."[121]

The national mood with regard to North America continued to improve. Reports of loyalists flocking to the British side continued to overshadow any other American news, the highlight being the new Georgia assembly's addresses of fidelity to Britain, which appeared in newspapers across the country in August 1780. Even the loss of Rhode Island did not noticeably dampen spirits in the press, because New England had long been written off and because the news arrived at the same time as reports of the battle of Camden in South Carolina—one of the most decisive British land victories in the war, in which Cornwallis made short work of the American forces. Although unofficial reports of Camden trickled into the press in the preceding weeks, the *London Gazette's* October 9 issue carrying Cornwallis's own account of his "complete victory" set off an eruption of harmonious praise. The *Morning Chronicle* rejoiced that the "great advantage obtained by Earl Cornwallis, over the . . . numerous [American rebel] army, is an additional proof that the British forces, officers and men, are superior in conduct and courage to their enemies."[122] Among the most publicly enjoyed aspects of the triumph was that the American commander had been none other than the victor of Saratoga, Horatio Gates. In the post-battle analysis in the press, several letters said to be from Cornwallis's officers circulated with claims that Gates had been so pompous as to request Cornwallis's surrender before the battle had begun, reminding the "noble Lord that a certain other general [Burgoyne]" had made the mistake of advancing beyond retreat.[123] In just one of the many gloating remarks that appeared in the British press, the *Morning Chronicle* printed a humorous piece purporting to be an advertisement posted by Gates in Philadelphia: "Strayed, deserted, or stolen, from the subscriber, on the 16 of August last, near Camden, in the state of South Carolina, a whole army."[124]

Anyone in regular contact with the British press would have been fully aware that the next target was Virginia. However, due largely to the loyalists' continued domination of the news that flowed from America to Britain, readers appeared confident that Virginia would prove less of an obstacle than originally imagined. Although the press remained wary of the most outrageous loyalist claims, either ignoring them or carefully identifying the sources as loyalist, editors and readers clearly believed that the southern colonies were full of supporters. As the usually cautious *Bristol Journal* informed its readers: "By some authentic private letters from Virginia, it appears, that the principal of the inhabitants and people of property of that province, have preserved an intimate loyalty, and secret deference for the Mother Country throughout that whole republican system, which has so long distracted America." The report continued, "a return of peace with Great Britain, and with it of trade, commerce, and wealth, is with them at present a most desirable object, and to which it is expected the reduction of the Carolinas will most favourably contribute."[125]

Meanwhile other reports, particularly from New York sources (both colonist and soldier), emphasized the woes of Congress. Regularly depicting Congress as being on the verge of collapse, newspaper coverage described the devaluation of the American dollar, corruption, and the suffering of colonists under its yoke. In a single, yet typical, day in January 1780, a reader's letter to the *Morning Chronicle* compared Congress to Cromwell's Parliament, noting that both misled their constituents into ruin; a letter from America in the *General Evening Post* insisted that Congress had been infiltrated by papists from Europe; and the *Morning Post* alleged that Congress's power was crumbling before an upsurge in loyalism.[126] Loyalist sources also depicted Congress's alliance with France as fragile, a claim that many in the British press now readily embraced. The Franco-American alliance was, the line of argument went, cobbled together out of convenience, whereas the British were cultural kin who stemmed from the same roots. Thus readers in Britain would not accept that France could have anything but the worst possible intentions for the colonists. As a letter in the *Stamford Mercury* cautioned, "France means them [the colonists] no good by the assurance and assistance . . . her only view is to weaken the power of Great Britain, and disable her colonies, so as to make them an easy prey to gallick [Gallic] ambition."[127] Such unnatural alliances, opponents of independence on both sides of the Atlantic concurred in the British press, had turned the populace against Congress. In consequence, throughout late 1780 and the first of half of 1781, most papers carried such claims as those of the *General Evening Post*, which remarked in December that "the people are universally disgusted with the tyranny of Congress, and desirous of a reconciliation with the Mother Country."[128]

Plied with positive news from the British war effort in America, many readers expressed expectations throughout the year for some sort of peace settlement. Important to note is that hardly anyone publicly prophesied a total British victory in a manner reminiscent of pre-Saratoga projections. The British had tried and failed to campaign in the northern colonies, and few papers printed calls for another attempt. Canada, all agreed, was safe, but readers would have been well aware from the tables and commentary that British forces were in no position to go on a major offensive campaign in the North. As virtually every paper explained to its readers, Britain's forces in the northern colonies had drained for campaigns in the Caribbean and the southern colonies, and Washington had entrenched his army too well.[129] Nevertheless, the possibility of any sort of peace short of total defeat was appealing, and false hopes abounded in the press. In the wake of Savannah, the *Bath Chronicle* informed its readers that "Government is in hourly expectation of news of the utmost importance from North America, the ground work thereof is confidently reported to be a secret negotiation, carried on with the Congress for a reconciliation with the mother country, on the plan held out to them by the [Carlisle] commissioners."[130] Following the capture of Charlestown, even more commentators chimed in, including the normally cautious *Bristol Journal*, which conclusively informed readers that the Americans' revolutionary zeal was dwindling: "The greatness and novelty of the Idea of Empire and Independency, affected the Colonists at first with extasy and rapture; But these, we may presume, are now in a great measure evaporated."[131] Loyalists who had taken refuge in Britain openly wrote in the press of "the present prospect of approaching peace," and a handful of observers began speculating which colonies would remain independent and which would rejoin Britain.[132] After the battle of Camden, even the king expressed public confidence in Cornwallis's prospects. In his widely reprinted November 1780 speech opening Parliament, he declared: "the signal successes which have attended the progress of my arms in the provinces of Georgia and Carolina, gained with so much honour to the conduct and courage of my officers, and to the valour and intrepidity of my troops, which have equalled their highest character in any age, will, I trust, have important consequences in bringing the war to a happy conclusion."[133]

As a result, the British press depicted the nation as entering 1781 brimming with confidence for the American theater of the war and the prospect of peace. A year later, public expectations for peace in America were greater still but not along such favorable terms. Primed by the successes of 1780,

British papers more readily endorsed loyalist reports from America than ever. Few questioned claims of loyalists flocking by the thousands to the British standard, and greatly exaggerated accounts of loyalist militias carrying out attacks on rebel positions also appeared regularly. Accounts of the deterioration of Congress and its army also continued, leading such papers as the *General Evening Post* to question whether or not the rebels could field an army for operations in the South at all. It pointed out that over half of the infantry battalions existed on paper only and that Congress "can no more raise them, and bring them into the field, than they can convert their pasteboard dollars into gold or silver."[134] In February the *Stamford Mercury* reported that the popular belief in British-occupied "New-York [was] that the rebellion was nearly at an end," and the general consensus in the British press agreed.[135]

Early press accounts of Cornwallis's operations in the southern colonies in 1781 made him appear unstoppable, and the campaign placed North America back in the public spotlight it had left three years earlier. Every newspaper marked Cornwallis's progress, but he moved so quickly that the press that summer was full of readers' complaints and editors' apologies over the lacking details. As the *Ipswich Journal* explained to its readers, Cornwallis's speed meant that "he can get nobody to carry home his dispatches . . . and the New-York Gazette must supply the place of the London Gazette."[136] When official reports did arrive via the *London Gazette*, newspapers printed them in full, rather than extracting them as usual, and spread them over several issues when necessary. The public discussion included at least some prophetic apprehension. A *Glasgow Journal* reader, among a small handful of others, voiced concern as early as June that Cornwallis had driven too deep into enemy territory and risked being trapped if the promised loyalists did not appear to resupply him.[137] However, such naysaying met with quick retorts from commentators attacking those "who do not weigh and examine the cases and decide instantly" that the worst will transpire. The public should have faith in Cornwallis.[138] The situation, proclaimed the *General Evening Post* after printing Cornwallis's latest dispatches in June, could not be better: "The provinces to the Northward have been already exhausted of troops; the Carolinians have in their turn been every-where defeated; and the Virginians are now in their turn experiencing the same fate."[139]

Although a handful of unsubstantiated rumors circulated in the London press early in the autumn of 1781, Cornwallis's troubles came as a shock to most readers when firm reports began to appear in late October. For the first time since France entered the war, the press focused almost exclusively on the American theater. The gravity of the situation in terms of its impact on the American war was never left in doubt. As the *Morning Post* remarked after informing its readers that Washington's army and a large French force were converging on Cornwallis's position in Virginia, "The next news from Virginia must be particularly important, as it is certain the whole success of the British army in the Southern Colonies must be entirely overturned if any misfortune should happen to the forces under Earl Cornwallis." Hope, however, was not lost: "Tho', when we contemplate the battles that commander has already fought, the difficulties his genius has surmounted on the past occasions, we may yet indulge a hope, that the intelligence from the next dispatches may be more favourable than many people at present imagine."[140] Two weeks later, armchair commanders assured readers of the *General Evening Post* (correctly as it turns out) that the French ships blocking Cornwallis's escape would not remain in the Chesapeake indefinitely and that Clinton would then be able to mount a rescue operation.[141] Unfortunately for Cornwallis and his army, the French managed to stay just long enough.

The press depicted the nation as greeting Cornwallis's surrender with great disbelief. Considering the rapidity with which his campaign had gone from triumphant to besieged in the press (due to a combination of delayed reports and the overly optimistic loyalist filters), the skepticism is not surprising. Early reports were dismissed in many papers when they began arriving. Even the widespread distribution of a reprint of the November 20 *Paris Gazette's* description of Cornwallis's surrender and the terms of capitulation, which circulated in late November, did not satisfy all of the public that the British had been defeated, and forums for die-hard ministry supporters and war hawks continued to print readers' denials. Only the *London Gazette's* issue three weeks later, which printed dispatches from Cornwallis and Clinton detailing the surrender, silenced the speculation and confirmed what the *Gazetteer* had declared a month earlier: "the dispute between us and the Americans is, undoubtedly, at this moment terminated; and America is at this instant as free as air."[142]

Yorktown forced the nation to accept that the war in America was now going as poorly as in the rest of the globe. The British press depicted the empire as in peril on all major fronts: the Caribbean, Europe, and India. In North America, the war had been lost. Although a few desperate optimists, either persuaded by the loyalist propaganda or part of the machine itself, hung on to hope that the rebellion would fail, virtually all other commentary in the press took American independence as a given. The question now, as it had been before Cornwallis's 1781 campaign sidetracked it, was whether or not the rest of the empire would survive.

The War that Britain Won and Winning the Peace

✳ The final stage of the conflict is consistently the most ignored period of the American Revolution and the global war it precipitated. One could easily be forgiven for thinking the war ended with the British surrender at Yorktown in the autumn of 1781, rather than nearly three years later, or for believing that the final years of the war were merely about tying up loose ends and dotting the *is* and crossing *ts* at the negotiations in Paris. A search in the British press for stories related only to North America during this period certainly highlights this view. As the *London Packet* forecast, the British army was "condemned to vegetate at New York" for the duration of the war.[1] Seven months later, the prediction held true. As a British officer declared in the opening lines of a letter home, which appeared in the *Stamford Mercury,* among other newspapers, "Everything here seems to be at a stand. The army is in such a state of inactivity."[2] Press coverage of America dropped dramatically during this period, particularly once the fiasco at Yorktown had been rehashed and analyzed. Virtually all commentary—save for the loyalists who continued to have a voice in the British press and pleaded upon deaf ears that the fight was not yet lost—was in agreement that North America was no longer a significant theater in the war. Yet interpreting the war through an American-focused lens grossly distorts the portrait of the world war that the British press was now covering.

From the American perspective, Cornwallis's surrender at Yorktown meant the final defeat of the British, and, according to the 1776 criteria for victory, it was, but the scope of the conflict had changed dramatically for the British by 1781. The global war that had begun with France's entry in 1778 had been going on longer than the preceding solely Anglo-American phase of the conflict. In the ongoing global war, which defined the press coverage and with it many Britons' engagement with the war, Yorktown merely resolved one theater—a theater that both the British government and the wider British public had made subordinate to other theaters four years earlier in the wake of Saratoga. For almost every combatant outside of North America, this period was arguably the most crucial. French and Spanish efforts to regain territories around the Mediterranean, Caribbean, and Asia peaked; the Dutch struggled to preserve what they could of their overstretched empire; and the rulers of Mysore sought to enlarge their own empire in South Asia. All of these enterprises could succeed only at Britain's expense.

What followed, however, was highly publicized and wholly unexpected British success. This was the slice of the conflict that Britain won—not only on the battlefields and oceans, but also in the hearts and minds of the reading public at home. In the British press, the monumental victories at the battle of the Saintes and the siege of Gibraltar more than redeemed previous losses at Saratoga or Yorktown. Britain humbled its European rivals, and at last the public had heroic, victorious commanders both at sea and on land. True, some of the American colonies had been lost, but the idea of restoring British rule in North America anywhere on a par with what it had enjoyed before the war had been written off by all but a handful in the press discussion years earlier. In consequence, at the war's conclusion the British did not depict themselves in the press as being vanquished or in mourning over the loss of the colonies. Instead, readers and editors embraced the end of the war with a mixture of relief and renewed faith in their nation. Britain had bloodied its ancient European rivals and preserved the bulk of its empire. Bells rang out, newspapers printed celebratory articles, and crowds greeted returning generals as if they had won the war, because in their minds they had triumphed. The press coverage thus ultimately reveals how un-American the war that would be remembered as the American Revolution had become in Britain by its conclusion.

Lord Cornwallis's surrender of the British army at Yorktown to the allied American and French forces on October 19, 1781, was the worst disaster that befell Britain during the war, and, unlike the fiasco at Saratoga four years earlier, it was a blow from which the British did not recover. The loss of men—over 8,000 troops along with one of Britain's best generals—was hard but not necessarily catastrophic to a national war effort that had over 100,000 regular troops and nearly that many men in the navy. The blow to the already shaky national morale, however, proved inescapable. As the *Edinburgh Magazine or Literary Amusement* remarked at the war's conclusion, the defeat resolutely persuaded the majority of the nation and House of Commons, "to abandon the offensive war in America, despairing of being able to reduce the colonies by force."[3] Even Lord North himself famously remarked, "Oh God, it is all over."

The buildup in the press in 1781 to Yorktown partly explains the intensity of the public reaction. As described in the previous chapter, the public (and government for that matter) had pinned a great deal of hope on Cornwallis's campaign. Although hardly anyone in the public discussion expected a return to pre-1775 British rule in America—expectations for the campaign had never been coherently articulated in the press—there was an almost universal sense that this was the last great British drive. The *London Packet* best summarized the suspense and expectation just days before the news reached Britain, stating, "Not only England but all of Europe stand in trembling suspense for the result of the contest in America."[4] Reflecting such public sentiments, George III privately described the moment as pivotal. Writing confidentially to North on November 3, he clearly stated his apprehension: "The moment is certainly anxious; the dye is now cast whether this shall be a great Empire or the least dignified of European States."[5]

As a result, the news of the surrender injected unparalleled defeatism into the public discussion. As the *London Courant* stated, "They [Americans] have fought nobly for it [independence], and have gained it."[6] Provincial newspapers entirely concurred, reprinting the dreary remarks of the metropolitan press or penning their own gloom. For example, the *Derby Mercury* described the release of Henry Laurens, the member of Congress captured at sea and imprisoned in the Tower of London, at the end of December, as "one among the numberless proofs, that even the Ministers no longer entertain a Doubt of American Independence."[7] In this rare instance the public voices spoke out in unison, and even the *General Evening Post,* normally a magnet for hawks, printed a letter from a reader declaring that his patience, and with it his support for the war, was at an end: "Seven years have elapsed! Your millions are spent! Nothing, worse than nothing, has been done! Your enemies are triumphant!"[8]

As with previous defeats, a great deal of public finger-pointing followed the news of Yorktown. As commander in chief in America, Sir Henry Clinton bore the brunt of the public criticism, which reached a fervor that winter

—so much so that he, like John Burgoyne and William Howe before him, published his own narrative of events as a pamphlet in order to salvage his public reputation. It did him little good, however, and, if anything, strengthened the resolve of his critics in the press, especially when upon his return he joined his fellow fired generals as a member of the Parliamentary opposition. "Sir Henry Clinton joins Opposition the moment he returns to England . . . we shall then see three unsuccessful generals in the lines of Opposition, that reguium peccatorum," chided *Ruddiman's Weekly Mercury* in Edinburgh.[9] Cornwallis's reputation proved more resilient, and throughout the scrutiny virtually all commentary depicted the long-favored general as a victim of Clinton's ineptitude. Although perhaps also the beneficiary of better publicists, Cornwallis benefited from the public credit earned from his string of victories, all won while Clinton sat seemingly idle in New York. Hence, the same above piece that criticized Clinton for joining the opposition to "cover himself" described Cornwallis as "the only general who has signalized himself in this war" and "an officer of higher reputation than any of them [Howe, Burgoyne and Clinton]." When the paroled Cornwallis returned to Britain in late January, he was celebrated wherever he went—all of which the newspapers around the country covered in detail for admiring readers. For example, the *Derby Mercury* described him passing through Exeter, where the mayor presented him with the freedom of the city. "So overjoyed were the People at his Arrival," the paper reported, "that he was carried from the London-Inn to the Guildhall on Men's Shoulders, accompanied by an incredible Number of Spectators, whose Acclamations upon the Occasion can be better conceived than described."[10]

Regardless of the finger-pointing and "Coolness," as the *Bristol Journal* described it, between Clinton and Cornwallis and their respective supporters, the ultimate political victim of Yorktown was North. Dissatisfaction with the war, especially the increased taxes it required, had seriously hurt his ministry in the general election of 1780, which left him with a tiny working majority in the House of Commons.[11] Yorktown was the final blow to the already weakened ministry, and most commentary in the press accepted it as such. Parliament's winter recess delayed any immediate action, but in late February the opposition won a motion—North's first major defeat—that called for a "stop to the American war," as the *Morning Chronicle* styled it.[12]

The debate took center stage in the press, with even provincial papers such as the *Stamford Mercury* taking the unusual step of devoting almost its entire issue to the event. No one in the press doubted the significance of the motion, and most shared the euphoric relief of the *Gazetteer,* which featured the unusual formatting step of a bold-faced headline that announced

"PEACE WITH AMERICA!"[13] North had no choice but to resign, despite the adamant reluctance of the king, who perhaps more than anyone had difficulty accepting a defeat at the hands of rebels who less than six years earlier had made the war personal with their insulting, public attacks on him in the Declaration of Independence. But George III did his duty and swallowed some of his pride. In response to an address on the motion from the House of Commons, he publicly called for the "restoration of harmony between Great Britain and the revolted Colonies" and the end of "offensive war on the continent of North America." According to the *Gazetteer,* the words were "said to be the Kings own, and not the fabrication" of an underling, and as he pronounced them, "His Majesty looked very pale, and much agitated."[14] Almost every newspaper and political magazine in the country printed the speech, because the implications of it were paramount: the war's most important supporter, who the press had reported throughout the conflict as confidently assuring victory, had admitted defeat.

Thus after nearly fourteen years as prime minister, North stepped down and was replaced by his longtime rival, the marquis of Rockingham, who the press rightly recognized as having been chosen to end the war in America and negotiate the best peace possible with the other powers. For years he and his supporters in Parliament, such as Edmund Burke and Charles James Fox, had suffered almost constant personal abuse in the press, as readers and editors alike vented their frustrations with Britain's war effort and the Americans' successes. Now such attacks were conspicuously absent even from those papers that hosted the most hawkish commentary. The absence likely stems at least partly from the fact that the Parliamentary opposition's reluctance to wage war with the colonies had been proven justified, but equally important is that North's fall and the king's admission had left the remaining war supporters leaderless. The reading public now yearned for peace in rare unison. Yet the shadow of defeatism cast by Yorktown proved to be short-lived. A series of unexpected major victories over Britain's enemies in other theaters swiftly rehabilitated the public's confidence in its leaders and armed forces. In consequence, the kind of peace Britain would have, and how the reading public would respond to it, would be redefined during the next seven months.

The tone in the press during the winter of 1781/2 was decidedly gloomy when forecasting what the next year of war would bring. A tiny handful of commentators managed to sound notes of optimism, such as the author of "Ode for the New Year"—written by a reader of the *General Evening Post*—who offered this bit of prose:

O world in arms assaults her [Britannia's] reign,
A world in arms assaults in vain.[15]

However, most papers, including the *General Evening Post,* were packed with far more calls for abandoning the war in America and taking a defensive stance against the Bourbon powers in hopes of securing the rest of the empire and forcing an honorable but swift peace. "Britain is not in a situation to undertake any enterprise of moment," *Ruddiman's Weekly Mercury* declared; "the war is to be spun out, in hopes that the enemy will be first exhausted, and think of offering terms of accommodation."[16] *Lloyd's Evening Post,* a favorite among the mercantile community and a bastion for hawkish commentary until Yorktown, presented its case against continuing the war in a language its business-minded readership would have appreciated—a full page table breaking down and then summing up the annual cost of the war to the penny (£9,336,401 3s 4d to be exact).[17] Clearly, the paper informed its readers, with such an investment not earning a profit, the time had come to withdraw it. Within the next few months, however, the tone of the public discussion in the press changed remarkably with the unequivocal naval victory in the Caribbean, which gave cause for a universal public elation and restored public confidence in Britain as an imperial, naval power.

The press's close coverage of the dismal news at the start of the year helped lower public expectations and, in consequence, made the victories that followed all the more shocking and uplifting. With the American mainland considered to be settled (judging by almost all commentary in the press) and the British coast secured, coverage of the war turned almost exclusively to the Caribbean. January opened with the arrival of news that France had captured St. Eustatia, which the British had captured from the Dutch in early 1781. Caught by surprise, the British garrison surrendered, according to the official account in the *London Gazette,* "with the smallest opposition."[18] The nation reacted with disgust as it read accounts of the British soldiers surrendering to a smaller enemy force in a matter of hours with only "trifling" efforts at defense. As the *Morning Post* remarked, the capture of the island "is certainly one of the most disgraceful Incidents which the British Flag has undergone during this War."[19] Worse still, Jamaica, a former Spanish possession, was widely (and rightly) assumed to be the next major target of the combined Spanish and French forces. This was bad news for any Britons on the island, the *General Evening Post* forecast, because "the fate of English property [if the island is taken] will be very unlike what it has been in the islands captured by the French . . . for the Spaniards consider Jamaica as their own property, and that they are only recovering what we wrested from them in the last century."[20] Letters from across the West Indies and throughout Britain poured into the press foretelling of an imminent invasion. The West Indian lobby was as active as ever, working to keep the colonies in the public spotlight. Its petition to the king, which had been signed by 201 planters and merchants living in London along with another 69 from the Bristol area, appeared in most newspapers throughout the country. The petition begged the king to beef up the inadequate protection of Jamaica and the other British West Indian Islands. "[I]t is with the utmost Concern, that your Petitioners are compelled to declare," they complained, "that the remaining Islands are still so unhappily destitute of Protection, that at no Moment of the War have they been exposed to more imminent Danger, than in the present awful Conjuncture."[21] Although Jamaica did not fall, St. Kitts, Nevis, and Montserrat did in quick succession, thus, in the words of the *London Evening Post,* "spreading a gloom upon the mercantile part of the metropolis" and leading to canceled orders for goods across the country.[22] Nationally reprinted reports from the *Bristol Journal* the following month that the French were "laying waste" to British estates on St. Kitts only heightened public concern and further drove up the price of the nation's favorite West Indian good, sugar.[23]

A letter to the *Salisbury Journal* from "A Constant Reader" summarized the national mood as portrayed in the press. In its "Description of the State of Great Britain," the letter describes Britain as a place "which neither law nor reason governs," its priests as "faithless," its generals as "plunderers," its senators as "Traytors," and its ability to wage war as "impotent."[24] Yet the national mood changed overnight in May when news arrived of Rodney's decisive victory over the French fleet under the command of the Comte de Grasse at the battle of the Saintes on April 12. News of the battle, which prevented the planned Spanish invasion of Jamaica and shattered French naval power in the West Indies, prompted public euphoria. The *General Evening Post,* like almost every other newspaper in the nation, devoted an entire issue to the event, featuring letters from Rodney, letters from his fellow officers, and commentary from readers.[25] Papers outside of London also offered their own supporting features and local perspectives. For example, the *Derby Mercury* printed the town of Derby's congratulatory address to the king on Rodney's victory, and the *Stamford Mercury* provided readers with a poem in honor of Rodney penned especially for the paper.[26] The elation was as universal as it was widespread. All political factions in both houses of Parliament immediately voted separate "Thanks to Admiral Rodney." In what *Lloyd's Evening Post* described as "a very elegant, open, manly speech," Admiral Lord Keppel, a member of the opposition that had previously complained about Rodney's treatment of the St. Eustatia population, led the lovefest.[27] Even the Corporation of London—long a hotbed of radicalism, American sympathy, and vociferous anti-North and anti-monarchy sentiment—sent a petition congratulating the king on the victory. And as time passed, the enthusiasm only grew. As declared in the *Derby Mercury,* "the late glorious News which we have received from the West Indies, is so splendid in itself, and of such vast Importance and Advantage to this Country, that the more we reflect on it, and the greater Consideration we pay it, the more evidently we must perceive, not only the Honour done the British Flag by it, but the great and essential Benefits the Nation must reap from it."[28]

The press once again presented Rodney as the perfect hero. Any tactical errors, loss of life, or previous behavior at St. Eustatia was ignored. Not only did Rodney return to Britain with his principle opponent as a prisoner— "the first Commander in Chief of a French army or Fleet who has been a prisoner in England since the reign of Queen Anne," explained the *General Evening Post*—he also brought the admiral's flagship and pride of the French navy, the *Ville de Paris,* in tow.[29] Rodney's official correspondence could not have been better scripted. In the opening lines of his report, printed first in a special issue of the *London Gazette* on May 18 and then in virtually every newspaper and magazine in the country, he eloquently announced his victory, appealing to the popular British attributes of modesty and the belief in providence: "It has pleased God, out of his Divine Providence, to grant his Majesty's arms a most complete victory over the fleet of his enemy." Embracing the essence of commradery and delight in doing one's duty—further ingratiating himself to an admiring public—he wrote of those British ships left out of the action in the following way: "Their Lordships [to whom Rodney was reporting] may easily imagine the Mortification it must have been to the sixteen gallant Officers commanding the Ships of the Rear, who could only be Spectators of an Action in which it was not their Power to join, being detained by the [calm waters]." The press also showed Rodney's human side, printing alongside these reports a less formal, more personal letter "to his Lady" assuring her of his safety.[30] Not surprisingly, by the end of the year a host of biographies began appearing in bookshops across the country and, subsequently, in extracted form in the press. All praised his name. The public elation had not waned that November when the City of London presented its official thanks to him. Like most provincial newspapers, the *Salisbury Journal* described the scene in great detail for its readers, who, though away from the events, had publicly shared Londoners' admiration for the admiral. After waiting on Rodney at his London home, the Lord Mayor and his delegation went in "procession to the London tavern, preceded by kettle drums, trumpets, French-horns, clarinets, bassoons, hautboys, &c. &c. where an elegant dinner was provided." Along the way the populace lined the streets "in surprising numbers, rending the air with the cry of 'Rodney for ever'; 'Rodney for ever'; insomuch that their acclamations reached the skies: At Charing-cross the horses were taken from the coach, and his Lordship (Lord Rodney) had the honour of being drawn (in the manner as worthy and great men have heretofore been honoured) by the people."[31]

The victory at the Saintes prompted a new British confidence not merely in the prospects for the West Indies but for the Atlantic war as a whole. As the opening verse of "a favourite song" entitled "Rodney Forever!" sung daily by the throngs of visitors that summer to Vauxhall Gardens—the popular metropolitan pleasure gardens that drew middling and elite crowds in the tens of thousands—proclaimed:

> Again Britannia smile,
> To save this drooping isle,
> See Rodney strikes his blow!
> For Rodney quickly will regain,
> Thy Sov'reign Empire o'er the main![32]

By July commentators speculated in newspapers across the country about attacks on the French coast—unthinkable just months earlier—and reclaiming the English Channel. "[T]here is not the last doubt but the British Flag will ride triumphant off Brest this Summer, and not be under the Disgrace of flying to Port when the Enemy's Fleet appears," declared a letter in the *Derby Mercury* in June.[33] For once in a long while, commentators did not panic at the lack of news from the fronts and accepted the situation as at least somewhat secure. "Nothing new has arrived in the Course of the Week from the West-Indies or Gibralter," declared the *Gazetteer*, "but it is at least a Comfort to be able to say, that our strength in these Situations is such, that we have nothing disagreeable to apprehend."[34]

Elation and bravado aside, printed commentary calling for a continuation of the war and redoubled effort against Britain's enemy was rare. Coverage throughout the nation made clear that the naval victory, regardless of how decisive, could not change the fact that the British forces both on land and at sea were outnumbered, overstretched, and incapable of defeating their worldwide enemies. As a widely reprinted remark from Keppel in the wake of Rodney's victory plainly stated, the French and Spanish could easily regain superiority in the West Indies by deploying some of their European forces, which could be accomplished with ease as "it is not in our power to stop them."[35] Readers' comments concurred, and editors consistently printed their views on the discussion, thus keeping the national discourse reasonably grounded. For example, a Londoner's letter to the *Morning Post* reminded fellow readers that "the present situation of this country notwithstanding the great victory obtained by Admiral Rodney, is yet as critical as at any period since the commencement of the war. We are surrounded by a host of foes and on every side a great superiority appears against us."[36] Rodney's victory had reduced the fatalism, but to vanquish it from the public discussion an equally dramatic and decisive land victory would be needed.

The successful defense and relief of Gibraltar in the summer and early autumn of 1782 generated more coverage and commentary in the British press than any other battle during the American Revolution or the global war into which it grew. Gibraltar's successful and highly publicized defense thus restored public confidence not only in the armed forces but in the nation itself. Combined with the naval victory in the Caribbean, overwhelming success at Gibraltar enabled the British public to embrace the war as a kind of victor. True, Britain had lost thirteen of its mainland colonies, but the discussion in the press had largely accepted this years earlier. Besides, as the intense coverage of Gibraltar emphasizes, the wider British public still gave greater weight to traditional European clashes.

Part of the siege's appeal was that the press coverage painted a familiar scene for the public during a war that had seemingly turned the world upside down. This war had shattered the traditional Protestant-versus-Catholic cosmology that seemed, albeit simplistically, to contemporaries to characterize the divisions in European struggles.[37] Catholic France had sided with the ultra-Protestant American colonists, and French Catholics in Quebec had joined the British effort to defeat them. Even the Dutch, longtime British allies, found themselves fighting on the same side as their former Spanish masters. In the battle for Gibraltar, the British public found the imagery with which they were accustomed: a besieged British minority facing superior numbers of Continental enemies. Images of the enemies' Catholicism—including reports of Catholic priests in enemy camps and Masses said for soldiers—that had been so familiar in the coverage of other conflicts but were largely understated during the present war became familiar in the press coverage of the siege, such as the *Morning Post's* description of the bishop of Paris giving absolution to the Comte d'Artois before his departure for Gibraltar.[38] In this aspect of the war, the nation could unite in a common spirit akin to the wars with the Bourbons of the past and wars with Revolutionary France that were to come. This part of the present war was, at least for the British reading public, comfortably like the others.

Recruiting advertisements during this period continued to emphasize Britain's European rivals as the main combatants, wholly ignoring the rebelling colonies. America was also conspicuously absent from printed tales of patriotism. A typical example directed at women appeared in the *Lady's Magazine* in July 1782. Appearing as part of a series of moral tales, the account describes a Mr. Townshend, who is of the modest middling sort but marries into wealth. Despite his comfort, he elects to answer the recruiting calls to defend his country against France and Spain by joining the navy. What follows is a description of his battles and eventually imprisonment in Martinique. When he returns home, he finds his wife and son thriving and infinitely proud of him. The accompanying illustration (see fig. 6.1), engraved especially for the story, depicts his wife and child waving good-bye as he again sails off to war. The magazine informs readers that the maxim the story is intended to illustrate is "that the man in a public line of life, who shall not be ready to sacrifice all his interests as an individual, to saving his country when endangered, is neither a good husband, a good father, or what is greater, a good patriot." Such confident language of purpose is entirely consistent with the public messages of the preceding Seven Years War and the French Revolutionary and Napoleonic Wars that followed, but, as previous chapters have described, this language is wholly absent from the early years of the conflict when the American colonists were the primary opponents. Such tales as that of Mr. Townshend, though fictitious, thus contrast remarkably with the earlier printed descriptions that appeared throughout the press of fathers being torn away from distraught wives and soldiers protesting deployment to America.

As a naturally fortified doorway between the Mediterranean and Atlantic, Gibraltar was an important component of the British Empire. Gibraltar had been a primary irritant in Anglo-Spanish tensions since its capture by the English in 1704, and, although Spain had ceded sovereignty of it in 1713, it remained a major war and foreign policy objective. The war between Britain and Spain that erupted out of the American Revolution was no exception. Prior to the outbreak of war with Britain in 1779, Spain had tried first to obtain Gibraltar by offering to act as mediator between Britain and France and, when this failed, attempted to blackmail Britain by offering to stay out of the war in exchange for it.[39] Once hostilities erupted, Gibraltar became the main sight of armed confrontation for Spain, whose government had equated its re-capture with victory in the war. With American independence effectively secured by Yorktown and peace negotiations beginning in earnest in the

FIGURE 6.1. "The Patriotic Parting," *Lady's Magazine* (July 1782). © British Library Board. All rights reserved.

summer of 1782, time worked against the Spanish besiegers. Joined by their French allies for one last attempt to take Gibraltar, the Spanish had either to storm it by land or prevent the arrival of the sort of massive seaborne re-supply effort that would enable the garrison to survive until a general peace.

Almost all of this was so thoroughly reported in the British press that it would have been known even to irregular readers. When war with Britain's European rivals seemed imminent in the summer of 1778, newspapers such as the *Exeter Flying-Post* described the impact that public concerns about Gibraltar had on the economy. According to the paper, insurance for ships sailing to Gibraltar rose 30 percent, because everyone knew that war with France would lead to war with Spain and that war with Spain meant an immediate siege of Gibraltar.[40] When peace stories began to circulate two years later, the *Gazetteer* confidently dismissed them as being "beyond ridicule" solely on the grounds that the Gibraltar issue had not been settled. "Those who are acquainted with the view of Spain know very well that Spain will never enter into any treaty," the paper explained, "except [one in which] Great Britain will put Gibraltar in their hands."[41] Ultimately, Gibraltar's symbolic significance outstretched its strategic importance. As the *Saint James's Chronicle* remarked at the high point of the siege, Gibraltar had "become of less real Importance" in terms of the Mediterranean; "yet suffering it [Gibraltar] to be wrested from us would be one of the most disgraceful Events of the present War."[42]

The press coverage of the three-year siege offered a little of everything for a reading public already engrossed in military operations: siege warfare, a land battle, long supply lines, the diplomacy of coalition forces, and, crucially, the potential for a great naval battle when the British went to relieve the garrison. As the siege lengthened, the stakes only grew. The buildup to the pinnacle of the siege in the late summer of 1782 only added to the drama. Since Spain's entry into the war three years earlier, Gibraltar had been a staple part of the news. Accounts of troop buildups, bombardments, and small engagements peppered the press with increasing regularity, but almost all commentary considered the fortress impregnable; however, public confidence in Gibraltar's security in early 1782 was shattered along with of the rest of the nation's morale, when, besides the disaster at Yorktown and the series of lost islands in the West Indies, Britain lost Minorca, its other key Mediterranean base and former Spanish possession. As with Gibraltar, the British at Minorca endured a lengthy siege, and, as with Gibraltar, public commentary fully expected the British island garrison to survive. As late as mid-January, the *Morning Post,* like so many other papers at the time, equated the two sieges, boasting that "the Spaniards are not likely to be much more fortunate in their Operations on that Island [Minorca], than they have hitherto been in their Attempts on Gibraltar."[43] Disease, however, took its toll, and the British forces capitulated in early February, the terms and account of which appeared in virtually every British newspaper in late March and early April. The press suddenly depicted Gibraltar as in peril. Adding to the national interest was the slowdown of the war elsewhere. By the summer of 1782 the North American theater was considered to be resolved and generated little news, Rodney's victory at the Saintes meant a lull in the Caribbean, and the perceived threat of an invasion of England was negligible.

Therefore Gibraltar dominated the press during the summer and early autumn of 1782. As Edinburgh's *Ruddiman's Weekly Mercury* remarked in late August, "The projected relief of Gibraltar is the general topic of conversation."[44] The press depicted the fate of the war as hinging on the outcome at Gibraltar. So crucial was this last hot zone of the European war, asserted the *Morning Post* and most other papers, that "the fate of Gibraltar" would determine the peace settlement: "On the good or bad success of these events, the future intentions of peace or war will be determined."[45] As a result, newspapers such as the *Derby Mercury* continually reminded readers, "The Attention of all of Europe is now turned with infinite Apprehension and Solicitude to the Fate of Gibraltar."[46]

Every paper in the country churned out coverage of unparalleled intensity of the siege that included tables of land forces, estimates of enemy ships, accounts of dwindling supplies, tables of the British relief force, vivid descriptions of the fortifications and weaponry, and, of course, copious commentary. Editors that summer offered readers almost every imaginable detail about the siege, such as *Ruddiman's Weekly Mercury's* lengthy description of Spanish gunboat designs.[47] Newspapers also carried reprinted articles from Spanish and French newspapers, such as the *Bristol Journal's* weekly serial "the journal of the siege of Gibraltar" that it claimed to be lifting from a paper from Paris, where "The siege of Gibraltar is constantly the subject of conversation."[48] Morale in France and Spain, these reprinted extracts clearly conveyed, was high. In its summary of the "letters received this day from France," the *Bristol Journal* affirmed that "the enemy are prepossessed of success in their attack on Gibraltar."[49] When editors ran out of current information, they printed old accounts, such as the *Derby Mercury's* lengthy description of the unsuccessful Franco-Spanish attempt to retake the peninsula in 1705.[50] Virtually every newspaper printed a detailed table of the relief fleet bound for Gibraltar under the command of Lord Howe, and London papers provided daily updates of its progress and movements along with a countdown to its estimated arrival at

Gibraltar. Once underway, most papers offered further tables and analysis of success, and on only one major fact did they all agree: the British would be outnumbered by the combined Franco-Spanish fleet waiting for them.

This intense coverage served to underline in readers' minds that an epic clash was both inevitable and unpredictable, and so the nation waited with bated breath over the summer for news of the outcome. The *General Evening Post* remarked, "the anxious expectation of the public is raised higher at this critical moment than it has ever been since the commencement of the war."[51] The language was as dramatic as it was at any other point in the war. As the *Bath Chronicle* declared in its coverage of the relief effort: "Every [enemy] Ship that can swim has received Orders to repair to Cadiz; and even some of the French West-India Ships that were come home to be repaired are now on their Way to the Place of Rendevous, without ever being in Dock." It continued: "Though they greatly exceed us in Number, when we consider that England never sent out a Fleet in better Condition than that now on the Point of sailing, it is not unreasonable to hope, that if there should be a Battle it will [be] *a proud Day, for Old England*."[52]

The British victory that followed surpassed even the most sanguine expectations. The land battle culminated in mid-September, when the Spanish and French forces unleashed their armada of floating batteries that waded into the harbor and proceeded to pound the garrison. The British responded by firing hot shot at the batteries, which caught fire and were destroyed, along with their crews of several thousand Spaniards and any hope of a successful assault. At sea, the besiegers fared little better. Although outnumbering Howe's fleet, the combined French and Spanish fleet blockading Gibraltar suffered from a combination of disorganization, poor weather, and bad luck, and at the beginning of October the British fleet relieved the garrison with little difficulty. News of the victories reached Britain in rapid succession. Although the *London Gazette* did not print the commanders' official reports for another month, editors tapped into every source available for details and confirmation, including foreign newspapers, private letters, and intercepted enemy correspondence.[53] In sharp contrast to the American theater, editors and readers alike reveled in the enemy bloodshed at Gibraltar. Calling the reports of the British destruction of the floating batteries and the repulse of the assault "glorious news" and rejoicing in the "prodigious slaughter" of the enemy's forces, the *Bristol Journal* was among the first papers to announce the garrison's victory.[54] Over the next few days, the reports circulated throughout the country, with such papers as *Ruddiman's Weekly Mercury* expressing equal delight over the "great carnage" that befell the besiegers and assuring readers that "though [the news] is not yet come officially, and therefore does not appear in the [London] Gazette, the public may depend upon it to be authentic."[55] News of Howe's relief of Gibraltar met equal adulation. The *Bristol Journal,* again one of the first to announce the news, opened its November 2 issue with "Gibraltar is Relieved!" followed by a glowing account of Howe. Like the reputation of the British armed forces, the once-maligned admiral had found redemption at Gibraltar, with such venues as even the *Saint James's Chronicle,* in which he had formerly been pilloried, printing an acknowledgment that "the Relief of Gibraltar by Lord Howe full answers the exalted Opinion the Public have ever entertained of that most excellent Commander."[56]

The siege also produced Britain's most acclaimed land commander of the war: George Augustus Eliott, Gibraltar's military governor. The experience in North America had badly damaged the reputation of the army's leadership in the press. Surrender, public feuding, and the constant second-guessing by armchair generals in the press had taken their toll on the public's perception of the military, and Thomas Gage, John Burgoyne, William Howe, and Henry Clinton had all become loathsome figures in the press. Eliott offered redemption, and editors and readers alike readily embraced him. During the summer of 1782, he became the public face of British resistance at Gibraltar, which in turn had become the symbol of Britain's defiance of its ancient enemies. Because Eliott had "become of late an object of universal attention," biographies of "the brave Governor of Gibraltar," as the *General Evening Post* described him, appeared in abundance in the press. Although differing in details, none carried anything negative, and all agreed that he was courageous and that the nation could place its confidence in him. As the *Morning Post* assured its readers during the height of the siege, "From the best information our correspondent can obtain of the state of Gibraltar, he finds that the people who last left the place are least apprehensive of its danger," because, "the brave Gen. Elliot has employed the assistance sent to him in the course of the summer to the greatest advantage."[57]

Fortunately for the editors and audiences in search of a hero, Eliott was not the quietly confident sort of commander. Instead he possessed that sort of bravado that readers and editors alike had adored in commanders in previous wars and sorely missed in the present conflict. When asked about the besiegers, Eliott, according to the *Gazetteer,* "speaks of the approaches of the enemy with contempt" and is ready to "repel the most vigorous attacks of the enemy, should they have the temerity to attempt a storm."[58] Another almost universally reprinted account depicted him as besting his enemies with the pen as well as the sword. Rubbing the strangling hold of the siege and the garrison's dwindling supplies in the British commander's face, the Spanish commander sent a parcel to Eliott, which, according to the accompanying note, included "a few little trifles for your table, of which I am sure you must stand in need, as I know you live entirely on vegetables." Eliott's letter of response delighted readers throughout Britain. Politely thanking the Spanish commander for the gift, Eliott asked him to send no more parcels, as he had resolved "since the beginning of the war . . . never to receive, or procure by any means whatever, any provisions or commodity for my own private use," because, he explained, "I confess I make it a point of honour to partake both of plenty and scarcity, in common with the lowest of my brave fellow soldiers." As for the jab about vegetables, Eliott concluded his response by explaining to his opponent that "The English are naturally fond of gardening and cultivation; and here we find our amusement in it, during the intervals of our public duty."[59] When Eliott's own gallant deeds and words were not forthcoming, commentators openly fabricated them. In a widely reprinted sketch of "Modern Characters," which included the individual's name followed by a few fictitious lines he or she might offer to the public if given the opportunity, the piece listed Eliott first and with the accompanying lines: "Know, my gallant soldiers, that valour is Superior far to numbers: there are no Odds against the truly brave."[60]

The public pinned its hopes on Gibraltar, and the gamble paid off. As Howe and his fleet sailed south, the *Morning Post*, like most newspapers, explained the stakes in clear terms: "Lord Howe's being permitted to relieve Gibraltar . . . will be the most convincing and unequivocal proof of the incapacity of our enemies, numerous as they are, to continue the war."[61] The resulting victory restored the nation's confidence, prompting a lasting change in tone in the public discourse and enabling the British to conclude the war as partial victors. "Nothing can be more truly honourable to the British flag; than the conduct of the fleet in the Straights of Gibraltar," declared the *Stamford Mercury*. "That the combined fleets of France and Spain, with the immense superiority they enjoyed, should keep at bay, and dare not advance to the enemy," it continued, "is a stigma which they will not easily be able to wipe away. The eyes of Europe were on the conduct of the belligerent nations; and on all hands the decision of the war seemed to depend on the event of this struggle."[62] While Rodney's victory at the Saintes had rehabilitated the nation's faith in the navy, Eliott's and Howe's fully restored it in Britain's armed forces as a whole. In a rare moment of harmony, readers' letters and editors from across the political and geographic divides reveled in the victory. As the *General Evening Post* proclaimed: "the Facts are clear; and all Europe must see and know, that Britain has, in the Face of the combined Fleets of the House of Bourbon,

The BELLIGERANT PLENIPO'S

FIGURE 6.2. "The Belligerant Plenipo's" (November 1782). This print emphasizes how Britain bested its European enemies. The five belligerents comment on the peace terms. From right to left: America delights in its new independence; Spain bemoans its inability to retake Gibraltar, whose absence is symbolized by the Spaniard's missing leg; Holland weeps over the loss of Ceylon and St. Eustatia, which is represented by a missing foot; France complains about the continued loss of Canada, represented by a missing arm. George III is surrounded by the missing appendages of his European rivals, and declares "I give them [United States] independence." Ireland floats above and delights in the trade benefits and increased legislative independence it negotiated during the war. BMC 6051. © Copyright the Trustees of the British Museum.

poured Relief into Gibraltar; and that those combined Fleets, with the Advantage of the Wind, did not chuse to hazard an Engagement with an inferior force."[63] The "sovereignty of the ocean" had been reclaimed.

In his speech opening Parliament on December 5, the king made observations akin to those offered by readers in the nation's press: consolation for the war's losses could be found in the victory at Gibraltar. "You must have seen with pride and satisfaction the gallant defence of the Governor and the garrison of Gibraltar," the king declared in the widely printed extract of the speech, "and my fleet, after effected the object of their destination, offering battle to the combined force of France and Spain on their own coasts." After such decisive victories, he concluded, Britain could accept an honorable peace: "Having manifested to the whole World, by the most lasting Examples, the signal Spirit and Bravery of my People, I conceived it a Moment not unbecoming my Dignity, and thought it a Regard due to the Lives and Fortunes of such brave and gallant Subjects, to shew myself ready on my Part to embrace fair and honourable Terms of Accommodation with all the Powers at War."[64] The unequivocal victory at Gibraltar, along with the unequivocal press coverage of it, enabled the nation to accept the end of the war in a favorable, if not somewhat triumphant, light.

The fall of the North ministry in February 1782 marked the beginning of a sustained discussion of the peace negotiations in the British press. North's replacements, first Rockingham and then, after his death in July, Shelburne, had been long-standing critics of the government and had risen to power on promises of securing an end to the war. Commentary throughout the press assumed that North's replacements would open negotiations with Britain's European and American opponents and, just as the British were ready for peace, so, too, were their opponents by the following autumn. Although at the start of the year Spain held hopes that drawing the war out might result in the capture of Gibraltar, the United States had met its objectives, and developments in central and eastern Europe, particularly an expansionist Russia, prompted France to seek a close to the war by the end of the year.[65] By April Britain had appointed representatives in Paris to negotiate informally and then formally with the other belligerent powers. Not until that winter, however, were terms agreed upon. Until then, speculation filled the press. Hardly anyone, however, expressed expectations that the negotiations might fail, and the overwhelming majority of commentary and coverage in the press agreed that America would be independent, but Britain would retain its position as the premier European imperial power.

Britain and France were at the center of the negotiations and the press's coverage of them. The American Congress, the Dutch, and the Spanish were, in varying degrees, clients of French leadership. Congress had met its military objectives by 1782 but was obliged by its alliance with France not to accept a peace until it, too, was satisfied; Spain would not begin direct negotiations until October, once Gibraltar clearly would not be taken by military force, and until then allowed France to negotiate informally on its behalf; and the demoralized Dutch effectively handed negotiating powers over to France. All sides had demands and expectations, but, with the important exception of North America, none of the governments expected a peace that would radically alter the balance of power in Europe or anywhere else. None had fought with sufficient success to merit a shift on a par with the terms that had so favored Britain following the Seven Years War. The discussion in the press largely reflected these realities, but this did not prevent the details from occupying large sections of print for the better part of six months. As *Ruddiman's Weekly Mercury* in Edinburgh remarked in May, the peace terms constituted the major discussion topic of the day, with "reports concerning a peace [being] at present more various and uncertain than ever." Little had changed four months later, when *Ruddiman's Weekly Mercury,* although now a little more war-weary and asserting that "we must have some peace made soon," again remarked that the peace terms remained the "very general topic of conversation."[66]

Discussion in the British press indicates that the public was acutely aware of the various peace scenarios and their consequences. This resulted partly from leaks made by rival negotiators: at one point both British secretaries of state, who were fierce rivals, had representatives in Paris.[67] The American delegation, too, was conflicted, and two of its chief negotiators, Benjamin Franklin and John Adams, were veterans of using the press to their benefit.[68] Newspaper and magazine editors also packed their pages with available accounts and maps of the various possessions that had become subjects of negotiation. In consequence, readers were well informed of the myriad of overseas territories that their government could swap, sacrifice, and gain like goods in a town market. British readers thus learned and speculated about such topics as the beaver trade in Canada, sugar output in St. Lucia, the strategic importance of Pondicherry, and the infrastructure of Puerto Rico. With the exception of the Floridas and Canada, however, North America figured little into the peace discussions in the press, further underlining that the British public had accepted independence.

Throughout 1782 and early 1783, public speculation of the terms varied wildly. This is hardly surprising, however, given the series of major British victories on land and at sea in 1782. And, too, the British government itself was divided for much of the process. Yet almost no commentary described the negotiations as anything nearing a capitulation. Even before the victories of 1782, the tone of the *Stamford Mercury* was typical in its declaration that peace "is the earnest wish of every true friend of his country; but it is to be hoped, that the ardency of their desire to obtain this happy event may not precipitate the parties who may be appointed to settle the terms of pacification, to offer or accept conditions derogatory to the dignity and interest of this country."[69] Some commentators continued to voice complaints about granting America total independence, such as one of the *Morning Post's* readers who called for one last-ditch campaign under Benedict Arnold as late as July, but such remarks were extremely rare and most likely connected to loyalists. As early as April, the previously hawkish *General Evening Post* was willing to concede American independence and grant Canada to France in exchange for the lost West Indian islands. Other commentary printed by the paper was willing to yield even more, including bases in India and Gibraltar if it fell.[70] The last bastions of anti-American sentiment, the *Morning Herald* and the *London Packet,* had accepted independence as a given by the end of the summer.[71]

The military successes of 1782 bred newfound public optimism in Britain for the peace terms. Victory in the Caribbean erased most of the gloom and replaced it with expectations that a handover of just a few territories would save the British Empire from ruin. In early September, the *Bristol Journal* was typical in its acceptance of what it described as the "very moderate" exchange of the captured West Indian islands for Canada, the loss of Gibraltar for the return of Minorca, and recognition of American independence.[72] In the wake of the successful defense and relief of Gibraltar, however, public commentary grew more confident. The *London Packet* still accepted (and lamented) the day "when an American Ambassador shall join the Corps Diplomatique in London," but it expected a much better deal from its European enemies.[73] Interestingly, the cabinet privately considered Gibraltar to be on the negotiating table. On December 3 it even voted in support of exchanging Gibraltar for a range of different combinations of French and Spanish West Indian islands and suffered the king's irritation when the deal failed.[74] However, the majority of sentiment expressed in the press vehemently opposed any exchange of Gibraltar after its "heroic" defense and pressured the government to refuse its exchange. As the *Saint James's Chronicle* noted, a "great Demur" had arisen among the public at the rumors of "giving up Gibraltar."[75] Warning that any terms involving the cession of Gibraltar "will be unpopular," *Ruddiman's Weekly Mercury* complained in a statement typifying the majority of commentary: "the glorious monument to British gallantry" must not "be sacrificed to Spain, under the specious name of Exchange."[76]

Public confidence increased so much during 1782 that most papers dismissed the growing threat in Asia. Press coverage of Asian events never rivaled the other theaters, and commentary was comparatively lacking (coverage consisted almost exclusively of news paragraphs, descriptions of the regions, and extracts of military dispatches). Yet, outside of North America, the war with Mysore was the least successful theater and would end with a peace that was at best a draw for Britain. The little commentary that existed in the press generally accepted Britain's position in the East Indies as stable. News of Sir Eyre Coote's successive victories over Haidar Ali's forces at Porto Novo, Polilur, where the British had been humiliated in 1780, and Sholingarh arrived with comfortable regularity in Britain in 1782 and 1783, leading papers such as *Ruddiman's Weekly Mercury* to declare confidently in June 1782 that "the last news from the East Indies may make us perfectly easy about the security of our dominion in that part of the world."[77] Reports of gains against the other European empires also continued to roll in, further boosting British confidence in its eastern empire. The *Bristol Journal* announced to its readers in May 1782 that Dutch Batavia had fallen, and Surat was next; a few months later the *Stamford Mercury* informed readers of British success at Padang and that Sumatra was next.[78] The reports were so positive that the *Derby Mercury* speculated in the spring that the "very seasonable" news of further Dutch losses in Asia would compel the Netherlands to seek a separate, early peace.[79] In consequence, arrival of the news in August of the battle of Sadras, an indecisive naval engagement with the French near Madras, and the defeat of a British-led land force by Haidar Ali's son, Tipu Sultan, barely dented public confidence. *Ruddiman's Weekly Mercury,* like the vast majority of other papers, thus remained as confident in the autumn as it had been in the previous January on the future of Britain's Asiatic interests, remarking in October that "the late expresses from India . . . give the most pleasing accounts of the present flourishing state of that government."[80]

The discussion of the war's conclusion was not without some regret in the press commentary, and almost all of it focused on the American loyalists. The loyalists, particularly in New York and Charlestown, had become adept producers of printed commentary by the end of the war, churning out magazines, pamphlets, and newspapers that regularly reached British audiences either directly or, more often, in extracted form in the British press. A letter from Charlestown printed in the *General Evening Post* in August described the "utter astonishment" that Britain planned to abandon America despite "the great naval victory we lately obtained, and the distresses of the rebel army."[81] Another loyalist's letter in the *Bristol Journal* concurred, complaining that "at a time when every thing appeared favourable to Great-Britain, her arms victorious in the East, her naval operations crowned with the most brilliant success in the West," the ministry was prepared to grant American independence and sacrifice the loyalists for "a most ignoble peace."[82] Combined, these accounts formed a voice of opposition in the British press to the peace terms.

Commentary in the press purporting to be British was mixed but largely sympathetic to the loyalists' plight. Some, however, was decidedly unsympathetic. A handful of readers' letters complained that the loyalists were suffering the consequences of their own apathy and that they should have done more to obstruct the rebellion. One such letter in the *Bristol Journal* called any government compensation for their losses "charity" that should stop.[83] Most publicly expressed views, however, took pity on the loyalists. Concluding with the remark "my heart bleeds for them," a widely reprinted letter from a British officer described the evacuation of Georgia in vivid detail, emphasizing "the picture of horror . . . of our worthy friends from Savannah, now encamped with their wives, children, negroes, and effects, on the burnings sands . . . would draw tears from the most obdurate."[84] The *Morning Post* called the prospect of abandoning the loyalists to the rebels "barbarous and cruel."[85] When the terms were announced, a number of commentators made their objections known once more. *Ruddiman's Weekly Mercury* offered a typical assessment, declaring the "abandoning of the loyalists" to be a "stain which must ever disgrace . . . those who assented to it."[86]

Some printed letters from America tried to put a brave face on the whole situation with claims of continued resistance to Congress's authority. A typical example is an extract reprinted from a loyalist newspaper in the *Whitehall Evening Post* that offered readers bold claims that the loyalists of New York "would defend themselves . . . while they had one drop of blood left."[87] Most of this boasting, however, was drowned out by a flood of much gloomier descriptions of the loyalists' morale. For example, in a single October issue of the *Stamford Mercury* a letter from New York decried, "the distress and agitation of the people is beyond description; they look upon themselves as consigned to ruin and wretchedness," and a separate British officer's letter described New Yorkers as reacting to news of the British decision to grant independence "with astonishment and distress . . . they were some time like people thunder-struck and stunned; they seemed incapable of doing any thing for their own relief, and abandoned to despair."[88]

Yet, despite coverage of the plights of the loyalists, hardly anyone in the British press advocated continuing the war in America on their behalf. The tone of the printed coverage recognized the situation as regrettable, but the ability of the loyalists and their plight to influence public opinion proved negligible. And as the war's official conclusion approached, press attention dwindled. The press universally depicted the British populace as wanting peace, and public patience with the slow, secretive pace of the peace negotiations often ran thin, generating regular complaints in the press. *Ruddiman's*

Weekly Mercury offered a typical protest in August, grumbling that the "Ministers who succeeded Lord North gave up on the American war and taught the public to believe, that this would be immediately followed by a peace with America, but the public see now that they have been imposed upon."[89] Seven and a half long years of war had been quite enough.

Concerns about the loyalists notwithstanding, the British publicly embraced peace. As the *London Evening Post* declared when terms at last seemed to be settled, "the public" was "in anxious expectation of peace."[90] The preliminary articles of the treaty and the king's speech proclaiming an end to hostilities appeared in virtually every newspaper and magazine in early 1783, and the nation let out a collective sigh of relief. The terms would not be formalized for the better part of a year—a treaty still needed to be settled with the Dutch, and the war with Mysore would continue into 1784—but during the winter of 1782/3 the British public accepted that the nation's least successful war of the century was finally over.

The public hardly took the terms as evidence of a crushing defeat. The rebelling colonies had been lost, but the vast majority of Britons had come to terms with this by degrees over the course of conflict and had fully accepted the inevitability of some sort of American home rule or independence years before. The press portrayed the merchant communities as being in "high spirits" at the prospect of peace allowing trade to resume and prosper. As *Ruddiman's Weekly Mercury* proclaimed in April 1783, "the Peace bids fair to prove beneficial to the home manufacturers and the natural productions of this country."[91] Widely reprinted reports as early as mid-February that "three American vessels . . . are now in the river, off the Tower [of London], with the thirteen stripes flying" and ready to trade certainly underlined the belief that American independence would not mean an end to Anglo-American commerce.[92] Moreover, the British armed forces had saved the empire from destruction with late decisive victories at sea and on land. The West Indies, the East Indies, naval supremacy, and Britain's preeminent place in Europe had been preserved, if not underlined. After all, Britain had been an empire divided and without allies, and yet the Bourbons still could not deliver a fatal blow. The situation in which, as the *London Packet* put it, "We are now about to make a Peace, formally and deliberately, with a People, whom, some Years ago, we were taught to despise as a naked Rabble, without Arms, Discipline, or Knowledge" was unsettling for some—particularly the often-quoted and still sour George III—but the national mood as exhibited in the press was decidedly upbeat.[93] Thus, as in many towns and cities, Worcester's churches rung a joyous "Musical Peal" on their bells for a reported three hours and thirty-five minutes in order "to congratulate the Public on the happy Prospect of Preliminaries of Peace being amicably settled between Great Britain and America."[94] This was not the behavior of a shamed and defeated populace.

When the "definitive terms," as the final version of the signed treaty was described, finally appeared in the press in September 1783, it provoked little comment. The peace was old news. The focus was instead on the future. As the *London Evening Post* remarked, the time had come to discover "whether the extraordinary Benefits proposed by the Americans from the Acquisition of Independence, will actually be realized by their Country."[95]

Part Three

A TRANSATLANTIC

CIVIL WAR

7

The Unlikely Hero

GEORGE WASHINGTON'S

TRANSATLANTIC APPEAL

✳ Throughout the American Revolution, the press in Britain portrayed the commander of the rebel army as the model of citizenly virtue and the ideal military leader. The nation and its press largely supported the effort to defeat the rebels, and most Britons ultimately considered the Continental Congress to be a den of self-serving scoundrels, but praise was heaped on George Washington, the American Cincinnatus, throughout the war. The general personified the dilemma that faced many Britons during the conflict: he was a quintessential English-American gentleman, despite being the enemy. He represented much of what the British Atlantic community thought admirable while commanding an army in a cause that many Britons believed would ruin the empire. He had fought for king and country in the Seven Years War and had even served with a number of the British officers who commanded the king's troops during the War of Independence. He was not from New England and so was not tarred with the radicalism most Britons associated with the region and blamed for the outbreak of hostilities. Nor was he a professional soldier. Washington was a successful member of Virginia's planting elite, thus having much in common with the country gentlemen who dominated the House of Commons.

Washington has long been a favorite subject for biographers, with each generation re-engaging and finding contemporary relevance in the life and actions of the revered American patriarch. He has been more scrutinized than perhaps any American, yet little is known about how this early American hero was received by the British nation against whom he won his celebrated fame. This is perhaps even more surprising when one considers the attention to Washington's image—Washington the monument as opposed to Washington the man—in the newly formed United States.[1] Washington was ever conscious that his actions and demeanor would be dissected, and he went to great pains to fashion himself as a gentlemanly citizen-soldier who had reluctantly left the comforts of private life to fulfill his duty to his country.[2] The British press guaranteed that the results of this self-fashioning were broadcast beyond an American audience, and common Anglo-American attitudes, such as a suspicion of standing armies and self-seeking men, ensured a potentially favorable reception in Britain. The result was a complimentary image of Washington that transcended British political divisions for the duration of the conflict. When an American-authored poem dedicated to Washington was reprinted in London in 1780, the *Monthly Review* and *Critical Review* expressed a rare consensus.[3] First, they agreed that the poem was poorly written; second, they praised its subject. In the same issue in which the *Critical Review* described Bostonians as a wretched people "used to tarring and feathering those who have been so unhappy as to offend them," it described the rebel leader's character as "very respectable" and proclaimed, "we have a high opinion of this *hero*." The *Monthly Review* concurred, describing Washington as "this modern FABIUS"—a reference to the then well-known paragon of ancient Roman Republican citizenly virtue, Quinus Fabius Maximus Verrucosus.[4] Washington reminded readers of Fabius in two main ways. Dubbed the "Cunctator" (Delayer) by his detractors, Fabius pursued a defensive military strategy when facing the legendary invasion of the Italian peninsula by Hannibal during the Second Punic War. Rather than attacking Hannibal directly, Fabius cautiously fought a war of attrition, wearing down the invaders by cutting off foraging parties and following a scorched earth policy. Although greatly criticized during his own day, Fabius was ultimately proved right by the more aggressive (and disastrous) tactics of the successors. Perhaps more importantly to his—and Washington's—legacy, Fabius twice relinquished the wartime dictatorial powers granted to him by the Roman Senate.

Washington's image in Britain ultimately highlights the complexity of British attitudes toward the American Revolution. Although historians have long recognized divisions in Britain over the conflict, they have tended to divide the British into neat pro and antiwar groups whose positions were de-termined by factors of politics, geography, and social class rather than devel-opments connected to the war itself. The previous chapters have challenged such an understanding of wider British public reactions, which, as seen in the press, were neither predetermined nor fixed. Instead, the war was a sub-ject of constant debate and negotiation in the public arena of the press. The reshuffling of generals, changes in government policy, public scrutiny of every scrap of news from America, and Britain's changing fortunes forced the British to have at least some degree of flexibility in their views of the war.

Between adamant support and opposition to the war existed an enor-mous gray area within which most publicly expressed sentiment existed. As a letter from a reader to the *Saint James's Chronicle* in March 1776 re-marked, sympathy for the colonists or reluctance to support the war did not necessarily make a Briton a seditious enemy of government: "I hope that the Friends of Peace and Harmony (in which number I mean to include myself) will not be regarded as Enemies to his Majesty, Haters of Monarchical Gov-ernment, or Friends of Rebellion."[5] Whether for pragmatic, ideological, or political reasons, few Britons were steadfast supporters or opponents of the war for its entirety. Even some of Britain's commanders, including Sir William Howe, John Burgoyne, Admiral Keppel, and Lord Cornwallis, ex-pressed varying degrees of reluctance to support the war at some point prior to their service in the conflict. Almost no one publicly reveled in the de-struction of colonial towns, and virtually no one expressed a desire to see Britain defeated. This was, after all, the British Empire at war with itself, and the reluctance in Britain to wage it is evident in the press throughout the conflict. Enemy casualties were less faceless than in previous American wars with France or the American Indians. Americans had familiar names, occu-pations, and habits, and the letters, diaries, and stories that packed the press constantly reminded British readers of this. An examination of the reception of Washington—universally admired yet a leader of a cause that threatened the empire—in the press highlights some of the ambiguity that characterized the British experience.

Washington's positive image in Britain was a product of his circum-stances as much as his own actions. First, the British press allowed an in-formed and free discussion; thus, in general, Washington received a fair hearing. Multiple lines of communication with North America, an extensive and relatively free press in Britain, and competition between newspapers for the latest information all worked to prevent his image from being monopo-lized by a handful of propagandists. Second, the character and conduct that made Washington a success in American circles won him favor in Britain. Third, Washington seemed to persevere against all odds. Regardless of his politics, it was difficult not to admire his tenacity. Fourth, the absence of serious British-born competition until late in the war made Washington's achievements shine all the more brightly. Finally, Washington's distance from the unpopular factional politics that plagued both sides of the Atlantic gave his image a unique luster. By avoiding public involvement in congressional politics, Washington distinguished himself from the body that most Britons held responsible for the war, thus allowing himself to be judged on his own merits.

To inform readers about Washington, British editors drew from a large range of sources, including official dispatches from the British forces in America, American loyalist and rebel newspapers, British soldiers, foreign correspondents, American exiles in Britain, veterans of the Seven Years War, rumors circulating around coffeehouses, and Washington's own correspondence. Coverage of Washington began when news of his appointment arrived in Britain in August 1775. Although favorably remembered by "many distinguished Officers in his Majesty's service" for his role in the Seven Years War, his was hardly a household name.[6] The press was swift to print what information it could gather, and short biographies of Washington soon appeared alongside descriptions of other key figures. Editors nevertheless attempted to provide sound information, correcting themselves when more accurate material surfaced.[7] Many of the initial accounts were wildly inaccurate, but the biographical errors they contained do not appear to have been the work of libelists, as the errors would not have benefited anyone.[8] *Town and Country Magazine* printed one of the strangest in October 1775, reporting that Washington's daughter had escaped to England after his servants accidentally killed her loyalist lover. Another popular early sketch that seems to have first appeared in the *Oxford Magazine* included such innocent mistakes as assigning Washington a Coventry birthplace and a family tie to the dukes of Albermarle, but when an officer who had served in America wrote in to the *London Chronicle* to set the record straight, his account was soon reprinted throughout the country.[9] By Christmas 1775 most readers would have been aware that Washington was, as the *Annual Register* for that year put it, "a gentleman of affluent fortune in Virginia . . . who had acquired considerable military experience, in the command of different bodies of the provincials in the last war."[10]

Washington received excellent treatment in the press from the start. Not surprisingly, newspapers printed some initial concerns that any general of a republican army might turn into another Oliver Cromwell, who most remembered in the press at that time as a dictator and tyrant, but accounts of Washington quickly put such fears to rest. Initial biographies of Washington, though brief, portrayed him in a generally favorable light. Though condemning the rebels, the *Scots Magazine* printed as its main portrait of the general an article that concluded, "He is a man of sense and great integrity; he is polite, though rather reserved; he is now in the prime of his life, an exceeding fine figure, (at least six feet height), and a very good countenance. There is much dignity and modesty in his manner."[11] Editors searching for American war news meant that the speeches and proclamations Washington gave to stir his troops, win over teetering colonists, or calm wary civic authorities reached British audiences. His correspondence with Congress and the British commanders also featured regularly in the coverage of the war, filling pages at a time and making him one of the age's most familiar figures. Washington handled himself admirably. Edmund Burke praised the general's literary style before the House of Commons, comparing it favorably to the unnecessarily "flowery" language of the British commander in chief, Thomas Gage.[12] More important, the message that Washington's words conveyed had a powerful impact on British audiences. Washington himself was acutely aware of the importance his words would carry, both to contemporary audiences and history, and he painstakingly crafted his speeches. Just as they won him hearts in America, Washington's speeches also gained the admiration of the British. When, like most papers throughout Britain, the *Dundee Weekly Magazine* printed his response to a congratulatory address from the New York Assembly on his appointment as commander in chief, the paper's extract made clear his modesty, self-subordination to civil authorities, and lack of personal ambition. "When we assumed the soldier, we did not lay aside the citizen," he assured audiences on both sides of the Atlantic, "and we shall most sincerely rejoice with you in that happy hour, when the establishment of American liberty, on the most firm and solid foundations, shall enable us to return to our private stations."[13] The *Scots Magazine* observed how this speech eased American fears that Washington might become another Cromwell, but Washington's self-presentation on this and other occasions also similarly persuaded observers in Britain.[14]

Among the most surprising elements of the British portrayals of Washington was that plenty of material existed for the construction of alternative depictions via the loyalist newspapers from New York that flooded into Britain after the autumn of 1776. Invaluable for condemning Congress and the cause of independence, these resources were not regularly used to denounce Washington. When negative comments appeared, editors were quick to attribute these to embittered loyalists, and they were rarely reprinted. Some positive commentary was even attributed to loyalists, such as a letter from a self-described Boston loyalist that appeared in the *Derby Mercury* after Washington's occupation of the town. It stated, in part: "they [rebels] will not match him as an Officer, I believe, in the whole Continent, and his prudent Regulations here confirm what I say."[15] Even Washington's status as a major slaveholder, regularly noted in biographical sketches, was not used to discredit him. Yet declining an opportunity to criticize a major figure was rare, as the British seemed to delight in denigrating everyone in the public eye—a point not lost on George III, his ministers, his commanders, or the opposition leaders in Parliament. As a German visitor to Britain remarked in July 1782, "It is shocking how they [newspapers] seize every opportunity for personal abuse."[16]

Public admiration of Washington, albeit sometimes given reluctantly, was genuine. Despite its politically charged context, the portrayal of Washington does not bear the markings of a party contest: it did not become a battlefield upon which various factions wrangled for their own ends. Representations do not appear to have been churned out by savvy propaganda machines, as most comments about Washington's character appeared in passing, usually in connection with other war news. Lengthy epistles of praise or debates on his character were rare, and those that appeared were consistently favorable. Most political factions benefited from a positive image of Washington, but any gain would have been slight. At some point in the conflict, all of the major parties called for a negotiated peace with America, and each would have gained from the popular perception of Washington as a virtuous man with whom Britain could negotiate. By the same token, however, if Washington's image was being publicly bolstered to serve a political end, then opponents of that end should have attacked the positive image in the press. But no one in Britain did. Besides, anyone interested in depicting the American rebels as decent folk would have focused their attention on Congress, because, as described below, Washington made every public effort from the start to defer all diplomatic matters to Congress without comment. Yet Congress was maligned in the press for most of the war.

The nation seemed to want to admire Washington, as opportunities to turn against him went largely ignored. Even minor public criticisms provoked swift responses. In a widely printed letter from "an Old Soldier" in 1778, Washington's abilities and character received a mixed review.[17] Although admitting that the American general had "performed wonders," the author depicted Washington's military skills as mediocre. Furthermore, the author questioned Washington's professed modesty. The

American general may not have been motivated by profit, "Old Soldier" noted, but "His ruling passion is military fame." The letter was among the most balanced assessments of Washington in Britain, but it soon met with widespread criticism. One irritated respondent summarized the more common view in a letter to the *Public Advertiser:* "the Americans are indebted, for the Stand they have hitherto made, to the Courage of the emigrant natives of this Island, and the Conduct of George Washington."[18]

Washington's positive image even managed to survive his controversial execution of Major John Andre, the British officer who arranged for the defection of Benedict Arnold in 1780. The *Gentleman's Magazine,* which carried Andre's trial in great detail, offered a typical assessment, concluding that although Washington had the right to execute Andre according to the rules of war, British commanders had set more merciful precedents.[19] The public's disdain was largely reserved for Arnold. As the *Westminster Magazine* declared in January 1781, "we cannot but condemn the conduct of General Arnold, as a departure from the principles which, though wrong in themselves, he seems to have had no honourable motive to abandon. However pleasing the Treason may be, the Traitor ever meets with contempt."[20] During the highly publicized Asgill affair in 1782—a debacle precipitated by the death of a rebel officer at the hands of loyalists, followed by Washington's threat to execute a randomly selected British officer and prisoner (Charles Asgill) in retaliation—the British perception of the American commander in chief prospered. Although Asgill became something of a tragic hero in the British press, Washington was not denounced for being his would-be executioner. Even the vehemently anti-American *Morning Post* assured its readers that so long as Washington was involved, Asgill was safe from harm. "We take this for granted," the paper asserted, "from the very excellent and humane character Mr. Washington has supported, during the whole course of the war."[21]

The press universally portrayed Washington as generous to his enemies, rising above the pressure of the civil war context in which resentment could easily spill onto the battlefield. Some of Washington's earliest correspondence that the press carried involved prisoner exchanges with Gage. In the printed extracts, Washington eloquently admonished Gage for mistreating American prisoners of war. Regardless of political disposition, Washington asserted, he adhered to his duty by properly treating and protecting the British prisoners from the "enraged people," and he was alarmed to hear that Gage was not doing the same with his prisoners.[22] Descriptions of plundering by German troops in New York and New Jersey contrasted sharply with Washington's reported orders on the eve of taking Trenton—held by a Hessian garrison—forbidding "plundering any person whatsoever, whether Tories or others." Accounts of his returning property pillaged by the Hessians to civilians after the battle won further praise.[23] The *Oxford Journal*, which catered to a traditionally Tory local market that loathed the American cause, called Washington "The Flower of American Chivalry."[24] Even the ministry-supporting *Morning Post* printed a letter supposedly intercepted from a French officer that described Washington's virtues and kindness to his opponents: "Gen Washington is continually recommending humanity, and when any prisoners are made, he is the first to desire that they may not be ill treated . . . his courage and disinterestedness are equal to his humanity."[25]

In victory he was portrayed as magnanimous. In March 1778 the *Public Advertiser* falsely announced that Washington had surrounded British-occupied Philadelphia but would have mercy upon the civilians and enemy soldiers alike. Learning that they were "in great Distress for Provision," Washington allegedly allowed nearby inhabitants "to carry whatever Provisions they please into the City." The paper surmised his reasoning: "he does not wish to reduce the British Army by Famine, as that would greatly distress the Inhabitants, being determined to clear his Country of these Invaders by other means."[26] False reports circulated that he had even graciously refused to accept Lord Cornwallis's sword at the British surrender at Yorktown, insisting that the British general keep it, an action widely noted as being "in praise of General Washington."[27] The *Edinburgh Magazine* printed a story that captured the British perception of Washington as both polite and true to the American cause.[28] According to the account, when Sir Guy Carleton, then commander in chief of the British forces in America, extended a dinner invitation to Washington near the close of the war, he declined, indicating that he could not "with propriety pay a visit to a garrison that was hostile to his country." But not wanting to appear impolite, Washington then sent a dinner invitation to Carleton, who accepted and was "entertained with great magnificence, and the most perfect propriety and politeness."

The American commander in chief's character was so unassailable in Britain that even John Burgoyne, the British general who surrendered his army at Saratoga in October 1777, relied on it to rehabilitate his own tarnished reputation. After his surrender, Burgoyne returned to Britain on parole to defend his conduct as leader of the ill-fated campaign. His defense in late May 1778 before the House of Commons, of which he was a member, received widespread coverage in the press.[29] Washington won initial favor with the public for receiving credit for what the *Exeter Flying-Post* and the rest of the press described as an intervention with Congress on behalf of

Burgoyne to enable the "unfortunate British officer to return to England on his parole" in order to defend his honor.[30] Washington's greatest coup, however, came when Burgoyne, during his defense, produced a letter that he had solicited from Washington, vindicating the defeated British general. Read in the House of Commons, this testimony was given prominence in the extensive press coverage of the event with newspapers across the nation printing it in full. The letter, which underlined Washington's gentlemanly characteristics of fair play and generosity to his enemies, was thus reprinted throughout Britain, allowing the public to read in Washington's own words his unbiased concern for honor and justice, whether it be his own or his enemy's.[31] "Far from suffering the views of national opposition to be embittered and debased by personal animosity," Washington assured in his letter, "I am ever ready to do justice to the merit of the gentleman and the soldier; and to esteem, where esteem is due, however the idea of a public enemy may interpose." The perceived justice of Washington's actions was contrasted with the ministry's efforts to deny Burgoyne either a full hearing in the Commons or a court-martial, although he demanded both. The *Public Advertiser* summarized the public mood in a comment after reprinting the letter: "Let every Englishman contrast the behavior of General Washington with that of the Junto [main advisors and leaders of the North government], since General Burgoyne's arrival."[32] The justice of the American commander shamed the ministry.

Much of Washington's appeal stemmed from his seemingly iron resolve in the face of certain defeat. Few expected Washington to survive the war, let alone win it. Although many commentators initially treated the American forces with caution, they largely dismissed Washington and his troops in the wake of their resounding defeat at Long Island. Desertion, lack of supplies, poor morale, insubordination, trouble with Congress, and virtually every other imaginable problem seemed to plague Washington and his troops. Even as news of Washington's appointment reached Britain, reports circulated that the rebellion would soon collapse due to the army's "Want of Bread as well as other Necessaries," and that "It is, therefore, proposed to throw away no more lives on a Rabble that seem ready to melt away of themselves."[33] One of the earliest appearances of Washington's name in the press was as the intended recipient of an intercepted letter from Congress apologizing to him for the poor quality of troops and few supplies.[34] Henceforth until his victory at Yorktown, every campaign opened and closed with claims that the forces Washington commanded were on their last legs. Facing such obstacles, Washington could not truly fail in the eyes of the British public: if he lost battles, he simply met expectations; if he was victorious, he had overcome impossible odds. The situation for his opponents was the exact opposite.

The opprobrium attached to the British leaders contrasts markedly with Washington's gentle treatment. Until near the end of the war, Britain had no commanders the public deemed worthy of significant celebration, and even then they came from outside the American theater.[35] Horace Walpole best described the deficiency of British leadership just weeks before the outbreak of war: "We are given up to profusion, extravagance and pleasure—Heroism is not at all in fashion. Cincinnatus will be found at the hazard table and Camillus at a ball."[36] The natural choice of a patriot hero was the king, but George III had not yet won widespread admiration and with it the affectionate title of "Farmer George."[37] Although his prime minister during most of the war, Lord North, enjoyed hefty majorities in Parliament, he was hardly a popular figure outside of its doors in the fashion of William Pitt in the last Seven Years War. As the previous chapters illustrate, politicians of any ilk simply were not in vogue during a transatlantic civil war that much of the nation publicly recognized as lamentable. Britain's commanders in the field fared little better in the press. In fairness, public expectations proved to be unreasonable. As described in detail earlier, in the wake of the overwhelming success in New York in 1776, public opinion expressed in the press expected a quick victory over the ragtag band of colonists that constituted Washington's amateur army. Anything short of a complete victory was failure. Moreover, romanticized military heroes like James Wolfe, who had died two decades earlier leading his troops in a spectacular victory over the French at Quebec, still loomed large in the national memory. A poem with him as its subject even won the Chancellor of the University of Oxford's prize on the eve of the American war.[38] Yet no Wolfe could be found among the officers who rotated through the revolving door of command in America. As a frustrated reader complained in the largely pro-war *General Evening Post* in the summer of 1779, "our Admirals and Commanders of our fleets and armies seem totally deficient of the spirit, animation, and bravery of the immortal Wolfe. . . . We have been upon the tip-toe of expectation, for these five years," the reader continued, "that every western wind would bring up peace, reconciliation or victory, from America: but every campaign ends with the disgust of our Generals and Officers by sea and land, and a change of men brings not change of measures, or means of terminating a destructive war."[39]

Thomas Gage, Washington's first British counterpart, suffered for having presided over the deterioration of Anglo-American relations in the 1760s and early 1770s. In the press, Gage appeared to be an impotent buffoon, issuing proclamation after proclamation for the colonists to cease their illegal meetings and obey British authority. Among the very pages carrying reprints of his proclamations were reports and letters detailing continued American defiance.[40] Like most newspapers in November 1774, an outraged *Exeter Flying-Post* reported that the American militia even "are exercised every day in view of Gen. Gage and his troops."[41] When news of clashes at Lexington and Concord spread through the British press in June, Gage bore the brunt of the criticism. If one believed the circulating colonial accounts, he had presided over "such cruel and inhuman proceedings of our army there, as never before disgraced the character of British soldiery," as the *Stamford Mercury* described it.[42] Even if one accepted Gage's own printed dispatches, then he still had lost all control of the situation and was under siege in Boston. The North ministry recalled him, but even then the disgraced commander received parting shots. The *Saint James's Chronicle* comically announced that Gage was returning to London disguised as his American wife, while she was to assume command of the troops at Boston—a post she would fulfill better than her husband.[43] The same paper later announced that Gage was carrying "with him the Portraits of Mess. Hancock, Adams, Washington, and Putman. We hope he means to apologize in the politest Manner, to a certain Royal Connoisseur, for not having been able to procure him the Originals."[44]

Gage's replacement, Sir William Howe, fared little better in the press. Howe recognized that the intensive press coverage of the war meant that he was being tried in the court of public opinion, and he made significant efforts to defend himself publicly. Unfortunately for Howe, this did little good.[45] He started his command on a bad footing by abandoning Boston. When news reached the British press in spring 1776, the most favorable reporting Howe received was a small applause for a meticulously executed retreat.[46] In contrast, Washington gained praise for showing "tenderness" to Howe by allowing him to evacuate unmolested.[47] In the wake of the evacuation, the Parliamentary opposition's self-appointed military expert, Isaac Barré, challenged the competence of William and his brother, Richard, Admiral Viscount Howe, before the House of Commons in a widely printed speech. Although he had served with both and professed to admire the character of both, Barré declared that he "did not think that the Administration could have picked out two Men more unqualified" for the job.[48] What followed in the press coverage only created supporters for Barré's assessment of William.

The public excitement that immediately followed Howe's victories around New York in 1776 dissipated that winter and spring, when restless commentators and readers rehashed events in the press.[49] The reported ease with which Howe and his commanders defeated Congress's forces began to work against Howe, as Britons began to wonder publicly why he had not defeated the Americans once and for all, and so his stock fell in the press. Washington, however, ultimately emerged as a capable general who, commanding amateurs, acquitted himself admirably. As a widely reprinted report that appeared in the *Ipswich Journal* concluded: "It is agreed on all hands that there never could be a finer disposition than that made by Gen Washington for retreat of his forces of Long-Island and New York."[50] Accusations of laziness, delay, and lack of confidence plagued Howe throughout his seemingly endless campaign to take Philadelphia in 1777. Washington, in sharp contrast, earned a reputation for diligence. As a reader recently returned from America remarked in a letter to the *Exeter Flying-Post*, "there cannot be a more active and vigilant commander than Mr. Washington, who always rises very early in the morning, and is seen riding thro' the different parts of the encampment before he eats or drinks any thing whatever."[51] When Howe took Philadelphia in the summer of 1777, he still did not win the public's favor, because it was overshadowed in Britain by the announcement of Burgoyne's surrender at Saratoga. Many provincial newspapers carried announcements of both in the same issue.

As Burgoyne's superior, Howe was held partly responsible for the disaster at Saratoga by commentators who feared that the surrender of New York would follow shortly, and he became a lightning rod for the public's dissatisfaction. Letters from American rebels printed in the British press taunted Howe for not being able to catch "our Fabian General," and staunch supporters of the war turned against him in frustration.[52] The Glasgow-based, pro-coercion *Caledonian Mercury* printed a reader's letter addressed to Howe in which the reader harshly condemned him: "The loss of America, the ruin of your country's greatness, an indelible disgrace fixed upon the honour of its arms, the lives of many brave men sacrificed to no purpose . . . these, Sir, form the melancholy catalogue of your achievements."[53] The usually sympathetic *Morning Post* carried criticisms of the British commander's strategy in a reader's letter. "The History of our American Campaigns must excite Laughter whenever it shall be published. . . . And what must the King of Prussia think of General Howe," the reader pondered, "who drew up his Army in Front of Washington's Lines, *looked at him*, then wheeled to the Right about and—*decamped?*"[54] The response to this query soon appeared in the *Public Advertiser*, which declared that the famous military leader Frederick II, too, was "said to be a great Admirer of General Washington."[55] "This attachment," explained the commentator, "may proceed from Resemblance

. . . of the General to the last Count Dawn, who always looked upon Victory as Uncertain; who never despised his Enemy; who always took Care to secure a Retreat . . . who never engaged rashly, but had the Art of preserving his Troops for some effective and noble Purpose; who, in short, knew how to out-wit his Adversary." The article concluded: "Such was the great Leopald Count Dawn, and such is the great General George Washington."

Howe's successors, Henry Clinton and Guy Carleton, did not suffer as much in the British press, but this was largely due to timing rather than any success of their own. Clinton replaced Howe in 1778, by which time Saratoga and France's entry into the war had resulted in most Britons giving up hope of a total victory in North America. As a widely reprinted letter from a British officer in New York explained in the summer of 1778, the British public had to be reasonable in its expectations of Clinton. "Clinton will do all that spirit and sense can do to remedy all our evils," he assured the public, "but human exertion is a limited thing . . . remember one thing, we do not contend with an army but with a country."[56] Of course, this did not stop readers from taking shots at Clinton, especially after Cornwallis's morale-boosting march through the Carolinas in 1780 and 1781 had ended in surrender at Yorktown. When Carleton replaced Clinton in the wake of the British surrender at Yorktown, no one expected him to do anything but preside over the peace and imminent British evacuation.

Unable to find a Cincinnatus among their own generals, Britons turned to Washington as the exemplary hero who served his country rather than himself. In a language that had become familiar in descriptions of Washington, the *Westminster Magazine* declared that:

> With one common voice he [Washington] was called forth to the defence of his country; and it is, perhaps, his peculiar glory, that there was not a single inhabitant of these States, except himself, who did not approve the choice, and place the firmest confidence in his integrity and abilities. . . . That nature has given him extraordinary military talents will hardly be controverted by his most bitter enemies. . . . [W]hen, I say, all this comes to be impartially considered, I think I may venture to pronounce, that General Washington will be regarded by mankind as one of the greatest military ornaments of the present age, and that his name will command the veneration of the latest posterity.[57]

Such high praise was considered sufficiently lavish to appear even in the American patriot press, which often fawned over the commander in chief. A highly flattering sketch of Washington, "[written] for the *London Chronicle*," was reprinted throughout Britain as well as later in newspapers in New Jersey,

For the London Chronicle.

A short Sketch of the LIFE *and* CHARACTER *of* Gen. WASHINGTON.

AS this gentleman always refused to accept of any pecuniary appointment for his public services, no salary has been annexed by Congrefs to his important command, and he only draws weekly for the expences of his public table, and other neceffary demands. General Wafhington, having never been in Europe, could not poffibly have feen much military fervice when the armies of Britain were fent to fubdue the Americans; yet ftill, for a variety of reafons, he was by much the moft proper man on the continent, and probably any where elfe, to be placed at the head of an American army. The very high eftimation he ftood in for integrity and honour, his engaging in the caufe of his country from fentiment and conviction of her wrongs, his moderation in politics, his extenfive property, and his approved abilities as a commander, were motives which neceffarily obliged the choice of America to fall upon him.

That nature has given General Wafhington extraordinary military talents, will hardly be controverted by his moft bitter enemies. Having been early actuated with a warm paffion to ferve his country in the military line, he has greatly improved his talents by unwearied induftry, a clofe application to the beft writers upon tactics, and by a more than common method and exactnefs. In reality, when it comes to be confidered, that at firft he only headed a body of men entirely unacquainted with military difcipline or operations, fomewhat ungovernable in temper, and who at beft could only be ftiled an alert and good militia, acting under very fhort enliftments, unclothed, unaccoutred, and at all times very ill fupplied with ammunition and artillery; and that with fuch an army he withftood the ravages and progrefs of near 40,000 veteran troops, plentifully provided with every neceffary article, commanded by the braveft officers in Europe, and fupported by a very powerful navy, which effectually prevented all movements by water; when all this comes to be impartially confidered, we may venture to pronounce, that General Wafhington may be regarded as one of the greateft military ornaments of the prefent age.

General Wafhington is now in the forty-feventh year of his age; he is a tall well-made man, rather large-boned, and has a tolerably genteel addrefs: his features are manly and bold, his eyes of a bluifh caft, and very lively; his hair a deep brown, his face rather long, and marked with the fmall-pox; his complexion fun-burnt and without much colour, and thoughtful. There is a remarkable air of dignity about him, with a ftriking degree of gracefulnefs: he has an excellent underftanding, without much quicknefs; is ftrictly juft, vigilant, and generous; an affectionate hufband, a faithful friend, a father to the deferving foldier; gentle in his manners, in temper rather referved; a total ftranger to religious prejudices, which have fo very often excited Chriftians of one denomination to cut the throats of thofe of another; in his morals he is irreproachable, and was never known to exceed the bounds of the moft rigid temperance. In a word, all his friends and acquaintance univerfally allow, that no man ever united in his own perfon a more perfect alliance of the virtues of a philofopher, with the talents of a general: Candour, fincerity, affability, and fimplicity, feem to be the ftriking features of his character, till an occafion offers of difplaying the moft determined bravery and independence of fpirit."

This Day was publifhed,

FIRE and WATER. A Comic Opera. In Two Acts. Performed at the Theatre Royal in the Hay Market.

By MILES PETER ANDREWS.

Printed for T. Cadell, in the Strand.

A NEW HUNTING SONG.

Sung by Mr. VERNON *at* VAUXHALL.

Set to Mufic by Mr. HERON.

SEE Phœbus begins to enliven the Eaft,
And fee the gay dawn wears away;
Come, roufe, fellow huntfman, relinquifh dull reft,
And join in the fports of the day.
No longer in floth let your fenfe remain,
Untainted the fweets of the morn;
Drive flumber away, and make one in our train,
To follow the found of the horn.

What mufic to ours can for fweetnefs compare,
What fports fuch a pleafure can yield?
What fcent fo refin'd as the new morning air?
What profpect fo bright as the field?
Let mifers for riches each tranfport forego,
'Midft their treafures diftrefs'd and forlorn,
We tafte ev'ry joy, and forget ev'ry woe,
So charming the found of the horn.

Such pleafures we feel while from vanity free,
Our hours pafs contented along;
In innocent paftime, in mirth, and in glee,
With a hearty repaft and a fong.
Ye mortals unbiafs'd by honours and wealth,
Thefe titles that forrow adorn,
Would you tafte the calm joys of contentment and health,
Then follow the found of the horn.

This Day was publifhed, Price 1l. 1s. in Boards,

Adorned with Copper-plates, and a new Map of Spain,

TRAVELS through SPAIN. With a view to illuftrate the natural hiftory and phyfical geography of that kingdom. In a feries of letters. Including the moft interefting fubjects contained in the memoirs of Don Guillermo Bowles and other Spanifh Writers. Interfperfed with hiftorical anecdotes. With notes and obfervations relative to the arts, and defcriptive of modern improvements. Written in the courfe of a late tour through that kingdom.

By JOHN TALBOT DILLON, Knt.
And Baron of the Sacred Roman Empire.

Printed for G. Robinfon, Paternofter-row.

SOCIETY for the Difcharge and Relief of Perfons imprifoned for Small Debts.

Craven-ftreet, Strand, Jul 24, 1780.

Benefactions fince the laft report, viz.		l.	s.	d.
Noah, Job, and Cornelius	—	2	2	0
Francis Paddey, Efq;	—	10	0	0
James Davifon, Efq;	—	10	0	0
E. Y. a Lady	—	5	5	0
R. A. by unknown	—	5	5	0
L. W.	—	5	5	0
W. J. 7th benefaction	—	5	5	0
		41	0	0

Difcharged from the feveral prifons in this metropolis and kingdom, 38 Debtors, under executions, for 79l. 4s. 6d.

Rejected 4 Petitions.

Approved the recommendations of 11 Petitioners. Referred for Enquiry 5 Petitions.

The books may be feen by Benefactors, and others inclined to fupport this Charity, between the hours of Eleven and Three, at No. 7, Craven-ftreet, where benefactions are received, and where the Society will meet on Wednefday the 13th of September, at Six o'clock in the afternoon.

Benefactions are alfo received at the Thatch'd-houfe Tavern, and by Mr. Neild, the Treafurer, in St. James's-ftreet; and by the following Bankers, viz. The London Exchange Banking Company in St. James's-ftreet; Meffrs. Hoares in Fleet-ftreet; Meff. Biddulph, Cocks, and Co. at Charing-crofs; Meffrs. Dorrien and Co. in Finch-lane, Cornhill; and Meff. Fuller, Son, and Co. in Lombard-ftreet; and at the feveral Bankers in Bath.

This Day was publifhed, Price 1s. 6d.

THE PRECEPTOR's ASSISTANT; Schoolmafter's Guide. Being a compendium of arithmetic, adapted to the ufe of fchools.

By JOHN SHIELD,
Mafter of the Academy at Iflington, in Middlefex.

Containing all the rules of arithmetic, in whole numbers, vulgar and decimal fractions, extraction of the fquare, cube, and biquadrate roots, duodecimals, menfuration of fuperficies and folid, with fome pleafing and ufeful recreations.

Printed for the Author, and fold by B. Law, Ave-Maria-lane; J. Brown, Cheapfide; and J. Prefton, Minories.

To be Sold by Public voluntary Roup,

Within the Britifh Coffee Houfe, Edinburgh, On Monday the 20th of November next, between the Hours of Five and Six in the Afternoon,

THE Lands, Barony, and Eftate of TILLICOULTRY, with the Teinds thereof, all lying in the parifh of Tillicoultry and county of Clackmannan.—This Eftate of great extent, and very low rented. A great deal of it is now inclofed, but no otherways improven; and there are few tacks upon it of any ftanding. There are feveral thriving young plantations and hedge-rows, and the old timber fit for cutting is of very confiderable value. There is a modern, large, and fubftantial manfion houfe, a complete fet of offices, and a fine garden well ftocked with wall-fruit of all kinds. The houfe ftands in the middle of the eftate, and is beautifully fituated at a proper diftance from the river Devon, in a healthy fporting country, near the port towns of Stirling and Alloa. The grounds abound with iron, ftone, and other ore, and there are inexhauftible fields of coal in different parts of the eftate level-free; the prefent working pits are in good order, confifting of a five-feet coal, lock-free, moft fubftantially fitted up, and the whole machinery in thorough repair. The kirk and manfe were lately built. The patronage of the parifh belongs to the eftate; and the valued rent is 3369l. 6s. Scots, which gives great political weight in this fmall county.—Along with the eftate of Tillicoultry will be fold the LANDS of TARBATFUIRD, lying in the fame county, and holding blench of a fubject fuperior. The free rent of the whole, including the average produce of the coal for the laft 18 years, amounts to about 1064l. fterling, and the far greater part of the cefs is paid by the tenants and feuers.

The title-deeds are clear, and, with the rental of the eftate and articles of the roup, are to be feen in the hands of Andrew Stewart, jun. Writer to the Signet; with whom, or John Robertfon Writer in Edinburgh, perfons inclining to purchafe may contract betwixt and the day of fale; and the houfe may be feen by applying to John Jamiefon, Writer in Alloa.

For BILIOUS DISORDERS, &c.

DR. JAMES's ANALEPTIC PILLS.

THE great efficacy of thefe PILLS in Rheumatifms has been fufficiently manifefted by the Cures which have been already publifhed. They are found equally ferviceable in bilious diforders, indigeftion, flatulencies, habitual coftivenefs, and the common complaints of the ftomach and bowels. For the ill effects of free living they are an excellent remedy, fpeedily removing that diforders which are occafioned by excefs in eating or drinking They are likewife very efficacious in gouty habits, where the ftomach and head are affected, as well as in what is called the rheumatic gout; and they are recommended as a prefervative againft paralytic complaints. They act principally as a gentle aperient, and require no particular regimen or confinement.

Sold, at 4s. a box, or one guinea fix boxes, by Francis Newbery, junior, removed to his New Medicinal Warehoufe No. 45, at the Eaft End of St. Paul's, on the Coach Way, five Doors from Cheapfide; and at Dr. James's late Houfe, in Bruton-ftreet; and by appointment no where elfe in London.

At the fame places only is fold, Dr. James's Powder for Fevers.

☞ The above medicines may be had in Dublin of Mr. Wm. Wilfon, in Dame-ftreet, who is appointed Sole Agent for Ireland.

FIGURE 7.1. "A Short Sketch of the Life and Character of Gen. Washington," *London Chronicle*, July 22, 1780.

Massachusetts, and Connecticut.[58] By the conclusion of the war, endorsements of Washington's character in the British press were virtually universal. The *London Packet* was the first of a host of London and provincial papers that carried the following Cincinnatus-style praise "from a reader" in 1782:

> General Washington, we are well informed had, at the outset of the American war, an estate of at least [£]8000 a year. He has received no pay from the Congress as Commander in Chief, except the expense of his table, which his friends insisted upon disbursing, as that is greatly increased by the post he holds in the army. He has often been solicited to reside in a House; but, determined to share the fate of his officers and soldiers, he prefers living in camp, nor does he indulge himself in any excesses at his table, contented to live with, and as his brother soldiers do. Possessed of this temper, he is the darling of his army, and will certainly be received by posterity as one of the most illustrious characters of the age in which he lived.[59]

Washington's seeming transcendence of the politics that fractured both sides of the Atlantic was central to the success of his image in Britain. Although at the center of political controversy that had become a rebellion, Washington was largely evaluated in the British press separately from the cause he endorsed. The press did not depict Washington as political at all. Neither his behavior as a member of Congress nor his role in pre-revolutionary Virginia politics received significant attention in the press. Such distance paid off, because throughout the war Britons wrote little in favor of politicians on either side of the Atlantic. As illustrated in the preceding chapters, political squabbling filled the press, as the political factions in Britain blamed each other first for the war and then for its failure. Opponents of the war and the ministry attacked North for pursuing a fruitless war that had grown from a mere skirmish in Massachusetts to a dangerous global conflict with Britain's European rivals. North's supporters, in turn, railed against his opponents for questioning the nation's leadership in a time of crisis and giving comfort to the enemy not, as a reader of the *Public Advertiser* explained, out of "regard to Patriotism and Principle" but in order to "uphold the drooping Cause of their selfish Ambition."[60] Congress appeared to be the same. Reports, both false and true, of corruption, backstabbing, and treachery appeared regularly in the press.

The almost apolitical depiction of Washington contrasted sharply with that of his British counterparts. Upon returning home in disgrace, many of Washington's adversaries entered the political fray by resuming seats in Parliament and turning publicly against their former employers. Burgoyne took up his seat in the House of Commons after returning on parole, and sat with the opposition; Howe and Clinton did the same when they returned. Like other newspapers that catered to pro-North readers, the *Morning Post* railed against these fallen generals, attacking their motives and character: "The Generals who had been so unsuccessful are returned home, they have, in order to save themselves from justice, united with Opposition, and have left nothing unattempted to incriminate the Administration."[61] *Ruddiman's Weekly Mercury* in Edinburgh did the same, remarking, "It is very natural to these officers, in order to cover themselves, to say that the war was, and is, and must be impracticable: but it is as natural for the public not to believe them."[62] Washington's credibility was never called into question; he generally was not held accountable for the war at all. His conscious, public subordination to civil authorities ultimately meant that the British public treated Congress, not Washington and his army, as the conflict's American protagonists. In consequence, throughout the war a single issue of a newspaper could praise Washington just inches away from a condemnation of Congress.

Congress received an altogether different hearing in the press than did Washington. Support and opposition to Congress closely followed political lines and attitudes toward the American cause and war in general. At Congress's inception in 1774, political reformers in Britain, particularly the London radicals who had long used the press to vocalize their views and rally support, welcomed Congress as one of their own. The ideology of the reformers, who were not a coherent group, ranged tremendously, but to varying degrees they espoused a quasi-republican outlook that reduced the power of the monarchy and made Parliament more representative of the wider British nation.[63] In Congress, which the press in the autumn of 1774 depicted as almost universally loved and supported in America, they found a potential model of reform.[64] In November 1774, the *Derby Mercury* described a "congressional party" in London at which attendees gave toasts first to the king and queen but then offered such ones as "May British swords never be drawn in defense of Tyranny." And they then toasted the health of an assortment of London radicals and members of the opposition in Parliament, including John Wilkes and Edmund Burke, as well as to congressional delegates Benjamin Franklin and John Hancock.[65] Newspapers that had devoted substantial space to parliamentary reform, such as the *Public Advertiser,* the *Gazetteer,* and the *Saint James's Chronicle,* initially carried commentary and news that favored Congress, typically depicting it as powerful and popular in America. In response to the appearance of Congress's first resolutions, a reader's letter in the *Saint James's Chronicle* poked fun at the false confidence and elitism of the ministry: "Have some Resolutions on

Paper of a few factious Demagogues, of some paltry Planters and merchants from New-York and Virginia, of some transported Felons, struck Terror into the Cabinet of Great-Britain?" the letter mocked, "I thought we had been told that America was to be chastised; that the Bostonians must be forced to fish up the drowned Teas, and swallow them drenched with the Waters of Bitterness."[66]

The welcome initially extended to Congress was a culmination of the previous support that American protesters found in England, where voting rights were restricted to practicing male Anglicans who met hefty property qualifications. Moreover, House of Commons constituencies had not changed to reflect the substantial population shifts of the eighteenth century, leaving urban areas grossly underrepresented while vanishing villages returned as many members as there were voters.[67] What this meant was that the aristocracy and country gentry dominated the Commons almost as much as they controlled the Lords, and elections with two or more candidates were relatively rare by this period.[68] This support is where North in particular derived his majorities in Parliament.[69] Yet all these under and unrepresented people paid taxes, and so American cries of "no taxation without representation" found a sympathetic audience particularly among the artisans, lower-middling sort, religious Dissenters, and urbanites—the very people who regularly read newspapers.

Yet such high hopes turned sour in the years that followed. A major blow was the Declaration of Independence, in which Congress broke with the tradition of reform and embraced rebellion—something even the radical reformers would not openly consider. Congress's resolutions and petitions to the king, which appeared throughout the British press, had pled its members' fidelity, and so supporting its calls for reform was hardly seditious. But the Declaration of Independence made the Americans rebels by their own admission, forcing former supporters to choose. Moreover, and as described in detail earlier, from the autumn of 1776 on, British soldiers and loyalists ensured a steady flow of accounts that depicted Congress in the worst possible light. Although many papers disregarded the most ridiculous claims, reports of Congress's abuses of its own citizenry gained currency in the press as the years wore on. Accounts of restrictions on the press, oppressive taxation, corruption, and jailing of political opponents all appeared regularly. As the author of one widely reprinted letter remarked, the colonists "are galled with most despotic chains of a designing Congress, who, under the pretence of opposing the arbitrary measures of a British administration, have themselves overturned the free press of America—ruined and imprisoned its conductors—banished their neutral brethren—, and seized upon all their fortunes and effects."[70] Thus, for many former supporters, Congress had seemingly abandoned its republican principles and become a band of petty tyrants. As even the *Saint James's Chronicle* remarked in April 1777 that the Americans were "fighting for the liberty of living under the most domineering, insolent and unfeeling Tyranny that can disgrace any Country."[71] Any remaining supporters became closeted. Within a couple of years of the fighting, printed defenses of Congress had all but disappeared in the British press.

For many of those readers and commentators who had opposed Congress from the start, Congress's behavior, both real and falsely depicted, coincided with their already poor opinion of any reforms that increased voting rights or reduced the power of the elite. This was not so much a coherent argument articulated against republicanism per se as it was a general social prejudice against the lower social ranks. For these Britons, John Wilkes and his London supporters who rallied and rioted for reform in the 1760s and early 1770s had merely been "rabble," and Congress was little different. A letter writer to the *General Evening Post*, which often played host to these views, described Congress's colonial enforcers as being "composed of barbers, tailors, cordwainers, &c. whose insolence and pertness would raise any Englishman's indignation."[72] Congress itself was regularly dismissed as a body dominated by New England artisans and tradesmen. That such low ranking people moved against British authority was no surprise, because, as one of many letter writers observed, for "men acquainted with human nature it is obvious, that in all countries the lower class of people are too much given to change, are easily imposed upon, and are ever ready to exclaim against all rulers."[73]

A close political association with Congress proved lethal to one's image in Britain. For example, Benjamin Franklin, the best-known colonist before the war, was treated harshly in the press. In its sketch of the "Life and Character of Dr. Franklin" in 1780, the *Political Magazine* labelled him the "author and encourager of the American rebellion."[74] "By his dark machinations," it declared, "this man has betrayed the Americans into arms against the mother country, which has cost them the lives of upwards of 100,000 of their people." When attempting to portray Edmund Burke as a traitor to his nation, a reader of the *Morning Chronicle* called him "the correspondent of Dr. Franklin."[75] Two years later, the *Political Magazine* attacked Franklin again in a collection of short descriptions of American leaders. "Ancient or modern history scarcely furnishes an example of such consummate hypocrisy, and hitherto successful duplicity," the magazine proclaimed, "and if the axe, or the haltar, are to be employed on this occasion, it were much to be wished the first example could be made of this hoary traitor."[76]

In sharp contrast, the press consistently depicted Washington as a gentleman in possession of all the expected traits of his social class. His letters portrayed generosity to his enemies, and his public refusal to accept payment for his services all demonstrated this. In consequence, an endorsement of the gentlemanly traits of Washington could simultaneously be a statement of support for the virtues of a government run by a landed elite, as Britain's unreformed Parliament was. Washington's virtuous image was often a tool for shaming Britain's leaders. In a January 1778 issue, the *Edinburgh Advertiser*, one of the most vehemently anti-American newspapers in the country, opened with a, by then, familiar attack on Britain's military leaders, blaming their self-serving character for the nation's woes. If Roman, Greek, and Crusader generals had fought without seeking pay and place, a reader declared, "Britain does not deserve a less noble sacrifice." For a modern example, the author turned to Washington, declaring, "Let us not, Mr. Printer, disdain to learn virtue even from a REBEL."[77]

For republican-minded reformers, Washington was also a laudable model of leadership—but for different reasons. Although depicted as one of the wealthiest men in America and the scion of the Virginian gentleman planters, Washington appeared in the British press as overtly self-subordinate to the republican civil authorities. According to the press, the relationship between Congress and Washington was not always harmonious, but Washington nevertheless answered to Congress. Whether or not Washington could in reality have usurped Congress is not the issue. Rather, in Britain, it was widely believed that he could have taken control at various points during the war. Reports of a faction-ridden, bankrupt Congress with a rapidly diminishing authority that was ripe for the usurping filled the press from late 1776 onward. Washington did not appear to take an interest in American politics. From the British perspective, Washington could have been a Caesar or a Cromwell but chose to be a Cincinnatus. As the *London Chronicle* admiringly stated in January 1782, Washington "will certainly be received by posterity as one of the most illustrious characters of the age in which he lived."[78]

Washington's image in Britain was so apolitical that he became an icon of transatlantic healing. In 1780, a British charity raising funds to support American prisoners of war in Britain published a poetical tribute to Washington along with a "Short Sketch of General Washington's Life and Character" (see fig. 7.2).[79] Like similar fund-raising drives that appeared throughout the war, the aim of this charity, the advertisement explained, was not to support the American cause but rather to "stamp a lesson on the minds of those unfortunate captives, and our American brethren in general, that they should not withdraw all national affection from [Britain]." The selection of Washington as the fund-raiser's showpiece attempted to capitalize on this

FIGURE 7.2. "George Washington, Commander in Chief of ye Armies of ye United States of America," frontispiece of *A Poetical Epistle to His Excellency George Washington, Esq. . . . To which is Annexed a Short General Sketch of General Washington's Life and Character* (London, 1780). BMC 5641, © Copyright the Trustees of the British Museum.

sense of damaged, but lingering, transatlantic affection. Washington's image was thus intended to represent everything good about the American colonists, and, even more, the British as a whole. As the *Westminster Magazine* concluded in its reprint of the biography, "It is somewhat singular, that even in England, not one reflection was ever cast, or the least disrespectful word uttered against him."[80]

Washington's popularity in Britain resulted from a mixture of his conduct and accidents of timing. His popularity also reveals as much about British attitudes toward the war as it does about the character of the man waging it for the Americans. To woo colonists and fulfill his own sense of how a commander should behave, Washington fashioned himself publicly as a citizen-soldier, ever ready to fight for his country without any expectation of material reward. Washington's reported endurance, perseverance, courage, generosity, and politeness appealed to British notions of good leadership and heroism. Such qualities shone all the more brightly in the context of Britons' dissatisfaction with their own leaders in Britain and America, who, despite successes, fell well short of the public's demand for total victory. Thus, the longer the war dragged on, the better Washington appeared by comparison. Moreover, his ability to distance himself from politics ensured his popularity despite general disdain for the American cause. Washington publicly followed the orders of Congress; if the orders were disagreeable, then Congress was to blame.

At the end of the war Washington conclusively proved that his declaration of duty to his country and public subordination to civil authorities were sincere. Like Cincinnatus, Washington very publicly disbanded his army and retired to his farm. His address upon retirement appeared in virtually every newspaper and magazine in Britain, and not a single commentator seems to have publicly questioned its sincerity. This final action ensured his legacy as a hero and the embodiment of an Anglo-American interpretation of citizenly virtues. Over a decade later, when Britain once more faced a republican threat, this time from France, Washington's heroic image lingered. In 1797, the Westminster Forum, a middling London debating society, debated whether or not Thomas Paine's printed attack on "the Character of General Washington . . . deserved the reprobation of every Friend of Liberty and Humanity." Two days later, the *Morning Herald* reported that the affirmative was "carried with universal approbation, by an audience consisting of upwards of five hundred persons, among whom . . . [were] several Noblemen, Magistrates, and Gentlemen of the first respectability of the Country."[81] In the context of a new revolution, this time a far bloodier and more radical one in Europe, Washington's apparent ability to have power without abusing it was all the more admirable.

The Controversy of Conducting the War

AFRICAN SLAVES, AMERICAN INDIANS,

AND GERMAN MERCENARIES

✳ In the Declaration of Independence, the American signers made the bold claim that the "history of the present King of Great Britain is a history of repeated injuries and usurpations, all having in direct object the establishment of an absolute tyranny over these states." In order "To prove this," they listed a myriad of "facts" to "be submitted to a candid world." Among them were a number of specific complaints about how George III was waging war against them. "He [the king] is, at this time, transporting large armies of foreign mercenaries," the Declaration railed, "to compleat the works of death, desolation and tyranny, already begun with circumstances of cruelty and perfidy, scarcely paralleled in the most barbarous ages, and totally unworthy of the head of a civilized nation." If this was not enough to demonstrate before the world the inhumanity and illegitimacy of the British sovereign, the Declaration laid a second charge, that "He has excited domestic insurrections amongst us, and has endeavored to bring on the inhabitants of our frontiers, the merciless Indian savages, whose known rule of warfare, is the undistinguished destruction of all ages, sexes and conditions."

There were a myriad of non-British peoples involved in the fighting in North America; however, the Declaration publicly singled out these three groups—black slaves, American Indians, and foreign troops—as particularly irksome and at least partly in the hope that these complaints would resonate with audiences outside of America. The Declaration was, after all, consciously distributed to the presses and courts throughout Europe. Although clearly propaganda, these complaints held elements of truth insomuch as they predicted elements of what the Anglo-American war would involve. Nearly half of the British expeditionary force that landed at Staten Island shortly after the Declaration's signing consisted of rented German troops; during the major campaigns in the southern colonies, blacks (both slave and free) typically outnumbered the regular troops in the British forces; and American Indians in the thousands allied themselves with the British, safeguarding troop columns and raiding frontier settlements. Without this assistance, the British would have been hard pressed to conduct a major land campaign. Yet—and despite the tone of outrage in the Declaration—none of these moves would have surprised anyone at the time. Arming slaves, allying with Indians, and renting foreign troops were all par for the course in European and imperial wars. Some German states and American Indian communities had even come to depend on it economically.

But this war was different for the British, and the public discussion in the press regarding the inclusion of "outsiders" in the war effort highlights this. Although wayward, the Americans were deemed undeserving by many readers of the full arsenal Britain typically deployed against its foreign enemies. Yet, as also revealed by the press coverage, Britons' opposition varied according to their own prejudices and historical experiences. In consequence, while Congress linked and expressed equal outrage at the involvement of slaves, Indians, and foreign troops, discussions in the British press did not.

The conflict between colonists and Britons in the decade before Lexington and Concord was a war of words. Fought publicly in the newspapers, periodicals, and pamphlets, this phase of Anglo-American hostilities set the civil-war tone that carried into the discussion of the armed hostilities that followed. Americans argued with fellow colonists, Britons argued among themselves, and everyone argued with each other, but most agreed on the central underlying principle that the colonists were "fellow nationals."[1] What this status actually meant and what obligations this carried on both sides of the Atlantic —taxation without representation, parliamentary sovereignty, etc.—constituted the heart of the debate. The language of the debate regularly emphasized that this was a family affair, although the contrast in selected terms—such as "brethren" and "children"—highlighted how differently the Anglo-American family could be perceived. For many on both sides of the Atlantic, the inclusion of outsiders in the fighting betrayed this family bond.

Employing the most alien descriptors available, such as "savages" for Indians and "Janissaries" for German troops, critics in Britain emphasized these groups' foreignness. Slaves, Indians, and foreign troops were deemed outsiders not only in nationality and ethnicity but also in motivation. Contemporaries realized that the reasons for participation varied enormously among these groups and individuals within the groups, but they seldom had anything to do with issues of taxation, representation, or the sovereignty of George III. No one publicly pretended that the New England farmer and runaway slave faced off in battle for the same reasons.[2] And, of course, these differences meant that blacks, Indians, and European mercenaries could be found, albeit in smaller numbers, fighting in Congress's forces. Ultimately, this foreignness made blacks, Indians, and Germans appear too flexible and therefore illegitimate in a war about ideology in the eyes of many contemporary American colonists and British readers alike. In consequence, complaints contained in the Declaration of Independence about these groups' participation would have struck a chord with British readers. The Declaration, however, did not raise the issue; rather, it fit into the ongoing discourse in the British press about how the war should have been conducted. The means with which the British government waged the war in America clearly mattered to many Britons at home. Although now errant, the colonists were British. As revealed in earlier chapters, some commentary in the press cried out for stiff retribution for the colonists, but most took a much more compassionate tone. This was, after all, a time when charities for the relief of American prisoners of war met openly and enjoyed widespread, popular support.[3]

At least some of the expressions in the press for leniency stemmed from strategic considerations: aggressive tactics would push more Americans into rebellion. As "An Englishman" remarked in a letter in the *Gazetteer,* tens of thousands of "foreign" troops, "inciting the slaves to revolt, and loosening the savages" upon the colonists was "driving" many colonists to the side of Congress.[4] That the issue of the war's conduct served as a convenient political truncheon for abusing the North ministry's prosecution of the war is also beyond doubt. After all, some of the most vociferous condemnations came from within Parliament's debating chambers. But this does not mean that sincerity, although always difficult to gage, was absent from these attacks. At one point in the debate over Indians, an incensed Lord Germain, the secretary of state for America who was heavily involved in running the American war, reportedly challenged Henry Luttrell, a leading opposition spokesman, to a duel.[5] Certainly the extent and breadth of some of the commentary in the press, particularly with regard to opposing the employment of Indians, suggests a genuine concern about the morality of such tactics and their poor reflection on the honor of the British nation.

An examination of British discussions in the press about the use of slaves, Indians, and foreign troops in the war effort underlines at least two of the major themes that run through this book. First, the British understood the war with the colonies to be inherently different from previous overseas conflicts. The colonists required different treatment than the French or Spanish, and the vast majority of Britons, including most of those in office, publicly professed that less severity was the best course of action. American cities would not be sacked, and rebel prisoners of war would not all be hung as traitors. Many commentators in the press extended this to the use of non-British forces, generally depicting them as undesirable tools in this particular war. Thus, although the British had cheered British officers who visited the horrors of Indian warfare on their enemies in the Seven Years War, the nation blanched at the prospect of the same fate befalling the colonists during the American Revolution.[6]

Second, the war fostered a great deal of internal reflection in Britain. As far as the discourse in the press reflected national opinion, Britons of every ilk verily believed that the outcome of the war depended on the decisions and efforts of Britain not America. In consequence, commentators in the press spent far more time remarking on British policies and actions than on the behavior of the colonists, and this is no more apparent than in the discourse on the conduct of the war in America. Certainly readers complained about the guerilla tactics of some of the rebel forces, but these complaints were rare in comparison to critiques of the behavior of the British troops and their allies. As a result, although readers were informed that Congress had foreign mercenaries in its pay, black troops in its army, and American Indian allies (albeit in smaller numbers than in the British forces), it had little impact on the national discussion in Britain. In this sense we are reminded that this was Britain's war, too—complete with discussions that had their own backgrounds and were not merely responses to American actions and complaints.

Britain's inclusion of black Americans, both free and enslaved, in its effort to subdue the colonies met with surprisingly little discussion in the British press. Of course, this is not to suggest that blacks played an unimportant role in the conflict. Their sheer numbers, which in colonies such as Virginia and South Carolina constituted between one-third and one-half of the population, made an impact inevitable, and numerous studies have chronicled their experiences and roles.[7] In the lawlessness that swept through much of the Southern colonies in the latter half of the conflict, escaping slavery, albeit often temporarily, became easier. Contemporaries such as David Ramsay estimated that one-quarter of South Carolina's slaves ran away, and Thomas Jefferson calculated that 30,000 Virginia slaves escaped from bondage.[8] Yet the subject provoked comparatively little commentary in the British press and was not a major part of the British reading public's experience of the revolution. Historians have marveled at how this history has been "lost," but a close study of the press reveals that it was never seriously chronicled in Britain in the first place.[9] Press coverage of black participation was confined largely to a handful of reports and letters from America—unlike the subjects of foreign troops and American Indian participants, both of whom blacks outnumbered. Few readers or editors weighed in on the matter, and neither the opposition in Parliament nor its supporters in the press appear to have attempted to capitalize on the subject in the ways they did with other aspects of the war. Nor do the North ministry's apologists or pro-war commentators seem to have taken much interest in the topic. Including a discussion of British press coverage of black participation here is important not least because it rounds out the broader examination of British public considerations of the groups about which the Americans complained about in the Declaration of Independence. The absence of a significant discussion in the British press is too glaring to ignore, considering that Britain was less than a generation away from abolishing the lucrative African slave trade and two generations away from ending chattel slavery altogether.

Like their white counterparts, blacks served in British and American armies in a variety of capacities, which ranged from camp cooks to George Washington's personal valet.[10] Only a small minority experienced combat, but both sides included free blacks and slaves in their regular fighting forces. Although Washington and many of his officers vociferously refused to include blacks in the Continental Army at the conflict's outset, by the war's end necessity had made blacks familiar faces in many regiments. Free and enslaved blacks were even more visible on the British side. The use of black slaves and freemen was not new to British military operations in the 1770s, nor did the American Revolution mark the end of the practice.[11] But, as in many other aspects, the American war posed a particularly unique set of problems. Arming French slaves or enlisting freemen from the British West Indies for foreign service was quite different than campaigning through a plantation system that the British sought to leave relatively intact. Nevertheless, blacks, by force or choice, aided the British cause in the tens of thousands. Some fought as soldiers in mixed or largely black regiments in the British army, while others augmented the Hessians' forces, who were probably the least racially prejudiced troops in the conflict.[12] Most, however, served in familiar roles as laborers, building roads and fortifications, and "beasts of burden," carrying soldiers' packs and officers' baggage. As many as half of the men in the British camps during the Southern campaigns from 1779 onward were black. And when rations ran short, these troops were the first to suffer, such as the more than five thousand blacks that Lord Cornwallis ejected from his fortifications and into the waiting rebel ranks during the siege of Yorktown. By the end of the war, at least 15,000–20,000 blacks lived within British-controlled zones—most of whom were later evacuated.[13]

During the war this part of the story received scant attention in the British press. This was not for lack of information. Blacks wrote no fewer than five petitions to the last two colonial governors of Massachusetts in the two years before the outbreak of fighting, some of which appeared in New England newspapers alongside articles complaining about the immorality of slavery.[14] The November 1775 proclamation of Virginia's last royal governor, Lord Dunmore, who offered freedom to able-bodied male slaves who rallied to the king's standard, appeared in full in many British newspapers, and Parliament debated it. The abysmal fate of disease, death, and eventual abandonment of those slaves who answered the call also received some coverage in the press in the form of printed letters from British soldiers and American colonists. But again, domestic commentary, either from editors or readers, was wholly lacking. Accounts of the British forces during the southern campaigns regularly included tables and details that noted the large number of blacks attached to the British army, so their continued participation was no secret. The *Morning Chronicle* was typical in its description of the celebrated repulse of the combined Franco-American forces at Savannah in the early autumn of 1779, noting the "4,000 negroes" accompanying the "3085 King's and European [German auxiliary] troops."[15] Yet commentary, positive or negative, was virtually absent. Accounts of loyalist evacuations, which appeared in every paper in the country from late 1781 on, typically noted a black presence—although not in the same moving language that described the anguish of whites. Yet, a significant national discussion of the future of these blacks did not appear in the press during the war.

The reasons for this absence can only be speculated, but clearly it was not a consequence of Britons lacking knowledge or interest in slavery. The history of Britain's relationship with race and slavery is as equally vibrant and complex, although different, as the American experience. Race and slavery were major topics of contemporary discussions. Like their continental counterparts, Scottish Enlightenment philosophers such as Adam Ferguson and Adam Smith expended a great deal of intellectual energy investigating the cultural diversity the British encountered abroad, and, unintentionally, their resulting classifications and explanations provided fuel for incarnations of modern racism.[16] Africans, both free and enslaved, living in Britain numbered in the tens of thousands and thus were common sights, particularly in London and port cities.[17] Moreover, the connection between chattel slavery and the popular products they produced—coffee, sugar, and tobacco—were well established by the 1770s, with images of slaves regularly appearing on the printed advertisements of the tens of thousands of shops that sold these goods, which peppered the national landscape.[18] In the decades that followed the American Revolution, abolitionists led popular boycotts of products produced by slave labor, particularly sugar, whose image became permanently stained with African blood in the minds of many consumers.[19]

The British public's particular type of awareness may at least partly explain why British commentators and readers generally ignored or dismissed American colonists' comparisons of their own plights with that of slaves. Although a popular rhetorical tool in the language of American commentators throughout the 1760s and 1770s, equating British policies with enslavement held little currency in the British press once the war started. Occasionally, London radicals might use the metaphor, but it received little endorsing commentary in the press. As a reader of the *Bristol Journal* remarked after reading the Declaration of Independence, "The language of the American Declarations and Addresses one would imagine that the parliament of Great Britain . . . had treated them with as great cruelty and as much injustice as they Americans treat their negro slaves."[20] Yet neither did the British newspapers and magazines devote much print to accusations of charges of American hypocrisy for demanding "liberty" while owning slaves.[21] When Lord Dunmore issued his proclamation or British generals enlisted the support of slaves, editors and readers did not cry out in the press that the rebels were reaping what they had sown. After all, to call the American colonists hypocrites would cut too close to home: the British, too, proclaimed the birthright of liberty as their own, yet their prosperity also relied on slave labor. Besides, when British critics wanted to accuse Congress of hypocrisy without highlighting their own, they had a wealth of material courtesy of the loyalist press from late 1776 onward that detailed (and often fabricated) Congress's brutal treatment of its free white citizenry, and this would have been more poignant to the free white British readers who constituted all but a tiny handful of newspaper readers in Britain.

Perhaps the most plausible explanation for the lacking discussion in the British press about African slaves' participation in the war is that no faction in Britain stood to gain from making an issue of it. There had been plenty of public rumbling building against slavery throughout the eighteenth century, but there was not a significant abolitionist movement until after the American Revolution.[22] Those connected to slavery had a decided upper hand in Parliament, where such groups as the West Indian lobby held considerable sway.[23] The North ministry never considered ending slavery in the rebelling colonies. To advocate such a move would have been suicide in that it would have alienated not only the West Indian lobby but potentially the loyalists in the South and everyone in Britain who was connected to slaves and the products they produced—all at a time when the government was prosecuting a less-than-popular war. It did not seriously entertain inciting mass slave revolts during the war, despite receiving a number of detailed proposals.[24] Unlike the employment of German troops or overtures to American Indians, the North ministry generally left the issue of slave emancipations up to officers on the ground. Dunmore's proclamation, for example, did not receive prior approval. When news of it reached Britain, the government apologists in the press who addressed the issue, such as those at the *Stamford Mercury,* downplayed its significance, explaining that this was not the result of a moral impulse, but instead it "was justified on the ground of necessity" in a climate where "it was impossible to raise men otherwise to recover our [British] rights."[25]

Those in opposition who potentially stood to gain from criticizing the move had similar reason to remain silent: the North ministry could not be toppled by any opposition party touting an abolitionist platform. Even Edmund Burke, the self-styled conscience of Parliament who publicly railed against the use of American Indians in the war and later attacked the East India Company via his role as prosecutor in the impeachment trial of Warren Hastings for the company's crimes against the people it ruled, was quiet on the subject of the "domestic insurrections" the British incited in America. But then for most of the war he represented Bristol, whose merchant community, which dominated local politics, had grown rich on the slave trade. Because no political faction would serve as a rallying point, the issue with regard to the American war was a nonstarter for the British, who took issue with slavery. As Horace Walpole, a close reader of the press and sometimes an American sympathizer, remarked, if the freedom of the slaves were at stake then choosing sides would be easy: "If all the black slaves were in rebellion, I should have no doubt in choosing my side."[26]

Moreover, British commanders did not visit the full horrors of a slave rebellion on the colonists, further allowing all sides in Britain to more easily balk at the issue. Dunmore's proclamation did not call for slaves to first slaughter their masters before rallying to him, and Cornwallis did not distribute large numbers of arms to bodies of slaves and then sail away, leaving them to wreak havoc on their white neighbors. Nor did he issue public proclamations threatening to unleash hoards of angry slaves on white colonists unless they surrendered—in sharp contrast to General John Burgoyne's heavily publicized tactics with regard to the Indians in his company as he marched through New York in 1777. American blacks were remarkably restrained, particularly in comparison to their Caribbean counterparts. The mainland South was not as Haiti would be in the Americas' next revolution. In consequence, the issues at hand in the limited public discussion were about depriving colonists of property and granting slaves freedom for service, not the indiscriminate slaughter of white planters by vengeful slaves. Had this been Britain's policy, the public response would have been remarkably different.

American Indian participation was among the most publicly detested aspects of the war in Britain. Although a period in which Britons agreed on little, public opposition to using Indians against the rebelling colonists remained loud, unwavering, and virtually universal throughout the conflict. Objections stemmed from two shared perceptions: first, the American Indian way of waging war was cruel; second, no matter what they had done, the American colonists, unlike previous French opponents, did not deserve to suffer Indian warfare.

Two centuries of colonization had left a largely negative image of Indians in the British popular imagination. There were, of course, multiple exceptions, because Britons' relationships with American Indians were as complex as they were diverse. Indians could be noble savage characters in London theaters, and genuine natives could be seen petitioning Parliament or testifying before the Board of Trade. Nevertheless, the recent press coverage of the Seven Years War in America, which had seen the vast majority of Indian combatants focus their efforts against the British and the colonists, had left the newspaper-reading nation with an incredibly narrow, jaded view of Indians in North America.[27] Images of thousands of slaughtered civilians and young, wounded British soldiers begging for mercy as they were scalped or burned alive received far more attention than the Indians who sacrificed themselves in honor of their alliances to the British or saw their own families suffer at the hands of European aggression. In consequence, by the era of the American Revolution, "Indian" was synonymous with militancy and cruelty in the press. For example, when reporting on a murder at "a little Public House at Kill y cwm" in Wales in 1772, the *Oxford Journal* drew on the popular image of Indian brutality as a reference point, describing the crime as "one of the most shocking Acts of wanton Cruelty and most savage Barbarity ever heard of.

It is of so brutal a Nature that Decency will not suffer the most distant Hint of the horrid Deed. . . . We shudder at the Barbarity of Indians, who roast their Prisoners alive; but the detestable, the hellish Brutality of these Villains is far more horrible."[28] Thus, when accusing the American colonists of mutilating fallen British soldiers at the battle of Concord, the *Dundee Weekly Mercury* labeled the acts "Indian cruel."[29]

During the American Revolution, the press reinforced this interpretation. As the *Ipswich Journal* reminded readers when it printed a supposed translation of an Indian war song, mercilessness and murder went hand in hand with Indian warfare, and revenge and bloodlust, not temperance and logic, were believed to be at the very heart of Indians' cultures:

> The war-song above-mentioned, is usually recited by the Indian tribes previous to an engagement, and seems dictated by the most unrelenting spirit of revenge. The general burthen of it is as follows: "I go to war to revenge the death of my brothers; I shall kill; I shall exterminate; I shall burn my enemies; I shall bring away slaves; I shall devour their heart, dry their flesh, drink their blood; I shall tear off their scalps, and make cups of their skulls."[30]

Editors and readers reminded the wider public that Indians would not distinguish between Briton, loyalist, or rebel any more than they would civilian from soldier. They were relentless, insatiable savages. As the *Scots Magazine* remarked in 1779, their thirst for blood was unquenchable, and their palates were indiscriminate: "their object and design in all wars, was not to fight, but to murder; not to conquer but to destroy: in a word, that their service was uncertain, their rapacity insatiate, their faith ever doubtful, and their action cruel and barbarous."[31]

Although general perceptions of Indians had not changed significantly since the Seven Years War, attitudes toward employing them in war had altered remarkably now that the enemy consisted of fellow British subjects. During the Seven Years War, the press had made heroes of men such as Sir William Johnson and Robert Rogers, whose abilities to amass Indian allies and fight like them against French and Indian enemies were widely celebrated.[32] Their brutal methods had not been tempered in press accounts, which included tales of scalping, cannibalism, and killing noncombatants. Indians who sided with the British, such as the Mohawk leader Hendrick, whose death at the battle of Lake George in 1755 was mourned in the British press, had been celebrated as worthy allies.[33] The change in the American Revolution was not in the way the Indians fought. As before, ranger companies formed under colonial leadership, including Rogers for a short time, and Johnson's heirs allied with those of Hendrick's to once again lead British fighting efforts in the New York backcountry. Yet in this war the British were publicly and vehemently opposed to visiting the horrors of Indian warfare upon their enemies. The *Exeter Flying-Post's* worry that the Indians massing at Quebec in the autumn of 1774 would be used to "make war on . . . the defenceless Protestant subjects in the back settlements" was wholly typical of British opinion displayed in the press. Such blatant restraint underlines the extent to which the British had accepted the American colonists as fellow nationals by the time of the American war, as well as the resilience of these sentiments in times of great discord. Such attitudes provoked frustration among the revenge-minded minority. As a reader complained in a letter to the *Public Advertiser,* "The Tomahawks and Scalping-knives in the Hands of Indian Auxiliaries, which were employed without Scruple under Mr. Pitt's Administration [during the Seven Years War], are now represented by Lord Chatham [Pitt's aristocratic title] as unlawful in War as the poisoning of Rivers. . . . And though we paid for French Scalps, coaxed and cultivated the Alliance of Indian Chiefs [in the Seven Years War]," the letter continued, "it is become shocking to suffer them to touch our American Brethren; even though these very loving Brethren can point their Bayonets at our Throats, immediately after taking Oaths of Pacification and Fidelity!"[34]

Events in the North American backcountry on the eve of the American Revolution ensured that the Indians were controversial even before fighting between the colonists and the British began. During the early 1770s, the British steadily withdrew their thinly stretched troops from frontier garrisons and redeployed them eastward in light of deteriorating Anglo-American relations.[35] In consequence, frontier tensions, which had been simmering for years, exploded into open hostilities that received acute coverage in the British press, which ensured fresh images of the brutality of Indian warfare in readers' minds. This meant that reports on early British efforts to secure Indian allies for a possible war with its own colonists appeared on the same pages as descriptions of massacred frontier families. In a November 1774 issue, amid reports of the latest news from Congress's meeting in Philadelphia and colonists arming for possible war, the *Glasgow Journal* devoted substantial space to describing in vivid detail how an Oneida raiding party in New York "roasted alive" its captives. "[T]hese ferocious bipeds," the account explained, have "an invariable rule to give entertainment to their friends far and near, and to render them more brilliant, their prisoners are brought forth, and put to death in the most excruciating manner."[36]

Not surprisingly, accusations that the North ministry was somehow involved in these raids soon appeared in London newspapers. The *London Packet*, a hotbed of anti-North commentary, remarked that "the great military skill shewn by the Indians in their last battle with the people of Virginia convinces all America that they have an assistance of a very unnatural nature; and since the language of the Court is, that they hope the Indians will scalp the greatest part of [colonists], it is easily to be discovered from what quarter they draw their new succour."[37] The *Saint James's Chronicle* concurred, declaring that the "Courtiers rejoice at this War hooping, it may be a Means to subdue the Spirit of the Colonies."[38] The provincial press was no less adamant. For example, within just two days in January 1775, the *Stamford Mercury*, usually a prime venue for anti-American sentiment, and the *Exeter Flying-Post* both claimed an article as their own, which declared that "It is the firm belief of the honest men of this nation, that the Indians are assisted by some very infamous hands, and that a new conquest of the colonists is attempting in a new and unnatural manner."[39]

When war between Britain and the American colonists erupted, the press closely followed Indian activities, but commentators generally portrayed them as an option best left alone. As the *Gentleman's Magazine* observed in September 1775, "introducing them upon the stage of action for the purpose of butchering our fellow-subjects . . . is equally impolitic and antichristian."[40] The problem, the *Derby Mercury* explained, was that it was impossible for British officers to persuade "these Savages to desist from their cruel practices." Even the *General Evening Post*, whose readers regularly denounced the rebelling colonists in the strongest terms possible, printed calls for caution in the employment of Indians. "They are an Enemy, who, when let loose," remarked a reader, "will probably make no Distinction between those that are Friends of Government and those that are Rebels."[41] Once news arrived that Indians were in the pay of the British, commentary in the press became harsher than ever. As the *Gazetteer* declared in December 1777: "What a dreadful mode of carrying on war is this, and calculated to gratify the insatiable revenge of those who direct such nefarious measures, but which are prohibited by the laws of every civilized nation throughout the world!—What English and Hessians must not in honour do, is left to be perpetrated by Savages."[42]

The widespread, public objection to the unrestrained use of Indians was one of the few themes that was both expressed across the political spectrum and remained relatively unchanged during the conflict. Unlike the use of slaves or German troops, complaints about Indians remained steadfast and virtually universal throughout the war. Only a tiny minority of the most ardent rebel-haters publicly viewed Indian involvement as a fit punishment for rebellion. William Markham, archbishop of York, made a public statement accepting Indians as viable tools for restoring "the supremacy of law" in America in a sermon, and he was ridiculed for it for the remainder of the war. As one reader remarked in the *Gazetteer*, "The ground on which the prelate ventured to tread . . . is so boggy and rotten that [he] could not prevent bemiring both himself and his subject in the dirt of worldly policy."[43] Even in the most ardent and detailed proposal that appeared in the press, the author, who claimed to have served in America alongside Indians in the last war, made clear his opposition to including them in any unchaperoned capacity. "The savages" should only be included if officers of sufficient quantity were able to control them, he explained, to ensure that they act "as bugbears, without allowing them to act as hell-hounds." Utilizing them in any other setting, he stressed, was unacceptable: "God forbid, however, that I should recommend the letting loose [of] these barbarians in all their native cruelty and ferocity! Rather than consent to this, I would willingly forego all the benefits arising from their service."[44] Even the *Gentleman's Magazine,* which tried particularly hard to follow a neutral-to-pro-coercion line in order to maintain the unmatched size of its readership, took a hard line against the use of Indians. After France's entry had turned most of the nation's attention away from the North American theater, the *Gentleman's Magazine* still carried a brutal account of Indian warfare with the intention of exhibiting "a striking instance of the ferocity of the Indian savages when employed in the service of civilised nations."[45] The lengthy account was that of the "massacre of the English garrison of Fort William Henry, in 1757," selectively extracted from Jonathan Carver's recently published *Travels through the Interior.* The passage offers vivid descriptions of babies being dashed against rocks, scalped women and children, and Indian savages who "drank the blood of their victims as it flowed warm from their fatal wounds."

The Indians' perspectives were almost never taken into account.[46] Public sympathy for their precarious situations did not emerge nor did readers admire the desire of many Indian communities to remain neutral. Even the swiftness with which some of the Indians, many of whom had been allied to the British Crown for generations, rallied to the British side met with disgust in the press. According to the British perspective, loyalty merely went to the highest bidder. As a widely reprinted extract from the *Annual Register* declared: "The Indians, ever light in act and faith, greedy for present, and eager for spoil, were not [with] difficulty induced, by a proper application of the one, and the hope of the other, concurring with their own natural disposition, to forget the treaties which they had lately confirmed with the colonists, and to engage in the design."[47] Nor did the public find solace in the handful of reports that appeared in the press describing Congress's efforts to win Indian allies. Indians fought alongside the American rebels throughout the war. Washington's army at Cambridge in 1775 included Stockbridge Indians, and, perhaps most famously, the Oneida and Tuscarora split with their Iroquois brethren and sided with the rebels (and suffered terribly for it).[48] Although a few commentators initiated some halfhearted attempts to deflect attacks on the ministry by emphasizing that the sin of employing Indians was a shared—and by implication excusable—one, this line of argument was wholly dismissed in the press. That Indians were supposedly necessary strategically or that they found employ in Congress's forces did not make a dent in the furor in the press. Such consistency underlines both the sincerity of the public complaints against using Indians in Britain's war effort and the great extent to which the conflict for the British was about independent reflection rather than mere reaction to American protagonists.

Public discussion about Indians peaked in late 1777 and 1778, during the uproar following General John Burgoyne's ill-fated campaign from Canada to New York. The campaign ended in the British surrender at Saratoga in October 1777, but the episode sparked a heated controversy in Britain that lasted until the end of the war. Burgoyne's campaign had been closely followed in the British press, which printed extracts from his journal and reports to his superiors alongside letters from officers and soldiers of varying ranks. There were high hopes that this campaign would slice the rebelling colonies in two and finally end the war, and so his defeat was a devastating blow to British morale at home. A substantial part of the debate focused on the several hundred Indians accompanying Burgoyne's army. As a reader remarked in a letter in the *Public Advertiser*, "the employing, or attempting to employ the Indians in America in our Service . . . is a reigning Subject of Conversation."[49] Because the plan consisted of an arduous journey from Canada through the New York wilderness, the North ministry viewed Indian allies as essential.[50] After all, this was the same region in which they had played such a crucial role in the Seven Years War, when the French had successfully used allied Indians to devastate the British frontier and isolate besieged British garrisons.

Although the Indians in Burgoyne's company did not cause devastation on par with that dealt by those who had fought with the French two decades earlier, the uproar in Britain surpassed the public outrage expressed from that time. The Indians who rallied to the British flag in 1777 were small in number in comparison to the support the French had been able to muster, and the colonists in the American army were far better prepared for wilderness warfare than the British troops had been in the last war. Nevertheless, Burgoyne and his superiors expected that public warnings of British readiness to unleash a "horde" of Indian warriors on the frontier communities would terrorize the colonists into submission. In June, Burgoyne distributed a proclamation that exaggerated the number of Indians in his company and threatened to unleash them on the civilian population. The press picked up on his intimidation tactics. As the *London Chronicle,* which printed the proclamation in full—as did most newspapers and magazines—explained, Burgoyne's move "was, doubtless, well calculated to intimidate and strike a general panic through the northern colonies; they had experienced the like in the late war; it was particularly dreaded, and, in the early stages of rebellion, would have produced instant submission."[51] However, as the *London Chronicle* and a host of others also recognized, the proclamation backfired. Instead of submitting, the apprehensive colonists seemingly flocked by the thousands to swell the ranks of the American army that ultimately defeated Burgoyne. As the vehemently pro-coercion *Edinburgh Advertiser* complained, the proclamation had only "inflamed the minds of the colonists; and giving them fresh cause for disgust, had nerved the arm of the contest with double vigour, by joining the moderate to the violent, and rousing every individual to resistance."[52]

Burgoyne's proclamation also backfired on the North ministry at home. The threat in his proclamation that "I have but to give stretch to the Indian forces under my direction, and they amount to thousands, to overtake the hardened enemies of Great Britain" was abhorred by the British public. As the *Annual Register* for 1777 dryly remarked, "this conduct was far from being generally approved at home."[53] The *London Evening Post* printed a scathing condemnation, noting that Indian allies were known to be uncontrollable savages in war: "It is an undoubted fact (says a correspondent) acknowledged by all who have served in America, that the Savages kill all they meet with. . . . Further it must be observed, the number of regulars appointed to restrain the impetuosity and barbarity of these Savages, is often not sufficient to govern or deter them from murdering in cold blood those who have laid down their arms, and surrendered." In consequence of such widely held knowledge, it concluded, "those who issue such sanguinary order, or connive them at all" are just as guilty, if not more so, as the Indians themselves.[54]

FIGURE 8.1. "The Allies, Par nobile Fratrum!" (February 1780). This print condemns Britain's alliances with American Indians. In it Lord North shares a cannibalistic meal of a child colonist with a group of American Indians, while William Markham, archbishop of York, brings boxes of tomahawks, scalping knives, and crucifixes. In the background the banner declaring George III as "Defender of the Faith" is in shreds, and a bible is turned upside down. Sickened by the sight, a starving dog vomits in the center foreground. BMC 5631, © Copyright the Trustees of the British Museum.

The most poignant portrayal of Indians' perceived inability, or unwillingness, to discriminate between friend and foe was the highly publicized death of Jane McRea, a loyalist engaged to an officer in Burgoyne's army. Although the circumstances of her death remain unclear, the British public, like most colonists, readily assigned full blame to the untameable ferocity of the Indians in Burgoyne's army.[55] The *Annual Register* for 1777, for instance, highlighted it as a particularly distressing example that "struck every breast with horror." It continued, "Every circumstance of this horrid transaction served to render it more calamitous and afflicting . . . the young lady is represented to have been in all the innocence of youth, and bloom of beauty. Her father was said to be deeply interested in the royal cause; and to wind up the catastrophe of this odious tragedy, she was to have been married to a British officer on the very day that she was massacred."[56]

Adding further fuel to readers' disapproval was a highly publicized exchange of letters between Burgoyne and Horatio Gates, the commander of the American army opposing the British advance. Even the fervently pro-ministry *Scots Magazine* printed the letters under the heading "Indian barbarity."[57] Gates blamed Burgoyne personally for the murder of this "young lady, lovely to the sight, of virtuous character" who was "dressed to receive her promised husband, but met her murderer employed by you." Gates also threatened to shame Burgoyne at home, demonstrating both the known propaganda value of the incident and the power of the press. "That savages of America should in their warfare, mangle and scalp the unhappy prisoners who fall into their hands, is neither new nor extraordinary," declared Gates, "but that the famous Lt-Gen. Burgoyne, in whom the fine gentleman is united with the soldier and the scholar, should hire the savages of America to scalp Europeans, and the descendants of Europeans; nay more, that he should pay a price for each scalp so barbarously taken; is more than will be believed in Europe, until authenticated facts shall, in every gazette, confirm the truth of the horrid deed." Burgoyne's publicized response to Gates was to deny any atrocities committed by Indians in his army and to offer the implausible explanation that McRea's death was an accident arising from a quarrel between two Indians over which individual would have the honor of protecting her. In the struggle she had accidentally been killed, claimed Burgoyne, and hence he had given the men pardons. Burgoyne also noted his "desire and demand" of Gates that "should it [Gates's letter] appear in print at all, this answer may follow it." Both Gates and the British press honoured this request, but it did Burgoyne little good.

The controversy surrounding the campaign's inclusion of Indians provoked heavily publicized criticism in Parliament, too, peaking on February 6, 1778, with the speech of Edmund Burke. Rising to his feet late that night in the House of Commons to hold forth for three and a half hours, Burke harshly condemned ministerial invitations to the Indians, declaring that they could not be rewarded in the usual British manner: "The Indians of America had not titles, sinecure places, lucrative government pensions, or red ribbons, to bestow on those who signalized themselves in the field; their rewards were generally received in human scalps, human flesh, and gratification arising from torturing, mangling, scalping, and sometimes eating their captives of war." According to Burke, this was no way to regain the affection of disgruntled colonists, and it certainly was no way to treat one's own countrymen.[58] Although spectators had been cleared from the galleries, highlights of Burke's speech were printed in newspapers throughout the country. The *Stamford Mercury* summarized the experience for its readers:

Burke rose and "began with an awful solemnity to prepare their minds, and incline them to adopt his sentiments and join him in his endeavours to make the House sensible as he was of the many barbarities which he said had been committed during the war in America." After "describing the savage ungovernable rage of the Indians let loose upon the unarmed, the aged, the infant, and helpless female; he painted them rioting in murder, lust, and rapine," and then he "inveighed most bitterly on those who by authorizing a treaty with barbarians may be justly deemed the authors of the calamities which attended the unhuman measure." In so doing, the paper explained, "[The North] Administration, Lord Dunmore, and General Burgoyne, were placed upon the carpet."[59]

Although Burke's motion condemning the ministry was soundly defeated in the House of Commons due to North's majority, the press hailed the speech as Burke's best ever. The *Public Advertiser* asserted that "It is agreed on all Sides, that Mr. Burke's Speech, on moving for an Inquiry about employing Savages . . . was the best and most fancif'l he ever delivered." Charles James Fox wrote in his diary entry for that day that Burke's wit "made North, Rigby, and Ministers laugh; his pathos drew tears down Barré's cheeks."[60] In the House of Commons itself, Colonel Barré called for the speech to be posted on the church doors under the injunctions of the bishops for a fast. George Johnstone declared that "he rejoiced there were no strangers [spectators] in the gallery, as Burke's speech would have excited them to tear the ministers to pieces as they went out of the house."[61]

Although the image of Hessian mercenaries scouring the American countryside for plunder is one of the most enduring popular impressions of the American Revolution, it is also largely false. Troops from Hessen-Kassel constituted the largest single contingent, but the 30,000 German troops who served in America also came from five other states. Moreover, they were not mercenaries in the manner of Friedrich Wilhelm Augustin, Baron von Steuben, who was instrumental in training Washington's army at Valley Forge, and the host of other European adventurers who sought to take advantage of the dearth of experienced officers serving Congress. Although often referred to as "mercenaries," the German soldiers employed in the British war effort were auxiliaries—regiments with their own officers whom the British government rented wholesale from German rulers. Nevertheless, in the British public discussion in the press, German auxiliaries came to symbolize what was wrong with the British war effort: lack of public support, poor leadership, and bad tactics. Important to note, however, is that almost all of the criticism bemoaned their necessity rather than calling for

FIGURE 8.2. "A Hessian Grenadeir" (August 1778). This satirical print pokes fun at the German troops' reputation for plunder. Standing at attention, the grenadier is weighed down with booty. BMC 5483, © Copyright the Trustees of the British Museum.

their dismissal. After all, the alternatives were either to accept the loss of the colonies without much of a fight or to send more Britons to that undesirable theater of war. The public consensus as expressed in the press, therefore, did not fully share Congress's declared abhorrence at the use of foreign troops. As were the cases with the inclusion of slaves and Indians, the type and strength of British objections to the employment of Germans were decidedly British in scope and content. Commentary in the press was neither a mirror nor merely a response to American discussions, and this further underlines the high degree of independence and uniqueness of the British domestic experience of the conflict.

Despite British and American complaints, the British government's decision to employ German auxiliaries in the war effort was hardly unorthodox. All of the major European powers had relied on them in the eighteenth century, and the practice was centuries old by the time of the American Revolution.[62] During the American Revolution, the Dutch, although at war with Britain, had a Scottish corps in its pay, and the French expeditionary force to America included German troops. The East India Company also actively recruited in Germany for soldiers. The British government was a major customer for the auxiliary trade during this period; Hessian soldiers had even fought for Britain at the battle of Culloden in 1746, which ended another rebellion against a reigning British monarch.[63] Germans had also been on British soil in the Seven Years War to help deter a French invasion. In the great struggle against Revolutionary France and Napoleon that followed, German soldiers, either by outright rental or through enormous alliance subsidies, numbered in the tens of thousands alongside British troops.

Centuries of intermittent warfare had forced German rulers to turn their states into the most heavily militarized places in Europe. Hessen-Kassel maintained an army in 1775 that was nearly the size of Britain's army at that time, although its population was only about 1/30 of Britain's. Even tiny states such as Anhalt-Zerbst, which had a population of about 20,000, still had armies of thousands of men—1,152 of which were rented to the British for service in America in April 1781.[64] Keeping such a large percentage of the able-bodied men in uniform was an impossible task for the German economies on their own, so rulers relied on renting troops in peacetime.[65] Moreover, extensive experience had made these soldiers, particularly those from Hessen-Kassel, some of the best in Europe. Although the ruling princes received the lion's share of the profits from the agreements, which regularly included so-called "blood money" clauses by which they gained additional funds in the event that his troops died, the individual soldiers benefited, too. The landgrave of Hessen-Kassel received just over nine pounds sterling per annum per soldier he provided to the British. Not surprisingly, he readily handed over 12,000 men, nearly half his army, for service in 1776 to the tune of an annual return of £110,000—roughly eleven times the value of the tea that colonists had dumped into Boston's harbor. The British government took on the responsibility of transporting and provisioning the soldiers. Because Britain paid the soldiers at the British rate, which was roughly three times their normal wages, the prospect of service in America was initially appealing.[66] Moreover, Germans had flooded into the British American colonies as immigrants for generations and prospered, leaving open the tantalizing possibility for poor German soldiers to stay once the war was over. And like many Britons, the Germans expected the war to be over quickly and with little fighting.[67] In consequence, the British had little trouble recruiting at the start of the war and by late spring of 1776 had a seemingly instant force of 20,000 German auxiliaries ready to crush the rebellion.

Most commentary and reporting in the press recognized that the British peacetime army, which was stretched thin across the burgeoning empire and reduced to a skeletal structure to save money, was not up to the task of a major military operation in America on its own. Moreover, reports of British soldiers in America deserting their posts were appearing almost daily in the press by the winter of 1774. Some commentators, such as a *Public Advertiser* reader who advocated replacing British soldiers in Boston with "Hanoverian Troops in British Pay," were discussing the necessity of foreign troops even before the First Continental Congress convened.[68] Letters from America that appeared in the British press before fighting began also anticipated the eventual arrival of German or Russian auxiliaries. Some letters, such as one from "a Gentleman of Military Distinction from Connecticut" that appeared in the *Saint James's Chronicle* in March 1775, even boasted that the colonists were so well prepared that they "need not blush to encounter an equal Number of Foreign Troops from any Quarter of the Globe."[69]

Early recruiting difficulties in Britain were highly publicized. American service was notoriously undesirable for British soldiers, particularly at a time when potential recruits were thought to have other economic opportunities. Stemming in no small part from the heavy press coverage of the Seven Years War, fighting in America was synonymous with scalping and other horrors.[70] As revealed in the popular 1776 ballad "Tears of the Footguards," which criticized the officers of the royal household regiments who had resigned their commissions when faced with service in America:

Protectress, Patroness of lilly Hands,
O interfere, and save me from those Lands
Where savage *Indians* thirst from human Blood,
And make Mankind their daily choicest Food.
O hear thy gentle Ensign's suppliant Strain,
I feel the Tomohawk within my Brain;
O spare me, modern *Venus,* hear my Pray'r,
And make my Terrors thy peculiar Care!
I can't support this bloody, civil Strife,
The very War-Hoops will destroy my life.[71]

Accounts of desertion among regiments in Britain appeared regularly in the press, as did stories of soldiers going to extreme measures to avoid service, such as a widely reprinted account of "a private soldier in the 36th regiment, now quartered in Salisbury [who] was, by order of a Court Martial, drumm'd out of the corps, for dismembering himself of his right thumb, lest he should be drafted for American service."[72] In response, most comment in the press accepted that employing German troops was the only viable option. As "Pacifius," a regular contributor to the *General Evening Post,* explained: "The upright and the honest will never scruple any expence to bring back the Colonies to their duty . . . If the actual force sent to America is not found to be sufficient, more Hessians, more Hanoverians, together with twenty or thirty thousand Russians, must make up the deficiencies." After all, "Pacifius" concluded, "The future greatness, or importance, of Old England is at stake."[73]

North's opponents in Parliament regularly used the ministry's reliance on Germans in 1776 and 1777 to highlight publicly the recruiting problems in Britain, declaring that they reflected a populace that was unhappy with the decision to go to war. As Sir Nathaniel Wraxall, who sat for the borough of Hindon in Wiltshire during the American Revolution, reflected privately at the war's conclusion, the employment of German auxiliaries, "though perhaps no more justly objects of moral or political condemnation than were the Swiss and German regiments permanently retained in the service of France, or the Scotch corps. then serving the pay of Holland, yet increased the popular awry and furnished the [parliamentary] Opposition subjects of obloquy and of declamation."[74] In the highly publicized House of Commons debates in 1776, opposition lords and members of Parliament let loose an array of quotable quips against foreign troops that translated into great press material. A particularly heated exchange at the end of February received

FIGURE 8.3. "Six-Pence a Day" (October 1775). This print emphasizes the undesirability of military service. Six pence was the daily pay of a private soldier, whereas the wages of the other workers illustrated were much higher—three shillings for a chairman, two shillings for a coachman, and one shilling for a chimney sweep. Moreover, a soldier faces dangerous service in America, depicted to the right, and his large family suffers due to his low wages. BMC 5295, © Copyright the Trustees of the British Museum.

close attention. In it Lord Cavendish called the decision to employ foreign troops "mortifying and humiliating" for Britain, and James Luttrell warned of the "danger" and stupidity of sending 16,000 poor and desperate Germans to a bountiful country that had previously enticed such people to settle and prosper. Surely, he argued, there would scarcely be a German left in the army within a year.[75] In a speech featured by papers across the country a week later, Lord Shelburne argued that if the ministry were correct in proclaiming a popular enthusiasm for the war, then it should have no difficulty raising British troops.[76] A letter from Philadelphia that appeared in the *Exeter Flying-Post* shared the sentiment and taunted the British for using foreign hirelings. "We are far from being dismayed at hearing that foreign mercenaries are hired to fight against us," the letter boasted, "[because] your

Administration have not prevalence enough among the inhabitants of Great Britain and Ireland to raise the quota of troops they intended to send over to subdue us."[77] Perhaps the most reprinted quip of the debates over foreign troops came from James Luttrell, who railed in March 1776: "Foreigners were to slaughter our oppressed Fellow-subjects in America. Foreigners are to fight our Battles, to protect our Coasts, to annoy our Enemies, to carry our Commerce, and to defend our Fortresses." He concluded with the darkest sarcasm: "Englishmen are too noble, too generous, too brave, too humane, to cut the Throats of Englishmen."[78]

During the early stages of the conflict, newspapers and magazines regularly printed commentary that concurred with the tenor of the opposition's remarks. As a reader of the *Saint James's Chronicle* observed, continental Europeans enjoyed so few liberties because their absolutist rulers kept foreign mercenaries in constant pay in order to stifle any opposition. The ministry's decision to employ German troops in America, the reader's letter concluded, revealed their minister's tyrannical "designs for the future."[79] Other critics expressed sympathy for the soldiers themselves, likening the soldiers, not the colonists, to African slaves. The *Stamford Mercury* described the practice as German princes "selling their subjects to carry war and destruction to the other side of the Atlantic," and after printing a table breaking down the number and origin of German troops to be used in the 1776 campaigns, the *Exeter Flying-Post* attacked the exchange of cash for soldiers, remarking, "Is not this very like the very business on the coast of Africa called the slave trade?"[80]

Most printed commentary, however, expressed little sympathy and much hostility toward the German troops, who were often portrayed as cruel drones in search of plunder. The Germans suffered throughout the war from a largely undeserved reputation as voracious pillagers who had little regard for civilian rights.[81] Descriptions of the Germans troops as "cutthroats" and "murdering hirelings" abounded, as did false reports of them slaughtering surrendering prisoners. After all, complained a reader of the *Saint James's Chronicle,* only an immoral man could accept such a service: "What god they must worship to be able to slaughter those who are innocent of any offense direct to them."[82] In consequence, most accounts of German troops harassing rebel and loyalist civilians received credit in the press. Although admitting that some of Congress-backed accounts of German "rapes, rapine, cruelty and murder" were "exaggerated," the *Annual Register* readily accepted many of them, depicting the auxiliaries as "naturally fierce and cruel, ignorant of any rights but those of despotism, and of any manners, but those established within the narrow precinct of their own government,

incapable of forming any distinction between ravaging and destroying
an enemy's country."[83] The *Annual Register* was notorious for taking every
opportunity to attack the North ministry, but even the usually supportive
Morning Post printed a lengthy anecdote—in order to demonstrate the
problem of "employing foreigners"—in which a young loyalist surgeon was
taken prisoner and almost killed due to the Hessians' inability to distinguish
loyalists from rebels.[84] Such coverage emphasized that the German troops,
while European and civilized, were still outsiders to the Anglo-American
quarrel, and critics regularly informed readers that such behavior carried
dire consequences for the war effort. After remarking in February 1778 that
"the Germans have not forgone their old trade of plundering . . . fore they
plunder friends and foes indiscriminately, the *Gazetteer* warned that such
practices would push more colonists to the rebel cause. "This behavior has
so incensed the people," it railed, "that the Congress will compleat their 85
battalions with ease."[85] Moreover, tension also existed with British forces.
Representative of numerous reports that appeared in the press, a letter first
printed in the *Public Advertiser* from an anonymous British officer in New
York complained that "German Affection to their Property (as they style it)"
slowed the movement of British forces and made them easy targets for the
rebel forces. The consequence, he concluded, was "a Lack of cordial Goodwill and Plenty of Jealousy" between all of the British and German troops.[86]

In the earliest years of the conflict, German troops simply could not
measure up to the admiration expressed for the citizen-soldiers Congress
commanded. Britain was, after all, a nation that shared with the American
colonists a tradition of abhorring standing armies and adulating militias. Although the British had abandoned this heritage in practice, they had not entirely released their respect for it. In consequence, the tactical effectiveness
of German auxiliaries also came under scrutiny from the start. Early complaints about expense—such as the *Saint James's Chronicle's* calculation that
17,300 foreign troops cost as much as 35,000 British troops—appeared
throughout the press, grating against the cost-conscious disposition of much
of the reading public.[87] Before the British vanquished Washington's forces
from New York in 1776—when British estimates in the press of the American citizen-soldier were at their height—many commentators doubted the
viability of foreign troops. As a reader of the *London Packet* remarked, "It is
the Observation of a great Philosopher and Politician, that a whole nation,
fighting for itself, is more powerful than ten Armies of ten Kings. . . . This is
the exact Situation of North America," the reader concluded, and thus "the
Vigour of Opposition and Defence in these People will be ten Times
stronger than all the Attacks of mercenary Troops hired to subdue them."[88]

Even after the German auxiliaries had proven their mettle at the battle of Long Island—for which they received scant praise in the British press—their alleged shortcomings remained subjects for derision and ridicule. The surprise defeat of the Hessian garrison at Trenton on Christmas Day 1776 fueled particular public concern. *Lloyd's Evening Post* was one of their few apologists, noting that the battalions at Trenton "were twice thanked (in orders) for their good behaviour during the late campaign."[89] Most papers spewed vicious criticism, such as the *Morning Post,* which implied cowardice in its assessment of the battle: "The Hessians in the late affair at Trenton have lost all the credit they gained at Long Island, for we have it from very good authority, that the battalions who were made prisoners only fired two rounds, and that with no small reluctance, and then threw down their arms." In the immediate aftermath of the British surrender at Saratoga, the German troops were again among the earliest targets for blame in the press. While describing British troops as heroic and their commander as "gallant," newspapers depicted the German troops as soft targets whom the American rebels habitually singled out.

Discussions in the British press about German troops all but ceased after the shift to the global war in the spring of 1778, when American victory appeared likely and escalation of the war with France's entry seemed imminent. Yet, the absence of comment on German troops after 1778 does not necessarily cast doubt on the sincerity of earlier complaints that appeared in the press. More likely the change reflects the larger shift in perceptions of the global war that the American Revolution had become. When the global conflict stripped space away from coverage of the American theater, many one-time important worries undoubtedly seemed increasingly ethereal. After all, complaints about the Germans had focused on the embarrassment of their necessity and the degree of their value to the British war effort. Few commentators advocated withdrawing them entirely or canceling the subsidy treaties with their princes. Therefore, even though the image of the German soldier was never fully rehabilitated during the conflict, it mattered less and less to a reading public far more concerned with preserving the empire and protecting Britain from invasion than the efficacy of using foreign troops to quell an overseas rebellion. Not until the end of the war did German troops receive anything resembling sustained coverage; at that time discussion centered on whether or not earlier predictions that they would settle in America would prove true. Like most commentary at the war's end, *Ruddiman's Weekly Mercury* [Edinburgh] concluded in November 1782 that the British decision to employ German auxiliaries would ultimately work to America's benefit, asserting that "the employment of so many German troops in America, from different parts of the empire, will be attended with one effect very favourable to that country. It will be the means of adding much to its populations, by the emigrations that will take place on a peace." Moreover, it declared, "this is an example that will doubtless be followed by the oppressed and half-ruined inhabitants of most arbitrary countries."[90] Most German soldiers did not return home, either as a result of desertion in order to stay in America or, more commonly, because they had died.[91]

That the press coverage of the American Revolution included a lengthy consideration of which tools could be ethically used to wage war in America is quite remarkable. Such considerations had occasionally entered into public discussions in past conflicts but not to the extent that they did during the American Revolution. During the Seven Years War, accounts of slaughtered enemies met with barely a hint of sympathy in the British press, and while the German troops were not popular when stationed in Britain, hardly anyone complained about using them to campaign against their enemies in Europe. British public concerns about the use of non-British combatants against the American rebels thus ultimately further exposes both how the nation understood the conflict to be inherently different and the widespread desire for a limited war. Expressions of reluctance to employ Germans and the outright condemnation of Indian alliances were virtually universal in the press. North supporters and apologists for these practices excused the government's actions almost entirely on grounds of necessity. No one publicly hailed the moves as masterstrokes. The opposition stemmed from a mixture of pragmatic concerns and, especially in the case of Indian alliances, moral outrage. The British public wanted victory in America but clearly not at all costs.

Equally significant, British discussions in the press about the use of slaves, Indians, and foreign soldiers further reveal national attitudes toward these groups themselves. Germans soldiers, although accepted as most like their British counterparts, were universally looked down upon as subjects of less enlightened societies. Depicted predominately as impoverished drones compelled to follow their rulers' bidding without regard to the moral consequences or the justness of the cause was anathema to the newspaper-reading British public, who reveled in a free press and relentlessly critiqued their own government. Although black slaves were the largest group of participants with grievances cited against them in the Declaration of Independence, they received far less attention than foreign troops and Indians in the press. In consequence, attempting to derive national opinions from such little evidence is impossible. Nevertheless, the lack of discussion underlines the argument that the wider British populace did not yet take issue with slavery —at least not to the extent that they were willing to accept the cost that reducing or eliminating it would carry—despite being well informed about it. The British press did not erupt with cheers for Dunmore's proclamation as a blow against the inhumanity of human bondage. Perhaps most striking is the disdain with which the wider British public regarded the Indians. The British press depicted Indians as cruel, martial figures and gave scant consideration to other aspects of Indian society. This had been part of the British heritage of the close press coverage of the Seven Years War in North America, and British war strategy in the American Revolution only encouraged this narrow representation. Not surprisingly, virtually no one complained when, at the conclusion of the war, the Indians, unlike the slaves and German auxiliaries who received at least some formal consideration and compensation from the belligerent nations, were abandoned wholesale by their British allies to the unforgiving citizens of the new American Republic.[92]

Allies or Foes, Republic or Anarchy?

DIVINING AMERICA'S FUTURE

✳ In September 1783, following over eight years of civil war between Britain and most of its mainland American colonies, the *Derby Mercury* posed a question that must have been in the minds of many of its readers: now that peace had been formalized and American independence finally settled, what would the former colonists do with it? The *Mercury*, like most newspapers and magazines, offered little in the way of definitive predictions, choosing instead to frame, rather than to answer, the question: "A Short Period will now discover whether the extraordinary Benefits proposed by the Americans from the Acquisition of Independence, will actually be realized to their country."[1] The United States was charting new territory, and contemporary commentators in the British press recognized this. In consequence, bold predictions were far more rare than cautionary tales when it came to divining America's prospects and the future of Anglo-American relations.

Almost no one in the press publicly accepted the Americans as unequivocal victors in the war. At the end of the war passing shots at the Americans appeared regularly, such as the widely reprinted letter from "A Veteran," who remarked, "Congress and Washington did not defeat Cornwallis, but rather it was the French army and navy."[2] Thus the American case against British tyranny—in favor of independence and for republicanism—had not been proven in the public arena of the press. Congress had not won because of the virtue of its cause, the consensus of comment concluded; rather Britain had grown weary, and the combined powers of France and Spain had raised the stakes beyond what most Britons were ready to gamble. As has been revealed in the previous chapters, the case for republicanism as embodied in Congress had been demonstrated to be morally lacking in the British public sphere by the end of the war. Few commentators openly admired the colonists for their victory or took it as a sign of British deficiency. According to the popular perception as depicted in the press, the greatest challenges to Britain's position had been posed by its ancient enemies, France and Spain, and, as the events of 1782 made clear, Britain passed these tests. Thus when the war ended the Hanoverian monarchy was more secure than ever, the Bourbons remained enemy number one, and popular interest in the empire and the benefits it might bring had not been soured.

When predictions for the future of Anglo-American relations and the success of the new American republic became a significant part of the national discourse at the war's conclusion, they did not emanate from a reading public who had been cowed by the conflict or shamed by the righteousness of the American cause. This was not a time of national despair or panic: Britain had, after all, successfully preserved its empire elsewhere. The public discussion mostly took place in a space of perceived national security and, therefore, was at least as self-assured as at any time since the conflict began. Thus, soul-searching and demands for massive imperial reform were not on the national agenda in the press. Even at its height in the last years of the war, the discussion about the Anglo-American future was far less intense than coverage of major campaigns or such topics as employing American Indians, the possibility of French invasion, and the actions of the first Congress. This ultimately explains why the later, long-term economic and political changes in Britain during the late eighteenth and early nineteenth centuries that historians have partly attributed to the American Revolution were not the immediate consequences of any groundswell of public agitation in the aftermath of defeat.

Commonly expressed assumptions in the press about the security of the empire and the continued threat of the Bourbon powers shaped the tenor of the British public's examination of the future of Anglo-American relations and the American republic in the press. Commerce was central to the public discussion. After all, before the war the colonies had been Britain's primary overseas market, and British merchants were anxious to see this relationship renewed. Those who accepted the emerging arguments of free trade were far more optimistic than those who associated territorial control with economic prosperity. Free traders were also more likely to assert the continued cultural similarities between the two countries, claiming that this would give the British an advantage over the French, whom most agreed posed the greatest danger to the mending of the Anglo-American relationship. In terms of the possibilities for Congress maintaining a functioning republic, hardly any comment gave it even the slimmest of chances. Britons' own history of experiments in republicanism in the seventeenth century had ingrained a pessimism that assumed outcomes of military takeovers, oppressive oligarchies, and anarchy. Yet the overwhelming consensus in the press, regardless of outlook, agreed that the American situation was ultimately unpredictable. Only time, readers and editors remarked again and again, would tell.

The long-term future of the America colonies had been a topic of discussion even before the American Revolution. Throughout the seventeenth and eighteenth centuries, British commentators had contemplated the future of the colonies, wondering whether and for how long Britain could maintain supremacy over them.[3] Others openly questioned if holding onto the colonies was in the nation's best interest, given that the growth of the colonies might ultimately shift the balance of power in the English-speaking world to the other side of the Atlantic and turn Britain into the junior partner. At the start of the war, Britons echoed many of these long-standing concerns. As the widely reprinted petition to the king signed by nine hundred Bristolians made clear, the vastness of America's size called for a peaceable conclusion, because, the petitioners explained, "[we] are convinced, from clear reason and severe experience, that [British] superiority, can hardly be preserved by mere force."[4] Adam Smith concluded in *The Wealth of Nations* that Britain would ultimately benefit from an independent America not only on the grounds of his standard free trade arguments but also because the rapid growth of America meant that the seat of power would otherwise move there in the next century.[5] The discussion in the press carried an abundance of commentary that concurred with this line of thinking, particularly in pieces that asserted the futility of the war. Although more elaborate than most, the *Saint James's Chronicle* in July 1776 was typical in its assessment of a careful breakdown of global populations by continent and country, claiming that Britain was a mere 1/50 of the size of British America. This, the piece concluded, "amounts to a Proof of the utter Impossibility of our ever subjugating the Americans."[6] As the conflict progressed, the theme of America's size surfaced with regularity, especially as Britons increasingly accepted the loss of the colonies as inevitable.

This is not to suggest that a majority of Britons expected defeat from the start. Plenty of commentary in the press remarked on postwar settlements that assumed Britain as the victor. During the winter of 1776, following the sweeping British success the previous autumn, editors and readers alike offered estimates of the number of troops needed for postwar occupation and called for stronger British control.[7] Yet beyond a loosely held consensus that the postwar occupation would require a "substantial" number of troops and that British executive authority in colonial governments would need to be stronger, commentary on the postwar Anglo-American relationship lacked cohesion and received scant coverage. Circulating pamphlets proposed elaborate plans for solving the British Atlantic's woes through such measures as a metamorphosis of Parliament into an imperial legislature with global delegations or the voluntary lopping off of America into a second British Empire akin to Byzantium, but such proposals, even on the rare occasions when extracts appeared in the press, provoked little discussion.

The acute imbalance in the press discussion in favor of assumptions of an independent postwar America resulted in overwhelming frustration with the war effort that characterized much of the press's coverage of the war. Pessimism for Britain's chances in America reigned, and predictions of success were panned except during a few brief windows. Frustration with the Howes' inability to vanquish the rebels once and for all in 1777, the surrenders at Saratoga later that year and Yorktown in 1781, and the length of the war in general meant that virtually every newspaper eventually professed the inevitability of American independence. Echoing years of commentary in other papers, the *London Packet,* at times a venue for some of the most hawkish commentary, admitted in the autumn of 1781, as the nation tensely waited for definitive news of the fate of the British army at Yorktown, that the outcome mattered little in the long run. The conflict had already revealed that an unwilling America could not be governed by Britain. "What an unhappy war is the present," it concluded, "wherein victory cannot insure success?"[8] When the time finally came for a sensible, sustained discussion in the press about the post-war future, it was late in the war—after even the government had publicly accepted the loss of the colonies. The initially hesitant tenor and eventually late timing of the discussion in the press underlines the lack of public confidence in the war. Whether supporting or opposing the case for prosecuting the war, the press coverage for all but a handful of brief periods largely assumed that Britain would not win, or at least that the colonies would not be brought back into the imperial fold on terms akin to their pre-war status.

The most detailed discussion in the press emerged in the later years of the war, when British defeat—and with it American independence—seemed inevitable to even the hardened proponents of the war. As detailed in previous chapters, the discussion in the British press clearly indicates that British acceptance of defeat came mainly in two waves: first, in the winter of 1777/8, following the surrender of the British army at Saratoga and France's entry on the side of Congress, and second, and with greater finality, following the arrival of news of the surrender of Lord Cornwallis and his army at Yorktown in the autumn of 1781. The vast majority of commentary about the future of North America, however, came in or after the second wave, and not until late in 1781 was there a sustained discussion in the press about postwar Anglo-American relations and the future of the American republic. At least in terms of long-term planning, the British public was not prepared to discuss the consequences of total separation, which suggests that many readers and editors retained hope after 1778 that some sort of accommodation short of independence might be reached (a hope that Yorktown apparently crushed). To be sure, newspapers and magazines in 1778 carried plenty of pieces melodramatically declaring the destruction of the British Empire and the consequent ruin of the British nation, but this material was more about complaining than forecasting. Although not without plenty of dissenters, the consensus of commentary was favorable with regard to the future of Anglo-American relations.

Nevertheless, pessimistic commentary about postwar Anglo-American relations was not in short supply. It abounded from all angles and in all geographies. Former proponents of conciliation declared that all their early warnings about the loss of trade and continued belligerent relations were about to come true. America, many declared, would be the "new Carthage," rivaling Britain militarily and economically. American tobacco, timber, wheat, rice, indigo, and more were all gone, they wailed. Even the fur trade would soon be lost as Americans swarmed westward, despite Britain's retention of Canada. "Thanks to the framers of the peace," who ceded much of the interior to the United States, complained *Ruddiman's Weekly Mercury* of Edinburgh, "the fur trade of Canada must necessarily be so small in future, that it really will not deserve the name of trade."[9] The inevitable consequence they universally depicted was national decline. In July 1783 the *Edinburgh Magazine* offered readers a lengthy comparison of Britain at the conclusion of the Seven Years War in 1763 to the current year. Representative of the pessimistic sentiment that appeared throughout the press, the magazine concluded that the unhappy contrast was obvious: "When we turn our eyes to the political state of this country in the present moment, this first reflection that occurs, is a painful comparison of what it so lately was, with what it now is. . . . In no other empire has humiliation so quickly succeeded to glory."[10] The loss of the mainland American colonies, the magazine and other commentators contended in an eighteenth-century domino theory, would reverberate through the empire, which they depicted as being bound together by trade. First the economies of West Indian islands that relied on American grain and markets would collapse, followed by the African slave trade that provided the West Indies with labor, and finally the East Indies, which relied on imperial markets for its cotton and tea trade. The best that could be hoped, the *Edinburgh Magazine* fretted in the next month's issue, was that the process would be slow. "Though without a spirit of prophecy, one may reasonably conclude, that Great Britain is past the zenith of her glory," the magazine admitted. "Yet," it offered as a kind of solace, "as the natural sun does not set immediately after shining . . . but descends by slow and silent, but resistless steps,—so it is to be hoped that the sun of Great Britain's glory, though just past the meridian, is not to disappear for ever."[11]

Another commonly expressed concern focused on emigration. The flow of people to the mainland colonies had been a subject of increasing worry in Britain during the 1760s and 1770s that the war had only temporarily hushed, and the widespread acceptance of American victory and independence served to reignite the debate in the last years of the conflict.[12] For pessimists, it signposted the nation's decline. Although nothing on a par with the mass emigration that characterized most of the nineteenth century after 1830, the flow of people from the British Isles on the eve of the war was substantial, particularly outside of England. More than 40,000 emigrants left Ulster ports in Ireland between 1768 and 1774, and as much as 3 percent of Scotland's population emigrated to America in the decade before the Revolution.[13] Many commentators in the press in the waning years of the war feared that this loss of manpower was a mere trickle that would quickly turn into a flood as the peoples of the British Isles raced to America in search of economic opportunities. Reports of German troops and British regulars remaining in America in large numbers, along with the often exaggerated descriptions of American government incentives, appeared regularly in virtually all of the British newspapers, and hardly any editors bothered to print dissenting accounts. Soon, most printed commentary agreed, civilians would follow the soldiers' lead. Such a loss of crucial manpower led to many laments in the press. As *Ruddiman's Weekly Mercury* concluded, "Emigrations from England, Scotland, and Ireland to America will be one of the heaviest blows this country received."[14]

Such public concerns ultimately reflected the mercantilist belief that emigration diminished the stature of one nation only to add directly to the wealth of another. One commentator even went so far as to calculate that the direct cost of each emigrant to Britain was ten pounds per annum in lost national earnings (£1.50 of which was lost tax revenue).[15] Such figures fostered anxiety. As a reader of the *Saint James's Chronicle* declared as the war concluded, "Let the Hours of Peace but once arrive and England, it is to be feared, will be bereft of one Sixteenth part of the Island's Population. And of Course," the reader grumbled, "those who remain in their native Country will be burthened one Sixteenth part more of the national debt."[16] Of particular concern was who would be emigrating: shipbuilders "discharged from the king's yards" at the war's end, the demobilized soldiers—"the number of 80,000 or 100,000" men "will most of them report to America," warned the *Stamford Mercury*. Worse still, it continued, the heavy tax burden left over from the war "will force innumerable multitudes of starving manufacturers likewise to seek a milder government [in America], in the article so essential to them, that of light taxation."[17]

Also worrying was that America's assets and infrastructure, which the British had worked so long to cultivate, would benefit their rival, France. Rumors of American coziness and even subordination to French interests abounded throughout the war, thanks in no small part to loyalist propaganda in American newspapers that made their way across the Atlantic. The extent to which British readers believed stories that Congress had ceded Rhode Island to France or that Philadelphians were celebrating the birth of the Dauphin "with great joy and festivity"—as reported in the loyalist press—is impossible to determine, but the message to those inclined to believe at least the tenor of the claims, if not their specificities, is clear.[18] As the *Morning Post* typically stated, "it is obvious they [colonists] have virtually become the subjects of France."[19] And for those of the mercantilist mind-set who advocated political control as a means of securing and extending commerce, French influence could only increase at the expense of British trade. The consequence of a postwar Franco-American trading alliance would have been nothing short of a disaster in the minds of these readers, who had been schooled by the press for nearly three decades that, in the words of the *Whitehall Evening Post* at the start of the last war in American in 1755, "whatever Nation remains sole Master of North America, must, in Consequence of that Acquisition, give Law in Europe."[20] As the *Public Advertiser* declared in 1778, "If France should obtain an exclusive Trade to America . . . she will be the most potent and opulent Power on the Globe, commercially considered."[21]

Far outweighing such negative predictions, however, were the more positive assessments, which heavily emphasized the continued cultural ties and the advantages of free trade. These optimists continually stressed that, despite the war, the British and Americans remained kin. This viewpoint had been a key part of the public discussion of the Atlantic empire since the Seven Years War and shaped the prevailing rhetoric of the major sides.[22] Virtually everyone agreed that the Americans were fellow nationalists, but they disagreed over the benefits and obligations the relationship entailed. As chronicled throughout this book, the idea of a shared culture was powerful at the outset of the conflict and endured throughout it—from the earliest petitions to the king calling for conciliation to the charities that raised funds for American prisoners of war. Britain's colonists in America, almost everyone agreed, were inherently different from the subjects that European empires, such as the Spanish, claimed dominion over. A piece in the *Salisbury Journal* remarked in October 1781 to news of uprisings in Spanish colonies that the Spanish subjects were justified in their actions, because they were "natives" who had been "subdued and cruelly oppressed by the Spaniards. . . . On the other hand," the article continued, Britain's American subjects were the benefactors of liberty and benevolence. "Thus," it concluded, "the Indians are seeking to shake off the yoke of slavery, but the North-Americans are like ungrateful children, who rebel against their parents."[23] Even the loyalists' calls in the press for continued British assistance relied heavily on the notions that the silent majority of colonists remained loyal countrymen and that Britons had an obligation to assist their beleaguered brethren.

Such ties, numerous readers' letters and editors' comments asserted throughout the country, ultimately mattered more to the Americans than the temporary convenience of an expedient French alliance. "[W]e have already established on a firm footing on the continent of America . . . ," a widely reprinted letter argued, "I mean language; to which add the strongest of nations—religion, laws and manners." The "particular connection by blood," the letter concluded would win out over "party spirit . . . [and] form a more advantageous intercourse than if the American States had still continued subjects to the British Crown."[24] The bitterness of war, many readers remarked in the press, would be temporary. As the *Morning Herald* summarized, "Time brings changes. American hatred against British subjects will subside."[25] Even the king, who had been personally insulted by the Declaration of Independence and chafed at the idea of American independence, was a visible promoter of this perspective. In his almost universally reprinted early December speech in 1782 opening Parliament, he publicly declared that the hostilities had ended. He professed that he ended the war reluctantly, bluntly stating that in admitting American independence, "I have sacrificed every consideration of my own to the wishes and opinions of my people." Yet hopefulness for the future characterized his highly publicized concluding remarks; independence was not the end, because "Religion—language—interest—affections—may, and I hope will yet prove a bond of permanent union between the two countries."[26]

The focus of such optimism was almost exclusively on renewed trade. Few in the press doubted the finality of the political settlement in which the former colonies emerged as an independent, foreign state, and hardly anyone expressed expectations of any sort of military alliance or that the colonies would one day return to the fold of the British Empire; however, the consensus of opinion in the press was equally accepting of the notion that America was a paramount component of the British economy. In consequence, newspapers in London and other port cities such as Bristol and Glasgow carried readers' rejoicings at the prospect of a return to peacetime Atlantic trade. Soon, the *Morning Post* declared with optimism at the end of 1782, "The Effects of peace will be very suddenly felt in this metropolis, by the immediate influx of foreigners and Americans, which pleasure, curiosity, and business would draw over."[27] Even in landlocked Oxford, the local paper remarked that merchants were "in high spirits, and many cargoes are now getting ready for the American market."[28]

Optimism with regard to Anglo-American trade generally emphasized the free trade thinking exemplified in Smith's recently published *Wealth of Nations*. Although hardly precise adherents to Smith's economic philosophy, commentators regularly asserted that Americans would make rational choices about trade, and such thinking would inevitably lead them to Britain, whose economy already fit advantageously with theirs. As a Scottish reader remarked, political animosity would not "prevent the people of Virginia, Maryland, and Carolina, from sending part of their tobacco and rice to England, if they can get a better part for their articles than in France."[29] History proved them right, as Anglo-American trade quickly accelerated beyond pre-war levels. Somewhat less accurate were publicly stated hopes that Britain could use free trade to subjugate an independent America into economic dependency and, hence, into a client state. As the *Gazetteer* argued as early as 1778 in a piece outlining the reasons for ending the war, American political divisions and America's "continued indebtedness to Europe for most of those articles which, to civilized nations, are reckoned even among the necessities of life" would prevent any genuine separation from Britain.[30] Thus, the piece concluded, admitting military defeat would ultimately yield victory for Britain, because the colonists would be as dependent as ever. Although client status proved to be a chimera, trade between the two nations quickly recovered and exceeded pre-war levels, and the desire to maintain this trade significantly influenced the foreign policy of the American Federalist party, and thus the U.S. government through 1800, during the republic's infancy.[31]

Whether a postwar American republic would survive was a question often raised in the British press during the war. Although a subject that usually appeared whenever the forces of Congress seemed to have an upper hand, it received particular scrutiny once it seemed an inevitable reality in the wake of the British surrender at Yorktown. *Ruddiman's Weekly Mercury* plainly laid out the subject that had been circulating in various forms throughout the press: "America seems now to be brought back to first principles, and to be in little better, in point of government, than a state of nature." Calling the new republic "a monster without a head," the paper concluded that unifying and ruling America would not be easy; after all, "One thing only do all the Thirteen States agree in, which, that each is sovereign and independent."[32] The outlook, according to the vast majority of commentary in the press, was decidedly gloomy for Americans. Although a handful of commentators expressed hope for America's future, few expected a republic to last.

Some commentary was optimistic. Just as they had conveyed support for American complaints about British governance in the years leading up to the revolution, many radicals in Britain expressed hope for the new republic's future. America's success put parliamentary reform definitely on the political agenda for many Britons.[33] Although political reform even remotely akin to what Americans enjoyed was not realized in Britain until the 1830s, American success proved to many reformers that it could be accomplished, and, in consequence, American independence prompted more calls for radical reforms in the war's aftermath. The reform movements of the 1760s symbolized by John Wilkes and his supporters and the Association movement during the American Revolution had focused largely on relatively mild objectives, such as reducing property qualifications for voting and increasing the number of Parliament's county seats, which had larger constituencies and were not part of the corrupt "rotten boroughs" that the landed elite controlled. In the wake of the American Revolution, however, reformers became more ambitious, calling for universal male suffrage in a language decreasingly based on English constitutional rights and increasingly on the rights of men.[34]

Although apparent in the correspondence and pamphlets of British radicals, this optimism was barely evident in the wider newspaper and periodical press at the end of the war. A piece in the *Edinburgh Magazine* at the end of the conflict claiming that "The virtue of an infant state, and the enlightened policy of Congress, will guard, for the present," against the potential threats of corruption and usurpation, was rare indeed. Most favorable remarks in the press instead held America's imitation of Britain as its best hope of success. The *Saint James's Chronicle* remarked favorably in January 1783 on reports from Philadelphia describing work on a new legal system that will be "framed after the British model," adding that "rigid attention" would be reserved primarily for "concisement and perspicuity."[35] The *Derby Mercury* printed concurring observations the following month, noting that laws would be "founded in general on British Laws" and altered only as absolutely necessary to conform "to the new Appearance of things which the Revolution produced."[36] But even with such imitation, few readers and commentators professed much hope for the endurance of republican government in America.

Far more prevalent in the press were pessimistic assessments of the republic's chances. As a reader of the *General Evening Post* bluntly stated in a letter in October 1780: "the democracy now gaining ground in America, should terminate as democracies always have done, in an oligarchy."[37] Despite a strong tradition in the British press of critiquing the monarchy, aristocracy, and elitism in general, printed responses to democracy as it was speculated to take hold in America suggest a more cautious reading public than such criticisms otherwise reveal. Most comment in the press—whether from readers, regular contributors, or editors—concurred that faith in the general populace, upon which the American republic was presumed to rely, was wholly misplaced. After 1776, the press coverage overwhelmingly depicted America as run by petty despots who used the mob to terrorize the more moderate (and reasonable) middling sort. The readiness with which British readers and editors, who were comprised primarily of the emerging middle class, accepted this portrayal further underlines their fear of the laboring ranks. Of course, it was the shops, breweries, and mills owned by the middle class that typically fell victim to rioters in the eighteenth century, most recently in the Gordon Riots that ravaged London in 1780.[38] Thus it is not surprising that magazines and newspapers such as the *Edinburgh Magazine* explained, "The government of the American nations has dissolved into the hands of the people. The people, as in other countries, are narrow minded, short-sighted, revengeful, and cruel. . . . The better kind of Americans," ("better" carries a classist meaning here) the magazine concluded, will be "unable to restrain the rage of the populace."[39]

The other perceived great threat came from the military. George Washington's reputation may have been second to none in the British press, but this was not enough to dispel British suspicions when it came to the mixture of armies and republics. The British Isles' own history, commentators reminded readers, bore out the inevitable result: tyranny. As *Ruddiman's Weekly Mercury* remarked in May 1783, the parallels were too much to ignore. "There appears a striking resemblance between the American army," it declared, "and the English under Oliver Cromwell." In particular the paper cited the grumblings of the army over issues of pay and conditions, which appeared regularly in the press and were often grossly exaggerated by loyalist prints from America. The demands and slowness to disband, the paper concluded, was just as "Cromwell and his army acted, till they drove the Commons from their seats, and government them with pleasure. How much further the parallel will run," it warned, "time only will discover."[40] No one needed to remind the British of the suffering under Cromwell, whose reputation as a tyrannical oppressor of liberty was still entrenched in British cosmology.[41] As a reader of the *General Evening Post* remarked on the topic of military rule in late 1780, "If the Army should, as in our civil wars, obtain the object of contention, America in that case will be equally miserable, because she must inevitably be the slave of a military government."[42]

To thwart the ambitions of the mob and the military, the new nation had Congress, but years of critical coverage, along with exaggerated and fabricated accounts of abuses and corruption, had all but destroyed its reputation in the British press. Although most of the especially vicious and outlandish reports stemmed from American loyalist prints, which most editors had treated with some caution, the representation of Congress as predominately corrupt and incompetent generally stuck. As described in earlier chapters, after the outbreak of armed hostilities and especially after news of the Declaration of Independence, Congress was increasingly portrayed as betraying the original principles of the revolution in the British press. With each passing year, fewer readers and editors publicly came to Congress's defense. By the final years of the war, when Britons gave particular attention to assessing the new republic's chances, Congress's apologists in the press had all but disappeared. *Lloyd's Evening Post* reported to its readers that under the current tax scheme imposed by Congress, Americans had traded a rate of six pennies per head before the rebellion for two guineas per head—the "Blessed effects of Independence!" it chided.[43] Collecting them in the anarchic conditions the press portrayed as pervading America was another matter. As the *Gazetteer* declared, "a great number of letters have come . . . corroborating the news, with accounts of the courts of justice being shut in several places, and the goals broke open, to liberate people who were confined for refusing to pay the taxes imposed by Congress."[44] Vague reports of colonies splitting from Congress, soldiers deserting, and local government collapsing into chaos peppered the British press throughout this period. As the *Bristol Journal* reported in September 1782, the national authority of Congress was an illusion, and "There is no authority now, except the authority of the mob."[45]

Perhaps most remarkable is the lack of bitterness toward America in the British press commentary as the war drew to a close. The loyalists and their supporters were not friends of an independent America, but in the final years of the war they largely reserved their public frustration and rage for those in the British government who let the war transpire and then end in failure under their watch. The overwhelming consensus in the press was gratefulness to see the war's conclusion. The conflict may have begun in rural Massachusetts, but it had drawn in Britain's feared European rivals and enveloped the globe, inciting tremendous public anxiety chronicled in (and to some extent fueled by) the press. Yet the press depicts the wider public as believing Britain triumphed over its ancient enemies both at sea and on land, affirming British superiority in the eyes of the populace. This renewed confidence enabled a degree of magnanimity that may not have been possible under other circumstances.

The consensus of public opinion at the end of the revolution on the future of Anglo-American relations and the new republic was remarkably accurate, underlining what adept analysts the British had become and highlighting the fairness with which they made their assessments. The desire for trade healed almost all wounds of the Revolutionary War, even when some of them were reopened in 1812. Trade accelerated rapidly, and the economies of both countries benefited. The United States never truly became a client state of Britain, but Federalist policies of the 1790s came dangerously close, as evidenced when the United States, though former allies of France, chose first to remain neutral when France and Britain went to war again in 1793 and then to fight the unofficial "Quasi-War" against France. Contemporaries, including Thomas Jefferson and James Madison, certainly expressed fears that such actions placed the United States into the service of Britain.

Britain's late military success also explains the lack of national soul-searching in the press at the war's conclusion. This was a populace that showed some of the earliest signs of nationalism and increasingly associated success overseas with the health of the nation at home, and one might expect greater reflection in the wake of losing one-quarter of the empire's free population. This is not to suggest that it did not happen at all, as evidence of it exists elsewhere, such as in pamphlets and government correspondence; however, in terms of a national pubic discussion that only the medium of the newspapers and periodical press could offer, such reflection was largely absent. But when taken in the context of the press coverage of the wider war, this absence is not all that surprising. After all, according to the consensus of reporting and commentary in the press, the rebelling colonies did not win on their own merits or stay true to the tenets of republicanism, and thus they did not prove the superiority of republicanism or the deficiency of the British system. Besides, the foreign powers that had tipped the balance in favor of the colonies had been defeated soundly by Britain elsewhere, thus further underlining British superiority. This also explains the certainty in the widely professed assumption in the press that republicanism would fail.

CONCLUSION

✳ In the late spring of 1794, over ten years after the war in America had concluded, Henry Sampson Woodfall, long-time editor of the *Public Advertiser,* received a letter of thanks from Adam Boyd of Augusta, Georgia.[1] The two men had never met —Boyd started the letter apologizing for the intrusion by stating, "I hope this informal entrance of a stranger will be forgiven"— but Boyd had read the *Public Advertiser* for decades and thus felt a certain intimacy with its editor. Boyd even remarked that he had hoped to travel to London and, while there, meet Woodfall, but renewed war between Britain and France and Boyd's advanced age had prevented it. Boyd praised Woodfall for printing the anti-ministry letters of "Junius," which had led to an anxious and expensive libel trial for Woodfall in 1770, and thanked him for not yielding to external pressure in the years that followed as he worked to preserve a free press.[2] Boyd also mourned the increased government intervention in the British press that emerged in response to the French Revolution.[3] "Times are changed," he declared, "and the free, independent principles and language of an American, illy suit the present condition of the once boasted land of liberty." The comment was not intended as a jibe, because he fully expected Woodfall to agree. Boyd concluded by offering a "sincere lament for the present state of your government," and, not harboring ill will toward his former fellow countrymen, hoped that change would be "effected without appeals to the sword and the guillotine."

Boyd's letter reflects many of the conclusions drawn in this book about the press during the era of the American Revolution. The press has never been a perfect mirror of public opinion, but during this period the preponderance of evidence points to its ability to reflect and engage with the opinions of its readers. The press was about profit, and the enormity of those profits shielded newspapers and magazines from the government and political party corruption that had distorted it in earlier decades. This is not to suggest that the press lacked bias or that it was wholly immune from corruption. Almost all newspapers and magazines had evident leanings—often designed to attract audiences in a highly competitive market—but these same publications also offered some balance and suffered public censure from readers and competitors alike when they did not. Thus even if a degree of corruption did exist, there was the expectation that it should not, as well as a genuine vigilance in identifying it. Moreover, readership was socially and geographically broad, and savvy editors recognized this. Advertisements that targeted professionals as well as artisans filled the pages of most papers, and the pen names and published addresses of many letters gave the appearance of a broad range of Britons weighing in on the debates.

Despite having never met, Boyd wrote his letter in a familiar tone, and the letter's language highlights the imagined intimacy the newspaper and periodical press created. During the era of the America Revolution, the British press reached millions of people across continents to forge and sustain a discourse on controversial subjects. This discourse was a relatively free one, and its facilitators, like Woodfall, won readers and profits for keeping it that way. The press's coverage also encouraged readers to be critics, helping turn ordinary Britons into astute and commenting observers of domestic and imperial policies. Like Boyd, they did not hesitate to offer their opinions in the relatively anonymous forum of the press, which potentially enabled people of all ranks, geographies, and genders to comment publicly on the actions of a governing elite to which they would not otherwise have access. Boyd's letter likely meant something to Woodfall, because, unlike much of his correspondence, he kept it. Perhaps he did so because it was so flattering or because it affirmed his international notoriety, but maybe Woodfall found in it confirmation of the power and importance of the medium to which he had dedicated his life.

An examination of the coverage in the British press of the American Revolution and the global war it precipitated reveals a great deal about British perceptions of both the conflict and the empire in general. The acknowledgement of American importance in the press was clear. America was a bread-and-butter topic of a lucrative industry that relied entirely on its ability to know what captured audiences' interest; if the subject did not sell copies, editors would have changed topics. Yet London magazines, literary magazines, local newspapers, London papers that focused on politics, London gossip rags, and magazines for women all covered the American Revolution. The decades of close coverage of America in the press made the empire tangible and significant for the millions of British readers who had followed the successful expansion of the empire in North America in the Seven Years War, debated the postwar imperial policies and the colonists' responses to them, and, finally, witnessed and commented upon a war that resulted in thirteen of the American colonies' independence. The empire in America mattered in the press for a host of reasons. Many Britons believed that America's markets and agricultural exports were vital to the economic stability and success of Britain and the rest of the empire. Others saw America as a source of manpower and tax revenue. Still others recognized America for its opportunities for impoverished, marginalized, and opportunistic people in Britain. America was also a symbol of British greatness and a monument to the superiority of British culture: several million people had built their societies in the New World on the English (and, after union with Scotland in 1707, British) model and prospered more than either their French or Spanish counterparts.

For all the wailing in the press during the early years of the war, the eventual independence of the rebelling colonies seems to have upset surprisingly few Britons by the war's conclusion. Partly this was because expectations for success in America were not high. Except for a few bright spots, the overwhelming tenor of the coverage and commentary in the press from the outset of the war did not expect a return to pre-crisis Anglo-American harmony. This had never been a popular war in Britain. The British—government, military, and public alike—had little interest in an all-out war of conquest, and the sincerity of the British effort to win in America after the first thirty months was dubious. For the British, the American Revolutionary War experience was equally, if not more, about the global imperial conflict with their European rivals, and Britain largely won this war.

The shift to a world war in 1778 reveals how globally minded British reading audiences had become. Just as the government redeployed its troops and ships away from North America to defend the home islands and other imperial posts, so, too, did the press shift its attentions elsewhere across the globe. Concerns for the Caribbean and Mediterranean soon outweighed those for North America, and Asia steadily emerged as a zone of increasing public interest and comment. Strategic and economic interests and future benefits of British imperial possessions were all subjects of an intense, knowledgeable discussion in the press. British readers were under no illusions about the significance of these far-flung possessions to the security, general prosperity, and comfort of life at home.

Much of the conflict after 1778, whether in Europe or abroad, was, of course, couched in the press in the familiar rhetoric of the Anglo-French and Anglo-Spanish rivalries. Nevertheless, we should not rush to assume the primacy of Europe over the empire in the hearts and minds of the reading public. After all, press coverage of North America and the West Indies (and, to a much lesser extent, India) exceeded that of the invasion scares and the Mediterranean. France and Spain received so much attention in the press largely because Britons perceived them to be the primary threat to their empire. Native threats, whether they were the armies of George Washington or of those of Tipu Sultan, were localized problems, and, except for menacing American privateers, they did not directly endanger the British Isles or the rest of the empire. According to the overwhelming consensus in the press, Britain largely won this global struggle, scoring major victories against France and Spain on land and at sea in Europe and abroad, and because Britain demonstrated supremacy over the primary threats to its empire as a whole, the reading public seems to have accepted the loss of slices of the periphery due to localized troubles. Moreover, the dismissal of Congress in the press and the emphasis on Washington and foreign assistance in the American victory served to undermine the value of republicanism, and so neither it nor a slate of liberal reforms were immediately embraced. Nor was the public convinced to rethink completely its imperial or foreign policies. Trade remained the primary motivation for empire, France the main enemy, and the new United States, though independent, would still be a major player in Britain's overseas commercial activities. In short, the British system still seemed to work. In consequence, as much as the conflict with America may have contributed to long-term changes in British social and imperial reforms, the immediate impact on the public's perception of either the nation or empire, in as much as it was reflected in the press, was slight.

As with every historical study, this one raises questions and topics for exploration that are outside of its scope. Histories from the American perspective have not been in short supply since before the war itself was concluded, but only recently have the perspectives of the British and Irish gained sustained, significant attention. Equally beneficial to our understanding of the conflict have been studies in recent decades of the experiences and motivations of previously excluded groups, such as American Indians, blacks, and women. Yet the international dimension remains under-explored.[4] The war touched five continents and had a significant impact on a host of other peoples, including those in Germany, the Netherlands, Spain, France, and the Indian subcontinent, but their experiences have not been adequately integrated into the wider global history of the American Revolution. An examination of the British press during this period demonstrates that the responses and experiences of ordinary Britons who stayed at home and did not engage directly in the conflict were significant and had consequences for peoples on both sides of the Atlantic. Similar considerations of other nationalities and cultural groups outside of North America may be equally revealing and ultimately add to the complexity of our understanding of the American Revolution.

The Anglo-American relationship during the late eighteenth and early nineteenth centuries is another area that has been neglected by historians interested in either side of the Atlantic, especially in comparison to earlier periods. The French Revolutionary and Napoleonic Wars continue to cast a shadow over this era for British historians, and historians of the early republican period of U.S. history are far more domestically focused than their counterparts in late colonial history. Yet if we are to understand the American Revolution as a radical cultural shift that extended beyond the war itself, as has been the recent trend, then it is worth considering a lengthier British perspective.[5] After all, the British were not mere observers who packed their bags and went home at the end of the war in 1783. Britain remained a strategic threat to the new United States both on land and at sea, postwar trade between the two countries soon exceeded the highest pre-war levels, America emerged as a commercial competitor, and British reformers continued to look at America as a laboratory for some of the reforms they hoped to achieve in Britain. Moreover, war again erupted between these two countries in 1812—a conflict that has been largely sidelined in American history and virtually ignored in British history.

The American Revolution's long-term legacy in British history is second perhaps only to its legacy in American history. Historians have persuasively identified the postwar acceleration of metropolitan control of the empire as an outcome of the revolution, and they have argued for its impact on the political reform movements in the next century.[6] Others have asserted that the loss of the colonists, who had been seen as fellow nationalists in the wake of the Seven Years War, ultimately forced a more cohesive British national identity based on the territorial confines of the British Isles.[7] Such a shift permanently tipped the balance toward Britain as an empire in which a minority of whites from the home nation largely ruled in the name of the national government rather than colonized overseas territories.

The greatest legacy of the British press coverage of the American Revolutionary era was that it accelerated the creation of a nation of imperial critics —Britons who were not directly involved in making policy but nevertheless felt invested in the process and justified in commenting publicly on it. The Seven Years War has often been credited with introducing the wider British public to the importance of the empire; the American Revolution should be recognized as the event that made them critical of it. Unlike the Seven Years War and the global phase of the American war, the conflict with the colonies was hugely unpopular; even those who supported it, as shown in this study, still publicly lamented it. As Stephen Conway has remarked, this was the first sustained public criticism of the use of military force as an instrument of government policy in British history, and, while the controversy surrounding the American Revolution did not create a groundswell of feeling against war in general, it sowed the seeds.[8] The length of the war, its expense, and its failures were all acutely covered in a widely accessible press that freely printed critical commentary. It is hard to imagine the intense public criticism of the East India Company in the 1780s, the showcase trial in the House of Lords of Warren Hastings (the governor of Bengal) for mismanagement and what were essentially crimes against humanity, or the rapid rise of the movement for the abolition of slavery and the slave trade without the groundwork for a popular public critique of empire that the sustained coverage of the American Revolution in the British press laid.[9] Such maneuvers as sugar boycotts in the 1790s to undermine West Indian slavery relied first on a popular awareness of the complex connections between behavior in the colonies and consumer choices and policy decisions in Britain and second on the belief that Britons outside of the government had the right to critique policy and the capacity to change it through popular action. Detailed press coverage of American boycotts of British goods in the 1760s and 1770s offered a blueprint for success.[10]

NOTES

ABBREVIATIONS

BL   British Library

BMC   British Museum Catalogue of Personal and Political Satires

JBS   *Journal of British Studies*

NA   National Archives, Kew (formerly the Public Record Office)

OHBE   *Oxford History of the British Empire*, ed. Wm. Roger Louise et al., 5 vol. (Oxford, 1998–1999)

Oxford DNB   *Oxford Dictionary of National Biography* (Oxford, 2004)

P&P   *Past and Present*

Walpole Correspondence
            The Yale Edition of Horace Walpole's Correspondence,
            ed. W. S. Lewis, 48 vols. (London, 1937–1983)

WMQ   *William and Mary Quarterly*

INTRODUCTION

1. George Crabbe, *The News-Paper: A Poem by Reverend George Crabbe, Chaplain to His Grace the Duke of Rutland* (London, 1785), 15–16.

2. *Edinburgh Magazine,* June 1759, p. 291.

3. H.V. Bowen, "British Conception of Global Empire, 1756–83," *Journal of Imperial and Commonwealth History* 26 (1998): 1–27; Bob Harris, "'American Idols': Empire, War and the Middling Ranks in Mid-Eighteenth-Century Britain," *P&P* 150 (1996): 111–41.

4. Eliga H. Gould, *The Persistence of Empire: British Political Cultures in the Age of the American Revolution* (Chapel Hill, NC, 2000), especially chap. 4.

5. John Wilkes to Junius, 6 Nov. 1771, reprinted in *Junius: Including Letters by the Same Writer under Different Signatures . . .,* ed. John Wade (London, 1865), ii. 104.

6. Troy Bickham, *Savages within the Empire: Representations of American Indians in Eighteenth-Century Britain* (Oxford, 2005).

7. *Morning Post,* 14 Sept. 1776.

8. *General Evening Post,* 1 Jan. 1778.

9. Often referred to as the "imperial school." See especially George Louis Beer, *British Colonial Policy, 1754–1765* (London, 1907); Charles McLean Andrews, *The Colonial Background of the American Revolution: Four Essays in American Colonial History* (New Haven, 1924); Lawrence Henry Gipson, *The British Empire Before the American Revolution,* 15 vols. (New York, 1936–1970); and Lawrence Henry Gipson, *The Coming of the Revolution, 1763–1775* (New York, 1954). For recent additions to the imperial school, see the following by P.D.G. Thomas: *British Politics and the Stamp Act Crisis: The First Phase of the American Revolution, 1763–1767* (Oxford, 1975); *The Townshend Duties Crisis: The Second Phase of the American Revolution, 1767–1773* (Oxford, 1987); and *Tea Party to Independence: The Third Phase of the American Revolution, 1773–1776* (Oxford, 1991); and P.J. Marshall, "Empire and Authority in the later Eighteenth Century," *Journal of Imperial and Commonwealth History* 15 (1987): 105–6; H.T. Dickinson, "Britain's

Imperial Sovereignty: The Ideological Case against the American Colonies," in *Britain and the American Revolution*, ed. H.T. Dickinson (London, 1998), 64–96.

10. Paul Langford, *A Polite and Commercial People, England, 1727-1783* (Oxford, 1989); Linda Colley, *Britons: Forging of the Nation, 1707-1837* (New Haven, 1992); and Frank O'Gorman, *The Long Eighteenth Century: British Political and Social History, 1688-1832* (London, 1997) are examples of how general histories of eighteenth-century Britain are increasingly including a discussion of the American Revolution.

11. Dror Wahrman, *The Making of the Modern Self* (New Haven, 2004); Stephen Conway, *The British Isles and the War of American Independence* (Oxford, 2000).

12. See Sheldon S. Cohen, *British Supporters of the American Revolution 1775-1783* (Rochester, NY, 2004); Jerome R. Reich, *British Friends of the American Revolution* (London, 1998); John Sainsbury, *Disaffected Patriots: London Supporters of Revolutionary America, 1769-1782* (Kingston, ON, 1987); Colin Bonwick, *English Radicals and the American Revolution* (Chapel Hill, NC, 1977); Robert E. Toohey, *Liberty and Empire: British Radical Solutions to the American Problem, 1774-1776* (Lexington, KY, 1978), J.H. Plumb, "British Attitudes to the American Revolution," in his *In the Light of History* (Boston, 1972); Thomas R. Knox, "Popular politics and provincial radicalism: Newcastle upon Tyne, 1769-1785," *Albion* 11 (1979): 224–41. Important exceptions to this are Paul Langford, "Old Whigs, Old Tories, and the American Revolution," *Journal of Imperial and Commonwealth History* 8 (1980): 106–30; Gould, *The Persistence of Empire*, especially chap. 5; and James J. Sack, who charts the resilient conservativism in the press during this period, in *From Jacobite to Conservative: Reaction and Orthodoxy in Britain, c. 1760-1832* (Cambridge, 1993).

13. On rising nationalism and loyalty to the state, see especially H.T. Dickinson, *The Politics of the People in Eighteenth-Century Britain* (London, 1994); Linda Colley, "The Apotheosis of George III: Loyalty, Royalty and the British Nation 1760-1820," *P&P* 102 (1984): 94–129; and Eliga H. Gould, "American Independence and Britain's Counter-Revolution," *P&P* 154 (1997): 107–41.

14. Pierre Jean Grosley, *A Tour to London: or, New Observations on England, and Its Inhabitants. . . translated from the French by Thomas Nugent* (Dublin, 1772) vol. 1, pp. 220–21.

15. Conway, *British Isles*, 315.

16. Peter Marshall, *Bristol and the American War of Independence* (Bristol, 1977), 6.

17. *The Diary of Abigail Gathern of Nottingham, 1751-1810*, ed. Adrian Henstock (Nottingham, 1980), 33.

18. On craftsmen's wages, see Maxine Berg, *Luxury and Pleasure in Eighteenth-Century Britain* (Oxford, 2005), 133–36.

19. John Brewer, *Party Ideology and Popular Politics at the Accession of George III* (Cambridge, 1976), 146–47, estimates that the size of a typical pamphlet edition during this period was 500. More successful writings sold between 1,500 and 3,000 copies, and a spectacular success sold 5,000. In contrast, a leading London paper sold between 3,000–5,000 copies of each issue, and a major magazine such as the *Gentleman's Magazine* sold about 10,000 copies per month.

20. One such pen-for-hire was James Macpherson, who was credited by North as being the greatest defender of the American war. Macpherson was well rewarded with an annual pension of £500 in addition to receiving £300 for the cushy job of secretary to the province of West Florida. See North to George III, March 1782, cited in Solomon Lutnick, *The American Revolution and the British Press, 1775-1783* (Columbia, MO, 1967), 18.

21. The most thorough examination of the pre-war crisis in the press can be found in F.J. Hinkhouse, *The Preliminaries of the American Revolution as Seen in the English Press, 1763-1775* (New York, 1926). The most extensive and often-cited study is Lutnick, *American Revolution and the British Press*.

22. Hannah Barker, *Newspapers, Politics, and Public Opinion in Late Eighteenth-Century England* (Oxford, 1998); Jeremy Black, *The English Press, 1621-1861* (Stroud, UK, 2001); C.Y. Ferdinand, *Benjamin Collins and the Provincial Newspaper Trade in the Eighteenth Century* (Oxford, 1997); Michael Harris, "The Structure, Ownership and Control of the Press, 1620-1780," *Newspaper History from the Seventeenth Century to the Present Day*, ed. George Boyce, James Curran, and

Pauline Wingate (London, 1978), 82–97; John Money, "Taverns, Coffee houses and Clubs: Local politics and popular articulacy in the Birmingham area in the age of the American Revolution," *Historical Journal* 15 (1971): 168–86; Jonathan Barry, "The press and the politics of culture in Bristol 1660–1775," in *Culture, Politics and Society in Britain, 1660–1800,* ed. Jeremy Black and Jeremy Gregory (Manchester, UK, 1991); John Feather, *The Provincial Book Trade in Eighteenth-Century England* (Cambridge, 1985).

23. Lutnick's dismissal of the provincial and Scottish press as unprofitable enterprises dominated by high political and government interests, *British Press,* 10–11, reflects the accepted view of the British press at the time, and, not surprisingly, papers published outside of London receive little consideration. On the importance of Britain outside the metropolis, the most influential examination has been by Peter Borsay, "The English Urban Renaissance," *Social History* 5 (1977): 581–603, followed by his *The English Urban Renaissance: Culture and Society in the Provincial Town, 1660–1770* (Oxford, 1989); and *Provincial Towns in Early Modern England and Ireland: Change, Convergence, and Divergence* (Oxford, 2002). See also Peter Clark, ed., *The Transformation of English Provincial Towns 1600–1800* (London, 1984); Roy Porter, "Science, provincial culture, and public opinion in Enlightenment England," *British Journal for Eighteenth-Century Studies* 3 (1980): 20–46; J.H. Plumb et al., *Life in the Georgian Town* (London, 1986); Hannah Barker, "Catering for provincial tastes? Newspapers, readership and profit in late eighteenth-century England," *Historical Research* 64 (1996): 42–60; Barry, "The press and the politics of culture in Bristol 1660–1775," in *Culture, Politics and Society in Britain, 1660–1800,* ed. Jeremy Black and Jeremy Gregory; Money, "Taverns, Coffee houses and Clubs"; Conway, *British Isles,* especially chap. 8; and Kathleen Wilson, *Sense of the People: Politics, Culture and Imperialism in England, 1715–1785* (Cambridge, 1995), chaps. 7–8.

24. See especially James Raven, Helen Small, and Naomi Tadmor, eds., *The Practice and Representation of Reading in England* (Cambridge, 1996); John Feather, "The Power of Print: Word and Image in Eighteenth-Century England," *Culture and Society in Britain, 1660–1800,* ed. Jeremy Black (Manchester, UK, 1997), 51–68; Don Herzog, *Poisoning the Minds of the Lower Orders* (Princeton, 1998), 52–60; Steven Pincus, "'Coffee Politicians Does Create': Coffeehouses and Restoration Culture," *Journal of Modern History* 67 (1995): 807–34; Jan Fergus, "Women, Class, and Growth of Magazine Readership in the Provinces, 1746–1780," *Studies in Eighteenth-Century Culture* 16 (1986): 41–53; Kathryn Shevelow, *Women and Print Culture: the Construction of Femininity in the Early Periodical* (New York, 1989); Paul Kaufman, "English Book Clubs and their Role in Social History," *Libri,* 14 (1964): 1–34.

25. The reprinted account appeared in the *London Evening Post* on 29 May 1775, just a month after its original publication in America, and later in almost every newspaper throughout Britain.

26. William Cobbett, ed. *Parliamentary History of England from the Norman Conquest to the Year 1803* (London, 1806–1820), 16: 1165–66.

27. Margaret Stead, "Contemporary Responses in Print to the American Campaigns of the Howe Brothers," in *Britain and America Go to War: The Impact of War and Warfare in Anglo-America, 1754–1815,* ed. Julie Flavell and Stephen Conway (Gainesville, FL, 2004), 95–115.

28. On the decided shift to partisanship in the American press during the 1760s and 1770s and the intimidation and manipulation of printers, see especially Jeffrey L. Pasley, *"The Tyranny of Printers": Newspaper Politics in the Early American Republic* (Charlottesville, 2001), 33–34; John C. Nerone, *Violence Against the Press: Policing the Public Sphere in U.S. History* (New York, 1994), 18–52; Richard Buel, Jr., "Freedom of the Press in Revolutionary America: The Evolution of Libertarianism, 1760–1820," in *The Press and the American Revolution,* ed. Bernard Bailyn and John B. Hench (Boston, 1981), 75–81; Paul Starr, *The Creation of the Media: Political Origins of Modern Communications* (New York, 2004), 65–68; and David Copeland, *Colonial American Newspapers: Character and Content* (Newark, 1997), 269–70.

29. Jack Greene, *The Quest for Power: The Lower Houses of Assembly in the Southern Royal Colonies, 1689–1776* (Chapel Hill, NC, 1963); J.G.A. Pocock, *The Machiavellian Moment: Florentine*

Political Thought and the Atlantic Republican Tradition (Princeton, 1975); Jon Butler, *Becoming American: The Revolution before 1776* (Cambridge, MA, 2000).

30. On limited mobilization before 1778, see Conway, *British Isles*, chap. 2.

31. Entry for 20 Aug. 1777, *The Journal of Samuel Curwen, Loyalist*, ed. Andrew Oliver (Cambridge, MA, 1972) 1:394.

32. Charles Goore Letterbook, William L. Clements Library, Goore to Sir William Meredith, 25 Jan. 1775.

33. Although he is primarily interested in the nineteenth and twentieth centuries, Bernard Porter has recently given many scholars pause in his argument against placing much stock in any kind of sustained, widespread, popular British imperialism in his study *The Absent-Minded Imperialists: Empire, Society, and Culture in Britain* (Oxford, 2004).

34. *Gazetteer*, 11 Aug. 1775.

1 — DISTRIBUTION, ORGANIZATION, AND READERSHIP

1. *General Evening Post*, 15 June 1776.

2. Ferdinand, *Benjamin Collins*, 167.

3. John Brewer, *Sinews of Power: War, Money and the English State, 1688–1783* (Cambridge, MA, 1990), especially chap. 8.

4. Pierre Jean Grosley, *A Tour to London: or, New Observations on England, and its Inhabitants. . . translated from the French by Thomas Nugent* (Dublin, 1772), vol. 1, pp. 220–21.

5. Benedict Anderson, *Imagined Communities: Reflections on the Origin and Spread of Nationalism*, revised edition (London, 1991).

6. Hannah Barker, *Newspapers, Politics and English Society, 1695–1855* (London, 2000), 30.

7. Michael Harris, *London Newspapers in the Age of Walpole: A Study of the Origins of the Modern English Press* (London, 1987), 55–57.

8. Harris, *London Newspapers*, 46.

9. Brewer, *Party Ideology and Popular Politics*, 142.

10. The black market for newspapers would have been very small due to their bulk and traceability. According to a letter to the Treasury from the General Post Office in 1782, newspapers were the vehicle for smuggling unstamped letters rather than the contraband itself: NA, T [Treasury] 1/577/9-11.

11. BL, Add MS. 38169. Records from this period also survive from the *Saint James's Chronicle* and *Hampshire Chronicle*, but neither of these offers the precise details on circulation, expenses, and sources of revenue that the *Public Advertiser's* ledgers do. Records of the *Gazetteer* survive for the period immediately following the American war. All have been considered in this study.

12. Lucyle Werkmeister, *The London Daily Press 1772–1792* (Lincoln, NE, 1963), 127.

13. For a description of Woodfall's experience with the still-anonymous "Junius" and his letters, see Robert R. Rea, *The English Press in Politics, 1760–1774* (Lincoln, NE, 1963), chap. 10.

14. On the cost of mills, see Maxine Berg, *Luxury and Pleasure in Eighteenth-Century Britain* (Oxford, 2005), 49.

15. Robert L. Haig, *The Gazetteer 1735–1797: A Study in the Eighteenth-Century English Newspaper* (Carbondale, IL, 1960), 147–48 and 215.

16. Haig, *The Gazetteer*, 224–25.

17. On the availability of review magazines, see Antonia Forster, "Review Journals and the Reading Public," in *Books and Their Readers in Eighteenth-Century England: New Essays*, ed. Isabel Rivers (London, 2001), 187.

18. On the earlier development of a national press, see Robert Harris, *A Patriot Press: National Politics and the London Press in the 1740s* (Oxford, 1993).

19. *London Courant*, 20 Jan. 1780.

20. John Feather, *The Provincial Book Trade in Eighteenth-Century England* (Cambridge, 1985), 48.

21. NA, T1/431/103 and T 1/577/9-11.

22. Brewer, *Party Ideology and Popular Politics*, 159.

23. Corpus Christi College, Oxford, Senior Common Room Wager Book, 1745–1810, C/21/4/1 (c.1768).

24. Ferdinand, *Benjamin Collins*, 125 and 128.

25. Ferdinand, *Benjamin Collins*, 21; Jeremy Black, *The English Press in the Eighteenth Century* (Philadelphia, 1987), 101; Black, *English Press, 1621–1861*, 112.

26. Barker, *Newspapers, Politics and English Society*, 29.

27. *Derby Mercury*, 5 July 1776.

28. Hannah Barker, "Catering for Provincial Tastes? Newspapers, Readership and Profit in Late Eighteenth-Century England," *Historical Research* 64 (1996): 42–60.

29. *Edinburgh Magazine*, preface to 1758, p. iv.

30. Ian Maxted, "Farley family," *Oxford DNB;* C.Y. Ferdinand, "The Salisbury Journal 1729–1785: A Study of a Provincial Newspaper" (D.Phil. thesis, University of Oxford, 1990), 85–86.

31. Wilfrid Prest, *Albion Ascendant: English History, 1660–1815* (Oxford, 1998), 165; Berg, *Luxury and Pleasure*, 3.

32. For commentary on the dearth of understanding in the eighteenth-century Scottish newspaper and periodical press, see Bob Harris, *Politics and the Rise of the Press: Britain and France, 1620–1800* (London, 1996), 11–12 and 21–22. For the handful of studies on the Scottish press, see John Dwyer, "The *Caledonian Mercury* and Scottish National Culture, 1763–1801," *Journal of History and Politics/Journal d'Histoire et de Politique* 7 (1989): 147–71; M.E. Craig, *The Scottish Periodical Press, 1750–1789* (Edinburgh, 1931); R.M.W. Cowan, *The Newspaper in Scotland: A Study of its First Expansion, 1815–1860* (Glasgow, 1986). For examples of the dismissal of the Scottish press in studies of Britain and the American Revolution, see especially Lutnick, *American Revolution and the British Press*, 10–11; and Alfred Grant, *Our American Brethren: A History of Letters in the British Press During the American Revolution, 1775–1781* (London, 1995), 8.

33. Harris, *Politics and the Rise of the Press*, 11.

34. *Bristol Journal*, 8 Nov. 1777; *Dundee Weekly Magazine*, 2 Sept. 1774.

35. Jeremy Black, *The English Press 1621–1861*, Stroud, Gloucestershire, UK, 2001, p. 112.

36. NA, T 1/577/9-11.

37. Cited in Black, *English Press*, 105.

38. Black, *English Press*, 104.

39. Dennis O'Bryen to Edmund Burke, March 1782, cited in Barker, *Newspapers, Politics and English Society*, 47; Brewer, *Party Ideology and Popular Politics*, 142.

40. Barker, *Newspapers, Politics and English Society*, 115.

41. Jan Fergus, "Provincial Servants' Reading in the Late Eighteenth Century," in *The Practice and Representation of Reading in England*, ed. James Raven, Helen Small, and Naomi Tadmoor (Cambridge, 1996), 162–74.

42. *Edinburgh Magazine*, preface to 1758, p. v.

43. Jacob M. Price, "Who Cared about the Colonies? The Impact of the Thirteen Colonies on British Society and Politics, circa 1714–1775," in *Strangers within the Realm: Cultural Margins of the First British Empire*, ed. Bernard Bailyn and Philip Morgan (Chapel Hill, NC, 1991), 427.

44. This is based on the provincial British population being just over 10 million and an average weekly distribution of newspapers and magazines (both provincial and metropolitan) of about 200,000 copies. For a more exact estimate, see E.A. Wrigley and R.S. Schofield, *The Population of England 1541–1871* (Cambridge, MA, 1981); Michael Flinn, *Scottish Population History* (Edinburgh, 1977).

45. Crabbe, *The News-Paper: A Poem*, 15–16.

46. *Derby Mercury*, 26 Sept. 1756.

47. Bickham, *Savages within the Empire*, 200–209.

48. *Joineriana: or the Book of Scraps* (London, 1772), 2:9.

49. *Morning Chronicle*, 20 Aug. 1780.

50. *Saint James's Chronicle,* 12 Oct. 1776.

51. Harris, *Politics and the Rise of the Press,* 25–26; Barker, *Newspapers, Politics and English Society,* 60–62; Karl Schweizer and Rebecca Klein, "The French Revolution and the Developments in the London Daily Press to 1793," *Journal of History and Politics/Journal d'Histoire et de Politique* 7 (1989): 171–86.

52. *Saint James's Chronicle,* 27 April 1776.

53. *Bristol Journal,* 16 March 1782 and 1 June 1782.

54. R.S. Schofield, "The Measurement of Literacy in Pre-Industrial England," in *Literacy in Traditional Societies,* ed. Jack Goody (Cambridge, 1968), 313–24.

55. Lawrence Stone, "Literacy and Education in England, 1640–1900," *P&P* 42 (1969): 102–9.

56. Margaret Spufford, *Small Books and Pleasant Histories: Popular Fiction and its Readership in Seventeenth Century England* (Cambridge, 1985), 92–94.

57. Brewer, *Party Ideology and Popular Politics,* 142; Harris, *Politics and the Rise of the Press,* 14.

58. David Vincent, *Literacy and Popular Culture, England 1750–1914* (Cambridge, 1989), 49. See also Naomi Tadmor, "'In the even my wife read to me': Women, Reading and Household Life in the Eighteenth Century," in *The Practice and Representation of Reading in England,* ed. James Raven, Helen Small, and Naomi Tadmor (Cambridge, 1996), 162–74; John Feather, "The Power of Print: Word and Image in Eighteenth-Century England," *Culture and Society in Britain, 1660–1800,* ed. Jeremy Black (Manchester, 1997), 61; Barker, *Newspapers, Politics and English Society,* 53–54; John Brewer, *Pleasures of the Imagination: English Culture in the Eighteenth Century* (London, 1997), 186–87.

59. Bryant Lillywhite, *London Coffee Houses: A Reference Book of Coffee Houses of the Seventeenth, Eighteenth and Nineteenth Centuries* (London, 1963).

60. Don Herzog, *Poisoning the Minds of the Lower Orders* (Princeton, 1998), 56–57; Paul Kaufman, "English Book Clubs and their Role in Social History," *Libri,* 14 (1964): 23; James Raven, "From Promotion to Proscription: Arrangements for Reading in Eighteenth-Century Libraries," *The Practice and Representation of Reading in England,* ed. James Raven, Helen Small, and Naomi Tadmor (Cambridge, 1996), 175; Brewer, *Pleasures of the Imagination,* 176–81; Bickham, *Savages within the Empire,* 51–53.

61. *London Magazine,* Aug. 1780, p. 355.

62. Brewer, *Pleasures of the Imagination,* 183–84.

63. John Trusler, *The London Adviser and Guide: Containing Every Instruction and Information Useful and Necessary to Persons Living in London* (London, 1786), 163–65.

64. *Gazetteer,* 4 Jan. 1776.

65. For a comprehensive listing of the various debating venues and the questions debated, see Donna T. Andrew, *London Debating Societies, 1776–1779* (London, 1994); on the Lyceum Theatre's debating society, see BL, "London III, Miscellany Institutions, Societies and other Bodies, Lyceum Theatre," TH.Cts. vol. 44.

66. *Town and Country,* Aug. 1770, p. 267.

67. *General Evening Post,* 23 Dec. 1777.

68. *General Evening Post,* 25 April 1781.

69. "Mr. Murray of Broughton's Plan to Promote the Prince's Administration," cited in Arthur Aspinall, *Politics and the Press c.1780–1850* (London, 1949), 445.

70. Latham seems to have first started a regular shared subscription on the eve of the Seven Years War and maintained it at least until his account diary stopped in 1767: *Records of Social and Economic History New Series XV: The Account Book of Richard Latham, 1724–1767,* ed. Lorna Weatherill (Oxford, 1990); *The Diary of Thomas Turner 1754–1765,* ed. David Vaisey (Oxford, 1984).

71. *Salisbury Journal,* 25 April 1757, cited in C.Y. Ferdinand, "The Salisbury Journal 1729–1785: A Study of a Provincial Newspaper." (D.Phil. thesis, University of Oxford, 1990), 220.

72. Barker, *Newspapers, Politics and English Society,* 56–59; Joshua Toulmin, *The History of Taunton, in the County of Somerset* (Taunton, 1791), 187.

73. Herzog, *Poisoning the Minds,* 58.

74. For the most recent studies of women as active participants in commerce, which amply demonstrate a high level of participation, see Hannah Barker, *The Business of Women: Female Enterprise and Urban Development in Northern England, 1760-1830* (Oxford, 2006) and Nicola Phillips, *Women in Business, 1700-1850* (Woodbridge, Suffolk, 2006).

75. Werkmeister, *London Daily Press,* 24-27.

76. Ian Maxted, "Farley family," *Oxford DNB.*

77. On Mary Say, see Haig, *The Gazetteer,* 145-48, 162-63, and 215; Ian Maxted, "Say, Mary," *Oxford DNB* (Oxford, 2004).

78. Harris, *Politics and the Rise of the Press,* 83; *Ipswich Journal,* 12 Aug. 1758.

79. *Morning Post,* 17 July 1779.

80. Naomi Tadmor, "In the even my wife read to me," in *The Practice and Representation of Reading in England;* Jan Fergus, "Women, Class, and Growth of Magazine Readership in the Provinces, 1746-1780," *Studies in Eighteenth-Century Culture* 16 (1986): 41-53. See also Kathryn Shevelow, *Women and Print Culture: the Construction of Femininity in the Early Periodical* (New York, 1989); Alison Adburgham, *Women in Print: Writing Women and Women's Magazines from the Restoration to the Accession of Victoria* (London, 1972), chap. 7.

81. Lorna Weatherill, "A Possession of One's Own: Women and Consumer Behavior in England, 1660-1740," *JBS,* 25 (1986), 139 and 142.

82. *The Diary of Abigail Gathern of Nottingham, 1751-1810,* ed. Adrian Henstock (Nottingham, 1980), 33.

83. *A Series of Letters between Mrs. Elizabeth Carter and Miss Catherine Talbot from the Year 1741 to 1770: To Which are Added Letters from Mrs. Carter to Mrs. [Elizabeth] Vesey between the Years 1767 and 1787* (London, 1809), 4:373.

84. *Letters from Mrs. Elizabeth Carter to Mrs. Montagu between the Years 1755 and 1800* (London, 1817), 2:310-11.

85. *London Chronicle,* 13 May 1775.

86. *Lloyd's Evening Post,* 24 July 1780.

87. Harris, *Politics and the Rise of the Press,* 40. Also see Barker, *Newspapers, Politics, and Public Opinion,* 38-41.

88. *Public Advertiser,* 14 July 1781, cited in Hannah Barker, "England, 1760-1815," in *Press, Politics and the Public Sphere in Europe and North America, 1760-1820,* ed. Hannah Barker and Simon Burrows (Cambridge, 2002), 95.

89. *Idler* no. 7, 27 May 1758.

90. *Oxford Magazine,* March 1774, pp. 85-86.

91. *Joineriana,* 2:6 and 11.

2 — POLITICS AND THE PRESS

1. See, for example, Arthur Aspinall, *Politics and the Press;* Werkmeister, *London Daily Press;* Lutnick, *American Revolution and the British Press.*

2. Harris, *London Newspapers in the Age of Walpole,* especially chaps. 6-7.

3. An act of Parliament (22 George III, c. 82) limited the total amount of domestic secret service money to £10,000. The vast majority of this was committed to other purposes, leaving precious little for press subsidies. See Aspinall, *Politics and the Press,* 67.

4. For a detailed discussion of subsidies, see Aspinall, *Politics and the Press,* chap. 3. On their limited impact, see also Black, *English Press, 1621-1861,* 137.

5. Brewer, *Party Ideology and Popular Politics,* 221; Barker, *Newspapers, Politics and English Society,* 84.

6. "Saint James's Chronicle, Minute Books," Manuscripts Department, University of North Carolina Library, Chapel Hill, North Carolina, 1: fol. 162 and 2: fol. 108-11 and 115-17.

7. Garrick almost never attended a meeting and seems, like many of the shareholders, to

have treated the paper as a way to diversify his investments.

8. Brewer, *Sinews of Power,* 34, argues that capital assets for private businesses rarely exceeded £10,000.

9. This is assuming that, like the *Public Advertiser* and *Saint James's Chronicle,* newspapers charged twice the amount of the tax for issues and advertisements.

10. The duty on coffee in 1774 was £115,126 8 shillings 8 pence: NA, T 64/276B/316.

11. John Feather, *The Provincial Book Trade in Eighteenth-Century England* (Cambridge, 1985), 4; G.A. Cranfield, *The Development of the Provincial Newspaper, 1700–1760* (Oxford, 1962), 256; Ferdinand, *Benjamin Collins,* 55.

12. C.Y. Ferdinand, "The Salisbury Journal 1729–1785," 86; Aspinall, *Politics and the Press,* 72; Barker, *Newspapers, Politics, and Public Opinion,* 105.

13. Roderick Floud and Deirdre N. McCloskey, *The Economic History of Britain Since 1700* (Cambridge, 1994), vol.1 (1700–1860), 2nd edition, table 7.3; Herbert S. Klein, *The Atlantic Slave Trade* (Cambridge, 1998), 97–100, argues that the average return for European investors in the African slave trade during this period was roughly 10 percent.

14. Wilfrid Prest, *Albion Ascendant,* 165.

15. *Gazetteer,* 23 Aug. 1780.

16. *London Chronicle,* 8 Jan. 1774.

17. *London Chronicle,* 3 April 1773.

18. *Gazetteer,* 1 Aug. 1780.

19. *Exeter Flying-Post,* 30 Jan. 1778; *London Courant,* 4 Jan. 1782.

20. Carl Philip Moritz, *Journeys of a German in England 1782,* tr. and ed. Reginald Nettell (London, 1965), 184.

21. Lutnick, *American Revolution and the British Press,* 28 and 33–34; For examples of shareholders accumulating profits to pay for legal fees, see Saint James's Chronicle, Minute Books, 1: fol. 162 and ii: fo. 108–11 and 115–17.

22. Robert W. Weir, "The Role of the Newspaper Press in the Southern Colonies on the Eve of the Revolution: An Interpretation," in *The Press and the American Revolution,* ed. Bernard Bailyn and John B. Hench, 99–113; Starr, *The Creation of the Media,* 59–60.

23. For the most detailed description of the development of a financially secure, increasingly provincial, and independent press in the American colonies, see Charles E. Clark, *The Public Prints: The Newspaper in Anglo-American Culture, 1665–1740* (New York, 1994), chap. 12. On the decided shift to partisanship in the American press during the 1760s and 1770s, see especially Pasley, *"The Tyranny of Printers,"* 33–34; Nerone, *Violence Against the Press,* 18–52; Richard Buel, Jr., "Freedom of the Press in Revolutionary America: The Evolution of Libertarianism, 1760–1820," in *The Press and the American Revolution,* ed. Bernard Bailyn and John B. Hench, 75–81; Starr, *Creation of the Media,* 65–68; Copeland, *Colonial American Newspapers,* 269–70.

24. William David Sloan and Julie Hedgepeth Williams, *The Early American Press, 1690–1783* (Westport, CT, 1994), 171.

25. Preface to the *Annual Register* for 1775.

26. *Morning Chronicle,* 27 July 1773. For Henry Bate's version, see *The Vauxhall Affray; or, The Macaronies Defeated* (London, 1773). For a summary of the affair, see Werkmeister, *London Daily Press,* 22–23.

27. Lutnick, *American Revolution and the British Press,* 24.

28. Werkmeister, *London Daily Press,* 34–40.

29. *Morning Post,* 9 June 1779.

30. Wilfrid Hindle, *The Morning Post, 1772–1937* (London, 1937), 8; Werkmeister, *London Daily Press,* 88.

31. Werkmeister, *London Daily Press,* 89.

32. P.D.G. Thomas, "The Beginning of Parliamentary Reporting in Newspapers, 1768–1774," *English Historical Review* 74 (1959): 623–36.

33. Mann to Walpole, 8 April 1775, *Walpole Correspondence,* 24:87.

34. *Morning Chronicle,* 29 Feb. 1780.

35. *Exeter Flying-Post,* 1 Sept. 1775.

36. Cited in David Ramsay, *The History of the American Revolution,* 2 vols. (1789; reprinted, New York, 1968), 2: 319. Weir, "Newspaper Press in the Southern Colonies," in *The Press and the American Revolution,* ed. Bernard Bailyn and John B. Hench, 99.

37. *Gazetteer,* 11 Dec. 1777.

38. *Morning Chronicle,* 2 May 1780.

39. Bodleian Library, MS. North b. 72, "Household account book of Lord North, 1763–64."

40. *Saint James's Chronicle,* 7 Nov. 1776.

41. *London Chronicle,* 9 April 1774.

42. *London Packet,* 21 Nov. 1781.

43. Walpole to Horace Mann, 18 Sept. 1774 and 4 Dec. 1777, *Walpole Correspondence,* 24:38 and 338.

3 — CRISIS AND CONFLICT BEFORE INDEPENDENCE

1. *Derby Mercury,* 22 July 1774.

2. *Derby Mercury,* 15 April 1774.

3. The bumbling, mismanagement, and distractions of a succession of British ministries, including North's, are vividly detailed in P.D.G. Thomas's three-volume history: *British Politics and the Stamp Act Crisis: The First Phase of the American Revolution 1763–1767* (Oxford, 1975); *The Townshend Duties Crisis: The Second Phase of the American Revolution, 1767–1773* (Oxford, 1987); and *Tea Party to Independence: The Third Phase of the American Revolution, 1773–1776* (Oxford, 1991).

4. Adam Smith, *An Inquiry into the Nature and Causes of the Wealth of Nations* (Dublin, 1776), 3:367.

5. Bickham, *Savages within the Empire,* especially chap. 2.

6. See especially Harris, "'American Idols,'" 111–41; Gould, *The Persistence of Empire;* P.J. Marshall, "A Nation Defined by Empire, 1755–1776," in *Uniting the Kingdom? The Making of British History,* ed. Alexander Grant and Keith Stringer (London, 1995), 208–22; Bowen, "British Conception of Global Empire," 1–27.

7. *London Evening Post,* 4 Feb. 1774.

8. *Gentleman's Magazine,* March 1774, p. 140.

9. *Gazetteer,* 2 April 1775.

10. *Glasgow Journal,* 3 Feb. 1774.

11. The letter appeared in various forms in most papers. See, for example, the *Glasgow Journal,* 10 Feb. 1774.

12. *Exeter Flying-Post,* 13 May 1774.

13. *London Evening Post,* 3 May 1774.

14. *Derby Mercury,* 18 March 1774.

15. See, for example, the *Glasgow Journal,* 23 June 1774; *Gazetteer,* 19 July 1774; *London Chronicle,* 19 July 1774; and *Bristol Journal,* 12 Nov. 1774.

16. *Derby Mercury,* 24 June 1774.

17. On the inability of the American press to remain independent during the American Revolution, see especially Pasley, *"The Tyranny of Printers,"* 33-34; Nerone, *Violence Against the Press,* 18–52; Richard Buel, Jr., "Freedom of the Press in Revolutionary America: The Evolution of Libertarianism, 1760–1820," in *The Press and the American Revolution,* ed. Bernard Bailyn and John B. Hench, 75–81; Starr, *The Creation of the Media,* 65–68; and Copeland, *Colonial American Newspapers,* 269–70.

18. *Stamford Mercury,* 1 Sept. 1774.

19. Paul Langford, "British Correspondence in the Colonial Press, 1763–1775: A Study in Anglo-American Misunderstanding before the American Revolution," in *The Press and the Ameri-*

can Revolution, ed. Bernard Bailyn and John B. Hench, 273–314.

20. *Edinburgh Magazine,* editor's preface to 1758, p. iv.

21. William L. Clements Library, Charles Goore Letterbook, Goore to Sir William Meredith, 25 Jan. 1775.

22. At this point few British newspapers bothered to note the specific American newspaper from which the story had been taken—something that would change later in the conflict.

23. *Saint James's Chronicle,* 6 Aug. and 14 July 1774; *Gazetteer,* 28 July 1774.

24. *Public Advertiser,* 26 Aug. 1774.

25. *London Chronicle,* 23 Aug. 1774; *Public Advertiser,* 1 Sept. 1774; *Saint James's Chronicle,* 17 Sept. 1774.

26. *London Evening Post,* 5 Nov. 1774.

27. *Bristol Journal,* 17 Dec. 1774.

28. *Ipswich Journal,* 7 Jan. 1775.

29. *Derby Mercury,* 23 Dec. 1774.

30. *Derby Mercury,* 11 Nov. 1774.

31. *Bristol Journal,* 12 Nov. 1774.

32. *London Evening Post,* 13 Oct. 1774.

33. *Public Advertiser,* 19 July 1774.

34. *Ipswich Journal,* 23 July 1774.

35. *Bristol Journal,* 13 Aug. 1774.

36. *London Evening Post,* 25 March 1774.

37. *Glasgow Journal,* 15 Sept. 1774.

38. *Saint James's Chronicle,* 12 Nov. 1774.

39. For example, Edmund Burke's famous "Speech on Conciliation with America" in March 1775, which represented the Rockingham Whigs' major effort, was defeated by a vote of 270 to 78. *The Writing and Speeches of Edmund Burke,* ed. Paul Langford, 3: *Party, Parliament, and the American War 1774–1780,* ed. Warren M. Elofson and John A. Woods (Oxford, 1996), 166.

40. Lutnick, *American Revolution and the British Press,* 50–53.

41. Jacob M. Price, "The Imperial Economy," *OHBE,* 2: tables 4.3 and 4.4 estimate annual British exports to North America in 1772–1773 at £2.649 million and imports from North America during the same period at £1.442 million. Even with re-exports and invisible earnings, such as shipping, the sum was far below the estimated cost of war.

42. Brewer, *Sinews of Power;* table 2.2 estimates the cost of the war at £109.368 million, or £13.67 million per annum.

43. On British isolation and foreign policy, see H.M. Scott, *British Foreign Policy in the Age of the American Revolution* (Oxford, 1990), especially chap. 9.

44. *Derby Mercury,* 17 June 1774.

45. *Exeter Flying-Post,* 3 June 1774.

46. *Derby Mercury,* 2 Dec. 1774.

47. *London Evening Post,* 1 Nov. 1774.

48. *Public Advertiser,* 1 Dec. 1774.

49. *Bristol Journal,* 4 March 1775.

50. *Saint James's Chronicle,* 8 April 1775.

51. *Saint James's Chronicle,* 22 Dec. 1774.

52. For the best analysis of the North ministry's miscalculations during this period, see Thomas, *Tea Party to Independence.*

53. *London Evening Post,* 26 March 1774.

54. *Stamford Mercury,* 19 Jan. 1775.

55. *London Packet,* 9 April 1774.

56. *Derby Mercury,* 19 Aug. 1774.

57. *Public Advertiser,* 14 Jan. 1775.

58. *Public Advertiser,* 9 Dec. 1774.

59. *Saint James's Chronicle,* 12 Jan. and 4 Feb. 1775.

60. *Public Advertiser,* 21 Dec. 1774.

61. *Public Advertiser,* 21 Dec. 1774

62. There is no shortage of work on the mixed motives of American sympathizers, but for the best summary, see James E. Bradley, "The British Public and the American Revolution: Ideology, Interest and Opinion," in *Britain and the American Revolution,* ed. H.T. Dickinson (London, 1998), 124–54. On the London radicals' use of the American cause, see Paul Langford, "London and the American Revolution," in *London in the Age of Reform,* ed. John Stevenson (Oxford, 1977), 55–78, and Sainsbury, *Disaffected Patriots.*

63. *Ipswich Journal,* 8 Oct. 1774.

64. *London Chronicle,* 18 Sept. 1774.

65. *Saint James's Chronicle,* 26 Jan. 1775.

66. For the best account of this often noted propaganda coup, see David Hackett Fischer, *Paul Revere's Ride* (New York, 1994), 271–76.

67. *Derby Mercury,* 9 June 1775.

68. *London Evening Post,* 10 June 1775.

69. *Exeter Flying-Post,* 8 June 1775.

70. See note 17 of this chapter.

71. *General Evening Post,* 9 June 1775.

72. *Stamford Mercury,* 1 June 1775.

73. William L. Clements Library, Ann Arbor, Michigan, Sackville Germain Papers, vol. 3: Germain to General Irwin: 30 May 1775.

74. *London Gazette,* 30 May 1775.

75. *Saint James's Chronicle,* 22 July 1775.

76. *Bristol Journal,* 1 July 1775.

77. *Saint James's Chronicle,* 4 July 1775.

78. *Derby Mercury,* 23 June 1775.

79. *London Evening Post,* 15 June 1775.

80. *Saint James's Chronicle,* 13 June 1775.

81. *Bristol Journal,* 17 June 1775.

82. *Ipswich Journal,* 1 July 1775.

83. *Oxford Journal,* 23 June 1775.

84. *London Evening Post,* 30 May 1775.

85. *London Chronicle,* 24 June 1775. The letter is dated June 6.

86. *Saint James's Chronicle,* 11 July 1775.

87. *Derby Mercury,* 23 June 1775.

88. Johnson to Thrale, 1 Aug. 1775, *Johnson Correspondence, The Letters of Samuel Johnson,* ed. Bruce Redford (Princeton, 1992–1994), 2:259.

89. *Derby Mercury,* 4 Aug. 1775.

90. *Derby Mercury,* 4 Aug. 1775.

91. *Dundee Weekly Magazine,* 11 Aug. 1775; *Bath Chronicle and Weekly Gazette,* 10 Aug. 1775.

92. *Oxford Magazine,* Sept. 1775, pp. 266–67.

93. *Ipswich Journal,* 29 July 1775. Gage had married an American-born woman, and the nephew was his through this marriage.

94. *Derby Mercury,* 18 Aug. 1775.

95. *London Evening Post,* 15 Aug. 1775.

96. Lady Sarah Bunbury to Lady Susan O'Brien, 6 July 1775, *The Life and Letters of Lady Sarah Lennox, 1745–1826* (London, 1902), 234–35.

97. *London Packet,* 18 Sept. 1775. The report subsequently appeared in most newspapers around the country.

98. For Cartwright's views on the subject, see his *American Independence the Glory and Interest of Great Britain* (London, 1774), selections of which appeared in the newspaper and periodical press.

99. See *Saint James's Chronicle*, 1 Feb. 1776 and the *London Packet*, 12 Feb. 1776.

100. *Derby Mercury*, 18 Aug. 1775.

101. *Dundee Weekly Magazine*, 29 Dec. 1775.

102. *Exeter Flying-Post*, 29 Dec. 1775.

103. *Dundee Weekly Magazine*, 29 Dec. 1775; *Saint James's Chronicle*, 6 Jan. 1776; *General Evening Post*, 4 Jan. 1775.

104. *Saint James's Chronicle*, 18 May 1776.

105. *Saint James's Chronicle*, 16 June 1776.

106. This was not for lack of availability, as it appeared in full in the *London Gazette*, 1 Sept. 1774.

107. *Exeter Flying-Post*, 3 Nov. 1775.

108. *Bristol Journal*, 9 Sept. 1775.

109. *General Evening Post*, 28 March 1776.

110. *General Evening Post*, 11 April 1776.

111. *Saint James's Chronicle*, 3 June 1775.

112. *Saint James's Chronicle*, 19 March 1776.

113. *Ipswich Journal*, 21 Oct. 1775.

114. Conway, *British Isles*, chap. 1.

115. *Saint James's Chronicle*, 6 Feb. 1776. Conway, *British Isles*, 13, estimates Britain's regular army troop strength in 1775 to have been about 36,000.

116. Bunbury to O'Brien, *The Life and Letters of Lady Sarah Lennox*, 234–35.

117. *General Evening Post*, 2 April 1776.

118. For the best summaries of the mainland American colonies' significance in the wider British Atlantic and imperial economies, see Price, "The Imperial Economy," *OHBE*, 2:78–104; and Nuala Zahedieh, "Economy," in *The British Atlantic World*, ed. David Armitage and Michael J. Braddick (New York, 2002).

119. On British tobacco trade and consumption, see especially Robert C. Nash, "The English and Scottish Tobacco Trades in the Seventeenth and Eighteenth Centuries: Legal and Illegal Trade," *Economic History Review* 35 (1982): 354–72; Carole Shammas, *The Pre-industrial Consumer in England and America* (Oxford, 1990), 177–80; James Walvin, *Fruits of Empire: Exotic Produce and British Taste, 1660–1800* (London, 1997), chap. 5.

120. *Bristol Journal*, 15 July 1775.

121. *Saint James's Chronicle*, 27 Feb. 1776.

122. *Derby Mercury*, 12 Jan. 1776.

123. *Saint James's Chronicle*, 12 March 1776.

124. *Saint James's Chronicle*, 31 Aug. 1775.

125. *General Evening Post*, 28 Aug. 1775; *London Evening Post*, 28 Aug. 1775.

126. *Derby Mercury*, 29 March 1775.

127. *Saint James's Chronicle*, 4 April 1776.

128. *Saint James's Chronicle*, 7 May 1776.

129. *Bristol Journal*, 2 March 1776.

130. *General Evening Post*, 15 June 1776.

131. *London Chronicle*, 18 Sept. 1775.

132. *Saint James's Chronicle*, 1 Feb. 1775.

133. *Saint James's Chronicle*, 30 July 1776.

134. *Bristol Journal*, 17 Aug. 1776.

135. *Gentleman's Magazine*, Aug. 1775, p. 361.

136. *Stamford Mercury*, 8 Aug. 1776.

4 — THE AMERICAN WAR

1. *Gazetteer*, 4 Jan. 1779.

2. *Lloyd's Evening Post*, 15 Jan. 1777.

3. *Morning Post,* 10 Jan. 1777.

4. *General Evening Post,* 1 Oct. 1776.

5. *Exeter Flying-Post,* 27 Sept. 1776.

6. *Saint James's Chronicle,* 1 Oct. 1776.

7. *General Evening Post,* 3 Sept. 1776.

8. *Ipswich Journal,* 17 Aug. 1776.

9. *Bristol Journal,* 19 Oct. 1776.

10. *Saint James's Chronicle,* 13, 22, and 24 Oct. 1776.

11. *General Evening Post,* 19 Sept. 1776.

12. Piers Makesy, *The War for America, 1775-1783* (Cambridge, MA, 1965), 97.

13. *General Evening Post,* 22 Oct. 1776. Her celebrated eldest son, George Augustus, Viscount Howe, died in 1758 during James Abercromby's ill-fated campaign against Fort Ticonderoga.

14. *Derby Mercury,* 25 Oct. 1776. It first appeared in the *London Gazette,* 19 Oct. 1776.

15. *Saint James's Chronicle,* 7 Nov. 1776.

16. *Saint James's Chronicle,* 12 Dec. 1776.

17. *Saint James's Chronicle,* 26 Nov. 1776.

18. Huntington Library, HM 54457 John Marsh diaries, 5:108-9.

19. In the wake of the Declaration of Independence, which turned colonial resistors into self-declared rebels, the line that war as unwinnable, rather than unjust, became the main public position of the leading opposition parties in Parliament—although many members still voiced concerns about the morality of the conflict. See especially Frank O'Gorman, "The Parliamentary Opposition to the Government's American Policy 1760-1782," in *Britain and the American Revolution,* ed. H.T. Dickinson (London, 1998), 97-123.

20. *Gazetteer,* 7 Jan. 1777.

21. *Morning Post,* 7 Jan. 1777.

22. "Germain, George," *Oxford DNB.*

23. *Saint James's Chronicle,* 12 Sept. 1776.

24. *General Evening Post,* 17 Oct. 1776.

25. *Saint James's Chronicle,* 22 Oct. 1776.

26. *Saint James's Chronicle,* 24 Aug. 1776; *General Evening Post,* 3 Oct. 1776.

27. *Stamford Mercury,* 15 Nov. 1776.

28. *Exeter Flying-Post,* 15 Nov. 1776.

29. *Lloyd's Evening Post,* 7 March 1777.

30. *General Evening Post,* 20 May 1777.

31. *London Evening Post,* 1 Jan. 1778.

32. *Morning Post,* 13 March 1777.

33. *Saint James's Chronicle,* 2 Nov. 1776.

34. *General Evening Post,* 6 Feb. 1777.

35. *Bristol Journal,* 10 Jan. 1778.

36. The most comprehensive study of loyalists in Britain is Mary Beth Norton's *The British-Americans: The Loyalist Exiles in England, 1774-1789* (Boston, 1972). The views of the loyalist exiles expressed here are greatly informed by it.

37. *The Journal of Samuel Curwen, Loyalist,* ed. Andrew Oliver (Cambridge, MA, 1972), 2 vols.

38. *Lloyd's Evening Post,* 17 Jan. 1777.

39. *Morning Post,* 20 March 1777.

40. *Derby Mercury,* 27 Sept. 1776.

41. *Saint James's Chronicle,* 21 Dec. 1776; *Dundee Weekly Magazine,* 7 March 1777.

42. *Stamford Mercury,* 26 Dec. 1776.

43. *Oxford Journal,* 10 Aug. 1776.

44. *Derby Mercury,* 16 Aug. 1776.

45. *Morning Post,* 1 Jan. 1777.
46. *Lloyd's Evening Post,* 3 Jan. 1777.
47. *Glasgow Journal,* 7 Jan. 1777.
48. *Lloyd's Evening Post,* 3 Jan. 1777.
49. *Morning Post,* 8 Jan. 1777.
50. *Morning Post,* 8 Jan. 1777.
51. *Morning Post,* 10 Jan. 1777.
52. *Bristol Journal,* 11 Jan. 1777.
53. *Bristol Journal,* 15 Feb. 1777; *Dundee Weekly Magazine,* 7 March 1777.
54. *Morning Post,* 6 Jan. 1777.
55. *Dundee Weekly Magazine,* 7 March 1777.
56. *Lloyd's Evening Post,* 8 Jan. 1777.
57. *Exeter Flying-Post,* 8 Feb. 1777.
58. *Lloyd's Evening Post,* 13 Jan. 1777.
59. See, for example, the *Morning Chronicle,* 18 March 1777.
60. *Morning Post,* 10 April 1777.
61. *Ipswich Journal,* April 19 1777.
62. *Bristol Journal,* 26 April 1777.
63. *Exeter Flying-Post,* 17 Oct. 1777.
64. See, for example, *Ruddiman's [Edinburgh] Weekly Mercury,* 24 Sept. 1777.
65. *London Evening Post,* 30 Oct. 1777.
66. Lutnick, *American Revolution and the British Press,* 104.
67. *Gazetteer,* 2 Dec. 1777.
68. *Edinburgh Advertiser,* 9 Dec. 1777.
69. *Morning Post,* 12 Nov. 1777.
70. *Bristol Journal,* 15 Nov. 1777.
71. *Morning Post,* 6 Dec. 1777.
72. Although the *London Gazette* did not print the terms until December 15, accurate and lengthy accounts of Burgoyne's defeat circulated widely in Britain from early December onward thanks to letters from America, reports via France, and extracts from American newspapers.
73. *London Chronicle,* 22 Jan. 1778.
74. *Morning Post,* 6, 7, and 13 Dec. 1777.
75. *Gazetteer,* 19 Dec. 1777.
76. *London Packet,* 17 Dec. 1777; *Ipswich Journal,* 10 Jan. 1778.
77. *Public Advertiser,* 2 Jan. 1778; 12 Jan. 1778.
78. *London Chronicle,* 18 Aug. 1778.
79. *Morning Post,* 23 Dec. 1777.
80. *Morning Post,* 20 Dec. 1777.
81. *Gazetteer,* 7 Jan. 1778.
82. *General Advertiser,* 5 Dec. 1777.
83. *Public Advertiser,* 4 March 1777.
84. *Morning Post,* 23 Dec. 1777.
85. *London Chronicle,* 17 Jan. 1778.
86. *Public Advertiser,* 2 Jan. 1778.
87. *Public Advertiser,* 6 April 1778.
88. *Gazetteer,* 4 April 1778.
89. Sheldon S. Cohen, *Yankee Sailors in British Gaols: Prisoners of War at Forton and Mill, 1777–1783* (Newark, 1995).
90. One of the petitions, addressed to Edmund Burke, appeared in full throughout the London and provincial press in late December 1777 and early January 1778; see the *Exeter Flying-Post,* 2 Jan. 1778.
91. *Exeter Flying-Post,* 2 Jan. 1778.

92. For details of the charity drive and the accounts of the Society for the Propagation of the Gospel, see Bickham, *Savages within the Empire,* 229–31. For a description of the hardships of the Anglican clergy during the war, see Nancy L. Rhoden, *Revolutionary Anglicanism: The Colonial Church of England Clergy During the American Revolution* (London, 1999).

93. Corpus Christi College, Oxford, Senior Common Room Wager Book, 1745–1810, C/21/4/1 (c.1778); *Gazetteer,* 4 Jan. 1779.

94. *Gazetteer,* 6 Jan. 1778.

95. *Gazetteer,* 7 Jan. 1778

96. *Exeter Flying-Post,* 30 Jan. 1778; *Stamford Mercury,* 22 Jan. 1778.

97. *London Chronicle,* 20 Jan. 1778.

98. *Gazetteer,* 4 Jan. 1778.

99. *Exeter Flying-Post,* 30 Jan. 1778

100. *General Evening Post,* 16 March 1776.

101. See Sainsbury, *Disaffected Patriots;* George Rudé, *Wilkes and Liberty: A Social Study* (Oxford, 1962); P.D.G. Thomas, *John Wilkes, A Friend to Liberty* (Oxford, 1996); Colin Bonwick, *English Radicals and the American Revolution* (Chapel Hill, NC, 1977); and Paul Langford, "London and the American Revolution," in *London in the Age of Reform,* ed. John Stevenson (Oxford, 1977), 55–78.

102. James Boswell, *The Life of Samuel Johnson* (Dublin, 1792), 2:211–12.

103. *Morning Post,* 25 May 1776.

104. *General Evening Post,* 29 Oct. 1776.

105. *Saint James's Chronicle,* 23 Sept. 1776.

106. *General Evening Post,* 4 Jan. 1776.

107. *General Evening Post,* 19 Sept. 1776.

108. O'Gorman, "The Parliamentary Opposition to the Government's American Policy" in *Britain and the American Revolution,* ed. H.T. Dickinson (London, 1998).

109. *Stamford Mercury,* 17 Nov. 1777.

110. *Public Advertiser,* 23 Feb. 1778.

111. *Morning Post,* 6 Dec. 1777.

112. *General Evening Post,* 5 Aug. 1777.

113. *Morning Post,* 15 Oct. 1777. "Paragraphical" refers to commentators in the press.

114. *Public Advertiser,* 4 May 1778.

115. *Morning Post,* 12 Dec. 1777.

116. Horace Walpole to Mason, 7 April 1778, *Walpole Correspondence,* 28:410.

117. Entry for 20 Aug. 1777, *Journal of Samuel Curwen, Loyalist,* 1:421.

118. Walpole to Horace Mann, 18 Feb. 1778, *Walpole Correspondence,* 24:354. The proposal circulated throughout the press following North's presentation of it to the House of Commons on February 17. It took about a week to appear in most newspapers across the country.

119. *Public Advertiser,* 19 Feb. 1778.

120. *Gazetteer,* 19 Feb. 1778

121. *Morning Post,* 23 and 24 Feb. 1778.

122. Although the Treaty of Amity and Commerce allied France with the United States, formally hostilities between France and Britain did not commence until June.

5 — THE GLOBAL WAR

1. Conway, *British Isles,* 11–13.

2. See especially Colley, *Britons,* chap. 1; David Armitage, *The Ideological Origins of the British Empire* (Cambridge, 2000), chap. 3; and Colin Haydon, "'I love my King and my Country, but a Roman catholic I hate': Anti-Catholicism, Xenophobia and National Identity in Eighteenth-Century England," in *Protestantism and National Identity: Britain and Ireland, c.1650–c.1850,* ed. Tony Claydon and Ian McBride (Cambridge, 1998), 33–52.

3. For just two of the briefer articulations of this shift, see Harris, "'American Idols': Empire, War and the Middling Ranks in Mid-eighteenth Century Britain," *Past and Present* 150 (1996); H.V. Bowen, "British Conception of Global Empire, 1756–83," *Journal of Imperial and Commonwealth History* 26 (1998).

4. Jeremy Black, *Natural and Necessary Enemies: Anglo-French Relations in the Eighteenth Century* (Athens, GA, 1986).

5. Alexander DeConde, "The French Alliance in Historical Speculation," in *Diplomacy and Revolution: The Franco-American Alliance of 1778,* ed. Ronald Hoffman and Peter J. Albert (Charlottesville, VA, 1981), 3.

6. *Saint James's Chronicle* 22 Aug. 1776; *Derby Mercury,* 20 Sept. 1776.

7. *Dundee Weekly Magazine,* 23 May 1777.

8. *Morning Post,* 2 July 1777.

9. *Ruddiman's Weekly Mercury,* 25 Sept. 1777.

10. *Exeter Flying-Post,* 1 Aug. 1777.

11. *Gazetteer,* 19 Aug. 1777.

12. *General Evening Post,* 13 Dec. 1777.

13. For the most thorough description of British diplomatic isolation in this period, see Scott, *British Foreign Policy.*

14. Richard Buel, Jr. argues that the navy's focus on supporting land operations prevented it from mounting an effective blockade until 1782, when the land war had largely ended, but even then it was not especially successful. *In Irons: Britain's Naval Supremacy and the American Revolutionary Economy* (New Haven, 1998), esp. 86 and 217–44. See also Mackesy, *The War for America,* 97–102.

15. George II to North, 25 March 1778, cited in Lutnick, *American Revolution and the British Press,* 124.

16. *Saint James's Chronicle,* 14 Dec. 1777.

17. *Morning Post,* 1 Jan. 1777; *Public Advertiser,* 24 March 1778.

18. *Bristol Journal,* 4 April 1778.

19. *Morning Post,* 1 March 1777.

20. *Morning Post,* 13 March 1777.

21. *Morning Post,* 3 March 1777.

22. Scott, *British Foreign Policy,* 252.

23. *Bristol Journal,* 10 Jan 1778.

24. *General Evening Post,* 5 Feb. 1778.

25. Huntington Library, HM 58204 Sale book of George Grant, fol. 89–20.

26. *Morning Post,* 3 Jan. 1778.

27. *Oxford Journal,* 8 Oct. 1778.

28. *Stamford Mercury,* 19 Nov. 1778.

29. On the rise of sugar consumption, see Walvin, *Fruits of Empire,* 117–24. The average annual duty on sugar between 1767–1771 was about £500,000: NA, Treasury miscellaneous records 64/276B/388. For the costs of naval ships and their maintenance, see Brewer, *The Sinews of Power,* 34–35.

30. On West Indian planters' presence and power in Britain in general, see Andrew Jackson O'Shaughnessy, *An Empire Divided: The American Revolution and the British Caribbean* (Philadelphia, 2000), esp. chap. 1 and 107, 206–8; Lillian M. Penson, "The London West India Interest in the Eighteenth Century," *English Historical Review* 30 (1921): 373–92; and James Raven, *Judging New Wealth: Popular Publishing and Responses to Commerce in England, 1750–1800* (Oxford, 1992), chap. 11. The number of MPs in the group depends on how one defines it, but contemporaries and historians place the number between 13 and 40: Sir Lewis Namier, *England in the Age of the American Revolution,* 2nd ed. (London, 1961), 234–36.

31. O'Shaughnessy, *Empire Divided,* 78–79.

32. *Stamford Mercury,* 8 Oct. 1778.

33. *Public Advertiser,* 13 Aug. 1778.

34. O'Shaughnessy partly credits the West Indian lobby, which placed pressure on the government both indirectly via the press and directly through meetings with MPs and ministers, with shaping government perceptions of the Caribbean and actions to prioritize it in his *Empire Divided,* 208–10.

35. Stephen Conway, *The War of American Independence 1775–1783* (London, 1995), 133–34 and 157–58.

36. *General Evening Post,* 21 Jan. 1779.

37. *Gazetteer,* 4 Jan. 1779.

38. *Bristol Journal,* 6 Feb. 1779.

39. *Glasgow Journal,* 12 Aug. 1779.

40. *General Evening Post,* 5 Oct. 1779.

41. *General Evening Post,* 4 Nov. 1779; *London Chronicle,* 4 Nov. 1779; *Whitehall Evening Post,* 4 Nov. 1779; *Bristol Journal,* 11 Dec. 1779.

42. *General Evening Post,* 30 Oct. 1779.

43. For a comprehensive account of Jones's exploits as reported in the British press, especially London, see Don Carlos Seitz, *Paul Jones, his exploits in English seas during 1778–1780, Contemporary Accounts Collected from English Newspapers, with a Complete Bibliography* (New York, 1917).

44. *London Courant,* 26 Nov. 1779.

45. Nicholas Rodgers, *Crowds, Culture, and Politics in Great Britain* (Oxford, 1998), 124.

46. *Gazetteer,* 29 June 1778.

47. *Morning Post,* 5 Nov. 1778.

48. *London Evening Post,* 2 Jan. 1779.

49. Rodgers, *Crowds, Culture, and Politics,* 130.

50. *General Evening Post,* 21 Jan. 1779.

51. Rodgers, *Crowds, Culture, and Politics,* 131–32.

52. For a more thorough discussion of the popular reaction to Keppel's acquittal, see Wilson, *Sense of the People,* 253–69; and Rodgers, *Crowds, Culture, and Politics,* chap. 4. Rodgers estimates that 168 towns and villages held celebrations.

53. *London Evening Post,* 2 March 1779.

54. *London Evening Post,* 23 Feb. 1779. Wilson, *Sense of the People,* 262–63.

55. See, for example, *General Evening Post,* 12 and 17 Sept. 1778.

56. *Gazetteer,* 18 July 1778.

57. For the best brief analysis of Ireland and the American Revolution, see Neil Longley York, "The Impact of the American Revolution on Ireland," in *Britain and the American Revolution,* ed. H.T. Dickinson (London, 1998); for an excellent comprehensive study, see Vincent Morley, *Irish Opinion and the American Revolution, 1760–1783* (Cambridge, 2002).

58. The Test Act of 1704 was not as rigorously enforced against Dissenters in Ireland as it was in England.

59. *London Courant,* 15 Dec. 1779.

60. *General Evening Post,* 18 Dec. 1779.

61. *Morning Chronicle,* 17 Feb. 1780.

62. Conway, *War of American Independence,* 142.

63. *General Evening Post,* 7 Sept. 1779.

64. For the best description of mobilization efforts and numbers, see Conway, *British Isles,* chap. 1.

65. *Morning Post,* 24 Sept. 1779.

66. *Gazetteer,* 10 Aug. 1779.

67. For the best exposition of this thesis, see Colley's *Britons.*

68. *Morning Post,* 19 June 1779.

69. *General Evening Post,* 22 June 1779.

70. *Morning Post,* 21 June 1779.

71. *Stamford Mercury,* 17 Feb. 1780.

72. *General Evening Post,* 7 Sept. 1779.

73. On the American rebels' generally favorable popular reception of the alliance, see William C. Stinchcombe, *The American Revolution and the French Alliance* (Syracuse, 1960), chap. 2.

74. *Morning Post,* 24 May 1779.

75. *Gazetteer,* 15 March 1779.

76. *London Gazette,* 21 April 1779; *General Evening Post,* 22 April 1779.

77. *Morning Post,* 23 Dec. 1779.

78. *Gazetteer,* 12 May 1779.

79. *General Evening Post,* 4 Oct. 1779

80. *General Evening Post,* 30 Oct. 1779.

81. *London Courant,* 29 Dec. 1779.

82. *Stamford Mercury,* 28 Sept. 1780.

83. *Salisbury Journal,* 15 May 1780.

84. *Salisbury Journal,* 15 May 1780.

85. *Gazetteer,* 25 May 1781.

86. *London Courant,* 3 March 1780.

87. *General Evening Post,* 25 April 1781.

88. Margarette Lincoln, *Representing the Royal Navy: British Seapower, 1750–1815* (London, 2002), esp. chap. 4.

89. *Glasgow Journal,* 18 Oct. 1781.

90. *Morning Chronicle,* 15 Jan. 1780.

91. North's experience is described in J. Paul de Castro, *The Gordon Riots* (Oxford, 1926), 37.

92. *London Courant,* 14 Jan. 1780.

93. *General Evening Post,* 27 May 1780.

94. Conway, *British Isles,* 13–24.

95. *Morning Chronicle,* 18 Jan. 1780.

96. *Bath Chronicle,* 13 Sept. 1781.

97. For the most comprehensive examination of the Anglo-Dutch War, see Friedrich Edler, *The Dutch Republic and the American Revolution* (Baltimore, 1911); for a concise assessment of the Dutch armed forces and their inability to substantially alter the shape of the global war, see Conway, *War of American Independence,* 66–68. Conway's analysis concurs with Jan Willem Schulte Nordholt, *The Dutch Republic and American Independence,* trans. Herbert H. Rowen (Chapel Hill, NC, 1982), who emphasizes the financial and commercial contributions of the Dutch to American independence over any military one.

98. *General Evening Post,* 23 Dec. 1781.

99. *Bristol Journal,* 17 Feb. 1780.

100. *London Packet,* 3 June 1781.

101. *Gazetteer,* 4 June 1781.

102. H.V. Bowen, *The Business of Empire: The East India Company and Imperial Britain, 1756–1833* (Cambridge, 2006), table 4.7. London shareholders also owned the majority of the total value of the company.

103. For an exhaustive study of the British press's coverage surrounding the Regulating Act, see J.R. Osborn, "India, Parliament and the Press under George III" (D.Phil. thesis, University of Oxford, 1999), chap. 4.

104. *Stamford Mercury,* 25 March 1779.

105. *Glasgow Journal,* 5 April 1781.

106. *Gazetteer,* 29 May 1781.

107. *Glasgow Journal,* 2 Aug. 1781.

108. O'Shaugnessy, *Empire Divided,* 171–73.

109. *London Evening Post,* 9 Aug. 1780.

110. *Gazetteer,* 24 Aug. 1780.
111. Matthew Mulcahy, *Hurricanes and Society in the British Greater Caribbean, 1624–1783* (Baltimore, 2006), 24–25.
112. Huntington Library, HM 58204 Sale book of George Grant.
113. The consensus is that white West Indians did not develop a creole culture until after the American Revolution. See especially Edward Brathwaite, *The Development of Creole Society in Jamaica, 1770–1820* (Oxford, 1978); Alan Karras, *Sojourners in the Sun: Scottish Migrants in Jamaica and the Chesapeake, 1740–1800* (Ithaca, NY, 1992), 47; and O'Shaughnessy, *Empire Divided,* esp. chap. 1.
114. Walvin, *Fruits of Empire,* 32–47 and 120; A.J.S. Gibson and T.C. Smout, *Prices, Food and Wages in Scotland, 1550–1780* (Cambridge, 1995), 233–34. S.D. Smith, "Accounting for Taste: British Coffee Consumption in Historical Perspective," *Journal of Interdisciplinary History,* 27 (1996), 183–214; and S.D. Smith, "Sugar's Poor Relation: British Coffee Planting in the West Indies, 1720–1833," *Slavery and Abolition,* 19 (1998): 68–69.
115. On public awareness of product origins and their associations with the empire, see Troy Bickham, "Eating the Empire: Intersections of Food, Cookery and Imperialism in Eighteenth-Century Britain," *P&P* 198 (2008): 71–110. Also see Timothy Morton, "Blood Sugar," in *Romanticism and Colonialism* ed. Timothy Fulford and Peter Kitson (Cambridge, 1998); and Clare Midgley, "Slave Sugar Boycotts, Female Activism and the Domestic Base of British Anti-Slavery Culture," *Slavery and Abolition,* 17 (1996): 137–62.
116. There were at least 62,000 groceries in Britain by 1800, or roughly a quarter of all shops in Britain. Sugar was a pillar of the grocery trade and so would have been sold in all of them. See Hoh-Cheung Mui and Lorna H. Mui, *Shops and Shopkeeping in Eighteenth-Century England* (Montreal, 1989).
117. For a more detailed description of the European financing of the slave trade during this period, see especially Herbert S. Klein, *The Atlantic Slave Trade* (Cambridge, 1998), chap. 4 and John Thornton, *Africa and Africans in the Making of the Atlantic World, 1400–1800,* 2nd edition (Cambridge, 1998), chaps. 2–4.
118. For a description of Rodney's motivations, abuses, and reactions in Parliament, see O'Shaughnessy, *Empire Divided,* 217–25.
119. *Stamford Mercury,* 3 May 1781.
120. *Exeter Flying-Post,* 8 March 1781.
121. *Gazetteer,* 11 July 1780.
122. *Morning Chronicle,* 11 Oct. 1780.
123. See, for example, the *Stamford Mercury,* 18 Oct. 1780.
124. *Morning Chronicle,* 18 Nov. 1780.
125. *Bristol Journal,* 29 July 1780.
126. *Morning Post,* 27 Jan. 1780.
127. *Stamford Mercury,* 17 Feb. 1780.
128. *General Evening Post,* 9 Dec. 1780.
129. For a widely reprinted example, see the *Morning Chronicle,* 30 Aug. 1780.
130. *Bath Chronicle,* 3 Feb. 1780.
131. *Bristol Journal,* 29 July 1780.
132. *General Evening Post,* 10 Aug. 1780.
133. *General Evening Post,* 2 Nov. 1780.
134. *General Evening Post,* 6 Jan. 1781.
135. *Stamford Mercury,* 15 Feb. 1781.
136. *Bath Chronicle,* 3 Sept. 1781.
137. *Glasgow Journal,* 14 June 1781.
138. *Stamford Mercury,* 7 June 1781.
139. *General Evening Post,* 7 June 1781.
140. *Morning Post,* 25 Oct. 1781.

141. *General Evening Post,* 6 Nov. 1781.
142. *Gazetteer,* 18 Nov. 1781.

6 — THE WAR THAT BRITAIN WON AND WINNING THE PEACE

1. *London Packet,* 13 March 1782.
2. *Stamford Mercury,* 10 Oct. 1782.
3. *Edinburgh Magazine or Literary Amusement,* 3 July 1783.
4. *London Packet,* 21 Nov 1781.
5. King George III to Lord North, 3 Nov. 1781, in *The Correspondence of King George the Third,* ed. J.W. Fortescue (1928), 5.
6. *London Courant,* 26 Dec. 1781.
7. *Derby Mercury,* 3 Jan. 1782.
8. *General Evening Post,* 13 Dec. 1781.
9. *Ruddiman's Weekly Mercury,* 27 Feb. 1782.
10. *Derby Mercury,* 31 Jan. 1782.
11. For an analysis of the election, see Ian R. Christie, *The End of the North Ministry 1780–82* (London, 1958), especially pp. 157–63.
12. *Morning Chronicle,* 28 Feb. 1782.
13. *Stamford Mercury,* 7 March 1782; *Gazetteer,* 28 Feb. 1782.
14. *Gazetteer,* 6 March 1782.
15. *General Evening Post,* 1 Jan. 1782.
16. *Ruddiman's Weekly Mercury,* 30 Jan. 1782.
17. *Lloyd's Evening Post,* 4 March 1782.
18. *London Gazette,* 12 Jan. 1782.
19. *Morning Post,* 17 Jan. 1782.
20. *General Evening Post,* 1 Jan. 1782.
21. *Derby Mercury,* 10 Jan. 1782.
22. *London Evening Post,* 28 March 1782.
23. *Bristol Journal,* 13 April 1782.
24. *Salisbury Journal,* 22 April 1782.
25. *General Evening Post,* 21 May 1782.
26. *Derby Mercury,* 23 May 1782; *Stamford Mercury,* 30 May 1782.
27. *Lloyd's Evening Post,* 28 May 1782. On Rodney in St. Eustatia, see chapter 5.
28. *Derby Mercury,* 30 May 1782.
29. *General Evening Post,* 2 Aug. 1782.
30. The letter appeared in the London papers shortly after the official reports, but in the provincial press, whose editors generally received both between issues, they typically appeared together.
31. *Salisbury Journal,* 2 Dec. 1782.
32. The full lyrics appeared in *Lloyd's Evening Post,* 26 June 1782, among other newspapers and magazines.
33. *Derby Mercury,* 13 June 1782.
34. *Gazetteer,* 11 July 1782.
35. *Lloyd's Evening Post,* 28 May 1782.
36. *Morning Post,* 17 July 1782.
37. Colley, *Britons,* 11–54. For a review of the most recent literature on the subject of Protestantism in Britain, see Tony Claydon and Ian McBride's *Protestantism and National Identity.*
38. *Morning Post,* 31 Aug. 1782.
39. On Spain's war objectives, see Scott, *British Foreign Policy,* 313 and 333; Stetson Conn, *Gibraltar in British Diplomacy in the Eighteenth Century* (New Haven, 1942), chaps. 8–9; and Esmond Wright, "The British Objectives, 1780–1783: 'If Not Dominion Then Trade,'" in *Peace and the*

Peacemakers: The Treaty of 1783, ed. Ronald Hoffman and Peter J. Albert (Charlottesville, 1986), 5–7.

40. *Exeter Flying-Post*, 11 Sept. 1778.
41. *Gazetteer*, 23 Oct. 1780.
42. *Saint James's Chronicle*, 26 Sept. 1782.
43. *Morning Post*, 17 Jan. 1782.
44. *Ruddiman's Weekly Mercury*, 21 Aug. 1782.
45. *Morning Post*, 30 Aug. 1782.
46. *Derby Mercury*, 15 Aug. 1782.
47. *Ruddiman's Weekly Mercury*, 4 Sept. 1782 and 28 Aug. 1782.
48. *Bristol Journal*, 28 Sept. 1782.
49. *Bristol Journal*, 10 Aug. 1782.
50. *Derby Mercury*, 29 Aug. 1782.
51. *General Evening Post*, 16 July 1782.
52. *Morning Herald*, 12 Sept. 1782.
53. The reports of Eliott and Howe appeared in the 27 Oct. and 8 Nov. issues of the *London Gazette* respectively.
54. *Bristol Journal*, 5 Oct. 1782.
55. *Ruddiman's Weekly Mercury*, 9 Oct. 1782.
56. *Saint James's Chronicle*, 29 Oct. 1782.
57. *Morning Post*, 30 Aug. 1782.
58. *Gazetteer*, 7 Sept. 1782.
59. *Bristol Journal*, 28 Sept. 1782.
60. *Morning Post*, 30 Aug. 1782.
61. *Morning Post*, 20 Sept. 1782.
62. *Stamford Mercury*, 14 Nov. 1782.
63. *London Packet*, 11 Nov. 1782; *General Evening Post*, 8 Nov. 1782.
64. The extract appeared in most papers during the first and second weeks of December. For example, see the *Derby Mercury*, 12 Dec. 1782.
65. Scott, *British Foreign Policy*, 333.
66. *Ruddiman's Weekly Mercury*, 1 May 1782 and 28 Aug. 1782.
67. Charles James Fox and Lord Shelburne initially each had representatives, Thomas Grenville and Richard Oswald respectively, pursuing sometimes conflicting courses. This came to an end in July with Rockingham's death, which resulted in Shelburne's elevation to Prime Minister and Fox's departure from the cabinet.
68. For a vivid description of the difficulties from Adams's perspective, see David McCullough, *John Adams* (New York, 2001), chap. 5. See also James H. Hutson, "The American Negotiators: The Diplomacy of Jealousy," in *Peace and the Peacemakers: The Treaty of 1783*, ed. Ronald Hoffman and Peter J. Albert (Charlottesville, VA, 1986), 52–69.
69. *Stamford Mercury*, 27 March 1782.
70. *General Evening Post*, 23 April 1782.
71. *Morning Post*, 17 July and 20 July 1782; *Morning Herald*, 29 July 1782; *London Packet*, 29 Aug. 1782.
72. *Bristol Journal*, 7 Sept. 1782.
73. *London Packet*, 25 Nov. 1782.
74. Conn, *Gibraltar in British Diplomacy*, 219–23.
75. *Saint James's Chronicle*, 24 Dec. 1782.
76. *Ruddiman's Weekly Mercury*, 11 Dec. 1782.
77. *Ruddiman's Weekly Mercury*, 12 June 1782.
78. *Bristol Journal*, 16 March 1782; *Stamford Mercury*, 30 July 1782.
79. *Derby Mercury*, 18 April 1782.
80. *Ruddiman's Weekly Mercury*, 16 Oct. 1782.
81. *General Evening Post*, 22 Aug. 1782.

82. *Bristol Journal,* 28 Sept. 1782.
83. *Bristol Journal,* 26 Oct. 1782.
84. *Ruddiman's Weekly Mercury,* 21 Aug. 1782.
85. *Morning Post,* 30 Aug. 1782.
86. *Ruddiman's Weekly Mercury,* 19 Feb. 1783.
87. *Whitehall Evening Post,* 26 Sept. 1782.
88. *Stamford Mercury,* 10 Oct. 1782.
89. *Ruddiman's Weekly Mercury,* 21 Aug. 1782.
90. *London Evening Post,* 14 Jan. 1783.
91. *Ruddiman's Weekly Mercury,* 16 April 1783.
92. *Stamford Mercury,* 13 Feb. 1783.
93. *London Packet,* 25 Nov. 1782.
94. *Derby Mercury,* 19 Dec. 1782.
95. *London Evening Post,* 9 Sept. 1782.

7 — THE UNLIKELY HERO

1. See especially Barry Schwartz, *George Washington: The Making of an American Symbol* (London, 1987); Marcus Cunliffe, *In Search of America: Transatlantic Essays, 1951–1990* (London, 1991); Garry Wills, *Cincinnatus: George Washington and the Enlightenment* (New York, 1984); Richard Brookhiser, *Founding Father: Rediscovering George Washington* (London, 1996); Paul K. Longmore, *The Invention of George Washington* (Berkeley, 1988); Joseph J. Ellis, *His Excellency George Washington* (New York, 2004); and the essays by W.W. Abbot, Edmund S. Morgan, and Gordon S. Wood in *George Washington Reconsidered* ed. Don Higginbotham (Charlottesville, VA, 2001).

2. Longmore, *The Invention of George Washington,* especially chap. 15.

3. *A Poetical Epistle to His Excellency George Washington, Esq. . . . To which is Annexed a Short General Sketch of General Washington's Life and Character* (London, 1780). The pamphlet was a slightly altered reprint of a pamphlet, which had appeared first in Annapolis, Maryland, in 1779, to which a new forward had been added. It was printed and distributed in London primarily by Charles Dilly and John Almon, two major London publishers and booksellers, but it also had advertised distributors in York, Cambridge, Bath, and Bristol. *Critical Review,* June 1780, pp. 472–74; *Monthly Review,* May 1780, pp. 389–91.

4. Many readers would have been particularly familiar with Fabius due to William Melmoth's popular *Anecdotes of some of the most Distinguished Characters of the Ancients.* His account of Fabius also appeared as the leading story in the *London Chronicle* on 7 March 1778.

5. *Saint James's Chronicle,* 2 March 1776.

6. *London Chronicle,* 26 Oct. 1775.

7. One notable example is the "spurious" letters, which were probably written by New York loyalists. A handful of London newspapers printed one or two, and they appeared together in pamphlet form; however, the pamphlet does not appear to have been widely circulated, and the letters were not widely reprinted in the provincial newspapers. Furthermore, they were largely rejected as being false, or at least questionable, and readers were warned to keep this in mind. For examples, see *Critical Review,* July 1777, p. 70; *Monthly Review,* June 1777, p. 70; *Scots Magazine,* June 1777, p. 320, and even the introduction to *Letters from General Washington to several of his Friends in the Year 1776 . . .* (London, 1777). The letters aroused no commentary and do not seem to have affected Washington's image in Britain. If anything, as the *Monthly Review* stated, "they would do great honour to General Washington, could his claim to them be indisputably established," p. 70.

8. Most inaccuracies mainly pertained to the extent of his wealth, military service, age, and relations. For examples, see *Annual Register* for 1775, p. 141; *Gentleman's Magazine,* Aug. 1775, p.

401; *Morning Post,* 4 Sept. 1775; *London Packet,* 22 Sept. and 20 Oct. 1775; *Scots Magazine,* Oct. 1775, pp. 561–62; and *London Chronicle,* 19 Oct. 1775.

    9. *Oxford Magazine,* Oct. 1775, p. 7; *London Chronicle,* 26 Oct. 1775.

    10. *Annual Register* for 1775, p. 141.

    11. *Scots Magazine,* Oct. 1775, pp. 562.

    12. *London Gazette,* 19 Sept. 1775; *Saint James's Chronicle,* 21 Sept. 1775; *Gentleman's Magazine,* Sept. 1775, pp. 446–49; *Proceedings and Debates of the British Parliaments Respecting North America, 1754–1783,* ed. R.C Simmons and P.D.G. Thomas (New York, 1987), 6:117.

    13. *Dundee Weekly Magazine,* 1 Sept. 1775.

    14. *Scots Magazine,* Aug. 1775, p. 436.

    15. *Derby Mercury,* 12 July 1776.

    16. Carl Philip Moritz, *Journeys of a German in England 1782,* trans. and ed. Reginald Nettel (London, 1965), entry for 14 July 1782, p. 184.

    17. *Lloyd's Evening Post,* 17 Aug. 1778; *Public Advertiser,* 17 Aug. 1778; *Gentleman's Magazine,* Aug. 1778, pp. 369–70.

    18. *Public Advertiser,* 22 Aug. 1778.

    19. *Gentleman's Magazine,* Supplement for 1780, pp. 610–16.

    20. A featured editorial in the *Westminster Magazine,* supplement for 1780, p. 690. For other examples, see *Morning Chronicle,* 17 Nov. 1780 and *London Packet,* 4 Jan 1782.

    21. *Morning Post,* 16 July 1782.

    22. See, for example, *Oxford Journal,* 19 Aug. 1775; *Derby Mercury,* 29 Sept. 1775; and *Scots Magazine,* Nov. 1775, pp. 587–88.

    23. For examples, see *Saint James's Chronicle,* 6 Aug. 1776; *Scots Magazine,* Feb. 1777, pp. 76–79; and March 1777, p. 141; *Gazetteer,* 22 Nov. 1777; *Public Advertiser,* 29 Aug. 1778; *The Detail and Conduct of the American War, under Generals Gage, Howe, and Burgoyne, and Vice Admiral Lord Howe,* 3rd ed. (London, 1780), pp. 41–43 and 100–109.

    24. *Oxford Journal,* 7 Dec. 1776.

    25. *Morning Post,* 2 July 1779. For the *Morning Post's* affiliation with the North ministry, see Lutnick, *American Revolution and the British Press,* 24–25; and Werkmeister, *London Daily Press,* chap. 1.

    26. *Public Advertiser,* 25 March 1778.

    27. *Morning Chronicle,* 1 Jan. 1782. Cornwallis feigned illness and left the surrender to an underling.

    28. *Edinburgh Magazine or Literary Amusement,* 21 Aug. 1783.

    29. Most papers carried the Parliamentary debate over several issues. The *London Chronicle,* for example, devoted substantial attention to the debate in the issues of 28 and 30 May and 18 June 1776. The *Morning Chronicle* generally was acknowledged as providing the best coverage of the Parliamentary debates, and its version therefore appeared in the majority of London papers as well as provincial papers.

    30. *Exeter Flying-Post,* 22 May 1778.

    31. The letter was usually printed alongside Burgoyne's testimony. It was printed separately in the *Gentleman's Magazine,* June 1778, pp. 1–2 and *Scots Magazine,* May 1778, p. 251. It was also reprinted as an appendix to the well-known Parliamentary reporter John Almon's account of *The Substance of General Burgoyne's Speeches on Mr. Vyner's Motion, On the 26th of May; and upon Mr. Hartley's Motion, On the 26th of May; with an Appendix, Containing General Washington's Letter to General Burgoyne* (London, 1778), which enjoyed at least four editions in 1778 alone.

    32. *Public Advertiser,* 17 June 1778.

    33. *Derby Mercury,* 4 Aug. 1775.

    34. *Gentleman's Magazine,* Sept. 1775, pp. 543–45. The letter was from Benjamin Harrison.

    35. General George Augustus Eliott, governor of Gibraltar, and Admiral George Rodney after the Battle of the Saintes; on their popularity, see chapter 6.

    36. Walpole to Horace Mann, 20 March 1775, *Walpole Correspondence,* 24:86.

37. On the unpopularity of George III during this period, see especially Colley, *Britons*, 195–217.

38. The award was the Chancellor's Academic Prize for the poem "Conquest of Quebec." The poem appeared in *Town and Country Magazine*, Jan. 1770, pp. 25–31.

39. *General Evening Post*, 7 Oct. 1779.

40. See chapter 3.

41. *Exeter Flying-Post*, 11 Nov. 1774.

42. *Stamford Mercury*, 8 June 1775.

43. *Saint James's Chronicle*, 23 Sept. 1775.

44. *Saint James's Chronicle*, 16 Sept. 1775.

45. On Howe's efforts to defend himself in the pamphlet and newspaper press, see Margaret Stead, "Contemporary Responses in Print to the American Campaigns of the Howe Brothers," in *Britain and America Go to War*, ed. Flavell and Conway, 116–42.

46. *Morning Chronicle*, 17 May 1776 and *London Evening Post*, 4 May 1776.

47. *Saint James's Chronicle*, 21 May 1776.

48. *Saint James's Chronicle*, 28 May 1776.

49. For examples, see *Lloyd's Evening Post*, 17 Oct. 1776; *Saint James's Chronicle*, 19 Oct. 1776; *Gazetteer*, 1 and 3 Nov. 1777 and 8 and 9 Dec. 1777; *Public Advertiser*, 2 Jan. and 24 Feb. 1778; *London Chronicle* 3 and 15 Jan. 1778; and *Gentleman's Magazine*, Feb. 1778, p. 89. The *London Chronicle* carried a series of letters from "F.D." attacking Howe in Jan. and Feb. 1779 as well as particularly fierce attacks from other readers on 3 and 15 Jan. 1778 and 24 July and 26 Aug. 1779.

50. *Ipswich Journal*, 17 Oct. 1776.

51. *Exeter Flying-Post*, 8 Aug. 1777.

52. For the quoted letter, see the *General Evening Post*, 23 Dec. 1777.

53. *Caledonian Mercury*, 30 Dec. 1778.

54. *Morning Post*, 6 Jan. 1778.

55. *Public Advertiser*, 18 June 1778.

56. *Stamford Mercury*, 3 Sept. 1778.

57. *Westminster Magazine*, Aug. 1780, p. 416.

58. See *New Jersey Gazette*, 6 Dec. 1780; *Norwich Packet* [Connecticut], 26 Dec. 1780; and *Continental Journal and Weekly Advertiser* [Boston], 4 Jan. 1781. I am grateful to Sarah Knott for these references.

59. *London Packet*, 4 Jan. 1782.

60. *Public Advertiser*, 8 June 1778.

61. *Morning Post*, 21 June 1779.

62. *Ruddiman's Weekly Mercury*, 27 Feb. 1782.

63. See Sainsbury, *Disaffected Patriots*; George Rudé, *Wilkes and Liberty: A Social Study* (Oxford, 1962); and Colin Bonwick, *English Radicals and the American Revolution* (Chapel Hill, NC, 1977).

64. See H.T. Dickinson, "'The Friends of America': British Sympathy with the American Revolution," in *Radicalism and Revolution in Britain, 1775–1848*, ed. Michael T. Davis (London, 2000), esp. 20–22. Dickinson argues that too much emphasis has been placed on the French Revolution's impact on British reform.

65. *Derby Mercury*, 18 Nov. 1774.

66. *Saint James's Chronicle*, 21 Dec. 1774.

67. The classic work on the subject is Sir Lewis Namier, *The Structure of Politics at the Accession of George III*, 2nd ed. (London, 1957). Roughly one-third of the members during this period came from constituencies with fewer than 100 eligible voters (more often than not tenants of the candidate's family).

68. On the political power of the landed elite, see J.C.D. Clark, *English Society, 1688–1832: Ideology, Social Structure and Political Practice during the Ancien Regime* (Cambridge, 1985); on numbers of contested elections, see O'Gorman, *The Long Eighteenth Century*, 139–40.

69. For an analysis of North's Parliamentary support, see Christie, *The End of the North Ministry*; Mary Kinnear, "Pro-Americans in the British House of Commons in the 1770s" (PhD diss., University of Oregon, 1973).

70. *General Evening Post*, 15 June 1776.

71. *Saint James's Chronicle*, 25 April 1777.

72. *General Evening Post*, 27 Feb. 1776.

73. *General Evening Post*, 28 Sept. 1776.

74. *Political Magazine*, Oct. 1780, p. 631.

75. *Morning Chronicle*, 12 Jan. 1782.

76. *Political Magazine*, July 1782, p. 445.

77. *Edinburgh Advertiser*, 20 Jan. 1778. The Scots' anti-American stance was generally more aggressive and public than elsewhere. See especially Conway, *British Isles*, 132–33, and Robert Kent Donavan, "The Popular Party of the Church of Scotland and the American Revolution," in *Scotland and America in the Age of the Enlightenment*, ed. Richard B. Sher and Jeffrey R. Smitten (Princeton, 1990), 81–99.

78. *London Chronicle*, 5 Jan. 1782.

79. *A Poetical Epistle to His Excellency George Washington, Esq.*

80. *Westminster Magazine*, Aug. 1780, p. 413.

81. *Morning Herald*, 2 Feb. 1797, cited in Donna T. Andrew, *London Debating Societies, 1776–1799* (London, 1994), 353.

8 — THE CONTROVERSY OF CONDUCTING THE WAR

1. See especially, Stephen Conway, "From Fellow-nationals to Foreigners: British Perceptions of the Americans, circa 1739–1783," *WMQ* 49 (2002): 3–38; Gould, *The Persistence of Empire*, especially chaps. 2 and 4; Bernard Bailyn, *The Ideological Origins of the American Revolution* (Boston, 1967); and Caroline Robbins, *The Eighteenth-Century Commonwealth Man* (Cambridge, MA, 1959).

2. Yet many of the motivations of the white colonists, British soldiers, blacks, American Indians, and Germans were similar—loyalty to friends, desire for material gain, and search for adventure. On the mixed motives of those who enlisted in the Continental Army, see especially John W. Shy's, "Hearts and Minds in the American Revolution: The Case of 'Long Bill' Scott and Peterborough, New Hampshire," in his *A People Numerous and Armed: Reflections on the Military Struggle for American Independence* (New York, 1976); and Charles Royster, *A Revolutionary People at War: The Continental Army and the American Character, 1775–1783* (Chapel Hill, NC, 1979).

3. See chapter 4.

4. *Gazetteer*, 30 March 1779.

5. *Gentleman's Magazine*, May 1778, p. 235.

6. Bickham, *Savages within the Empire*, 102–8.

7. See especially Gerald W. Mullin, *Flight and Rebellion: Slave Resistance in Eighteenth-Century Virginia* (Oxford, 1972); Peter M. Voelz, *Slave and Soldier: The Military Impact of Blacks in the Colonial Americas* (New York, 1993); Benjamin Quarles, *The Negro in the American Revolution* (Chapel Hill, NC, 1961); David Brion Davis, *The Problem of Slavery in the Age of the American Revolution* (Ithaca, 1975); most recently, Simon Schama, *Rough Crossings: Britain, the Slaves and the American Revolution* (London, 2005); and Judith L. Van Buskirk, "African Americans in the Revolutionary War and Its Aftermath," in *War and Society in the American Revolution*, ed. John Resch and Walter Sargent (DeKalb, IL, 2007).

8. Ray Raphael, *A People's History of the American Revolution: How Common People Shaped the Fight for Independence* (New York, 2002), 330–31.

9. Schama's *Rough Crossings* does much to recover this aspect of Atlantic history and argue its long-term significance.

10. Troy Bickham, "Billy Lee," *Oxford DNB* (Oxford, 2004).

11. Voelz, *Slave and Soldier*, especially chap. 5.

12. Charles W. Ingrao, *The Hessian Mercenary State: Ideas, Institutions, and Reform under Fredrick II, 1760–1785* (Cambridge, 1987), 154; Rodney Atwood, *The Hessians: Mercenaries from Hessen-Kassel in the American Revolution* (Cambridge, 1980), 165–66; Elliot Hoffman, "Black-Hessians: American Blacks and German Soldiers," *Negro History Bulletin* 44 (1981): 81–82.

13. Evacuation was just the beginning for blacks. A few remained in military service, while most remained slaves—either following their masters or being sold into slavery in the West Indies by ruthless profiteers. Still others moved to Nova Scotia and then to Africa as colonizers of the new British colony, Sierra Leone. For a comprehensive look at these sagas, see Schama, *Rough Crossings*.

14. Schama, *Rough Crossings*, 15.

15. *Morning Chronicle*, 17 Jan. 1780.

16. See Robert Wokler, "Apes and Races in the Scottish Enlightenment: Monboddo and Kames on the Nature of Man," in *Philosophy and Science of the Scottish Enlightenment*, ed. Peter Jones (Edinburgh, 1988); Roxann Wheeler, *The Complexion of Race: Categories of Difference in Eighteenth-Century British Culture* (Philadelphia, 2000), esp. 176–233; Bickham, *Savages within the Empire*, chap. 5; H.M. Hopfl, "From Savage to Scotsman: Conjectural History in the Scottish Enlightenment," *JBS* 17 (1978), 19–40.

17. Gretchen Holbrook Gerzina, *Black London: Life before Emancipation* (London, 1995), 5.

18. On the availability of these products in Britain, see especially Walvin, *Fruits of Empire*; on their association in consumers' minds with slavery, see Bickham, "Eating the Empire."

19. Timothy Morton, "Blood Sugar," in *Romanticism and Colonialism*, ed. Timothy Fulford and Peter Kitson; Midgley, "Slave Sugar Boycotts."

20. *Bristol Journal*, 26 Aug. 1776.

21. See the *London Packet*, 22 Sept. 1775 and the *Monthly Review*, Nov. 1776, p. 348. The more partisan pamphlet press, which tended to respond more directly to the American pamphlets that deployed the language of slavery, was more vocal on this issue. For examples, see *The Thoughts of a Traveller Upon our American Disputes* (London, 1774) and *An Answer to the Declaration of the American Congress* (London, 1776).

22. Christopher Leslie Brown, *Moral Capital: Foundations of British Abolitionism* (Chapel Hill, NC, 2006). Andrew Jackson O'Shaughnessy argues that the loss of the mainland colonies made the remaining slave-owning colonies more vulnerable to the abolitionist groups that formed after the war in *Empire Divided*, 238–48.

23. O'Shaughnessy, *Empire Divided*, esp. chap. 1 and pp. 107, 206–8; Lillian M. Penson, "The London West India Interest in the Eighteenth Century," *English Historical Review* 30 (1921): 373–92.

24. For examples, see Johan Bouchan to Lord Germain, Secretary of State for America, 27 Nov. 1775 and a proposal from Sir John Dalrymple "On the Expedition to the Southern Colonies," also sent to Germain, in the Sackville Germain Papers, William L. Clements Library, Ann Arbor, Michigan.

25. *Stamford Mercury*, 12 Feb. 1778.

26. Walpole to William Maon, 14 Feb. 1774, *Walpole Correspondence*, 28:135–36.

27. For a more comprehensive discussion of British perceptions of American Indians and the role of the Seven Years War, see Bickham, *Savages within the Empire*.

28. *Oxford Journal*, 7 March 1772.

29. *Dundee Weekly Magazine*, 11 Aug. 1775.

30. *Ipswich Journal*, 3 Jan. 1778.

31. *Scots Magazine*, April 1779, p. 179.

32. On Roger's fame, see *Gentleman's Magazine*, April 1758, p. 169 and Oct. 1758, pp. 498–99; *London Chronicle*, 6 May 1758; *Ipswich Journal*, 10 June 1758; *Scots Magazine*, Aug. 1758, p. 438; *Edinburgh Chronicle*, 17 May 1759; *Gentleman's Magazine*, May 1759, pp. 203–4; *Derby Mercury*, 18 Jan. and 8 Feb. 1760; and *Edinburgh Magazine*, Jan. 1760, p. 48. On Johnson's fame, see the *London Gazette*, 30 Oct. 1755; *Derby Mercury*, 7 and 14 Nov. 1755; *Gentleman's Magazine*, Nov. 1755, p. 519; *Whitehall Evening Post*, 27 Dec. 1755; *Evening Advertiser*, 1 Jan. 1755; *Ipswich Journal*,

3 Jan. 1755; *London Magazine*, Sept. 1756, p. 431; *Royal Magazine*, Oct. 1759, pp. 167–68; *Scots Magazine*, appendix for 1762.

33. *Gentleman's Magazine*, Nov. 1755, p. 519. This account of the battle and Hendrick's death appeared throughout the British press.

34. *Public Advertiser*, 9 Jan. 1778.

35. Bickham, *Savages within the Empire*, chap. 4; and Jack M. Sosin, *Whitehall and the Wilderness: The Middle West in British Colonial Policy, 1760–1775* (Lincoln, NE, 1961), chap. 9.

36. *Glasgow Journal*, 25 Nov. 1774.

37. *London Packet*, 13 Jan. 1775.

38. *Saint James's Chronicle*, 15 Jan. 1775.

39. *Stamford Mercury*, 19 Jan. 1775 and *Exeter Flying-Post*, 20 Jan. 1775.

40. *Gentleman's Magazine*, Sept. 1775, p. 446. Early British efforts to secure Indian allies first appeared in 1774. For examples, see *London Chronicle*, 5 and 9 Aug. 1774 and *Public Advertiser*, 24 Aug. 1774. Reports increased considerably in 1775. For examples, see *Ipswich Journal*, 7 Jan. and 1 July 1775; *Saint James's Chronicle*, 12 Aug. and 7 Aug. 1775; *London Packet*, 22 Sept. 1775; *Gentleman's Magazine*, Oct. 1775, p. 495.

41. *General Evening Post*, 25 Oct. 1776.

42. *Gazetteer*, 16 Dec. 1777.

43. *Gazetteer*, 20 Aug. 1777.

44. The letter, signed "An Old Soldier," appeared in newspapers throughout the country and across the political spectrum. See, for example, the *London Chronicle*, 22 Oct. 1776 and *General Evening Post*, 26 Oct. 1776.

45. *Gentleman's Magazine*, Feb. 1780, pp. 69–72. Although the *Gentleman's Magazine* does not give credit to Jonathan Carver, the selective extract is taken directly from his travel account, which otherwise is a fairly sympathetic treatment of Indians. See Jonathan Carver, *Travels through the Interior Parts of North America, in the Years 1766, 1767, 1768* (London, 1778), 312–29. Ian Steele has provided an excellent examination of the episode that significantly reduces the death toll and explains the sequence of events in his *Betrayals: Fort William Henry and the Massacre* (Oxford, 1990).

46. One notable exception appeared in the *London Chronicle* on 20 June 1776 in the form of a lengthy supposed "Old Indian's Speech to his Countrymen." He complains of white intrusions on Indian lands and his pleasure at seeing the Europeans kill one another. The article was not widely reprinted and provoked no further commentary in the press.

47. *Scots Magazine*, Dec. 1778, p. 648.

48. For an excellent case study of the impact of the war on one of the revolution's Indian allies, see Karim M. Tiro, "The Dilemmas of Alliance: The Oneida Indian Nation in the American Revolution," in *War and Society in the American Revolution*, ed. Resch and Sargent.

49. *Public Advertiser*, 9 Jan. 1778.

50. See Germain MS, vol. 5: William L. Clements Library, Ann Arbor, Michigan, Sackville Germain Papers, Germain to Burgoyne, 23 and 26 Aug. 1776.

51. *London Chronicle*, 22 Jan. 1778.

52. *Edinburgh Advertiser*, 13 Feb. 1778.

53. *Annual Register* for 1777, p. 144.

54. *London Evening Post*, 16 Dec. 1777.

55. For a short summary of the importance of the murder of McRea in the post-war, anti-Indian sentiment in the United States, as well as a comprehensive examination of the roles of Indians in the war, see Colin Calloway, *The American War of Independence in Indian Country* (Cambridge, 1995), 295. See also June Namias, *White Captives: Gender and Ethnicity on the American Frontier* (Chapel Hill, NC, 1993), chap. 4.

56. *Annual Register* for 1777, p. 156.

57. *Scots Magazine*, Dec. 1777, pp. 648–49. The cited extracts of Gates's letter are from this magazine, although the letters appeared in various forms throughout the press.

58. Because the House of Commons was closed to visitors, several versions of the speech cir-

culated. The most widely reprinted first appeared in the 7 Feb. 1778 edition of the *Morning Chronicle*, which was renowned for its Parliamentary reporting.

59. *Stamford Mercury,* 12 Feb. 1778.

60. *Memorials and Correspondence of Charles James Fox,* 4 vols., ed. Lord John Russel (London, 1853–1857), 1:171.

61. *Memorials of Fox,* 355.

62. Atwood, *The Hessians,* 1.

63. Bernard Uhlendorf, ed., *Revolution in America: Confidential Letters and Journals of Adjutant General Major Baurmeister of the Hessian Forces* (New York, 1954), 6.

64. Uhlendorf, *Revolution in America,* 10.

65. Ingrao, *The Hessian Mercenary State,* 136–36.

66. For details of the treaty between Hessen-Kassel and Britain, see Uhlendorf, *Baurmeister of the Hessian Forces,* 6–8; and Ingrao, *Hessian Mercenary State,* 138.

67. Ingrao, *Hessian Mercenary State,* 138.

68. *Public Advertiser,* 3 Sept. 1774. Although George III was also the Elector of Hanover, troops still had to be rented from the state's army, which was independent of the British command, and Britons treated them as foreigners in the press.

69. *Saint James's Chronicle,* 28 March 1775.

70. For press coverage of American warfare during the Seven Years War, see Bickham, *Savages within the Empire,* chap. 2.

71. *The Tears of the Foot Guards, Upon Their Departure for America: Written by an Ensign of the Provincial Army,* 2nd ed. (London, 1776), 6.

72. *London Packet,* 25 Oct. 1775.

73. *General Evening Post,* 19 Sept. 1776.

74. Henry B. Wheately, ed., *The Historical and Posthumous Memoirs of Sir Nathaniel Wraxall, 1772–1784* (London, 1884), 1:355.

75. For an example of the coverage of the debate, see the *Saint James's Chronicle,* 2 March 1776.

76. *London Chronicle,* 9 March 1776.

77. *Exeter Flying-Post,* 28 June 1776.

78. *Saint James's Chronicle,* 28 March 1776.

79. *Saint James's Chronicle,* 29 June 1775.

80. *Stamford Mercury,* 6 March 1777; *Exeter Flying-Post,* 8 March 1776.

81. For more balanced assessments of Hessian conduct, see Don Higginbotham, *The War of American Independence* (New York, 1971), 131 and Stephen Conway, "The Great Mischief Complained of," *WMQ* 47 (1990): 370–91.

82. *Saint James's Chronicle,* 25 Oct. 1776.

83. *Annual Register* for 1777, p. 11.

84. *Morning Post,* 2 July 1777.

85. *Gazetteer,* 28 Feb. 1776.

86. *Public Advertiser,* 29 Aug. 1778.

87. *Saint James's Chronicle,* 16 April 1776.

88. *London Packet,* 18 Nov. 1775.

89. *Lloyd's Evening Post,* 1 March 1777.

90. *Ruddiman's Weekly Mercury,* 13 Nov. 1782.

91. Ingrao, *Hessian Mercenary State,* 157–62.

92. On Britain's mistreatment of its Indian allies at the conclusion of the war, see Colin Calloway, *Crown and Calumet: British Indian Relations, 1783–1815* (Norman, OK, 1987), esp. 5–11.

9 — ALLIES OR FOES, REPUBLIC OR ANARCHY?

1. *Derby Mercury,* 11 Sept. 1783.

2. *Morning Chronicle,* 11 Jan. 1782.

3. J.M. Bumsted, "'Things in the Womb of Time': Ideas of American Independence, 1633 to 1763," *WMQ* 31 (1974): 533–64.

4. *London Gazette*, 7 Oct. 1775.

5. Adam Smith, *An Inquiry into the Nature and Causes of the Wealth of Nations* (Dublin, 1776), 2: 498–500. See also Dickinson, "'The Friends of America,'" in *Radicalism and Revolution in Britain*, ed. Michael T. Davis, 19; and Andrew S. Skinner, "Adam Smith and America: The Political Economy of Conflict," in *Scotland and America in the Age of Enlightenment*, ed. Richard B. Sher and Jeffrey R. Smitten (Princeton, 1990), 148–62.

6. *Saint James's Chronicle*, 9 July 1776.

7. The *General Evening Post* and the *Morning Post* were particularly guilty of carrying such overly optimistic remarks. See especially *General Evening Post*, 28 Sept. 1776 and 1 Feb. 1777; *Morning Post*, 13 Jan. 1777.

8. *London Packet*, 21 Nov. 1781.

9. *Ruddiman's Weekly Mercury*, 19 Feb. 1783.

10. *Edinburgh Magazine or Literary Amusement*, 3 July 1783.

11. *Edinburgh Magazine or Literary Amusement*, 14 Aug. 1783.

12. For the most extensive study of emigration on the eve of the war, see Bernard Bailyn, *Voyagers to the West: A Passage in the Peopling of America on the Eve of the Revolution* (New York, 1986). See also W.A. Carrothers, *Emigration from the British Isles* (London, 1929); Eric Richard, *Britannia's Children: Emigration from England, Scotland, Wales and Ireland since 1600* (London, 2004), chaps. 5–6. For a more detailed examination of British and American perceptions of emigration to America during the 1780s, see Marilyn C. Baseler, *"Asylum for Mankind": America, 1607–1800* (Ithaca, 1998), chap. 5.

13. Jacob M. Price, "Who Cared about the Colonies? The Impact of the Thirteen Colonies on British Society and Politics, circa 1714–1775," in *Strangers within the Realm*, ed. Bernard Bailyn and Philip Morgan, 427.

14. *Ruddiman's Weekly Mercury*, 13 Nov. 1782.

15. *Leeds Mercury*, 25 Oct. 1785, cited in Baseler, *"Asylum for Mankind,"* 156.

16. *Saint James's Chronicle*, 7 Jan. 1783.

17. *Stamford Mercury*, 14 Nov. 1782.

18. Accounts of the celebrations first appeared in *Ruddiman's Weekly Mercury*, 25 Sept. 1782, but were subsequently printed in most papers.

19. *Morning Post*, 20 July 1782.

20. *Whitehall Evening Post*, 4 Sept. 1755.

21. *Public Advertiser*, 24 March 1778.

22. See especially Conway, "From fellow-nationals to foreigners," 3–38; Gould, *The Persistence of Empire*, esp. chaps. 2 and 4.

23. *Salisbury Journal*, 15 Oct. 1781.

24. *Edinburgh Magazine or Literary Amusement*, Aug. 1783, p. 202.

25. *Morning Herald*, 20 Dec. 1782.

26. The king's speech of 5 December reached most readers within a week.

27. *Morning Post*, 29 Nov. 1782.

28. *Oxford Journal*, 16 April 1783.

29. *Ruddiman's Weekly Mercury*, 14 May 1783.

30. *Gazetteer*, 18 July 1778.

31. On the recovery of Anglo-American trade and the decline of Franco-American influence and trade, see especially Peter Marshall, "The First and Second British Empire: A Question of Demarcation," *History* 49 (1964): 13–23; P.J. Marshall, "The Eighteenth-Century Empire," in *British Politics and Society from Walpole to Pitt, 1742–1789*, ed. Jeremy Black (London, 1990), 87–90; and William C. Stinchcombe, *The American Revolution and the French Alliance* (Syracuse, 1960), chap. 9.

32. *Ruddiman's Weekly Mercury*, 28 May 1783.

33. Dickinson, "'The Friends of America,'" in *Radicalism and Revolution*, ed. Michael T. Davis, 1–29.

34. Dickinson argues persuasively that too much emphasis has been placed on the French Revolution with regard to this shift in "The Friends of America," 20–22. For an alternative view of the significance of the French Revolution on British thinking, see Lynn Hunt, *Inventing Human Rights: A History* (New York, 2007), esp. chap. 4.

35. *Saint James's Chronicle*, 15 Jan. 1783.

36. *Derby Mercury*, 6 Feb. 1783.

37. *General Evening Post*, 17 Oct. 1783.

38. See especially E.P. Thompson, "The Moral Economy and the English Crowd in the Eighteenth Century" and "Custom, Law and Common Right," reprinted in his *Customs in Common* (London, 1991); and John G. Rule, "Wrecking and Coastal Plunder," in *Albion's Fatal Tree: Crime and Society in Eighteenth-Century England*, ed. Douglass Hay et al. (London, 1975).

39. *Edinburgh Magazine or Literary Amusement*, Sept. 1783, p. 318.

40. *Ruddiman's Weekly Mercury*, 21 May 1783.

41. This was in contrast to the American colonies, particularly New England, where Cromwell's reputation was more favorable. See Peter Karsten, *Patriot-Heroes in England and America: Political Symbolism and Changing Values over Three Centuries* (Madison, 1978), esp. 53–56.

42. *General Evening Post*, 9 Dec. 1780.

43. *Lloyd's Evening Post*, 26 July 1782.

44. *Gazetteer*, 19 Sept. 1782.

45. *Bristol Journal*, 21 Sept. 1782.

CONCLUSION

1. Letter from Adam Boyd of Augusta, Georgia, 3 April 1794, in BL, Add MS 27780: "Letters to H. S. Woodfall, 1763–1790," fol. 48.

2. For a description of Woodfall's experience with the still-anonymous "Junius" and his letters, see Rea, *The English Press in Politics*, chap. 10.

3. Fearful of revolution at home, the British government passed new acts and stepped up enforcement of old ones that restricted a number of personal liberties, including those of assembly and the press. The government also invested substantial amounts of secret service money in subsidies for writers and editors and increased taxes on newspapers, magazines, and advertisements, partly to raise money in a time of war but also to curtail readership. The extent of the government's enforcement and success has been a matter of debate. On the British press in this era, see especially Stuart M. Andrew, *The British Periodical Press and the French Revolution* (London, 2000); and Hannah Barker, "England, 1776–1815," in *Press, Politics and the Public Sphere*, ed. Hannah Barker and Simon Burrows, 97–99.

4. For two recent examples of the potential of the global history vein of the American Revolution, see David Armitage, *The Declaration of Independence: A Global History* (Cambridge, MA, 2007); and Lynn Hunt, *Inventing Human Rights: A History* (New York, 2007).

5. For the best articulation of this view, see Gordon S. Wood, *The Radicalism of the American Revolution* (New York, 1991).

6. See especially C.A. Bayly, *Imperial Meridian: The First British Empire and the World, 1780–1830* (Cambridge, 1989); P.J. Marshall, "Empire and Authority in the Later Eighteenth Century," *Journal of Imperial and Commonwealth History*, 15 (1987): 105–22; Stephen Conway, "Britain and the Revolutionary Crisis, 1763–1791," in *OHBE* 2: 345–46; H.T. Dickinson, "'The Friends of America': British Sympathy with the American Revolution," in *Radicalism and Revolution: Essays in Honour of Malcolm I. Thomis*, ed. Michael T. Davis (London, 2000), 1–29.

7. Colley, *Britons*, esp. 143–45; Gould, *The Persistence of Empire*, esp. chap. 6.

8. Conway, *British Isles*, 315–25.

9. The contrast between the language, depth, and extent of public interest in India before and after the American Revolution is most vividly detailed in J.R. Osborn, "India, Parliament and the Press under George III" (D.Phil. thesis, University of Oxford, 1999); Schama makes a case for the connection between the rise of the British abolitionist movement and the American Revolution in *Rough Crossings*.

10. On the cultural significance of consumer boycotts during this period, see T.H. Breen, "'Baubles of Britain': The American and Consumer Revolutions of the Eighteenth Century," *P&P* 119 (1988): 73–104; Timothy Morton, "Blood Sugar," in *Romanticism and Colonialism*, ed. Timothy Fulford and Peter Kitson; Midgley, "Slave Sugar Boycotts."

SELECTED BIBLIOGRAPHY

PRIMARY SOURCES

Manuscripts

British Library
European Magazine minutes, Add. MS 38728
Letters to Henry Sampson Woodfall, 1763–1790, Add. MS
John Almon papers, Add. MS 20733
Public Advertiser accounts, Add. MS 38169
London III, Miscellany Institutions, Societies and other Bodies, Lyceum Theatre,
    TH.Cts. vol. 44

British Museum
British Museum Catalogue of Personal and Political Satires

Bodleian Library, University of Oxford
Household account book of Lord North, 1763/4, MS. North b. 72

Corpus Christi College, University of Oxford
Senior Common Room Wager Book, 1745–1810, C/21/4/1

Huntington Library, San Marino, California
John Marsh diaries, HM 54457
Sale book of George Grant, HM 58204

National Archives, Kew
Audit Office, General Account of Stamp Studies, AO 3/955-75
Gazetteer books and correspondence, C 104/67-8
Hampshire Chronicle advertising account books, E 140/90-1
Prerogative Court of Canterbury and related Probate Jurisdictions: Will Registers
Treasury: minutes, entry books, and correspondence pre-1920, T 1 and T 64

University of North Carolina Library, Manuscripts Department, Chapel Hill, North Carolina
Saint James's Chronicle minute books

William L. Clements Library, Ann Arbor, Michigan
Charles Goore Letterbook
Sackville Germain Papers

Newspapers and Periodicals

Annual Register
Bath Chronicle and Weekly Gazette
Bristol Journal
Caledonian Mercury
Critical Review
Daily Advertiser

Derby Mercury
Dundee Weekly Magazine
Edinburgh Advertiser
Edinburgh Chronicle
Edinburgh Magazine
Edinburgh Magazine and Review
Edinburgh Magazine or Literary Amusement
European Magazine and London Review
Exeter Flying-Post
Gazetteer and New Daily Advertiser
General Advertiser
General Evening Post
Gentleman's Magazine
Glasgow Journal
Idler
Ipswich Journal
Lloyd's Evening Post
London Chronicle
London Courant
London Evening Post
London Gazette
London Magazine
London Packet
Monthly Review
Morning Chronicle
Morning Herald
Morning Post
Oxford Journal
Oxford Magazine
Political Magazine
Public Advertiser
Ruddiman's [Edinburgh] Weekly Mercury
Saint James's Chronicle
Salisbury Journal
Scots Magazine
Stamford Mercury
Town and Country Magazine
Universal Magazine
Westminster Magazine
Whitehall Evening Post

Published Works

Almon, John. *The Substance of General Burgoyne's Speeches on Mr. Vyner's Motion, On the 26th of May; and upon Mr. Hartley's Motion, On the 26th of May; with an Appendix, Containing General Washington's Letter to General Burgoyne.* London, 1778.

The Ambulator; or, the Stranger's Companion in a Tour Round London. London, 1774.

[Bate, Henry]. *The Vauxhall Affray; or, The Macaronies Defeated.* London, 1773.

Boswell, James. *The Life of Samuel Johnson.* 2 vols. Dublin, 1792.

Britannica Curiosa. 2nd ed. London, 1777.

Carter, Clarence Edwin, ed. *The Correspondence of General Thomas Gage with the Secretaries of State, 1763–1775.* 2 vols. New Haven, 1931.

Cartwright, F.D., ed. *The Life and Correspondence of Major Cartwright.* 2 vols. London, 1826.

Cartwright, John. *American Independence the Glory and Interest of Great Britain.* London, 1774.

Carver, Jonathan. *Travels through the Interior Parts of North America, in the Years 1766, 1767, 1768.* London, 1778.

The Correspondence of King George the Third. 6 vols. Edited by J.W. Fortescue. London, 1927–1928.

Crabbe, George. *The News-Paper: A Poem by Reverend George Crabbe, Chaplain to His Grace the Duke of Rutland.* London, 1785.

The Detail and Conduct of the American War, under Generals Gage, Howe, and Burgoyne, and Vice Admiral Lord Howe. 3rd ed. London, 1780.

The Diary of Abigail Gathern of Nottingham, 1751–1810. Edited by Adrian Henstock. Nottingham, 1980.

The Diary of Thomas Turner 1754–1765. Edited by David Vaisey. Oxford, 1984.

Grosley, Pierre Jean. *A Tour to London: or, New Observations on England, and Its Inhabitants . . . translated from the French by Thomas Nugent.* 3 vols. Dublin, 1772.

Horace Walpole's Correspondence. 48 vols. Edited by W.S. Lewis. New Haven, 1937–1983.

Johnson, Samuel. *The Yale Edition of the Works of Samuel Johnson, vol. ii: The Idler and Adventurer.* Edited by W.J. Bate and John M. Bullitt. New Haven, 1963.

Joineriana: or the Book of Scraps. 2 vols. London, 1772.

Letters from General Washington to several of his Friends in the Year 1776. In which are set forth a fairer and fuller view of American politics. Than ever yet transpired, Or the Public could be made acquainted with through any other Channel. London, 1777.

Letters from Mrs. Elizabeth Carter to Mrs. Montagu between the Years 1755 and 1800. 3 vols. London, 1817.

The Life and Letters of Lady Sarah Lennox, 1745–1826. Edited by Henry Fox. London, 1902.

The London Guide. London, 1782.

Memorials and Correspondence of Charles James Fox. 4 vols. Edited by Lord John Russel. London, 1853–1857.

Moritz, Carl Philip. *Journeys of a German in England 1782.* Translated and edited by Reginald Nettell. London, 1965.

Oliver, Andrew, ed. *The Journal of Samuel Curwen, Loyalist.* 2 vols. Cambridge, MA, 1972.

A Poetical Epistle to His Excellency George Washington, Esq. . . . To which is Annexed a Short General Sketch of General Washington's Life and Character. London, 1780.

Redford, Bruce, ed. *The Letters of Samuel Johnson.* 5 vols. Princeton, 1992–1994.

Reflections on the Present State of the American War. London, 1776.

Remarks on the Conduct of the Opposition with Regard to America. London, 1777.

Remarks on General Burgoyne's State of the Expedition from Canada. London, 1780.

Remarks upon General Howe's Account of his Proceedings on Long-Island in the Extraordinary Gazette of October 10, 1776. London, 1778.

A Series of Letters between Mrs. Elizabeth Carter and Miss Catherine Talbot from the Year 1741 to 1770: To Which are Added Letters from Mrs. Carter to Mrs. [Elizabeth] Vesey between the Years 1767 and 1787. 4 volumes. London, 1809.

Smith, Adam. *An Inquiry into the Nature and Causes of the Wealth of Nations.* 3 vols. Dublin, 1776.

The Tears of the Foot Guards, Upon Their Departure for America: Written by an Ensign of the Provincial Army. 2nd ed. London, 1776.

Toulmin, Joshua. *The History of Taunton, in the County of Somerset.* Taunton, 1791.

Trusler, John. *The London Adviser and Guide: Containing Every Instruction and Information Useful and Necessary to Persons Living in London.* London, 1786.

Uhlendorf, Bernard, ed. *Revolution in America: Confidential Letters and Journals of Adjutant General Major Baurmeister of the Hessian Forces.* New York, 1954.

Weatherill, Lorna, ed. *Records of Social and Economic History New Series XV: The Account Book of Richard Latham, 1724–1767.* Oxford, 1990.

Wheately, Henry B., ed. *The Historical and Posthumous Memoirs of Sir Nathaniel Wraxall, 1772–1784.* 5 vols. London, 1884.

The Writing and Speeches of Edmund Burke. 12 vols. Edited by Paul Langford. Oxford, 1981–2000.

SECONDARY SOURCES

Adburgham, Alison. *Women in Print: Writing Women and Women's Magazines from the Restoration to the Accession of Victoria*. London, 1972.

Altick, Richard J. *English Common Reader: A Social History of the Mass Reading Public*. Chicago, 1957.

Anderson, Benedict. *Imagined Communities: Reflections on the Origin and Spread of Nationalism*. revised edition. London, 1991.

Andrew, Donna T. *London Debating Societies, 1776–1779*. London, 1994.

Andrew, Stuart M. *The British Periodical Press and the French Revolution*. London, 2000.

Andrews, Charles McLean. *The Colonial Background of the American Revolution: Four Essays in American Colonial History*. New Haven, 1924.

Armitage, David. *The Declaration of Independence: A Global History*. Cambridge, Mass., 2007.

———. *The Ideological Origins of the British Empire*. Cambridge, 2000.

Armitage, David, and Michael J. Braddick, eds. *The British Atlantic World*. New York, 2002.

Aspinall, Arthur. *Politics and the Press c.1780–1850*. London, 1949.

———. "Statistical Accounts of the London Newspapers in the Eighteenth Century." *English Historical Review* 63 (1948): 201–32.

Atwood, Rodney. *The Hessians: Mercenaries from Hessen-Kassel in the American Revolution*. Cambridge, 1980.

Bailyn, Bernard. *The Ideological Origins of the American Revolution*. Boston, 1967.

———. *Voyagers to the West: A Passage in the Peopling of America on the Eve of the Revolution*. New York, 1986.

Bailyn, Bernard, and John B. Hench, eds. *The Press and the American Revolution*. Boston, 1981.

Bailyn, Bernard, and Philip Morgan, eds. *Strangers within the Realm: Cultural Margins of the First British Empire*. Chapel Hill, NC, 1991.

Barker, Hannah. *The Business of Women: Female Enterprise and Urban Development in Northern England 1760–1830*. Oxford, 2006.

———. "Catering for provincial tastes? Newspapers, Readership and Profit in Late Eighteenth-Century England." *Historical Research* 64 (1996): 42–60.

———. *Newspapers, Politics and English Society, 1695–1855*. London, 2000.

———. *Newspapers, Politics, and Public Opinion in Late Eighteenth-Century England*. Oxford, 1998.

Barker, Hannah, and Simon Burrows, eds. *Press, Politics and the Public Sphere in Europe and North America, 1760–1820*. Cambridge, 2002.

Barker-Benfield, G.J. *The Culture of Sensibility: Sex and Society in Eighteenth Century Britain*. Chicago, 1992.

Baseler, Marilyn C. *"Asylum for Mankind": America, 1607–1800*. Ithaca, 1998.

Bayly, C.A. *Imperial Meridian: The First British Empire and the World, 1780–1830*. Cambridge, 1989.

Beer, George Louis. *British Colonial Policy, 1754–1765*. London, 1907.

Berg, Maxine. *Luxury and Pleasure in Eighteenth-Century Britain*. Oxford, 2005.

Berkhofer, Robert F., Jr. *The White Man's Indian: Images of the American Indian from Columbus to the Present*. New York, 1978.

Bickham, Troy. "Eating the Empire: Intersections of Food, Cookery and Imperialism in Eighteenth-Century Britain." *P&P* 198 (2008): 71–110.

———. *Savages within the Empire: Representations of American Indians in Eighteenth-Century Britain*. Oxford, 2005.

———. "Sympathizing with Sedition? George Washington, the British Press, and British Attitudes during the American War of Independence." *WMQ* 59 (2002): 102–22.

Bissell, Benjamin. *The American Indian in English Literature in the 18th Century*. New Haven, 1925.

Black, Jeremy, ed. "Continuity and Change in the British Press, 1750–1833." *Publishing History* 36 (1994): 39–85.

———. *Culture and Society in Britain, 1660–1800.* Manchester, UK, 1997.

———. "The Development of the Provincial Newspaper." *British Journal for Eighteenth-Century Studies* 14 (1991): 159–70.

———. *The English Press 1621–1861.* Stroud, Gloucestershire, UK, 2001.

———. *The English Press in the Eighteenth Century.* Philadelphia, 1987.

———. *Natural and Necessary Enemies: Anglo-French Relations in the Eighteenth Century.* Athens, GA, 1986.

———. *War for America: the Fight for Independence 1775–1783.* London, 1991.

Black, Jeremy, and Jeremy Gregory, eds. *Culture, Politics and Society in Britain, 1660–1800.* Manchester, UK, 1991.

Bonwick, Colin. *English Radicals and the American Revolution.* Chapel Hill, NC, 1977.

Borsay, Peter. "The English Urban Renaissance." *Social History* 5 (1977): 581–603.

———. *The English Urban Renaissance: Culture and Society in the Provincial Town, 1660–1770.* Oxford, 1989.

———. *Provincial Towns in Early Modern England and Ireland: Change, Convergence, and Divergence.* Oxford, 2002.

Bowen, H.V. "British Conception of Global Empire, 1756–83." *Journal of Imperial and Commonwealth History* 26 (1998): 1–27.

———. *The Business of Empire: The East India Company and Imperial Britain, 1756–1833.* Cambridge, 2006.

———. *Elites, Enterprise and the Making of the British Overseas Empire, 1688–1775.* London, 1996.

Bowman, Larry G. *Captive Americans: Prisoners of War During the American Revolution.* Athens, OH, 1976.

Boyce, George, James Curran, and Pauline Wingate, eds. *Newspaper History from the Seventeenth Century to the Present Day.* London, 1978.

Brathwaite, Edward. *The Development of Creole Society in Jamaica, 1770–1820.* Oxford, 1978.

Breen, T.H. "'Baubles of Britain': The American and Consumer Revolutions of the Eighteenth Century." *P&P* 119 (1988): 73–104.

———. *The Marketplace of Revolution: How Consumer Politics Shaped American Independence.* Oxford, 2004.

Brewer, John. *Party Ideology and Popular Politics at the Accession of George III.* Cambridge, 1976.

———. *Pleasures of the Imagination: English Culture in the Eighteenth Century.* London, 1997.

———. *Sinews of Power: War, Money and the English State, 1688–1783.* Cambridge, MA, 1990.

Brookhiser, Richard. *Founding Father: Rediscovering George Washington.* London, 1996.

Brown, Christopher Leslie. *Moral Capital: Foundations of British Abolitionism.* Chapel Hill, NC, 2006.

Buel, Richard, Jr. *In Irons: Britain's Naval Supremacy and the American Revolutionary Economy.* New Haven, 1998.

Bumsted, J.M. "'Things in the Womb of Time': Ideas of American Independence, 1633 to 1763." *WMQ* 31 (1974): 533–64.

Butler, Jon. *Becoming American: The Revolution before 1776.* Cambridge, MA, 2000.

Calloway, Colin. *The American War of Independence in Indian Country.* Cambridge, 1995.

———. *Crown and Calumet: British Indian Relations, 1783–1815.* Norman, OK, 1987.

Carrothers, W.A. *Emigration from the British Isles.* London, 1929.

Christie, Ian R. *The End of the North Ministry 1780–1782.* London, 1958.

Clark, Bob. *From Grub Street to Fleet Street: An Illustrated History of English Newspapers to 1899.* Burlington, VT, 2004.

Clark, Charles E. *The Public Prints: The Newspaper in Anglo-American Culture, 1665–1740.* New York, 1994.

Clark, Dora Mae. *British Opinion and the America Revolution.* New Haven, 1930.

Clark, J.C.D. *English Society, 1688–1832: Ideology, Social Structure and Political Practice during the Ancien Regime.* Cambridge, 1985.

——. *The Language of Liberty, 1660–1832: Political Discourse and Social Dynamics in the Anglo-American World.* Cambridge, 1994.

Clark, Peter, ed. *The Transformation of English Provincial Towns 1600–1800.* London, 1984.

Claydon, Tony, and Ian McBride, eds. *Protestantism and National Identity: Britain and Ireland, c.1650–c.1850.* Cambridge, 1998.

Cohen, Sheldon S. *British Supporters of the American Revolution 1775–1783.* Rochester, NY, 2004.

——. *Yankee Sailors in British Gaols: Prisoners of War at Forton and Mill, 1777–1783.* Newark, 1995.

Colley, Linda. "The Apotheosis of George III: Loyalty, Royalty and the British Nation 1760–1820." *P&P* 102 (1984): 94–129.

——. *Britons: Forging of the Nation, 1707–1837.* New Haven, 1992.

——. *Captives.* New York, 2003.

Conn, Stetson. *Gibraltar in British Diplomacy in the Eighteenth Century.* New Haven, 1942.

Conway, Stephen. *The British Isles and the War of American Independence.* Oxford, 2000.

——. "From fellow-nationals to foreigners: British perceptions of the Americans, circa 1739–1783." *WMQ* 49 (2002): 3–38.

——. "The Great Mischief Complained of." *WMQ* 47 (1990): 370–91.

——. *The War of American Independence 1775–1783.* London, 1995.

Copeland, David. *Colonial American Newspapers: Character and Content.* Newark, 1997.

Cowan, R.M.W. *The Newspaper in Scotland: A Study of its First Expansion, 1815–1860.* Glasgow, 1986.

Craig, M.E. *The Scottish Periodical Press, 1750–1789.* Edinburgh, 1931.

Cranfield, G.A. *The Development of the Provincial Newspaper, 1700–1760.* Oxford, 1962.

——. "A Handlist of English Provincial Newspapers and Periodicals, 1700–1760: Additions and Corrections." *Transactions of the Cambridge Bibliographical Society* 2 (1956): 269–74.

Craven, Maxwell. *Derby: An Illustrated History.* Derby, 1988.

Cunliffe, Marcus. *In Search of America: Transatlantic Essays, 1951–1990.* London, 1991.

Davis, David Brion. *The Problem of Slavery in the Age of the American Revolution.* Ithaca, 1975.

de Castro, J. Paul. *The Gordon Riots.* Oxford, 1926.

Dickinson, H.T., ed. *Britain and the American Revolution.* London, 1998.

——. "'The Friends of America': British Sympathy with the American Revolution." In *Radicalism and Revolution in Britain, 1775–1848,* ed. Michael T. Davis. London, 2000.

——. *The Politics of the People in Eighteenth-Century Britain.* London, 1994.

Dwyer, John. "The *Caledonian Mercury* and Scottish National Culture, 1763–1801." *Journal of History and Politics/Journal d'Histoire et de Politique* 7 (1989): 147–71.

——. *Virtuous Discourse: Sensibility and Community in Late Eighteenth-Century Scotland.* Edinburgh, 1987.

Edler, Friedrich. *The Dutch Republic and the American Revolution.* Baltimore, 1911.

Ellis, Aytoun. *The Penny Universities.* London, 1956.

Ellis, Joseph J. *His Excellency George Washington.* New York, 2004.

Elofson, Warren M., and John A. Woods, eds. *Party, Parliament, and the American War 1774–1780.* Oxford, 1996.

Favell, M. Kay. "The Enlightened Reader and the New Industrial Towns." *British Journal for Eighteenth-Century Studies* 8 (1985): 17–35.

Feather, John. *The Provincial Book Trade in Eighteenth-Century England.* Cambridge, 1985.

Ferdinand, C.Y. *Benjamin Collins and the Provincial Newspaper Trade in the Eighteenth Century.* Oxford, 1997.

——. "The Salisbury Journal 1729–1785: A Study of a Provincial Newspaper." D.Phil. Thesis, University of Oxford, 1990.

Fergus, Jan. *Provincial Readers in Eighteenth-Century England.* Oxford, 2006.

——. "Women, Class, and Growth of Magazine Readership in the Provinces, 1746–1780." *Studies in Eighteenth-Century Culture* 16 (1986): 41–53.

Fischer, David Hackett. *Paul Revere's Ride*. New York, 1994.

Flavell, Julie, and Stephen Conway, eds. *Britain and America Go to War: The Impact of War and Warfare in Anglo-America, 1754–1815*. Gainesville, FL, 2004.

Fleming, Thomas. *The Perils of Peace: America's Struggle for Survival After Yorktown*. New York, 2007.

Flinn, Michael. *Scottish Population History*. Edinburgh, 1977.

Floud, Roderick, and Deirdre N. McCloskey. *The Economic History of Britain Since 1700*. 2nd ed., 2 vols. Cambridge, 1994.

Fulford, Tim. *Romantic Indians: Native Americans, British Literature, and Transatlantic Culture 1756–1830*. Oxford, 2006.

Fulford, Timothy, and Peter Kitson, eds. *Romanticism and Colonialism*. Cambridge, 1998.

Gerzina, Gretchen Holbrook. *Black London: Life before Emancipation*. London, 1995.

Gibson, A.J.S., and T.C. Smout. *Prices, Food and Wages in Scotland, 1550–1780*. Cambridge, 1995.

Gipson, Lawrence Henry. *The British Empire Before the American Revolution*. 15 vols. New York, 1936–1970.

———. *The Coming of the Revolution, 1763–1775*. New York, 1954.

Goody, Jack, ed. *Literacy in Traditional Societies*. Cambridge, 1968.

Gould, Eliga H. "American Independence and Britain's Counter-Revolution." *P&P* 154 (1997): 107–41.

———. *The Persistence of Empire: British Political Cultures in the Age of the American Revolution*. Chapel Hill, NC, 2000.

Grant, Alfred. *Our American Brethren: A History of Letters in the British Press During the American Revolution, 1775–1781*. London, 1995.

Greene, Jack. *The Quest for Power: The Lower Houses of Assembly in the Southern Royal Colonies, 1689–1776*. Chapel Hill, NC, 1963.

Gruber, I.D. "Lord Howe and Lord George Germain: British Politics and the Winning of American Independence." *WMQ* 22 (1965): 225–43.

Haig, Robert L. *The Gazetteer 1735–1797: A Study in the Eighteenth-Century English Newspaper*. Carbondale, IL, 1960.

Harlow, Vincent T. *The Founding of the Second British Empire 1763–1793*, 2 vols. London, 1952.

Harris, Bob. "'American Idols': Empire, War and the Middling Ranks in Mid-Eighteenth-Century Britain." *P&P* 150 (1996): 111–41.

———. *A Patriot Press: National Politics and the London Press in the 1740s*. Oxford, 1993.

———. *Politics and the Rise of the Press: Britain and France, 1620–1800*. London, 1996.

Harris, Michael. *London Newspapers in the Age of Walpole: A Study of the Origins of the Modern English Press*. London, 1987.

Hay, Douglass, et al. *Albion's Fatal Tree: Crime and Society in Eighteenth-Century England*. London, 1975.

Herzog, Don. *Poisoning the Minds of the Lower Orders*. Princeton, 1998.

Higginbotham, Don, ed. *George Washington Reconsidered*. Charlottesville, VA, 2001.

———. *The War of American Independence*. New York, 1971.

Hindle, Wilfrid. *The Morning Post, 1772–1937*. London, 1937.

Hinkhouse, F.J. *The Preliminaries of the American Revolution as Seen in the English Press, 1763–1775*. New York, 1926.

Hoffman, Elliot. "Black-Hessians: American Blacks and German Soldiers." *Negro History Bulletin* 44 (1981): 81–82.

Hoffman, Ronald, and Peter J. Albert, eds. *Diplomacy and Revolution: The Franco-American Alliance of 1778*. Charlottesville, Virginia, 1981.

———. *Peace and the Peacemakers: The Treaty of 1783*. Charlottesville, VA, 1986.

Honor, Hugh. *The New Golden Land: European Images of America from the Discoveries to the Present Time*. New York, 1975.

Hopfl, H.M. "From Savage to Scotsman: Conjectural History in the Scottish Enlightenment." *JBS* 17 (1978): 19–40.

Hunt, Lynn. *Inventing Human Rights: A History.* New York, 2007.

Hunt, Margaret R. *The Middling Sort: Commerce, Gender, and the Family in England, 1680–1780.* Berkeley, 1996.

Hunter, Jean. "The Lady's Magazine and the Study of Englishwomen in the Eighteenth Century." In *Newsletter to Newspapers: Eighteenth Century Journalism,* ed. Donovan H. Bond and W. Reynolds. Morgantown, WV, 1977.

Ingrao, Charles W. *The Hessian Mercenary State: Ideas, Institutions, and Reform under Fredrick II, 1760–1785.* Cambridge, 1987.

Jones, Peter, ed. *Philosophy and Science of the Scottish Enlightenment.* Edinburgh, 1988.

Karras, Alan. *Sojourners in the Sun: Scottish Migrants in Jamaica and the Chesapeake, 1740–1800.* Ithaca, NY, 1992.

Karsten, Peter. *Patriot-Heroes in England and America: Political Symbolism and Changing Values over Three Centuries.* Madison, 1978.

Kaufman, Paul. "English Book Clubs and their Role in Social History." *Libri* 14 (1964): 1–34.

Kinnear, Mary. "Pro-Americans in the British House of Commons in the 1770s." PhD diss., University of Oregon, 1973.

Klein, Herbert S. *The Atlantic Slave Trade.* Cambridge, 1998.

Knox, Thomas R. "Popular politics and provincial radicalism: Newcastle upon Tyne, 1769–1785." *Albion* 11 (1979): 224–41.

Kupperman, Karen Ordahl, ed. *America in European Consciousness, 1493–1750.* Chapel Hill, 1995.

Langford, Paul. "The English Clergy and the American Revolution." In *The Transformation of Political Culture: England and Germany in the Late Eighteenth Century,* ed. Eckhart Hellmuth. Oxford, 1990.

———. "Old Whigs, Old Tories, and the American Revolution." *Journal of Imperial and Commonwealth History* 8 (1980): 106–30.

———. *A Polite and Commercial People, England 1727–1783.* Oxford, 1989.

Lillywhite, Bryant. *London Coffee Houses: A Reference Book of Coffee Houses of the Seventeenth, Eighteenth and Nineteenth Centuries.* London, 1963.

Lincoln, Margarette. *Representing the Royal Navy: British Seapower, 1750–1815.* London, 2002.

Longmore, Paul K. *The Invention of George Washington.* Berkeley, 1988.

Louis, William Roger, ed. *Oxford History of the British Empire.* 5 vols. Oxford, 2001.

Lutnick, Solomon. *The American Revolution and the British Press, 1775–1783.* Columbia, MO, 1967.

Makesy, Piers. *The War for America, 1775–1783.* Cambridge, MA, 1965.

Marshall, P.J. "The Eighteenth-Century Empire." In *British Politics and Society from Walpole to Pitt, 1742–1789,* ed. Jeremy Black. London, 1990.

———. "Empire and Authority in the later Eighteenth Century." *Journal of Imperial and Commonwealth History* 15 (1987): 105–22.

———. "A Nation Defined by Empire, 1755–1776." In *Uniting the Kingdom? The Making of British History,* ed. Alexander Grant and Keith Stringer. London, 1995.

Marshall, Peter. *Bristol and the American War of Independence.* Bristol, 1977.

———. "The First and Second British Empire: A Question of Demarcation." *History* 49 (1964): 13–23.

Marston, Jerrilyn Greene. *King and Congress: The Transfer of Political Legitimacy, 1774–1776.* Princeton, 1987.

McCullough, David. *John Adams.* New York, 2001.

Middlekauf, Robert. *The Glorious Cause: The American Revolution, 1763–1789.* New York, 1982.

Midgley, Clare. "Slave Sugar Boycotts, Female Activism and the Domestic Base of British Anti-Slavery Culture." *Slavery and Abolition* 17 (1996): 137–62.

Money, John. "Taverns, Coffee houses and Clubs: Local politics and popular articulacy in the Birmingham area in the age of the American Revolution." *Historical Journal* 15 (1971): 168–86.

Morley, Vincent. *Irish Opinion and the American Revolution, 1760–1783.* Cambridge, 2002.

Mui, Hoh-Cheung, and Lorna H. Mui. *Shops and Shopkeeping in Eighteenth-Century England.* Montreal, 1989.

Mulcahy, Matthew. *Hurricanes and Society in the British Greater Caribbean, 1624-1783.* Baltimore, 2006.

Mullin, Gerald W. *Flight and Rebellion: Slave Resistance in Eighteenth-Century Virginia.* Oxford, 1972.

Namias, June. *White Captives: Gender and Ethnicity on the American Frontier.* Chapel Hill, NC, 1993.

Namier, Sir Lewis. *England in the Age of the American Revolution.* 2nd ed. London, 1961.

———. *The Structure of Politics at the Accession of George III.* 2nd ed. London, 1957.

Nash, Robert C. "The English and Scottish Tobacco Trades in the Seventeenth and Eighteenth Centuries: Legal and Illegal Trade." *Economic History Review* 35 (1982): 354-72.

Nerone, John C. *Violence Against the Press: Policing the Public Sphere in U.S. History.* New York, 1994.

Nordholt, Jan Willem Schulte. *The Dutch Republic and American Independence.* trans. Herbert H. Rowen. Chapel Hill, NC, 1982.

Norton, Mary Beth. *The British-Americans: The Loyalist Exiles in England, 1774-1789.* Boston, 1972.

O'Gorman, Frank. *The Long Eighteenth Century: British Political and Social History, 1688-1832.* London, 1997.

Osborn, J.R. "India, Parliament and the Press under George III." D.Phil. thesis, University of Oxford, 1999.

O'Shaughnessy, Andrew Jackson. *An Empire Divided: The American Revolution and the British Caribbean.* Philadelphia, 2000.

Oxford Dictionary of National Biography. 60 vols. Oxford, 2004.

Pasley, Jeffrey L. *"The Tyranny of Printers": Newspaper Politics in the Early American Republic.* Charlottesville, VA, 2001.

Penson, Lillian M. "The London West India Interest in the Eighteenth Century." *English Historical Review* 30 (1921): 373-92.

Phillips, Nicola. *Women in Business, 1700-1850.* Woodbridge, Suffolk, UK, 2006.

Pincus, Steven. "'Coffee Politicians Does Create': Coffeehouses and Restoration Culture." *Journal of Modern History* 67 (1995): 807-34.

Plumb, J.H. "British Attitudes to the American Revolution." In *In the Light of History.* J.H. Plumb. Boston, 1972.

Plumb, J.H., et al. *Life in the Georgian Town.* London, 1986.

Pocock, J.G.A. *The Machiavellian Moment: Florentine Political Thought and the Atlantic Republican Tradition.* Princeton, 1975.

Porter, Bernard. *The Absent-Minded Imperialists: Empire, Society, and Culture in Britain.* Oxford, 2004.

Porter, Roy. "Science, Provincial Culture, and Public Opinion in Enlightenment England." *British Journal for Eighteenth-Century Studies* 3 (1980): 20-46.

Prest, Wilfrid. *Albion Ascendant: English History, 1660-1815.* Oxford, 1998.

Quarles, Benjamin. *The Negro in the American Revolution.* Chapel Hill, NC, 1961.

Raphael, Ray. *A People's History of the American Revolution: How Common People Shaped the Fight for Independence.* New York, 2002.

Raven, James. *Judging New Wealth: Popular Publishing and Responses to Commerce in England, 1750-1800.* Oxford, 1992.

Raven, James, Helen Small, and Naomi Tadmor, eds. *The Practice and Representation of Reading in England.* Cambridge, 1996.

Raymond, Joad. *The Invention of the Newspaper: English Newsbooks 1641-1649.* Oxford, 1996.

Rea, Robert R. *The English Press in Politics, 1760-1774.* Lincoln, NE, 1963.

Reich, Jerome R. *British Friends of the American Revolution.* London, 1998.

Resch, John and Walter Sargent, eds. *War and Society in the American Revolution: Mobilization and Home Fronts.* DeKalb, IL, 2007.

Rhoden, Nancy L. *Revolutionary Anglicanism: The Colonial Church of England Clergy During the American Revolution.* London, 1999.

Richard, Eric. *Britannia's Children: Emigration from England, Scotland, Wales and Ireland since 1600.* London, 2004.

Rivers, Isabel. *Books and Their Readers in Eighteenth-Century England: New Essays.* London, 2001.

Robbins, Caroline. *The Eighteenth-Century Commonwealth Man.* Cambridge, MA, 1959.

Rodgers, Nicholas. *Crowds, Culture, and Politics in Great Britain.* Oxford, 1998.

Rogers, Nicholas. *Crowds, Culture, and Politics in Georgian Britain.* Oxford, 1998.

Royster, Charles. *A Revolutionary People at War: The Continental Army and the American Character, 1775–1783.* Chapel Hill, 1979.

Rudé, George. *Wilkes and Liberty: A Social Study.* Oxford, 1962.

Sack, James J. *From Jacobite to Conservative: Reaction and Orthodoxy in Britain, c. 1760–1832.* Cambridge, 1993.

Sainsbury, John. *Disaffected Patriots: London Supporters of Revolutionary America, 1769–1782.* Kingston, ON, 1987.

Schama, Simon. *Rough Crossings: Britain, the Slaves and the American Revolution.* London, 2005.

Schwartz, Barry. *George Washington: The Making of an American Symbol.* London, 1987.

Schweizer, Karl, and Rebecca Klein. "The French Revolution and the Developments in the London Daily Press to 1793." *Journal of History and Politics/Journal d'Histoire et de Politique* 7 (1989): 171–86.

Scott, H.M. *British Foreign Policy in the Age of the American Revolution.* Oxford, 1990.

Seitz, Don Carlos. *Paul Jones, his exploits in English seas during 1778–1780, Contemporary Accounts Collected from English Newspapers, with a Complete Bibliography.* New York, 1917.

Shammas, Carole. *The Pre-industrial Consumer in England and America.* Oxford, 1990.

Shapiro, Barbara. *A Culture of Fact: England, 1550–1720.* Ithaca, 2000.

Sher, Richard B., and Jeffrey R. Smitten, eds. *Scotland and America in the Age of the Enlightenment.* Princeton, 1990.

Shevelow, Kathryn. *Women and Print Culture: the Construction of Femininity in the Early Periodical.* New York, 1989.

Shy, John W. *A People Numerous and Armed: Reflections on the Military Struggle for American Independence.* New York, 1976.

Simmons, R.C., and P.D.G. Thomas, eds. *Proceedings and Debates of the British Parliaments Respecting North America, 1754–1783.* 5 vols. New York, 1987.

Sloan, William David, and Julie Hedgepeth Williams. *The Early American Press, 1690–1783.* Westport, CT, 1994.

Smith, S.D. "Accounting for Taste: British Coffee Consumption in Historical Perspective." *Journal of Interdisciplinary History* 27 (1996): 183–214.

———. "Sugar's Poor Relation: British Coffee Planting in the West Indies, 1720–1833." *Slavery and Abolition* 19 (1998): 68–69.

Sommerville, C. John. *The News Revolution in England: Cultural Dynamics of Daily Information.* Oxford, 1996.

Sosin, Jack M. *Whitehall and the Wilderness: The Middle West in British Colonial Policy, 1760–1775.* Lincoln, NE, 1961.

Sparrow, Andrew. *Obscure Scribblers: A History of Parliamentary Journalism.* London, 2003.

Spufford, Margaret. *Small Books and Pleasant Histories: Popular Fiction and its Readership in Seventeenth Century England.* Cambridge, 1985.

Starr, Paul. *The Creation of the Media: Political Origins of Modern Communications.* New York, 2004.

Steele, Ian. *Betrayals: Fort William Henry and the Massacre.* Oxford, 1990.

Stevenson, John, ed. *London in the Age of Reform.* Oxford, 1977.

Stinchcombe, William C. *The American Revolution and the French Alliance.* Syracuse, 1960.

Stone, Lawrence. "Literacy and Education in England, 1640–1900." *P&P* 42 (1969): 102–9.

Thomas, J.P. "The British Empire and the Press, 1763–1774." D.Phil. thesis, University of Oxford, 1982.

Thomas, P.D.G. "The Beginning of Parliamentary Reporting in Newspapers, 1768–1774." *English Historical Review* 74 (1959): 623–36.

———. *British Politics and the Stamp Act Crisis: The First Phase of the American Revolution, 1763–1767.* Oxford, 1975.

———. *John Wilkes, A Friend to Liberty.* Oxford, 1996.

———. *Tea Party to Independence: The Third Phase of the American Revolution, 1773–1776.* Oxford, 1991.

———. *The Townshend Duties Crisis: The Second Phase of the American Revolution, 1767–1773.* Oxford, 1987.

Thompson, E.P. *Customs in Common.* London, 1991.

Thornton, John. *Africa and Africans in the Making of the Atlantic World, 1400–1800.* 2nd ed. Cambridge, 1998.

Toohey, Robert E. *Liberty and Empire: British Radical Solutions to the American Problem, 1774–1776.* Lexington, KY, 1978.

Vincent, David. *Literacy and Popular Culture, England 1750–1914.* Cambridge, 1989.

Voelz, Peter M. *Slave and Soldier: The Military Impact of Blacks in the Colonial Americas.* New York, 1993.

Wade, John, ed. *Junius: Including Letters by the Same Writer under Different Signatures. . . .* London, 1865.

Wahrman, Dror. "The English Problem of Identity in the American Revolution." *American Historical Review* 106 (2001): 1245–48.

———. *The Making of the Modern Self.* New Haven, 2004.

———. "Virtual Representation: Parliamentary Reporting and Language of Class in the 1790s." *P&P* 136 (1992): 83–113.

Walvin, James. *Fruits of Empire: Exotic Produce and British Taste, 1660–1800.* London, 1997.

Weatherill, Lorna. "A Possession of One's Own: Women and Consumer Behavior in England, 1660–1740." *JBS* 25 (1986): 131–56.

Werkmeister, Lucyle. *The London Daily Press 1772–1792.* Lincoln, NE, 1963.

Wheeler, Roxann. *The Complexion of Race: Categories of Difference in Eighteenth-Century British Culture.* Philadelphia, 2000.

Wills, Garry. *Cincinnatus: George Washington and the Enlightenment.* New York, 1984.

Wilson, Harold S. *History of the Post in Derby, 1635–1941.* Nottingham, 1990.

Wilson, Kathleen. *Sense of the People: Politics, Culture and Imperialism in England, 1715–1785.* Cambridge, 1995.

———. *This Island Race: Englishness, Empire and Gender in the Eighteenth Century.* London, 2003.

Winkler, K.T. "The Forces of the Market and the London Newspaper in the First Half of the Eighteenth Century." *Journal of Newspaper and Periodical History* 4 (1988): 22–35.

Wood, Gordon S. *The Radicalism of the American Revolution.* New York, 1991.

Wrigley, E.A., and R.S. Schofield. *The Population of England 1541–1871.* Cambridge, MA, 1981.

INDEX

*Page numbers in **bold** refer to illustrations*

Adams, John, 177
Adams, Sam, 10, 60, 71, 99
advertisements (newspaper), 22–23, 24, 25, 27, 32–33
African Americans: British use of, 208, 209; included in loyalist evacuation accounts, 211; lack of press coverage of explained, 209–3, 233; military service, 210–11, 213–14; mistreatment of by British army, 211; offered freedom for service, 212, 213; Parliamentary opposition leaves issue alone, 212–13; precedents for arming, 207, 210
Agincourt, battle of, invoked, 146
American Indians: alliances not surprising, 207; British use of, 208; celebrated in Seven Years War, 215–16; Congress's alliances with ignored, 218; impossible to control, 217, 218, 220; murder Jane McRea, 221–22, 223; negative depictions consequence of Seven Years War, 214, 218; Parliamentary opposition condemns use of, 222–23; perspectives ignored, 218; proponents for use of attacked, 218; public opposition to use of, 214, 216, 217–18, 220
Amherst, Jeffrey, Baron, 78
American Revolution: as a civil war, 4, 5, 57, 72–73, 74, 77–78, 80, 86, 111–12, 185–87, 207–8, 209, 216, 229, 241
André, John, 191
armed forces (American), 65, 68, 155; accused of abuses, 77; advantages over British, 68, 80–81; as citizen-soldiers, 93–94, 108, 230; disintegrating, 101–2, 139, 156; disparaged, 93, 102; naval power, 121–22, 129; poorly equipped, 193–94, 101–2; praise for, 75–77, 91; tactics complained of, 209; threat to postwar republic, 245
army (British): accused of brutality, 71–72; celebrated, 91; depicted as lacking leadership, 194; desertion in, 64, 226, 227; as liberators, 100; mobilization of chronicled, 81–82; protests American service, 77–78; public confidence in, 96, 103–4; recruitment for, 135–37, **138**, 146, 226, **228**; reputation re-

deemed after Gibraltar, 173–75; thought insufficient for American operations, 80–81, 226
Arnold, Benedict, 178, 191
Asgill, Charles, 191
Asia, 142, 147–49, 178–79, 239

Baldwin, Henry, 45, 46
Barré, Isaac, 53, 195
Bate, Henry (after 1780 Bate, Dudley), 50–51
Bath Chronicle, 47
book clubs. *See* circulating libraries and book clubs
Boston (Mass.), 60, 61, 68–69, 70, 79
Boston Tea Party, 60, 70
Bristol, 8, 86, 213, 236
Bunker Hill, battle of, 75–77
Burgoyne, John: and controversy over use of American Indians, 219–23; defends murder of Jane McRea, 202; defense of conduct in Parliament, 192–93; joins opposition in Parliament, 199–200; resignation rumored, 78; returns to Britain, 106–7; surrenders at Saratoga, 106
Burke, Edmund, 8, 30, 50, 85, 99, 112, 189, 200, 202, 213, 222–23

Camden, battle of, 153
Canada, 78–79, 238
Carleton, Sir Guy,192, 197
Caribbean. *See* West Indies
Carlisle Peace Commission, 116–17
Cartwright, John, 78
charity for American prisoners, 88, 203–4, 109–12
Charlestown (Charleston), 153, 155, 179
Chatham, William Pitt, earl of, 112–13, 194
Church of England, 85, 99–100, 110
circulating libraries and book clubs, 24–25, 38–39
Clinton, Sir Henry, 153; blamed for defeat at Yorktown, 160–61, 197; joins opposition in Parliament, 200
coffeehouses, 29, 34–37, 38–39, 52, 63, 99, 143
Coercive Acts (1774), 61
Collins, Benjamin, 26–27